THE NIGHT WATCH

DAVID ATLEE PHILLIPS

THE
NIGHT
WATCH

New York   ATHENEUM   1977

Library of Congress Cataloging in Publication Data

Phillips, David Atlee.
    The night watch.

    Autobiographical.
    Includes index.
    1. United States. Central Intelligence Agency.
2. Phillips, David Atlee. 3. Spies—Biography.
4. United States—Foreign relations—Latin America.
5. Latin America—Foreign relations—United States.
I. Title.
JK468.16P54   1977   327'.12'0924   [B]   76-11855
ISBN 0-689-10754-4

Copyright © 1977 by David Atlee Phillips
All rights reserved
Published simultaneously in Canada by McClelland and Stewart Ltd.
Manufactured by The Book Press, Brattleboro, Vermont
Designed by Harry Ford
First Printing January 1977
Second Printing April 1977

This book is for Dick Welch

PREFACE

In early December 1974 I was a happy man. Despite vicissitudes over the years, including family tragedy, my private life was pleasant and rewarding. Professionally, I was pleased with the course of my career. After twenty-five years in secret operations I was promoted that December to GS-18, the ultimate rank a CIA officer can achieve except for the presidentially appointed Director or Deputy Director of the Agency. I was a Division Chief, charged with managing the affairs of several hundred people, a budget of many millions of dollars, and CIA operations in twenty-odd countries in Latin America and the Caribbean. My salary was $36,000 a year. At fifty-two I had eight more years of service before reaching the age when the CIA asks its executives to retire. I was one of a handful of candidates in line for the position of Chief of the Clandestine Service, the CIA Directorate which conducts espionage and covert action worldwide. The attractive alternative to a more senior assignment in Washington was at least one more overseas tour—I had already served in eight countries—in a major CIA station, perhaps Paris or London. The material well-being was comforting: of seven living children five had to be educated, the youngest being four years old.

The storm which changed my life broke just before Christmas of 1974. In the tumult which ensued I felt compelled to abandon what had been an exciting and—I had believed until then—honorable career working in the peculiar service of intelligence. Suddenly the image of CIA people was tarnished in almost daily revelations and sensational headlines. One of my own children repudiated my profession.

William E. Colby, the soldier-priest at the helm of the CIA during the tempest, categorized three kinds of secrets. First, "bad secrets," which conceal ineptitude or misconduct. I write candidly about bad secrets. Then, "nonsecrets," the details of intelligence work which are now public knowledge; in an era when clandestine operations have been the subject of intensive media and congressional scrutiny, I can write about things which only a year ago were sacrosanct. Finally, Colby said, there are "good secrets": those which protect the identities of American intelligence sources (the people and technical equipment producing intelligence) and methods (the manner in which men and machines obtain the information). I have used literary license when necessary to protect good secrets.

A thick, green tome was published in Washington in early 1976. *The Final Report of the Select Committee to Study Governmental Operations with Respect to Intelligence Activities.* It is better known as the Senate Church Committee Report. It said, "...In some respects, the intelligence profession resembles monastic life with some of the disciplines and personal sacrifices reminiscent of medieval orders. Intelligence work is a life of service, but one in which the norms of American national life are sometimes distressingly distorted."

This book is about the men and women who have worked in American intelligence. It is also about the distortions of their trade and the moral conflicts they must resolve in order to be effective, indeed to survive, in the challenging business of espionage, illegal in every country in the world.

I hope this memoir—sometimes painful in the writing—will be useful to those who ponder whether our country can or should conduct secret operations within the kind of open society we have in America, especially the United States after Vietnam and Watergate.

David Atlee Phillips
Bethesda, Maryland, 1976

CONTENTS

Chapter 1
CHILE 1950–1953
PAGE 3

Chapter 2
GUATEMALA 1954
PAGE 30

Chapter 3
WASHINGTON, CUBA, LEBANON, CUBA 1955–1959
PAGE 55

Chapter 4
WASHINGTON—THE BAY OF PIGS 1960–1961
PAGE 85

Chapter 5
MEXICO 1962–1964
PAGE 112

Chapter 6
THE DOMINICAN REPUBLIC 1965–1967
PAGE 144

Chapter 7
WASHINGTON 1968–1969
PAGE 187

Chapter 8
BRAZIL, VENEZUELA 1970–1972
PAGE 213

Chapter 9
WASHINGTON 1973–1974
PAGE 236

CONTENTS

Chapter 10
WASHINGTON 1975
PAGE 264

EPILOGUE
PAGE 283

INDEX
PAGE 297

x

THE NIGHT WATCH

1

CHILE 1950–1953

Santiago, 1950. The lunch was typically Chilean: fish soup, fried conger eel, ground corn steamed in its husk and, for dessert, *cherimoya*, a succulent South American fruit. I wondered why the diplomat from the American embassy in Santiago had invited me to such a remote restaurant on the outskirts of the city. As we sipped coffee he explained. "I'm the local chief for the CIA," he said. "We want you to give Uncle Sam a little help in your spare time."

"The CIA?" I had heard only vague reference to the organization—a quarter of a century ago it was the least known of United States agencies.

"The Central Intelligence Agency," he said. "We're in the business of espionage and secret operations."

"Doesn't the FBI do that in Latin America?"

"They did, during World War II and until recently, when the CIA took over. Or at least began to operate. J. Edgar Hoover didn't like losing the responsibility and in most countries of Latin America the FBI burned its files and dismissed its agents rather than turn them over to us. I was the first CIA officer in one of the Central American republics and the only thing I found when the Bureau left was a row of empty safes and a pair of rubber gloves in what had been an FBI darkroom. But I was able to recontact most of the Bureau's sources, because I hired the ex-FBI chief's driver, and he knew where I could find them." The CIA man—I'll call him Brad—stirred his coffee thoughtfully. He said ruefully, "You know, I have a feeling J. Edgar is never going to forgive us for taking over this territory."

My first reaction to being approached by American intelligence was one of curiosity. "You don't look like a spy," I said to Brad. He didn't like the observation. "I'm not a spy," he said flatly. "A spy is a grubby little person who sells secrets for money, or maybe a fine person who works for another country because he doesn't like his own. I'm a career government employee, an intelligence officer, a manager of spies."

"You want me to be a spy?" I asked.

"No, an agent." Brad spoke in simple terms, as if explaining to a child. "An agent is not always a spy, but someone who helps us, one way or another. If you work for us you will be put under a contract which will outline your duties."

"Why me?"

"You have three of the four things most necessary in working in foreign intelligence. Cover, because you have a business to explain why you are in Chile, and what you are doing. Access, because the business gives you an excuse to move around, meet people, and ask questions. Language, which you have already learned."

"And the fourth, that I don't have?"

"Experience."

"How can I help? There's not much spare time right now. I signed the final papers on a new printing press this morning." I was the owner and editor of the weekly English-language *The South Pacific Mail*. It was printed at the shop of a daily newspaper in Valparaiso, the port city for Santiago; it was losing money, and I had decided some months before that moving the business to Santiago and buying printing equipment for commercial work was the only formula which would save the foundering paper.

"I know about your buying new equipment," Brad said. "That's one reason we decided to approach you. Have time for a drive in the country? I'll give you the details where we can talk privately."

The path over the years leading to the lunch in Santiago and my initiation into American intelligence began in Fort Worth, Texas, in 1922—appropriately enough on October 31, Halloween, suitable birthday for a spook. My father died when I was five, leaving my mother, three older brothers, and a portfolio of oil stocks which turned to ashes in the market crash of 1929. We were the poorest rich people in Fort Worth. A founder of a local country club, my father left us a life membership and the deed to a house on the fourth green. Even teenagers were not allowed to play on weekends without a caddy. I joined the local blacks at the caddy house at four in the morning to queue for a caddying job; the morning stipend allowed me to pay a caddy and play in the afternoon. My mother went to work. She was determined to offer each of her four sons his choice of colleges, a task she accomplished by great personal sacrifice, and by becoming in time a successful business executive. I chose

4

William and Mary in Virginia. My record the first year was marred when I failed to appear for final exams. I had attended a weekend prom at a now defunct girls' school in Washington and accepted, perhaps in an alcoholic haze, an invitation from a convivial fellow to ride with him back to school. I slept well in his car, but unfortunately his school turned out to be Yale.

I returned to Fort Worth to study at Texas Christian University and live at home, from whence, mother pointed out, I should be able to find my way to school. I tried a number of jobs. The most difficult was selling cemetery lots door to door, a corrosive occupation but one which, like selling used cars, develops talents useful in a career of espionage. But I was a failure. My supervisor was testy in explaining that I must not use as part of my sales spiel the fact that the lots at the cemetery had a wonderful view. One morning I rang a doorbell, determined to sell. The door opened and a pleasant old lady, withered and tottering and ninety-five if a day, smiled and asked how she could help me. I simply couldn't do it. I asked her if she would like to buy a locomotive, tipped my hat when she allowed she didn't really need one, and went off to New York to become an actor.

After two years of dismal rounds of producers' offices and survival on grainy cheese sandwiches from corner stores, I began to suspect that I was not destined to be a great actor. I had time to think about it during World War II. I had been touring for thirteen months with a third-rate company of *Junior Miss* when, early one morning, an FBI agent awakened me at the Manx Hotel in San Francisco. He was civil in explaining that I had done nothing wrong; indeed I had been punctilious in advising my draft board each time I changed residence. But the months of one-night stands and the stack of postcards advising of my diurnal changes of address—the stack quite high by now—was confusing the Selective Service people. They wanted me to drop in, that very day, to the induction center. So I became an armed tourist in Europe. During eleven missions out of Italy I sat in the nose turret of a B-24 bomber. The B-24 was a good airplane but ours did not survive the anti-aircraft fire and enemy fighter attacks we encountered on our eleventh mission over Austria. I parachuted with the rest of the crew near the Adriatic coast. German soldiers with guns at the ready waited as we descended. I spent the next year in a prison camp.

My first intelligence work was as a member of the camp's escape committee. Eventually I learned enough to escape myself, but only with the assistance of a brave Frenchman named Pierre. Cold and disheartened, I was trying to sleep in a rain-drenched forest outside Nuremberg after bolting from a column of marching Allied prisoners. Pierre literally stepped on me. He was a forced-laborer in Nuremberg, and soon returned

5

with civilian clothes, money, and a compass. He also provided me with a tin of hot venison stew: the reason he frequented the forest was to poach deer which belonged to a fat German air force marshal named Goering. I was determined to repay Pierre somehow after the war. I asked him for his address in France, so I could write to him, and learned my first lesson in what is known in the intelligence trade as tradecraft. Pierre smiled and noted down *my* address in Texas—should I be captured again by the Germans they would find nothing to incriminate him.

After seventeen days of sleeping under bushes and seventeen nights of skulking across the German countryside I found a column of American tanks clanking down a dirt road. I jumped in front of the first tank, shouting my appreciation for being liberated from the Nazis. A sergeant aimed a sub-machine gun at my nose and challenged me to prove I was an American. I couldn't. "What's the name of Betty Grable's husband?" he asked. I didn't know that bandleader Harry James was. "If you don't know who's the luckiest man in the world you can't be no American," was the retort. I finally talked my way past the tank gunner and back to the United States, after a short stop in Wiesbaden to be interrogated by military intelligence officers on the area in which I had been hiding since escape. I met General Omar Bradley, who assigned to his personal cook the task of helping me regain some of the sixty-five pounds I had lost in the prison camp. The cook was a peacetime chef from the El Morocco nightclub in New York, so I ate well.

Six months after the war I heard from Pierre, who had returned to his native village near Lyon. I mailed him a package of chocolates and cigarettes and in a letter asked him what I could possibly do to repay him for his gallant assistance. He replied that he did indeed need help; that since the war he had grown bald. The United States, he knew, was a country where no problem remained unsolved. Would I please send him something to make his hair grow again?

I consulted a dermatologist, who suggested a hair piece. I remonstrated, emphasizing that it was important that I really try to help Pierre. I was told the only way a bald man could grow hair was by some sort of massage, a ten-million-to-one shot. So I mailed Pirere a massage machine. He replied some weeks later that he appreciated the rich gift, but that unfortunately there was no electricity in his village. I despaired of helping, but was cheered when I received a heartening letter from him: "While I do not find your little machine useful for my own problem," he wrote, "I have found it to be most rewarding financially. Each Sunday morning I go to the nearest village which does have electricity and I rent your machine to the local baldies, explaining that it will regenerate their hair. We are all being patient. Meanwhile I make enough to pay for the week's wine and bread. How can I ever thank you?"

Again I turned to being an actor, touring in road shows of *You Can't Take It with You* and *The Man Who Came to Dinner*. When it became obvious that my talent was modest, I decided to be a radio announcer, and was given an opportunity after working at NBC as a guide. Unfortunately I did not heed the advice of Martin Block, one of America's first disc jockeys with his popular "Make-Believe Ball Room Time." He warned me to be careful in correcting bloopers, counseling it was better to allow a mistake to slide by so that the listener would at least wonder if he really heard it. My big chance came when I was to say "and now we take you to the smoky city of Pittsburgh and the music of..." It came out "smoky shitty." Alas, I failed to remember Block's admonition and tried to correct my error, the final sentence in my radio announcer's career being "and now we take you to the smoky, shitty city of Pittsburgh..."

Perhaps I could be a dramatist. My first play was a comedy about my experiences in the German prisoner-of-war camp. Herman Shumlin, one of Broadway's top producers, optioned the play but delayed production fearing the public was not ready for wartime humor. Shumlin's associate, a young lawyer, disagreed with him. While they debated timing, *Stalag 17* was produced and became a hit. Shumlin and his partner separated. I often reflect on whether my life might not have been different had David Merrick taken my play with him when he broke with Shumlin.

There was a guarantee of $200 a month from Shumlin's option for at least a year. I had a serious talk with the airline stewardess I met in Fort Worth on my first visit after being mustered out of service. Helen agreed (a) to marry me and (b) to live in South America where I could continue to write in a place where $200 would go a long way. We chose Chile on the basis of an encyclopedia article which said that in Chile it was possible to ski in the Andes in the morning and swim in the Pacific on the same afternoon. Later we found this to be true, if it did make for an arduous day.

We were surprised to find that it was snowing the day we arrived in Santiago from the port of Valparaiso. We had no way of knowing then—July 14, 1948—that it had been the first snow to fall on the Chilean capital in thirty-seven years. We had failed to comprehend that if you go far enough south you outdistance the birds; that it is possible to travel just as far on the other side of the equator as it is on "our" side. That on the other side the world has summer in winter, a reversal of seasons. Thus by choosing July as our arrival date we had inadvertently hit the middle of winter. We had come to a land where oysters are eaten in the months without "r." We were almost as far from New York

7

as Moscow is, farther south than the tip of South Africa.

Our adjustment to a new life was made easier because Helen and I both knew Spanish; I had studied the language casually in college and seriously while visiting a brother who lived in Mexico, and Helen had learned conversational Spanish while an airline stewardess.

We spent our first six months in gray and drab Santiago, hardly a jewel of a city but one enhanced by a perfect setting in the lush central valley of Chile with the snow-covered Andes looming over the capital. I wrote, selling a juvenile play and sending another comedy to an agent in New York. I attended classes at the University of Chile and joined a local theater group of the English-speaking community. Word came from Shumlin that *Stalag 17* had pre-empted production of my play. Money was running out, so my wife Helen and I decided to return to the United States. But, just after we spent our remaining funds on two airplane tickets, an unexpected opportunity arose to buy *The South Pacific Mail*, Latin America's oldest English-language newspaper. The British owner had sent his son to the London School of Journalism, planning to turn the family business over to him, but the son was killed in World War II. The father died, leaving the paper in debt, and the family was delighted to find a young American incautious enough to take the paper and its debts off their hands for a small payment I borrowed. After trading in our two return tickets, Helen and I moved to the port of Valparaiso, where the paper was printed in a local newspaper plant. After a year it became obvious that our journal would never survive unless we could afford a printing plant and augment our income from advertising with profitable, commercial printing. We moved back to Santiago and purchased some old, secondhand presses.

The morning I signed the contract for the printing equipment I received a telephone call from the man I had thought to be a diplomat from the American embassy, inviting me to lunch.

The Cold War had begun to heat up in 1950; Joseph Stalin was still living. The combination of a printing press and a clearable American —then—was irresistible to the local CIA chief.

As we drove slowly through the countryside and up the road to the mountains the CIA Station Chief told me that an investigation of my background, and Helen's, had been carried out over a period of several months, which explained letters from Texas reporting that "credit investigators" had been asking questions. When the CIA first learned of my intention to buy the printing equipment the thought occurred to them that having available a secure printing facility would be useful. Brad asked if I could operate the presses myself. I told him I could not handle the largest alone, but could do so with the two smaller ones. He said

8

that was fine, and that I should be prepared for some night work in the print shop after the Chilean employees had gone for the day.

"May I tell my wife?" It occurred to me that Helen might have a healthy curiosity about unexplained nocturnal absences.

"By all means," Brad said. "It is a myth that intelligence men don't say anything to their wives about their work. If you can't trust her discretion, you shouldn't be in the business. If you can't tell her, it's better that you not try to help us."

"Another thing," I said. "I'm in rehearsal for a play with the little theater group here. Almost every night. Will I have to give that up?"

"No." Brad paused. "As a matter of fact, you should stay in amateur theatricals. It might be a good way for you to meet agents you will be handling."

"What does that mean?" I asked.

"That comes later," Brad said. He went on to inform me that I would be paid a monthly salary of $50.00, to be deposited in my Texas bank after going through a financial cover company in New York, and would have a local expense account of $12.50 monthly. I was pleased. In Chile in 1950 fifty bucks a month would hire a full-time maid, buy a supply of firewood, and pay for a dozen bottles of good wine.

Brad said we would see each other only rarely. Routine meetings would be held in a "safe house" with my "case officer," one of his subordinates. He explained: a safe house could be an apartment or office or hotel room, chosen for its security, where I would meet with my case officer, the CIA official who would be my contact and manager. He then gave me a hand-drawn map directing me to an apartment. "Sort of like an account executive in an advertising agency," Brad said. "You will see each other about twice a week. Your first meeting in this safe house will be next Tuesday afternoon at 3 P.M. and your case officer will be known to you in alias as Linda."

Linda? In Spanish it means pretty.

"You mean my case officer is a woman?"

"That's right," Brad said, grinning.

"Won't it look funny if anyone sees I'm meeting with a woman in an apartment?"

"Nothing funny at all," Brad said, "about a man and a woman meeting regularly, particularly when two men meeting are suspected of being homosexual. A man and woman trysting in Chile will be natural and acceptable enough to outsiders."

I thought: Not to Helen.

That night I told Helen about my new part-time job. She shrugged, amused, and said that it would be good to have the extra money. We were expecting our first child. I failed to mention to Helen that my case

9

officer was a woman. Brad, in his countryside briefing, had told me that one tenet of the intelligence business was confining knowledge of our business to a "need-to-know" and this seemed to be a good time to put it into practice. As a matter of fact, I was rather excited about the prospect of meeting a woman for huggermugger purposes in a Santiago apartment. All the spy stories I had read described free-spirited, beautiful women with long legs and sometimes with round heels. The more I thought about it, the more intriguing the prospect became. In fact I began to savor the meeting with "Linda."

On Tuesday before the meeting I showered, used deodorant unsparingly, and dressed in my Sunday suit. I followed the map given me by Brad and found a gloomy building of rundown offices and shabby apartments. A dark arcade on the ground floor bisected the building. Stairs littered with trash led to the third floor. I had to light a match to find the apartment number, and knocked on the door with what I hoped was a properly conspiratorial rap. I checked my tie and ran my comb quickly through my hair. I was really quite keyed up. Perhaps I should have purchased a flower for my lapel?

Linda opened the door.

Linda was certainly a formidable-looking woman. She inspected me through glasses which might have been fashioned from the bottoms of Coca-Cola bottles, then tossed her head in an ungracious invitation to enter. I followed her into the dismal apartment. Linda's hair was short, cut in masculine style and her clothes heavy and . . . practical. She wore no make-up at all. I found myself staring at her shoes, which had metal tips on the toes, much like the footwear used by Chilean copper miners. Linda was obviously a practical woman. My boss.

Linda had an agenda, and she methodically ticked off the items one by one. I must always check to be sure I was not being followed when entering and departing from the safe house area. I could telephone her during the day at one number and at night at another, always using an alias to identify myself. Another false name—this time a pseudonym, or full alias with first name and middle initial—would be used when signing CIA reports or receipts. Any unusual contact with suspicious strangers was to be reported in writing. I should henceforth proceed on the assumption that my telephone calls were being monitored and my mail being read.

"I have a lot to learn," I told Linda.

"Of course," she said. She stared at me through the Coca-Cola bottoms. "When can you go to Conus for training?"

"Conus?"

"The Continental United States," Linda explained.

"To school?"

"For three weeks," Linda said. "In New York. A special training course in tradecraft. Specifically, to prepare you for your first operational assignment."

"And that will be?"

"We intend to dangle you," my case officer said.

"Dangle?"

"A dangle operation is when something or someone of interest is intentionally put into the path of another intelligence service with the hope it will bite. In this case, you will be the bait. We plan to plant the word around Santiago that you are not really a newspaper editor, but the chief of American intelligence for Chile. We believe Soviet intelligence, the KGB, will approach you and try to cultivate you, in an attempt to find out who you are and what you are doing."

It occurred to me that I should have asked Brad for sixty bucks a month.

"What good will that do?" I asked.

"We will be able to identify the KGB contact, what his method of operation is, and what he is interested in. Of course he will learn nothing about American intelligence because you don't know anything."

That made sense. I told Linda I would be able to travel to New York within the next couple of weeks. She handed me an envelope, indicating that it contained tourist-class airfare and per diem for one week in New York. I was to account for all expenses, keeping receipts. She gave me contact instructions for meeting a CIA man in New York.

I decided to test the system. "Linda, I often have a pain in my back, way down low. I really should travel first-class on such a long trip."

Linda chortled, literally slapping her thigh. Oh, well, just thought I'd try.

Linda ended the meeting by standing up abruptly. "I'll leave first," she said. "See you here next Monday at ten in the morning. Be sure you're not followed. And don't forget to turn off the radio, the water and the lights before you leave here."

For the first time I realized a radio was blaring, and the water running in a tiny kitchen sink. I was impressed. That was to thwart any bugs. Linda may not have been a raving beauty, but she was professional.

As a starving actor in New York I had lived in a number of flea-bags, so it was pleasant to enjoy a clean and comfortable hotel for a change in that city. Government travelers are given per diem, the daily payment which is an allowance for food and lodging, usually more than enough in smaller cities but never enough for large ones. As instructed by Linda, I waited in my room for a telephone call from "Jack," who was to be my training officer. We met and he took me to a brownstone in the East Seventies. It was a CIA safe house for training overseas personnel who were under cover, or anyone whose job was so sensitive that he was not allowed to visit Washington or the Agency training retreat in nearby Virginia. There were other agents in the safe house, but I never saw them. When I went to the john my instructor would check first to be sure it was not occupied by another student.

During the first week Jack was the only training officer I saw. His task was to teach me basic tradecraft, especially the techniques of conducting and countering surveillance. Jack was a slight man with a scarred face; he lighted one cigarette from another throughout the day. I was reassured since he looked and acted more like a spy than the intelligence officers I had met in Santiago. He had grown up in Europe where his father had been a peripatetic executive for an American oil company, and spoke half a dozen European languages fluently. He was a "street man," an officer who specialized in meeting and recruiting spies and running dark alley operations, as opposed to the operations officers who spend much of their time at desks and work hard for promotion and positions of management responsibility. I learned that, when I told a case officer on the telephone I would meet him at the Roxy Theater at eleven, I really meant under the clock at the Biltmore at twelve. I found that I would meet agents using an alias, perhaps never revealing my true name. I learned recognition procedures: "You go into the men's room at the movie with a copy of *Newsweek* in your left hand. You say to the agent, 'Haven't we met in Cairo?' If he answers 'No, but I seem to remember you from Alexandria,' the meeting is okay." Jack taught me how to make a "brush pass," when a case officer ostensibly bumps into his agent accidentally but when they part there has been a quick exchange of documents, perhaps folded into identical newspapers. I practiced loading "dead drops," public but usually unobserved receptacles where papers or packages can be stashed and picked up later without any personal meeting. Jack taught me how to use "danger signals"—an X scrawled on a wall with blue chalk might mean that it was all right to have a subsequent meeting, while a circle was a warning that the encounter must be aborted.

Surveillance exercises were on the streets of New York; sometimes Jack would be joined by colleagues who acted as a team. I tried to elude them. Once I purchased a ticket to a Broadway show where a friend from my acting days was stage manager and through his good offices slipped out through the stage door to Shubert Alley. Jack was leaning against a wall waiting and shook his head in disgust at such an obvious ploy. I considered the whole thing fun and games, and enjoyed it, even if my feet were sore. But Jack was bored, and often mentioned how anxious he was to get back to overseas operations. Later I realized why he thought it so dull: I was a neophyte in the intelligence business, taking the freshman course. It was some years later before I graduated into the more esoteric graduate schools of tradecraft.

The second week my tutor was "Paul," a morose man with a red face who looked like a bartender but was a specialist in Communism. I didn't like Paul very much, because he gave me homework assignments which kept me up to the morning hours, but when the week was over I knew the history of the Marxist revolution and the intimate biographies of Communist and Socialist leaders in the major countries of the world. The final test was an oral presentation to Paul, repeated several times until it was accepted as convincing, in which I pretended to be an American Communist.

The third and final week concentrated on the techniques of propaganda and political action. My teacher was a genial professorial type who, to my surprise, stuttered. I had presumed that everyone working with the CIA passed a rigid physical exam which rejected those with the slightest handicap. I enjoyed my classes with "Edgar." We drank countless cups of black coffee while he taught me the arcane arts of clandestine and black broadcasting, the former being transmissions with an identified sponsorship from an unspecified location, the latter ones claiming to emanate from a political group which did not really exist or, falsely, from one which did. Edgar was especially devoted to the rumor technique and recounted stories of orchestrated rumor campaigns which were decisive in affecting political and military events. He explained the political potential in organized groups of women, students, and laborers. He was evangelical in describing the political and propaganda coups he had orchestrated during World War II as a member of O.S.S.

I asked Edgar, "Why am I being taught this?"

"Your file," Edgar replied, "indicates you have the qualifications we look for in a propaganda specialist."

"But I don't intend to spend more than part-time working for the 'company.'" I had already learned that term, and that CIA headquarters in Washington was called the "Pickle Factory" by many of its people.

"I've heard that before," Edgar said, and gave me a reading assignment for the next day.

Edgar had asked me to read the portentous exchange between George F. Kennan—writing under the nom de plume of "Mr. X"—and Walter Lippmann in *Foreign Affairs*. The debate concerned the virtues of the United States policy of containment, whose success was forecast by Kennan and witnessed in Europe and whose folly was recognized by Lippmann and witnessed in Southeast Asia. Edgar philosophized the next morning. The objective of the containment policy lay in halting the advancing frontiers of the Soviet empire into the territory which bore the optimistic if perhaps naïve cachet the "Free World." Its method lay in building an armed alliance which would restrain Soviet armies and those of the Soviets' allies. Containment, then, had spawned a Cold War —a term coined by Bernard Baruch. Containment shifted the effort of conquest to the terrain of subversion. A contest was under way between political adversaries—the Soviet Union and the United States—which avoided the engagement of armed forces. In this less-than-a-hot war, intelligence services had become instruments of Soviet and American foreign policy. Without gainsaying the vital and immense role played by the Marshall Plan, for example, in constructing the economic fortifications of Western Europe, the pickets and skirmishers of the Cold War were the contending KGB and CIA, and the agents and intermediaries who collaborated with them.

"And our most recent and best information," Edgar concluded, "is that the Soviets intend to carry the Cold War into Latin America. With their Communist parties in place already in every country, they certainly have the capability. We want to be ready. Maybe you can help us."

I thought about Edgar's exposition on the plane flying back to Chile. Not a chance. I had no intention of being a professional intelligence officer. I was concerned with making *The South Pacific Mail* a paying proposition, a goal which seemed hazy and distant and certainly not to be achieved without priority attention. No, not a chance would I become a Cold Warrior.

In Santiago things had slipped badly at *The South Pacific Mail*, and I decided that I needed someone on the staff capable of running the paper during my future absences. I hired a young Australian, Rick Bowers, who had been teaching at a British school. Times were tough, and money was short. Meeting the weekly payroll was often the result of anguish. Rick and I worked long and tedious hours getting the paper out, especially during the early months when we were both learning the rudiments of the printing trade. Soon we obtained commercial contracts which, using the presses when they would otherwise be idle, began to pay off. Some debts were paid, but the accountant was still using red ink.

Managing a newspaper with a readership primarily British, but also catering to Americans, Europeans, and Chileans, was tricky. Each editorial was a walk on a nationalistic tightrope. The British readers, not overjoyed that an American youth had usurped their journal, were not always gracious in their comments. When I wrote the first in a series of columns about the local softball league of the American community, one British correspondent insisted that the stories be abandoned. "I am not interested in soft balls," he wrote. Once I needed to fill one column

14

of the final page before the paper went to press. We had set in type a promotion advertisement for such occasions, a two-column announcement that "*The South Pacific Mail* is the Newspaper Most Read on the West Coast of South America." I had to fill only a one-column space, so I narrowed the two-column announcement by omitting some words and using initials. The result gave British readers cause for merriment: "*The South Pacific Mail* is the Newspaper Most Read on the W.C. of South America." Rick was once irritated with a reader who had written a really nasty letter complaining about the quality of Rick's reporting on the British cricket games in Santiago. Rick stopped the press just before the last copy of the next issue was printed. Under the offending letter he inserted a slug of type which read: "Fuck you, Dear Reader." Just a joke, of course. Rick wanted the satisfaction of reading the admonition in type. Exhausted after the week's work, Rick and I relaxed in the shop, doing away with most of a bottle of rum. A delivery boy, unnoticed, came in and gathered up a load of papers, including the one with the X-rated exhortation. We never did find out to which customer that copy was delivered.

I continued to act in amateur shows. I even played a major role in one Chilean film—this because I had written the screenplay and included as one character a gringo engineer who mirrored my own physical appearance. At a meeting with Linda she told me Brad had decided I was ready to handle an intelligence "source." She explained that would mean I would be an "outside" case officer who would meet and debrief a trusted and dependable spy.

"How do I meet him?" I asked.

"You already have," Linda said. "At our request he volunteered for backstage work with your group. That provides the cover you both need—you can claim that you met and became friends during the play."

So the quiet little man I thought had joined our little theater group "to improve my English" was really a spy, perhaps a better actor than any of us. As Linda predicted, I was able to meet him and transact our business securely long after the play was over. This method of meeting and staying in contact with agents was one I later used in several countries —nowhere did an amateur group spurn the offer of a local citizen to help backstage and "to improve his English."

Next, Linda told me, Operation Dangle had begun. The word had been put out that I was not a newspaper editor, but the chief of American intelligence in Chile. She did not say how, but later I learned that a double-agent—an opportunist who worked both sides of the espionage street—had been allowed to discover my alleged role, with the CIA knowing he would report back to his other, Marxist sponsors. (Subsequently I learned that scores of agents are on the payrolls of the world's intelligence services precisely because they are disloyal and can be used as conduits of dis-information.)

I waited. Anyone who approached me was suspect: a stranger asking for directions on the street; a foreign diplomat being friendly at a cocktail party; an insistent insurance salesman; a Chilean soliciting funds for charity. What did a KGB agent look like? How did he act?

When anyone expressed any interest in me I would give Linda his name at our next meeting. It would sometimes take several days—cables had to be sent to and from other countries and Washington—before she would tell me that checks were negative.

As I understood the rules of the mysterious game, there was no reason to tell Linda of people with whom I became acquainted at my own initiative. I didn't tell her, for instance, of a new Chilean friend I was seeing fairly frequently. He was a genial fellow who had mailed an announcement to *The South Pacific Mail*, offering to pay for English-from-Spanish translations of a study he had written on Santiago's colonial architecture. I of course snapped up the offer, not even printing his advertisement. We saw each other often. He was always meticulous, explaining that he wanted everything to be just right since his study was to be printed by a London historical society. I didn't complain as long as he paid, which he did generously.

Linda, incidentally, had changed. She no longer wore the thick glasses which had intimidated me before, and her selection of clothes was more feminine. For the first time I became aware that she had a rather good figure. At one of our meetings I told her she was looking very nice, and she smiled.

The telephone rang at *The South Pacific Mail*. Helen was calling from the hospital. The doctor had just told her that an immediate operation was necessary, following numerous false alarms about the birth of our first child. Something had gone wrong. "Hurry," Helen said, "Little Caesar will be born within the hour."

There were no cabs in sight on the street, so I hustled to the nearest corner where I saw a crowd of people which, I thought, was pushing its way into a bus. I say "thought" because as I reached the corner the bus toppled over on its side. The mob had been pushing the bus *over*, not pushing *into* the bus. A woman screamed and a frightened tot jumped from an open window. I headed for the central plaza, hoping to find better transportation.

In the plaza a typical Latin riot was erupting. Two more buses lay on their sides, one with its wheels still spinning. Students were rushing back and forth, shouting and cursing. A fat woman who had been trampled sat on the sidewalk, legs askew, staring blankly as oranges spilled from her market sack into the gutter. An old man cringed behind a lottery kiosk. For a moment, stunned, I stood motionless. A machine gun sputtered across the plaza. I moved then.

Crouching behind an automobile I had time to reconstruct what had happened. The day before, municipal authorities had announced a steep increase in bus fares and provoked a commuters' strike. Some buses had been stoned, a few tires punctured. But now the citizens of Santiago, encouraged by rabble-rousers, were on a rampage, upsetting buses all over the city and shouting defiance at the police.

Machine gun bursts continued to echo between the buildings around the plaza. An army half-track packed with soldiers skidded to a stop in front of the Workers' Insurance Building, known to Chileans as the Tower of Blood. (In 1938 thirty-odd teenage students were senselessly slaughtered there.) The machine gun burped again. The soldiers were shooting above the heads of the rioters whenever they massed.

I ducked into a side street, determined to run the mile to the clinic. Just as I rounded the corner, a half dozen thugs grabbed me and lifted me bodily against the wall of a bank.

When violence breaks out in Latin America the fury of the mob is likely to be turned on any foreigner, especially the *yanqui*. In this case my blond hair was like an American flag, and the rowdies who grabbed me had been drinking. I knew I was in real trouble when the ringleader shouted in my face: "Yankee, what are you doing in our country?"

"*Was ist los? Was ist los?*" I shouted back, trying desperately to remember my prison-camp German. "*Raus! Ich liebe dich! Ich liebe dich!*"

The ringleader of the gang inspected me suspiciously. Then he released his grip on my collar, allowing me to breathe again. Turning to his cohorts he said, with a sneer, "Let him go, fellows. Just another kraut." And he led his gang away in search of other buses or *yanquis* who might still be upright.

There was no place to hide. Shopkeepers were anxiously rolling down the heavy iron grilles which protect their businesses against looting in times of crisis. But finally I found an open door and darted in. It was a florist's shop. It occurred to me that I really did need some flowers for Helen's room at the hospital. So I bought some gladiolas. In fact, I purchased every single long-stemmed gladiola the florist had and arranged them in my arms so that they completely covered my face. Camouflaged by the floral hedge, I stepped into the street and headed toward the hospital.

The ploy worked fine. A fragrant Birnam Wood sort of thing. No one could see the *yanqui* countenance behind the mass of blooms, and those who cared must have thought me a delivery boy, burdened with an

17

unusually large order. One cheery soul, panting as he hustled toward the plaza to see the bloodshed, yelled at me, "You people will have a lot of business tomorrow."

In our first luncheon meeting Brad told me one reason I had been approached by the CIA was that I spoke fluent Spanish. While the CIA has an excellent language school, there is no substitute for learning on the job in the country where the language is spoken. In Latin America there is one difficulty: most Latins are so courteous that they seldom correct a foreigner's mistake, even if a young woman at a formal dinner party translates her high school Spanish literally to say "I'm warm" and comes out with something a great deal more electrifying concerning an intense sexual desire.

A tourist does not really need Spanish in Latin America. One can travel from Panama to Tierra del Fuego and always find shopkeepers who speak sufficient English to sell you something. But if you make the return trip to sell something to them, you won't find a Latin who can say "cat" in English.

In our first months in Chile, while I was staying at home and writing, I did not improve my Spanish significantly. Once in business, I perfected it pronto. There is no better way—despite a myth to the contrary—to be precise in learning a language than to have accuracy make the difference between profit and loss.

It was not so easy for Helen. Wives must learn in the kitchen and deal with servants who sometimes speak atrocious Spanish.

I recall one young American bride's problem in Santiago. Her husband was a new arrival at the American embassy, and the Ambassador was invited for dinner. The bride's Spanish was so limited that she could carry on only the most rudimentary conversation with her maid. She did get across the point that the Ambassador was going to be on hand, and that she wanted everything properly served. Especially, she told the maid, she wanted the fish served with a lemon in the mouth. The maid seemed to think this was a silly idea. She protested, even threatened to quit. But the young American wife insisted: "*Con un limón en la boca, con un limón en la boca,*" she repeated over and over again. Finally the maid agreed to serve the fish that way, stupid as the idea was. That night the visiting Ambassador straightened up when the fish was served on a silver tray, by a maid who stubbornly held a lemon in her tightly clenched teeth!

Language problems work both ways, and the language barrier can be a hurdle even for one who has fluent command of a second tongue. One night at a dinner party in Santiago I was seated next to a charming

18

Chilean lady who spoke excellent English. Helen was visiting in the United States and my companion inquired about when she was returning. I said in a few days.

"Oh, I'm so glad," my dinner partner said, "because she's bringing me two chastity belts."

I stammered a bit and then asked my friend if she were not possibly thinking of something else. She insisted that she had the right items in mind.

"Are you sure?" I asked.

"Of course I'm sure," was the reply from my dinner partner, who was beginning to be a bit testy. "They're for my children—two Hop-A-Long Chastity Belts!"

Brad's tour as Chief of Station in Santiago ended. He introduced me to his replacement, "Bob," who had just arrived from another Latin American country. The new chief was a pleasant man with an insurance salesman's quick smile. I was becoming accustomed to the fact that intelligence officers look like other people.

Linda too was preparing to leave Chile for a new post. As her time remaining in Santiago diminished, she grew increasingly frustrated and impatient. Operation Dangle was her baby, and she was disappointed that nothing had developed. At the end of one of our meetings she said we would meet again on Thursday morning.

"Linda," I said, "could we postpone that until Friday? I'm doing a translation job for a fellow and I have to work with him on Thursday."

"All right." Then Linda asked, "Who is he?"

"A Chilean."

"Why didn't you tell me about him?"

"Oh, he's not a candidate for Dangle," I said. "He didn't approach me. I approached him."

"Where does he work?"

"I don't know." I began to have a queasy feeling. "But I do have his name and post office box, if you want to check him out."

"Post office box?" Linda cast her eyes heavenward. "I think I'd better check him out. It's not impossible that our target dangled himself in order to meet our dangle."

Several days later Linda contacted me for an emergency meeting at the safe house. I had a premonition about what she was going to tell me. I was right.

"You've been had," Linda said. "We had no traces on the name of your friend. But he made a mistake and went back to the post office box he had rented, and we followed him home. We checked out his real name and...there was our Dangle prize. He's a member of the Com-

19

munist Party and has made a dozen trips to Moscow. The one we were fishing for." Linda grimaced. "You should have told me about him in the beginning."

"I'm sorry, Linda. I'll do better next time."

"How?" Linda asked herself, shaking her head slowly from side to side. "How did we ever beat the British?"

I presumed she was referring to the revolution two hundred years ago. In any event it didn't seem a very gracious thing to say. "What do I do now?" I asked.

"Disengage," Linda said. "He has too much of a head start on you—he's been absorbing everything he's learned about you while you . . ." She kindly left the sentence unfinished. "Never mind. Fortunately we have someone else close to him, so we can take it from there."

A week later Linda and I met for the last time in the safe house. Despite my clumsy handling of the case, she was content with the outcome of Operation Dangle and anxious to depart for her new post. She told me that in the future I would be meeting with the new chief.

It was time to say good-bye. After reminding me to turn off the radio and shut off the water, Linda stretched up on her toes to kiss me on the cheek. I felt very warm toward her; it had been fun. And what a change! I had never seen such a metamorphosis. Linda looked really quite attractive, petite and chic. She was wearing a cashmere sweater which revealed what was a really fine figure, and her lips were red with an impudent dab of lipstick.

"Linda, I'm going to miss you," I said. "It's been great—professionally and personally. To tell you the truth I didn't feel that way when we first met, but you've changed so much. You're really a good-looking gal."

Linda laughed. "I won't win any prizes," she said. "You see, I've been in the business of meeting men in safe houses for a long time, and I've learned how to keep them safe. Sometimes I meet local agents, Latins. A Latin feels he simply has to make a pass at any woman he is alone with, just to be macho. And the Americans I deal with aren't much better. So I learned to turn you guys off in the beginning. It's made life a lot easier."

And Linda kissed me good-bye, not on the cheek this time, but on the lips.

Bob and I met for the first time in a safe house, a new one. He wasted no time. "We want you to attempt to make a recruitment. Our best agent in the Communist Party is aging, and illness keeps him away from Party activity much of the time. We need a new penetration, a source who is well enough wired in to give us solid information, not only on what they can do but on what they intend to do. Before she left Linda wrote a target study on our candidate, who is named Juan."

"A target study?" I asked.

"Trade term," Bob said. He smiled, looking all the world like the principal of a junior high school. "We've selected Juan for recruitment, and the target study is a compilation of everything we know about him. From information gathered by other agents, from several weeks of surveillance, and from his government file, which we were able to borrow from...a friend. Briefly, Juan is a hard worker and respected in the Party. He often acts as a courier and has traveled to the Bloc countries. Will you have a go at trying to recruit him?"

I hesitated. Just how deeply was I being drawn into this murky business? But finally I agreed. "Okay. Tell me about him."

"Juan owns a small bookstore which specializes in Marxist literature," Bob said. "He grew up in a broken middle-class family. His father deserted it when Juan was ten. He and his brothers and sisters had to work to keep things going, particularly after their mother became an invalid. Juan scratched his way through the university, where he was converted to Marxism. Five years ago he joined the Communist Party. He is married and has one child. According to our best sources he is beginning to have second thoughts about the extent of Soviet control over the local Party. His Communist colleagues have begun to note this."

"Any other soft spots?" I asked.

"The vulnerability paragraph in the study is skimpy," Bob said. "But we do know that things have been rough for him financially. He receives some money from the Party, but he needs more."

"Is money important to him?"

"Probably not," Bob said. "But it is to his wife. She's a bit of a harridan and doesn't like his politics. She wants him to drop the proletariat emphasis of his bookstore and solicit a more lucrative trade. In short, she's tired of being poor and wants Juan to get off his Socialist duff and make some money. That's about it. At our next meeting I'll give you a file which contains everything we know about him. His friends, personal habits, his daily routine. Before you approach him you'll have to know him well."

"How do I meet him?" I asked.

"That's up to you," Bob said. "You might consider buying some books."

"How much time do I have?"

"I would like you to meet him, cultivate him, gain his confidence, and make the pitch within three months. Six months maximum. If he won't cooperate by then, we drop the case and work on another."

I spent two weeks absorbing the information in the file Bob gave me. I walked past Juan's bookstore and staked out the shabby apartment house where he lived. I became completely engrossed in the history and character of a man I had never met. One thing was evident from the file which Bob had not mentioned: Juan had become a Communist because he really believed that was the way to a better world for his children. Also, despite the pressure from his wife, he remained a sincere and dedicated Marxist. I suspected Juan would spit in my eye when I asked him to be an informer.

It also occurred to me that this was pretty tricky business. What if Juan only pretended to accept my offer and at Party instructions played along to see what they could get out of it? Even though I would approach him in alias, he might well find out that I was the owner of *The South Pacific Mail* and a handful of metal shavings in the press would put me out of business temporarily while a single stick of dynamite would bankrupt me.

Something else bothered me even more. I began to fret about questions of the morality and personal ethics of this business. I was setting out to persuade a human being to betray his cause and his comrades. Was it really worth it? Did the U.S. government have a vital need for Juan's information? It was a long time before these hard questions were completely resolved in my own mind.

One morning I entered Juan's bookstore and began to browse. I selected a newly published volume of poems by the Chilean poet Pablo Neruda; Juan accepted my payment with a grunted *gracias*. I did not return for a week. This time I waited until Juan and I were alone. When I asked for a little-known book of Marxist esoterica Juan was suspicious. He squinted his eyes. "You are an American?"

"Yes."

"Your Spanish is good. Where did you learn of this book?"

"In my university." I was learning to lie easily. "Do you have a copy?"

Juan found the book, slipped it into a paper sack and counted out my change. I tried to continue the conversation but he cut me off abruptly.

In the following weeks I purchased several other books; each was Socialist and each successively more militant or obscure. Juan's doubts about his new and regular *yanqui* client increased. Once he asked, "Are you from the American embassy?" I indicated that I was in Chile doing some private research. "Are you a Socialist?" he asked. I said no, but that I was interested in the Socialist movement because that was the subject of a research paper I was writing.

During the next several visits I was taciturn, waiting for Juan to take the initiative in further discussion. Finally he did. "Why are you writing about Socialism?"

"I'm working on a private grant," I said. "Visiting a number of Latin American countries doing the research."

"Why don't you go to your embassy and talk to the FBI?" Juan's voice was thick with sarcasm. "They know all about us."

"Us?"

"Yes." Juan spoke evenly. "I am a Communist."

"Oh, I didn't know," I lied. "Anyway, there are no FBI people at the embassy now. But I have talked to the diplomats there. Now I need to learn the other side of the story to do a serious study."

"How do I know you are not from the FBI, despite what you say?"

"You don't," I said. "But if you are a Communist I certainly would like to talk to you about the Party here, and what its goals are."

Juan's eyes narrowed. We had arrived at a crucial point in the re- cruitment process. Finally he spoke. "All right. I don't mind talking to you about it. Perhaps your research paper will be a better one if you listen to me."

Now one of two things had happened: either Juan had accepted the idea of a confidential relationship with me, which meant his recruitment could be accelerated; or he had decided to inform the Party and to pretend to carry on such a relationship.

I reported to Bob, who was pleased. "Good," he said. "The operation is very much alive." My enthusiasm was dampened when Bob said that henceforth each time I left Juan's bookstore one of CIA's local sur- veillance teams would conduct counter-surveillance; that is, to be sure members of Juan's Communist Party or the KGB were not following me to check me out. I had never given my name to Juan.

During the next three weeks I had long, rambling discussions with Juan, some in the backroom office of his bookstore. Juan was candid in saying it was best that his friends not know of his frequent meetings with an American. A second crucial step in the recruitment process: Juan had accepted not only a confidential relationship, but a clandestine one.

Juan spoke only in general terms of the Party and its goals. He was more specific about his own conversion, and why he rejected the capitalist ethic, and of his disenchantment with the Chilean government, although he admitted it was democratic and better than the traditional military regimes of Latin America. I was honest with Juan. I told him that I was not impressed with Communism, indeed that I was an anti-Com- munist. Soon we were engaged in heated dialectic debate and—recalling the long hours of Paul's training sessions in New York—I tried to counter his points one by one. Some of our conversations carried on into evening hours after the bookstore was closed, over a bottle of Chilean *pisco*.

Juan discussed his family life without reserve. He told me of his concern that his child should have the educational opportunities which

23

had been made so difficult for him. He described the bickering between him and his wife over money matters, and her nagging insistence that he abandon the Party. I was surprised to learn something that was not in Bob's file: both Juan and his wife were fervent believers in astrology. A strange quirk for Juan, who was an atheist, but he said he read a daily astrology column in the principal newspaper each morning and that he and his wife had found the predictions in the column largely accurate. I couldn't understand the anomaly of a dedicated Marxist who was devoted to the questionable art of astrology and influenced by a daily horoscope.

After almost five months had passed Bob became impatient. "When will you make the recruitment pitch?" he asked.

"Soon," I said. "He's not quite ready. The relationship is fine, he trusts me. But not to the point where he will spy for me. I need something else, something to increase the odds."

It came to me a week later.

I called Bob for a special meeting. I said I was ready for the pitch but I would have to ask him to make another recruitment to help me with mine. Bob was intrigued by my request and said he would try to do what I asked. Three days later we met, and he said it was done. "Then I'll make the pitch a week from Tuesday," I said, and gave Bob a note I had written out for him before the meeting. He read it and smiled.

A week from that Tuesday I went by Juan's shop, pretending to be in a hurry, but saying I had something important to discuss with him. Could I return for a *pisco* after his store closed? He agreed. That night I made the pitch. I told Juan that my sponsors in the United States liked what I had done so far and had decided to enlarge the project. They believed an expanded work was in order, perhaps a book. I had been asked to stay on in Chile to put it together; they would pay well. But, I explained to Juan, I couldn't do it without his help. Unless he could provide me with more information about the Party, with details on its activities and members, I could not justify the time and expense involved.

Juan listened to the pitch, saying nothing. He was clutching the *pisco* glass so tightly his knuckles were white. Then I said it: "Juan, why don't you help me? Of course I would help you—give you half the money I receive."

Juan was quiet for a long time; he poured himself another drink. Then: "The truth is that I've been thinking of giving up Party work. That would be no good for ... your purposes."

I agreed. "No, you would have to stay in the Party. In fact, I would want you to increase your participation, working hard, perhaps some day becoming a member of the Central Committee. I'll pay your expenses. You'll have enough money to keep your wife happy, to save some for your son's education."

Juan leaned back in his chair, exhaling for a long time, as if weary but relieved. "*Hecho*," he said. "Done." In Spanish, an oral contract.

Juan had become a spy.

Later Juan talked with me about that evening. He analyzed and rationalized his reasons for accepting my offer. There was no question in his mind that he was working for United States intelligence, although he never said that. He did say that our long political conversations had influenced him; that my description of life in the United States had swayed him and had changed some of his concepts; that he had concluded that the Western way was the best way; and that he was being a better Chilean by cooperating with me and abandoning Communism. I was not sure how true any of this was, and still am not. Perhaps I did convert him.

On the other hand, in Juan's case the money was definitely a factor. He later told me about the morning of the day I made the pitch, and how he and his wife had read the astrology column with their customary enthusiasm. They had both been excited, as the horoscope said Juan would receive that day a financial offer which would change his life, allow him to continue in his work, and to solve his money problems—an offer which he must not refuse. Juan took a clipping from his pocket and read the horoscope to me.

I knew what the horoscope said because I wrote it. The assistance I asked of Bob was that someone approach the astrology columnist and bribe him to use a prepared prediction. The text I wanted was written on the piece of paper I gave Bob ten days before my offer to Juan.

I had made a recruitment, the first of a number of similar ones I was to make over the years. Bob was euphoric; he said it was a good job, professionally done, successful because of perseverance and imagination.

I wasn't sure whether I was pleased with myself or not.

The South Pacific Mail accountant began to use black ink. The commercial printing market improved. Among the routine jobs was the publication of a book in phonetics to record an anthropologist's conversations with members of a remote Chilean Indian tribe which had no alphabet or written language. We published a guidebook for tourists and Christmas cards in English and Spanish. A British friend was co-host with me on a radio program in English, sponsored by my paper. We survived the appearance of a visiting British soccer umpire who, when asked his opinion of Chileans as soccer players, responded, "They'll never learn to play the game. They don't have the brains for it."

25

I opened a liquor store called Sandy Mac's. The plan was to attract customers from the English-speaking community through free advertising whenever unused space was available in *The South Pacific Mail*. The first manager was hired through an ad seeking a bilingual person who could run the grog shop. I was pleasantly surprised when an Oxford graduate accepted the job. He explained that he was bored and just wanted something to do—it turned out he was dry and wanted something to drink. When I visited the store at the end of the opening day I found him swaying behind the counter, his eyes glazed in a rapture of fulfillment. They should have been; they were floating over the contents of several bottles of scotch. We hired another manager, settling for a fellow with lousy English and a stomach ulcer.

Helen and I took stock in January of 1954. We were into our sixth year in Chile. Daughter Maria was followed, implacably, by son David, Jr., and another daughter, Atlee. *The South Pacific Mail* and its satellite activities were doing well. We were tempted to settle permanently in Santiago, but decided that the children should have at least a few formative years at home. And then perhaps some day we could all return to Chile. Meantime Rick could run the paper, of which he now owned a percentage.

An American journalist and lecturer on Latin American affairs visited Santiago and I heard him speak. He was not very articulate. It occurred to me I too could lecture on Latin America. I made a ten-minute tape, illustrative of the type of speech I thought I could deliver, and mailed it to an agent in New York. A commitment to represent me for a two-year lecture tour in the United States came in the return mail. It was only later, visiting the lecture agent in New York, that I learned that his bureau represented the speaker I had heard in Santiago and I had been contracted to replace him.

My speaking tour of women's clubs, civic groups, and college audiences was to begin in the fall of 1954. I told Bob early in the year. He began to turn over my chores to others. Helen and I planned to spend the summer of 1954 in Europe, a trip I had arranged without cost by placing a series of advertisements for shipping companies and airlines in the newspaper in return for tickets for the entire family.

One thing we knew we would miss in the United States was the luxury of maids. A full-time, live-in servant in Chile then cost $35.00 a month, so we had become accustomed to that most pleasant of sounds, the clinking of dishes being washed by someone else in the kitchen after dinner.

We had had a number of maids in Chile. None were educated, and few gifted. One was with us only briefly. When Helen asked her to put a roll of toilet paper in the john she found the maid, an hour later, laboriously attempting to roll the paper from its original tube onto the roller in the bathroom wall, an effort surpassed only by a friend's new maid who, when asked to light the oven to cook dinner on her first day of work, built a fire of sticks and logs in the gas oven.

My favorite maid was Rosa, a diminutive sexagenarian Indian woman, a direct descendant of the fierce Araucanian tribe which was even in the nineteen fifties facing extinction (when Pedro de Valdivia, the Spanish gold seeker, went to the land of the Araucanians they gave him gold— molten and poured down his throat). Rosa was responsible for my aban- doning the hobby of painting. I had been struggling with oil painting, and in a converted bedroom-studio there were two dozen of my best efforts. When it was time for us to leave Chile I asked Rosa what she wanted for a farewell gift. I was deeply touched when she said she wanted one of my paintings. "You see," I told Helen, "this illiterate Indian woman has an instinctive appreciation for the finer things." Then, to the maid, "Of course, Rosa, you may go into my studio and take your choice." Shortly Rosa returned with her favorite of my works—my palette!

We certainly would miss our friends. Living in a foreign community overseas leads to friendships which are close and enduring. We had many Chilean friends we might never see again. Another group consisted of American friends, many from the American embassy, which we might be seeing again in the future. Dick and Nancy Cushing; Dick was the embassy press attaché, a former AP reporter, and we would serve with them again in several countries. Ted and Phyllis Long; Ted was a young Third Secretary at the embassy, who once remarked on a classmate at Princeton I had never heard of then named Bill Colby. Another former AP reporter, Allen Stewart, with whom I would play golf around the South American continent in the next two decades, and his wife Marian. There was a young American couple I met at the University of Chile; "Wally" was a brilliant scholar who was to become an outstanding CIA street man, and with whom I would serve in other countries.

Then there was an American neighbor who lived down the street. His name was "Jake," and he became an excruciating bore because of his detailed descriptions of his job selling detergents for an American com- pany. Jake and his wife and Helen and I once enjoyed a marvelous week camping alongside a turbulent Andean stream, spending long evening hours before a fire on which the women cooked the tasty mountain trout we had caught during the day. Jake almost spoiled the outing with his enthusiastic recital of the virtues of detergents and the vital role they played in his life.*

* Three years later someone tapped me on the shoulder in the halls of CIA headquarters in Washington. It was Jake. "Want to buy some soap?" he asked with a wicked smile. We had been deep-cover CIA colleagues, living within shout-

One of my final assignments in Chile was routine. Bob asked me to attend a Marxist political rally and report on the proceedings. I sat in the rear of a dingy auditorium and observed the motley gathering, which was boosting the theme of the popular front. I was fascinated by one of the speakers, a small man wearing thick glasses who strutted around the stage like a bantam rooster, making his political points skillfully. Despite his less than 'impressive appearance he was a brilliant dialectician and was sincere and convincing when expounding his Marxist theories. I told Bob later that the man was worth watching. Bob noted the name: Salvador Allende.

Bob had one more assignment for me. "Now we will find out if your recruitment of Juan will stick. The turnover. Perhaps he was charmed by you as a person and will refuse to cooperate with a new case officer. That will be the real test—when you tell him you are leaving." Juan and I met for the last time in our safe house. I told him I was leaving and that henceforth he would be seeing another American. Juan shrugged, signed his monthly salary receipt, and wished me well. I wished him the best, too, and meant it.

Rick took over the management of the paper while Helen and I put our affairs in order for the Europe trip and our return to the United States. Bob called me late one evening during this period. He wanted to see me; a message had arrived from Washington which needed to be answered at once. He picked me up a few blocks from my house. We drove up the road leading to the mountains. There was a full moon and it was bright as daytime with the light reflected from Andean snows.

"Brad cabled from Washington, asking you to accept a special assignment. You would have to leave at once, tomorrow if possible."

"Not a chance," I said. "We have tickets for Europe and the packers are coming next week."

"Okay," Bob said. "I'll tell headquarters."

Of course I was curious. "What kind of assignment?"

Bob said he had no idea.

"Where?" I asked. Again Bob didn't know.

"How long would it take?"

"That I do know. The message says you would have to be away from your family for at least four months. Perhaps more."

I was intrigued. While cutting it close, I did have six months before the lecture tour in the States would begin. "This is ridiculous," I told Bob.

---

ing distance of each other in Santiago, and I had never suspected. He had known about me, however, and plagued me with his detergent cover story just "for the hell of it," as he noted.

"I can't leave Helen with three kids, expect her to pack, and go God knows where for God knows how long."

"I understand," Bob said. He looked at me closely. "The only other thing the cable said was you were to buy a ticket to New York on Pan American and that at one of the stops you would be contacted."

I finally asked Bob to wait until the next morning before responding to the cable. I wanted to talk to Helen. Her reaction surprised me: she told me to go ahead; otherwise I would spend the rest of my life wondering what would have happened had I accepted the assignment. Anyway, she added, the prospect of traveling through Europe with three babies in tow seemed less and less attractive as the departure date for England neared. She would pack, move to the United States, and wait until she could join me.

"All right," I finally said. "But I promise you one thing—this is the last time! I want to settle down and make a normal life for us. I'm going to quit the spy business."

Helen smiled.

There was a festive farewell party in *The South Pacific Mail* shop. Helen drove me to the airport.

The four-engine DC-6 flew up the spine of the Andes, peaks surpassed in height only by the Himalayas. I didn't know where I was going, or what I was going to do. I only knew I had a one-way ticket to adventure.

I was excited as hell.

2

GUATEMALA 1954

To hell with Brad, and to hell with the CIA—I was in what was called in Fort Worth in my youth the cross-bar hotel. Arrested and fingerprinted like a common criminal as well as dumped into a cell of the Fort Lauderdale jail with half a dozen hoodlums. Just wait until I got out, so I could tell Brad to take his CIA, its secrets and false documents, and stuff them in an appropriate orifice.

It was March of 1954 when I left Chile on that Pan American flight without knowing my final destination. At the Miami airport a CIA man met my plane to tell me I would not be traveling further. My first question was to ask what the assignment was; he told me to be patient and I would be briefed shortly. Meanwhile he introduced me to a security type who provided me with false documents, confused me with arcane instructions, and drove me to a safe house north of Miami. I needed new clothes. Early one morning I deposited a cash per diem advance against expenses in a Hollywood bank and then bought a suit and some shirts at a clothing store just down the street. The store manager asked me how I would pay when I picked up the suit after alterations. I told him with a check from the nearby bank. When I returned for my clothes that night, I wrote out the check and handed it over. A large man who looked like a bear and a small one who looked like a fox emerged from the back of the store where they had been observing the transaction and declared I was under arrest. "For intent to defraud," was the reason given when I asked why; "a bum check." The store manager had telephoned the bank during my absence and had been told that I had no account. This was wrong, but perhaps I should have warned him the account was new. The store manager had then summoned the local police; they had skulked behind a curtain waiting for me to return and pay with what they thought to be a bouncing check.

"Let's see your identification," the big detective ordered. I opened my wallet and realized, with a jolt, that most of the documents in it were mint-fresh phonies printed by CIA in a false name. These documents would only generate further complications since my check, now in the massive paw of the detective, was signed in my true name. Sifting through the phony documentation I finally found a limp Chilean driver's license and a tattered Chilean identity carnet. I explained that I had returned from a long absence outside the country, had opened the bank account just that morning, and the check was perfectly good as they could verify by calling the bank and asking for the new accounts person. The smaller law officer pointed out that the bank was closed. Producing the deposit slip, I suggested that the store hold my check until morning and keep their bloody clothes. Then everybody would be happy. The detective looked at the store manager, who shrugged his acquiescence. By this time a group of customers was watching the scene with some interest.

Just as I thought the matter was resolved, the big detective asked an embarrassing question: "What you got in the envelope?"

Tucked under one arm I had a manila envelope. It had been given to me by the security man. Inside were a dozen classified papers, including instructions on finding the safe house, recognition signals for persons who would be showing up there, and two documents which showed my smiling face over false signatures. It was patent that the contents of the envelope would not help my case.

"I'm sorry," I said. "I can't tell you."

It's only a short drive from Hollywood, Florida, to the County Jail in Fort Lauderdale. On arrival I insisted on speaking with the senior official on duty. The Chief of Detectives agreed to see me alone, after the arresting officers had frisked me carefully. The Chief told me I could make one telephone call, so I dialed the number given me for such emergencies, the office of the CIA security man who had given me the manila envelope. There was no answer. "I'm going to tell you the truth," I said to the Chief, who was regarding me suspiciously over the rim of a grimy coffee cup. "The check is good; it's simply a case of a new account not being known when the store manager called. And I can't show you or anyone else the contents of this envelope." The Florida law officer stared at me, saying nothing.

"I'm with the Central Intelligence Agency," I said. "I'm on a ... mission."

The Chief of Detectives let his eyes roll toward the ceiling, where he

31

inspected a myriad of flyspecks, one by one. Still, he didn't speak.

"As soon as I contact someone at that telephone," I said, "you will be told to let me go."

The detective deigned to glance my way. "Who?"

"A fellow named..." I broke off the sentence—that idiot security man hadn't even given me his last name. "You'll see," I said, lamely. "Meanwhile, will you please let me go?"

The reply was negative. The Chief said I could keep trying the number until there was an answer. He would offer the hospitality of the county until the connection was made. I was taken to the desk of the booking sergeant, fingerprinted, and formally booked. When I was told I could not keep the manila envelope in my possession, I put my wallet into it and wrapped the entire envelope with several swaths of Scotch tape, until it was girdled with the adhesive. Then, across each piece of tape I wrote my signature. I announced that the contents were national secrets and not to be tampered with. The booking sergeant and the Chief of Detectives were mildly interested. They stowed the envelope in a safe and me in an adjoining jail cell which was already crowded with six prisoners.

When the policemen departed, one of the inmates asked me for a cigarette after introducing himself as Popeye. He looked like Faulkner's Popeye rather than the comic strip character. I extended my pack to him. He confiscated the entire pack and distributed the cigarettes, over my protests, to the other prisoners. I asked if I could have just one. Popeye said no, that the rule was new cons could share the available cigarette supply only after the first two days.

I sat on an upturned bucket, despondent, and let my chin fall into my cupped hands. The communal cell was filthy; the jailhouse stench of stale urine was demoralizing; and durance vile it certainly was. Goddamn the CIA!

Two hours later I was allowed out of the cell long enough to make another telephone call. Again, no answer. Back in the cell my morale remained low but my anger subsided. After all, I had anticipated some adventure. Soon it was obvious that Popeye and his cronies were small-time criminals, awaiting arraignment on a number of minor charges: insulting a magistrate, shoplifting, breaking and entering, and, in the case of one charmer, indecent exposure. But they all played the tough-guy role. They were alternately arrogant and sullen, strutting and posturing and, to my dismay, often spitting on the already polluted floor.

"What about you?" Popeye asked me. "First time in the clink?"

I glared at Popeye, then at his cohorts. Then I summoned my best Stanislavski and curled my lip in disdain. "First time?" I snorted. "The last time I was in stir it was for more than a year." That was true; I did not elaborate by adding that my last and only hitch had been served in a German prisoner-of-war camp.

Popeye and Company were impressed. They gathered around me. "What you in for this time?"

"Bank job. Cops was waitin' for me down in Miami. Bastards!" I hawked and spat on the floor at Popeye's feet.

"Geez." Popeye was pop-eyed. "A bank job! They gonna throw away the key on ya!"

"Naaw." I projected an image of ineluctable lack of concern. "I got connections. Soon as I get ahold of my lawyer he'll spring me before breakfast."

"Why was the law waitin' for ya?" Popeye asked. "Somebody squeal?"

"Yeah," I said. "My woman." I tried to spit again, but couldn't muster the saliva.

"Geez," said Popeye. "What you gonna do to her?"

I narrowed my eyes and drew one finger across my neck.

"Geez," said Popeye.

"What about one of them cigarettes?" I asked Popeye.

"You bet," he said. "Take two."

I finally talked to the security man on the telephone. He seemed blithely unconcerned about my plight; he even found it somewhat amusing. But he did show up later with a document from the local FBI office, chatted briefly with the Chief of Detectives, and arranged my release. I said good-bye to Popeye and his motley crew, after a short lecture to them on the perils of a life of crime without having proper legal counsel available on a retainer basis. In the car with the security officer I relaxed and, to my surprise, even could laugh about the incident.

But I didn't laugh three days later when the CIA asked me to appear in court and *plead guilty* to the charge of intent to defraud. It appeared this was the easy way to resolve the matter, because the judge would have no problem in giving me a suspended sentence on a guilty plea, but could not declare me innocent without a documented hearing which would reveal my intelligence connection. I protested, saying I didn't want the conviction on my record, not to speak of a criminal background and fingerprints forevermore in the central files of the FBI in Washington. I did plead guilty before the judge, *in camera*, and my sentence was suspended.

When I saw Brad I expressed my displeasure in emphatic terms. "And now," I asked, "will you please tell me what my mission is? Otherwise I might go to jail again and wither there without knowing why I abandoned my family in Chile." Brad said I would be briefed the very next day by two visitors from CIA headquarters. One of them would be Tracy

33

Barnes, a senior officer from the DDP, the Directorate of Plans—a euphemism for the overseas arm of CIA's Clandestine Service.*

Tracy Barnes was the first super-grader I had met. (CIA employees work in the normal government grade structure, with GS-18 being the highest rank. Those achieving GS-16 or over are super-graders and described as senior officers. Brad was a GS-15, the rough equivalent of a colonel in the military; Tracy was a CIA general.) Barnes was an exceptionally pleasant man with a ready smile and a casual manner. He wore a subdued plaid sports jacket, a button-down shirt and old school tie, and gray flannel slacks and loafers. He was very urbane with an easy confidence (Groton, law degrees from Harvard and Yale; twice on missions behind enemy lines in the O.S.S., he worked for Allen Dulles in Switzerland during World War II). I liked him instantly.

Barnes was accompanied by an aide, who was introduced only as Howard. He too exuded urbaneness but not with Barnes's quiet flair. He was dressed less conservatively and wore a tropical straw hat with the brim snapped down over his eyes. He fiddled constantly with a pipe and its paraphernalia.

"It's Guatemala," Barnes said. "The Arbenz government there has been drifting more and more to the left. His Guatemalan Labor Party has two thousand disciplined members and a decidedly Marxist leadership. Jacobo Arbenz is responding more and more to overtures from Moscow."

"The labor federation might be important," I said, "but in Latin America it's the army that counts." Barnes's aide nodded in agreement.

Barnes continued. "That's what I'm told. In this case the enlisted military seems to be largely apathetic, and the senior officers generally support the President. One who doesn't is Carlos Castillo Armas, a colonel who recently tunneled out of prison in Guatemala City and is now in exile. He's organizing anti-Communist resistance against the Arbenz government and will invade if he can recruit enough soldiers and obtain enough military hardware."

"I gather," I said, "that he will find this support."

"Yes," Barnes replied. "That's why we're here."

"But Arbenz became President in a free election," I said. "What right do we have to help someone to topple his government and throw him out of office?"

Barnes ducked that. For a moment I detected in his face a flicker of concern, a doubt, the reaction of a sensitive man. "It's not just a question

* Tracy Barnes is a true name. In this book CIA personnel (as well as some others who should not be identified) not previously identified in the media or those still working for the Agency are introduced with a first-name alias, chosen at random, as in the case of "Brad."

of Arbenz," he said. "Nor of Guatemala. We have solid intelligence that the Soviets intend to throw substantial support to Arbenz. Weapons. There are six thousand soldiers in the Guatemalan army, twenty-five hundred constabulary, and several government-organized paramilitary units. Given Soviet backing, that spells trouble in all of Central America. An easily expandable beachhead, if you want to use the current term."

Barnes's assistant tamped and lit his pipe. "Guatemala is bordered by Honduras, British Honduras, Salvador, and Mexico. That means it's unacceptable to have a Commie running Guatemala." He smiled pleasantly.

"I'm still not sure that gives us the right to intervene," I said. "Why does CIA have the job?"

"CIA was created by Truman in 1947," Barnes said. "Our charter was clear enough about three of our functions—collection of intelligence, counter-intelligence, and protection of sources and methods—but then, gave us a catch-all assignment of performing 'such other functions and duties as the National Security Council may, from time to time, direct.' This is one of those unlisted functions." Barnes stood up. "To be even more specific, our marching orders on this operation come from President Eisenhower. He has asked us to assist the Guatemalans who are opposed to Arbenz."

"There could be a civil war," I said. "A lot of people might be killed."

"Yes," Barnes said, soberly. "We will try to do it without bloodshed, if that's possible." Barnes excused himself; he had to return to Washington. His aide would brief me further, and he would be commuting between Washington, Florida, and Central America as the political action officer for the project.

When Barnes left his assistant made a suggestion. "What about a drink and some lunch? I know a place where the bartender makes the best daiquiris in Miami. Used to work at Floridita in Havana. Ever tried a *mulata*? Three kinds of rum, dark and sexy."

"Let's go," I said to Howard. "Any reason I'm not supposed to know your last name?"

"Not at all. Hunt. E. Howard Hunt."

During the next few days I found myself liking E. Howard Hunt, Jr. He was friendly, anxious to help me, and considerate. His credentials seemed impeccable: Brown University, O.S.S. in China, a successful and prolific writer. After two well-written serious novels and *Bimini Run*, which was made into a film, he had produced a series of spy thrillers. As a frustrated writer, I was impressed. It was evident from the outset that Howard was unusually conservative for a CIA officer. While there were some right-wingers in the Agency the majority of the people I had met fit the pattern of Ivy League, O.S.S., and liberal. CIA conservatives often referred to Communists, as Howard had, as "Commies," while the typical officer selected his political sobriquets more carefully, making it clear whether he was speaking of a Communist, Marxist, or Socialist (because the distinction could be important, if not vital, in writing intelligence reports as well as planning and conducting most operations).

Howard Hunt's penchant for the devious was apparent in almost any conversation. For example, most propaganda undertaken covertly is handled in this fashion only because it cannot be handled overtly, but Howard was inclined to consider the option of using the Department of State or the United States Information Agency only if the effort were not possible by CIA stealth.

Hunt also displayed, on occasion, a proclivity for the bizarre and even macabre. I recall that, when briefing me on Arbenz, he recounted the circumstances of the suicide of Arbenz's father: the Swiss-born druggist had filled his mouth with water before inserting a .45 pistol into his pursed lips and pulling the trigger. "Like a bomb," Howard said. "It's the water that does it. Really effective. Whole head is blown off."

Howard Hunt flew off on one of his trips and Brad described my role in the upcoming operation. Castillo Armas would have three old B-26 bombers and several cargo and fighter planes, a few to be flown by Guatemalans, but most by foreign mercenaries. A staging area for the military effort had been arranged with the leader of a country bordering Guatemala. Another neighboring country would harbor a rebel clandestine radio station, which would pretend to be broadcasting from within Guatemala. A team of radio technicians, writers and announcers, including two women, was being recruited in Guatemala City. They would convene in Florida for planning sessions before going off to the third country where the transmitter was now being erected. I was to act as an adviser to the radio team.

Meanwhile, Brad said, he wanted me to travel to Guatemala for a week to absorb everything I could about the country's history, customs, people, and, most important, the political mood of the populace. "A single mistake in the broadcasts, the slightest error in detail," he warned, "will make it difficult to convince listeners that the station is inside Guatemala. If a program mentions red fireplugs, for instance, when they really are green."

"Which colors are they?" I asked.

"You'll see," said Brad. "And we want you to return via Washington. The top people want to meet you."

"What's the line of command?" I asked Brad.

"I'm your boss in the field. Then the Chief of the Western Hemisphere Division in Washington, Colonel J. C. King, then Tracy, his boss Frank Wisner the DDP, Richard Bissell, and finally Dulles himself."

36

"Do I have to use false documents?" I asked. "I would probably like the jail in Guatemala City even less than the one in Fort Lauderdale."

"We've thought of that." Brad grinned. "So we've arranged for you to travel with one of the most proficient officers in CIA. He has to make an orientation trip too and will help you stay out of . . . trouble."

When I met my traveling companion I was inordinately impressed. "Peter" was a real operator. Unlike most of the CIA officers I had met previously who had served under official cover in United States embassies, Peter was a deep-cover type known for his tradecraft savvy and derring-do. He spoke with a slight German accent; he was in fact of German origin and had fought in the underground against Hitler. He took the intelligence business very seriously, openly scorning those who took shortcuts which might endanger the security of an operation. He was outspoken in expressing his disagreement with anyone, never hesitating to confront headquarters if he, while serving in the field, thought an instruction to be wrong. (Some years later Peter was in charge of an operation in Southeast Asia, and his difference of opinion with headquarters led to a week-long exchange of emotional cables, a communications debate known in CIA as a "pissing contest." Finally Peter brought the argument to an end with a cable which has since been dear to the hearts of all field operators: "Is headquarters still in friendly hands?" he queried.)

We shared a hotel room the night before our departure for Guatemala. What the hell was Peter doing? He was sitting on his bed, cutting up his clothes with a razor blade!

"What are you doing?" I asked.

"Can't you see?" Peter said. "I'm sitting on my bed cutting the laundry marks out of my clothes."

Truly professional. When Peter offered me the razor blade I declined, explaining that my clothes were new, and had never gone to the laundry— I had recovered them once the Hollywood store manager found I really did have a bank account. "The label from the store, then," Peter said. I did as he advised, feeling more spylike than at any other time during my brief career with CIA.

Peter and I flew to Guatemala, where he steered me through the shoals which confront the clandestine operator traveling abroad with false documents. Leading two lives, being two persons, was becoming increasingly easy for me.

From Guatemala City I flew to Washington and, for the first time, saw the inside of CIA headquarters. I was disappointed to find that, except for the Director's office, which was in a fine building, most CIA people worked in shabby, rundown wooden buildings alongside the reflecting pool between the Lincoln and Washington monuments. (It was not until 1962 that the CIA moved to its modern, suburban retreat at

Langley, Virginia.) I met, briefly, the hierarchy which presided over CIA operations: Dulles, Wisner, Bissell, Helms, and several others. They were pleasant but businesslike, and all had developed to a fine point the bureaucratic talent of signaling an end to a meeting without really announcing it. One senior official, formerly a lawyer and one of Thomas Dewey's "gangbusters" in New York in the thirties, was not so subtle. The first thing that met my eye in his office was a desk plaque which read: BE BRIEF. BE BLUNT. BE GONE.

Howard Hunt was hospitable, inviting me to his rather grand home, which I assumed was a luxury which came from his government salary augmented by the income from his spy thrillers. He and his quite attractive wife Dorothy were gracious and entertaining. On my return to Florida I asked Brad, "Just where does Howard Hunt fit in this? Is he my boss?"

"Sort of," Brad said. "But not really. I know Hunt, and I want to give you some advice. Listen to the music when he sings, but don't pay any attention to his lyrics."

I was puzzled but didn't ask him to elaborate.

Brad then asked me, "Did you find out what color the fireplugs are in Guatemala City?"

"Yes. Thanks a lot." I had found there were no fireplugs in the Guatemalan capital.

The members of the team which would conduct the clandestine radio broadcasts—all Guatemalans—assembled in Florida near Miami with their sponsors. There were three young men who were to become the leaders of the group, two of whom I can identify: Mario López Otero and José Toron Barrios, known as "Pepe." They were bright, talented, and hard workers. Howard Hunt flew down for meetings. He knew of the spartan conditions they would soon face, as the jungle transmitter was being set up in an old cow barn, and living quarters would be in a dilapidated shack. Howard suggested, at the end of our discussions, that we take them out for a night on the town in Miami. He named one of the larger and gaudier nightclubs. I asked Howard if it was really a good idea for us to be seen in public with the Guatemalans. He thought a moment and made his judgment: "It's okay."

Howard was a generous host at the nightclub; of course CIA would be taking care of the tab. I was nervous as the evening wore on. Perhaps I should have consulted Brad. Maybe the decision by Howard was the kind of lyric Brad had warned me about.

I was jolted when a flashbulb illuminated our entire group. A camera girl had just taken a photograph of an adjoining table; while she had not been interested in us there was no question Howard or I—or both of us—

might be discernible in the background, sitting at a table with nine Guatemalans about to participate in a secret operation. That, I knew from my training days in New York, was a no-no. Howard looked at me. He too was concerned.

I skipped after the camera girl through the crowded nightclub, catching her just as she was about to enter her darkroom. I whispered, "How would you like to make twenty bucks?"

She looked at me, up and down, then shrugged. "Why not? But I don't get off till four in the morning, honey."

"No," I said, slightly flustered. "I'll give you twenty for that negative, if you will go back and tell the people that it's no good and take another photo." I peeled off two bills, then another. "And there's ten more in it for you if the next picture does *not* include my table in the background."

The camera girl strained to look at the table where Howard sat with the Guatemalans, two of them pretty young women. "Sure, honey," she said. "I understand. Night on the town, huh?"

Returning to the table, I suggested it was time to return to the safe house where we were all staying. Howard demurred, saying he wanted to visit another club. Two of the Guatemalans went off into the night with Howard, leaving eight of us in the station wagon I was driving. After a few minutes on the highway out of Miami we were inundated by a tropical deluge. I could hardly see. The tires splayed curtains of water on both sides of the station wagon. The windshield wipers barely disturbed the opaque film of water surrounding the car. A sedan in front of me stopped abruptly. I slammed on the brakes, but too late. I smashed into the left rear of the car and then my station wagon slid off the highway into the median.

My reaction was one of absolute fury. Goddamn Howard Hunt, goddamn CIA—I was going to end up in the Fort Lauderdale jail again!

The other driver staggered from his car, swaying. He must be hurt! What would I say to the police? How would I explain my seven Guatemalans, whose documents were questionable? Fortunately we were only half a mile from the safe house, and Pepe and Mario knew where it was. I gave the safe house key to Pepe, telling him to get the hell out and back there—pronto! Guatemalans spilled out both sides of the station wagon, quickly disappearing into the rainstorm. I ran to help the driver of the car in front. He wasn't hurt. He was drunk, but amiably so. In the driving rain he shook hands, introducing himself as Harvey. The two of us managed to push his car off the highway, and then went across the way to an all-night restaurant. Harvey was cheerful as he drank black coffee; disoriented as he was he accepted my plea that he had better shape up before the police came to investigate the accident. The police arrived, took notes, and instructed Harvey and me to appear in traffic court the next morning. They said I was the guilty party—Florida state law assumes any driver hitting another from behind to be negligent. As we chatted Harvey continued to be pleasant, even solicitous. "Hope none of your friends were hurt," he said.

One of the policemen turned to me. "What friends?"

I could not tell him the truth. "Why, there were no friends," I lied. My god! I was lying to a U.S. policeman.

Harvey shook his head in disbelief. "I coulda sworn that wagon was jammed with people."

The next day I went to court, but not to jail. After consultation with the CIA security officer I intercepted Harvey outside the court. He said repairs for his car would be something over a hundred dollars, and I gave him two hundred from a fund given me by the security officer. The court session was short. The judge did warn Harvey that the police report indicated a suspicion of drunken driving, which would be on the record.

Outside Harvey confided, "You know, the truth is I was drinking. In fact I was stinko. I was even seeing things. I coulda sworn your wagon was chock-full of people."

I nodded sympathetically.

"You ever see that car in the circus where a dozen clowns come out? That's what it was like. Like a Mickey Mouse comedy—they was people leaving your car in all directions." Harvey shook his head from side to side.

In late April Pepe and Mario and their team went to Central America to prepare for the clandestine radio broadcasts to Guatemala. I went along as an observer and adviser. A few days before the first transmission Pepe described the objective of the broadcasts: "Our audience is divided into five parts. Two percent are hard-core Marxists; 13 percent are officials and others in sympathy with the Arbenz regime; 60 percent of the listeners can be characterized as neutral, a soap-opera audience, generally uninformed and apathetic; 23 percent are moderately well informed and deplore the country's drift toward Communism, but they are frustrated because they can do nothing about it; and, finally, 2 percent are militant anti-Communists, some of them in exile. Our job," Pepe continued, "is to intimidate listeners in the first two groups, and then to influence the mass of neutral types in the third group—especially the middle class in Guatemala City—and induce them to join the fourth and fifth categories. We can expect some propaganda mileage from leaflet drops, but it's the radio broadcasts which must do the basic job."

Mario explained the technique. "Credibility will be our major problem. We must begin with the big lie—that we are really broadcasting from within Guatemala. Given the absolute necessity for that deception, we must be very careful to avoid saying anything which can be proved false. The smallest mistake will be used by Arbenz to ridicule us. If we must lie again, we have to be sure it's a big one and worth the risk. Once we have established credibility we must define the issues for each of the groups Pepe spoke about and, at the proper time, tell them what action is expected of them. Timing is important, as we don't want our supporters to act prematurely and be arrested. We must always be positive, must always take the initiative, acting never reacting."

The station was to call itself the Voice of Liberation; its slogan was to be *Trabajo, Pan, y Patria*—Work, Bread, and Country. Too distant from Guatemala City for conventional medium-wave signals, it was to be on the short-wave band. This was not a problem in the Guatemala of 1954. The majority of the radio sets in the country received short-wave since Guatemalans were accustomed to foreign broadcasts, especially from Mexico. Also, major Guatemalan stations broadcast short-wave simultaneously with regular local transmissions. In rural areas all radio sets were short-wave, as those living on farms and ranches depended on short-wave broadcasts from the capital for weather information, crop and market statistics, and—there was no television—entertainment.

The first broadcast was scheduled for May 1, Labor Day, a very special holiday in Guatemala. No one worked. The government closed down, commerce stopped, and, most important, there were no newspapers or radio broadcasts—even the powerful government station went off the air for the day. The radio dial was soundless except for short-wave programs from Mexico. A vast, captive audience was available for Mario and Pepe, if only Guatemalans could be told of the first broadcast and persuaded to tune in to it. But you can't or shouldn't advertise the inauguration of a clandestine radio station in the newspapers.

Pepe and Mario did just that. A colleague was dispatched to Mexico City to send cables to the major newspapers of Guatemala. The message asked each editor to publish a half-page advertisement in his paper the day before Labor Day. It intimated—but did not say—that the program would originate in Mexico, and would feature a galaxy of Latin stars: Maria Felix, the beauteous Mexican actress, a well-known trio, several famous singers, and Cantinflas! The Mexican comic was then—as now— perhaps the best-known man in Latin America and the mention of his name would guarantee a large listening audience. The radio frequency where fortunate Guatemalans could find this spectacular array of talent was to be printed in large type, the cable from Mexico instructed the editors. In a businesslike aside, the message said a representative of the Mexican entrepreneur would visit Guatemala the day after Labor Day to pay for the advertising space. Editors were delighted at the prospect of filling half a page of the edition before the holiday, traditionally a

41

thin one. Without exception, they printed the advertisement. (And, in fact, they were paid. Another associate of Pepe and Mario dropped off an envelope stuffed with cash after the holiday. This consideration was not lost on Guatemala's newspaper publishers, an elite and extremely important minority.)

The listeners who tuned in to the first broadcast of the Voice of Liberation were not entirely deceived: Maria Felix, the trio, the famous singers, and Cantinflas did appear on the program—on records. Mario and Pepe apologized to their listeners, explaining that the need for this deception only came about because the Arbenz regime would not tolerate free and open political debate. This was true; only forty-eight hours before, the government had announced censorship of all Guatemalan media. And the listeners were ready to accept the deception about the Mexican entertainers because they found themselves enjoying the only kind of show which tops Cantinflas in Latin America—the kind of exciting political extravaganza that tempts most Latins to begin thinking about being with the winner and, once that decision is made, figuring how and when they should jump on the bandwagon.

Pepe and Mario knew they had just over six weeks to build toward the climax of their propaganda campaign before Colonel Carlos Castillo Armas would lead his army of exiles across the border into Guatemala on June 18—D-Day. By then the Voice of Liberation had to create the proper psychological climate for rebellion and transform a part of the listening audience into activists. To do this the basic premises of the rebel movement were defined in the initial broadcasts. Next, special programs were designed to influence specific groups. The women announcers exhorted Guatemalan women to sway their husbands and sons. Soldiers were told why their duty lay with the rebels rather than with those who would sell out the country to foreigners. Workers were wooed, youth was cajoled. There was a revolutionary something for everyone. Decision time was drawing near! Would the listener be with the winners or the losers?

On May 1, when the campaign started, the Guatemalan capital and countryside had been quiet. Within a week there was unrest everywhere. Two weeks later the unrest became anxiety and, in some sectors, panic. The Voice of Liberation was responsible for the unrest, but the heightened concern had its origin in Washington, not in Guatemala, because of a portentous announcement made by the Department of State on the fifteenth of June.

An intelligence report had arrived in Washington a few days before the announcement. It was the product of a classic intelligence coup. A source—a spy—had observed a ship embarking from the port of Stettin in the Baltic. Its cargo was arms, destined for Arbenz in Guatemala. One

42

version is that the information reached Washington by microdot, a photographic negative so small it was glued to a letter so that it would appear to a censor to be a period. Developed and enlarged at CIA headquarters, the secret message revealed that the M/S *Alfhem* was loaded to the Plimsoll line with Czech military equipment.

The Department of State announcement that Soviet-supplied arms were in Guatemala—the ship was that day being unloaded in an Atlantic port—provoked consternation throughout Central America. The shipment contained 2,000 tons of weapons, enough to supply the 6,000-man Guatemalan army several times over. The Arbenz government said nothing, but the Voice of Liberation aired the story stridently. In the beginning the theme used was that the immensity of the shipment proved that under tutelage of its Soviet sponsors, Guatemala entertained expansionist notions.

But a new and important piece of intelligence reached Mario and Pepe soon: Arbenz, distrusting his senior military officers, had decided to distribute the newly arrived weapons to a countryside militia controlled by his loyal labor federation. It was vital to hammer home to the Guatemalan military the portent of this decision. Mario and Pepe called on Castillo Armas's rebel air force. Thousands of leaflets were dropped in daring low-level flights over Guatemala City and other towns. The message, accompanied by similar explanations on the radio broadcasts, was that Arbenz planned the destruction of the military, which was to be replaced by a civilian proletariat constabulary, a prospect disturbing even to antimilitary civilians. Now there was a crack in the fortress of government rule and control. Senior military officers began to think of their own interests and Arbenz, realizing this, distrusted his commanders even more than before. The crack was to widen in the days to come.

On the eighth of June Arbenz announced the suspension of civil liberties. In effect a state of siege was imposed. Individual Guatemalans began to plan for the political climax they could see coming. The Chief of the Guatemalan Secret Police began to make indiscriminate arrests in the capital. The middle class stirred. Arms were taken from secret hiding places and oiled; ammunition was checked. Opponents of the government met and conspired. The market women of Guatemala City marched in protest, the first sign of organized resistance. The lines were being drawn. In five weeks what had been a placid country was in turmoil.

One major goal of the Voice of Liberation was to neutralize the Guatemalan air force. Several broadcasts recounted the stories of brave Soviet aviators who had served the cause of freedom by defecting with their fighter planes to the West. Shortly thereafter a well-known Guatemalan aviator fled the country in his plane, landing in a nearby country. The defector was brought to the tumbledown shack which served as a studio. Pepe and

Mario asked him to tape a special broadcast, an appeal to his former colleagues, urging them to defect with their aircraft and instructing them how to do it safely. "Not a chance," was his reply. "My family is still in Guatemala City." This argument did not impress Pepe and Mario; their families too were in the Guatemalan capital. They nonetheless treated the defector well. That evening the three of them relaxed over a bottle of scotch. The pilot was a good aviator and a poor drinker. He became expansive, verbose. Pepe refilled his glass frequently. The pilot was sitting on the floor of the shack, his back against an old sofa.

"If you did broadcast a plea to your air force friends," Mario asked, "what would you say?"

The pilot was eloquent and fiery in the best Latin tradition as he delivered a hypothetical speech to his friends persuading them to defect with their planes and to join Castillo Armas and his rebels.

"Have another drink," Pepe said. "And how would they know what to do?" The pilot, in a warm scotch mist, outlined the procedures he would recommend to be used by fleeing pilots who might wish to land safely in rebel territory.

The aviator had had a long day; soon his eyes closed and he was dozing. Mario and Pepe removed the tape recorder they had hidden in the sofa cushions. It was only an hour's work to cut up the tape, then splice it together again so that only the voice of the pilot—in what appeared to be a voluntary exhortation—remained in an impassioned request to his flying friends to join the winners. The tape was broadcast the next morning. From that moment the Guatemalan air force was grounded. Arbenz, fearing his pilots would defect with their planes, did not permit the flight of a single military aircraft for the duration of the conflict.

The government ordered a blackout in Guatemala City and other large towns, cutting off electricity. The edict was announced as a defensive measure against bombing by the rebels, but some believed the real reason was to deny Guatemalans the opportunity of hearing the Voice of Liberation. Whatever the motive, the result was increased tension in the populace. Further, it was not effective. Some inhabitants of the capital had battery radios, and all the electricity in the countryside was from batteries or gasoline generators. Farmers listened to nighttime programs, then brought the message to Guatemala City market along with their vegetables and the market women recounted the news from the rebel radio as they counted out change to their customers.

The blackout did affect, however, some of Castillo Armas's air operations. Two C-46 cargo planes were making almost nightly flights to airdrop supplies to rebel partisans encamped in the hills around the capital. Small fires marked the drop zone. The rebel pilots could

44

not find these small signal fires without the lights of Guatemala City as an orientation point. The flyers finally approached Mario and Pepe asking for help. The Voice of Liberation broadcast an appeal to sympathizers in the capital, asking them to place lighted candles in tin cans and to put the cans in their patios, explaining the reason for the request. Many Guatemalans, frustrated because of their inability to support the rebels, found a way they could participate actively—candles flickered in hundreds of courtyards, and the rebel pilots made their drop on target.

The next day Arbenz's Chief of Secret Police drove through the neighborhoods of Guatemala City, announcing that anyone apprehended assisting the enemy by lighting candles would be executed. That night the city was black, and the rebel air mission had to abort. The game continued: Mario and Pepe next took advantage of the government's original proclamation that the blackout was to inhibit rebel bombing. "The Voice of Liberation thanks its valiant supporters," the announcer intoned. "Each night our planes find most of the city lighted by the candles of patriots. Only the military reservations, controlled by the government, remain blacked out. This is invaluable to our pilots. Should it become necessary to bomb the capital, they will know where to drop their bombs—on the dark areas of the city."

That night candles burned as never before in all parts of Guatemala City, including some in military camps!

One month had passed since the first broadcast of the Voice of Liberation. Headlines in newspapers in the capital read: TERROR IN THE STREETS, UNREST IN OUR REPUBLIC, and WHERE ARE WE HEADING? The climate for revolt had been created. Arbenz sent one thousand farmers to the mountains to search out the location of the rebel transmitter. An ingenuous Guatemalan official approached the U.S. military attaché, requesting the American to provide direction-finding equipment which could pinpoint the radio. One prominent politician accused Arbenz of operating the station as an excuse to curtail civil liberties. The regime was not astute at all in its public reaction to the clandestine radio. Silence would have been the wiser course. Instead the government added to the stature and credibility of the broadcasts by ill-advised statements and reactions. Mario and Pepe decided it was time for the Voice of Liberation to pretend to move and convey to listeners the impression the radio was operating under dangerous conditions. The rebel broadcasters prepared a dramatic charade in which they carefully rehearsed what would appear to be their own demise. There was the sound of shots, muffled commands of "hands up," and urgent whispering by Pepe to Mario that "they've found us! Take off!" It was their plan to return to the air the next day claiming they had eluded government soldiers and set up shop in a new loca-

45

tion. The government in Guatemala City was cooperative. A gullible Arbenz commentator was completely taken in by the sham raid and announced triumphantly to the nation that the rebel radio lair had been found and destroyed. Thus, when the Voice of Liberation returned to the air the next day—"from a new location"—it had the cachet of government authentication. The big lie was now accepted, even by skeptics who had assumed the station was outside the country. They had been told by the government that the radio had been overrun by the Guatemalan army, thus it must be within Guatemala. The women announcers no longer participated in the broadcasts, Mario and Pepe explaining their new situation was too precarious for distaff rebels. Credibility enhanced, the Voice of Liberation was accepted as authentic by foreign newsmen in Guatemala City who were scratching for facts denied them by the Arbenz government. The *New York Times* ran a story based on rebel information, labeling it as coming from "an authoritative source." *Life* described the radio station as being "deep in the jungle."

D-Day. On the eighteenth of June the radio station announced that Colonel Carlos Castillo Armas and his troops had invaded. It was true: several trucks had crossed the border without opposition, Castillo Armas out front in a battered station wagon, to bivouac six miles inside Guatemala. Mario and Pepe used indirection to make their propaganda points: "At our command post here in the jungle we are unable to confirm or deny the report that Castillo Armas has an army of five thousand men." In fact the army was a hundred fifty ragtag recruits. "There are reports of a battle at Esquipulas, but we do not yet have a tally of the dead." There were no casualties; there had been no battle. Rumors buffeted the country.

The B-26 bombers and World War II fighters of the rebel air force began to fly noisy missions. In several parts of the country they made low-level strafing runs. When the news reached the capital, government soldiers began to sandbag positions in anticipation of Guatemala City being bombed. A young Guatemalan rebel pilot, Carlos Cheeseman, converted his single-engine Cessna into a bomber. His "bombardier" dropped a homemade bomb of dynamite sticks and a hand grenade on an oil tank at Puerto Barrios igniting a conflagration which could be seen at night from miles away. The airplanes of the rebel air force soon became known as *sulfatos*. The word means laxative, and the planes were so called because of the effect they were alleged to have on Guatemalan leaders.

Not all of the rebel air forays were successful. On one occasion a mercenary fighter pilot, respected for his ability in the cockpit but known to be less talented intellectually, was instructed to strafe the concrete blockhouse of the government's radio transmitter, the objective being to silence

Arbenz's station. "But be careful," he was warned. "Just down the road is the transmitter of an evangelical station, and there are two American missionary ladies there. You can tell the difference because the Arbenz station is all concrete and the mission has a red tile roof." The pilot returned from the assignment, claiming success. "Are you sure you hit the right place?" he was asked. "Absolutely," he replied, "you should have seen them red tiles flying!"*

Another mercenary pilot hit the mark but with unhappy results. After aborting a mission because of bad weather he made a personal decision "not to waste his bomb" and dropped it, with unerring precision, on a freighter in the port at Puerto Barrios, claiming later that he presumed the ship to be unloading Soviet weapons. The cargo was cotton, which absorbed much of the water in the port as the ship sank to the bottom. The ship was insured by Lloyd's of London.**

Seven weeks had passed since the inaugural broadcast of the Voice of Liberation, and several days since the "invasion." It was clear there would be no military solution, with one side or the other winning a decisive battlefield victory. Castillo Armas had neither the men nor the matériel to do so, and the government, confused and lacking faith in the military, particularly its air force, lacked the will to engage the enemy. Mario and Pepe continued an imaginative psychological warfare campaign. They made a tape in which a rebel announcer mimicked the voice of a Communist leader and transmitted the program at a frequency just next to that of the government station, a technique known as snuggling. Unwary listeners thought they were listening to an official broadcast. The Arbenz station reacted by adopting a new identification theme, sonorous chimes much like those of Big Ben, announcing, "Unless you hear these chimes, you are listening to impostors." It was a simple matter for Mario and Pepe to record the chimes and use them in their next rebel broadcast. And they continued to be Machiavellian in their use of dis-information to foment rumor: "It is *not* true that the waters of Lake Atitlán have been poisoned," they would say. Speculation that they might have been would then spread throughout the area.

But the stalemate continued. Pepe and Mario were becoming distraught and discouraged. They had been preparing twenty-minute programs every hour on the hour for the weeks since D-Day and were glassy-eyed with fatigue. They feared that the bluff and bravado of

* The American missionary ladies, fortunately, were not in residence at the time.
** Press reports, some years later, claimed that CIA quietly settled a claim, after much negotiation, with Lloyd's for $1,000,000.00.

psychological operations could no longer substitute for actual military capabilities.

Mario and Pepe met with the rebel high command to prepare a last-ditch effort. Despite the threat of bombing Guatemala City being carried constantly in broadcasts none had occurred. It was decided to drop a single bomb on the capital. On the twenty-fifth of June a rebel pilot let one fall in the middle of the parade ground of the largest military encampment. The noise was tremendous and an ominous column of black smoke rose above the capital. No one was hurt, but the inhabitants of Guatemala City prepared for the worst, many of them fleeing the city.

Pepe and Mario decided now was the time for a final big lie. The Voice of Liberation broadcast that two columns of rebel soldiers were converging on Guatemala City. In fact, Castillo Armas and his makeshift army were still encamped six miles inside the border, far from the capital. The highways were crowded, but with frightened citizens fleeing Guatemala City and not with soldiers approaching it. The radio skillfully created the illusion that the capital would soon be under attack. Dramatic appeals were made to the refugees on the highways, instructing them to make way for rebel trucks. Simulated military messages were broadcast to "rebel commands." Pepe and Mario again used indirection to make their propaganda points: "To Commander X, to Commander X. Sorry, we cannot provide the five hundred additional soldiers you want. No more than three hundred are available; they will be joining you at noon tomorrow." And, "To Commander Y, to Commander Y, please detach and send to Commander X three hundred of your men, to arrive at noon tomorrow." In fact there was no Commander X, no Commander Y, and not even three men available. There was only the hope that Arbenz and his loyalists would give up hope.

The bomb was dropped on a Friday night and the radio announcement of two imaginary columns of soldiers was broadcast on Sunday morning, the twenty-seventh of June. Arbenz resigned in a nationwide radio speech that night. He drove to the Mexican embassy to seek asylum, and six hundred of his supporters followed him there and to other foreign embassies.

The revolution was over.

Castillo Armas and his men were flown to a landing field outside Guatemala City, then marched triumphantly into the capital. A hurriedly recruited band played the theme music of the Voice of Liberation. Mario and Pepe were in the vanguard, wearing battle fatigues and hand-stitched shoulder patches.

One of Arbenz's top military officers, a graduate of the French military academy at St.-Cyr and a capable commander and strategist, was loyal to the end. Arbenz had not trusted him sufficiently to allow him to seek out the tiny invasion force, which he could have crushed easily. The colonel from St.-Cyr did not take asylum in a foreign embassy. He stayed in his barracks and, for several days, wept.

Several of us were flying back to Washington. Tracy Barnes had sent a message to Brad, saying that we were to report to the White House. President Eisenhower was pleased and wanted to hear the details of the operation. Brad and Peter, as well as other CIA officers who had been involved in the operation, were on the plane. Among them were "Hector," a handsome para-military officer, and his sidekick "El Indio," a massive American of Mexican and Indian extraction I had seen only briefly during the revolt but was to work with in other operations over the years. Each of us was to speak at the presidential briefing for ten minutes, and we worked on our notes during the flight. Hector and I were concerned after Brad let us read his speech. Brad had been working long hours—perhaps twenty hours a day for two weeks—and the strain was showing. His report was confused, concentrating on his role in Korean operations several years before. Hector and I attempted to persuade him to change the presentation, but he refused.

Two limousines were waiting for us at Washington's National Airport. We were driven directly to the home of Allen Dulles on Wisconsin Avenue. I noted, as we drove into the grove of trees which shielded the Director's home from the street, that there were no guards. (Nor, when visiting the homes of Directors of Central Intelligence in later years, did I ever see a guard.) Dulles was casually dressed, fiddled with his pipe and occasionally touched his ample mustache. He was the actor central casting would have selected to play the role of spy-master.

"Tomorrow morning, gentlemen," Dulles said, "we will go to the White House to brief the President. Let's run over your presentations." It was a warm summer night. We drank iced tea as we sat around a garden table in Dulles's back yard. The lighted shaft of the Washington Monument could be seen through the trees. Tracy, J. C. King, Peter, Hector, El Indio, and I spoke. Finally Brad rehearsed his speech. When he finished Allen Dulles said, "Brad, I've never heard such crap." It was the nearest thing to an expletive I ever heard Dulles use. The Director turned to me: "They tell me you know how to write. Work out a new speech for Brad." That night and into early morning hours Hector and I helped Brad with a new report at the hotel, stressing his command role in the operation rather than Korean recollections.

We went to the White House in the morning. Gathered in the theater in the East Wing were more notables than I had ever seen: the President, his Joint Chiefs of Staff, the Secretary of State—Allen Dulles's brother, Foster—the Attorney General, and perhaps two dozen other

49

members of the President's Cabinet and household staff. Young John Eisenhower stood in the back of the room. I stood beside him as my colleagues reported, one by one, on their particular role in the operation. After my turn at the podium Herbert Brownell, the Attorney General, said to me, "Very smooth, you could be a professional speaker." (This was comforting, as I was scheduled to begin my lecture tour the following month.)

The lights were turned off while Brad used slides during his report. A door opened near me. In the darkness I could see only the silhouette of the person entering the room; when the door closed it was dark again, and I could not make out the features of the man standing next to me. He whispered a number of questions: "Who is that? Who made that decision?"

I was vaguely uncomfortable. The questions from the unknown man next to me were insistent, furtive. Brad finished and the lights went up. The man moved away. He was Richard Nixon, the Vice President.

Eisenhower's first question was to Hector: "How many men did Castillo Armas lose?" Hector said only one, a courier who had infiltrated Guatemala to try to join a partisan group before the invasion; none had died in the invasion. Eisenhower shook his head, perhaps thinking of the thousands who had died in France. "Incredible."

The President's next question was directed to Peter, who snapped to attention when Eisenhower said, "Those were interesting remarks about the military academy in Guatemala City. Do you know who founded that school?"

"Sir?" Peter was taken aback. He prided himself in knowing every detail of any operation he was involved in, and the historical query caught him off guard.

"Who created it?" snapped the President. "Who was the founder of the academy?"

"I'm afraid I don't know, sir," Peter admitted.

"Well, by god, I did!" Eisenhower said, immensely pleased with himself.

Nixon asked a number of questions, concise and to the point, and demonstrated thorough knowledge of the Guatemalan political situation. He was impressive—not at all the disturbing man he was in the shadows.

Eisenhower turned to his Chief of the Joint Chiefs. "What about the Russians? Any reaction?"

General Ridgway answered. "They don't seem to be up to anything. But the navy is watching a Soviet sub in the area; it could be there to evacuate some of Arbenz's friends, or to supply arms to any resisters."

Eisenhower shook hands all around. "Great," he said to Brad, "that was a good briefing." Hector and I smiled at each other as Brad flushed with pleasure. The President's final handshake was with Allen Dulles. "Thanks, Allen, and thanks to all of you. You've averted a Soviet beachhead in our hemisphere." Eisenhower spoke to his Chief of Naval Operations. "Watch that sub, Admiral. If it gets near the coast of Guatemala we'll sink the son-of-a-bitch." The President strode from the room.

The CIA officers involved in the Guatemalan operation went on to other chores. Tracy became chief of the important CIA office at Frankfurt in Germany. Howard Hunt was assigned to the American embassy in Tokyo. Hector, Peter, and El Indio received promotions and new assignments. Another of the field officers who had been involved did not fare well. Shortly after the White House meeting Tracy escorted him into the office of Allen Dulles. Dulles was still ebullient about the success of the Guatemalan operation, which had followed a similar one in Iran the year before. To the officer he said, "I have good news for you. Your next job will be as Chief of Station in Madrid, and we're going to promote you to GS-16."

"The COS assignment is great," the officer said. "But I've been thinking about promotion. I really believe I deserve a double promotion."

Tracy had worked with Dulles for a long time. Later, in describing the encounter to me, he said he had never seen so ungenial a look on the face of our customarily genial Director. The officer, as a GS-15, was suggesting the rough approximation of a military officer requesting that he be jumped from colonel to two-star general, skipping the brigadier grade. Dulles told the officer he would have to think about that.

"Ambition is acceptable in CIA," Tracy told me. "But don't ever try the power play. The only time you can get away with that is when you're being hired." He was certainly right in the case of this officer. One of the chiefs of CIA's Guatemalan field operation never made it to Madrid or to another COS assignment. When he retired from CIA some twenty years later he was still a GS-15, while the others of us who worked with him in 1954 had received four or five promotions.

I returned to Guatemala for a one-month temporary duty assignment. There were some five weeks free before I was to begin my lecture tour, and I accepted a request that I go to Guatemala City as part of a team which would assist the new government in sifting and evaluating the documents left behind when Arbenz and his friends abruptly went into foreign embassies. The papers we found were an intelligence gold mine, filled with nuggets of information which explained the motivation and plans of the Arbenz regime: government files, copies of diplomatic messages, the private papers and even diaries of the top Communist leaders, left behind in their haste to leave Guatemala after Arbenz's resignation. The CI-nicks—counter-intelligence officers—who worked with me were ecstatic. These were pearls which could be fondled for years. (Within CIA, counter-intelligence officers are sometimes held in disdain by operations officers. The CI-nicks are seen as information misers gloating over their stashed jewels but never doing anything with them. Operations officers believe intelligence should be passed around and, if advantageous, used, that even the finest gems of information lose their luster unless brought into the light.) My task was to glean from the documents information to be disseminated abroad, especially in Latin America, which would demonstrate the extent of Soviet involvement with the regime of Arbenz.

The month in Guatemala City was pleasant. Several evenings I spent at the bridge table with Ambassador Jack Puerifoy and his attractive wife. The Ambassador was a flamboyant character, the only American envoy I ever knew to carry a pistol. I played golf on the up-and-down course in the hills just outside the capital with clubs borrowed from a friend in the embassy and shoes loaned to me by an obliging locker room attendant. The shoes were uncommonly comfortable, fitting just right. After my final round I asked the attendant if he were interested in selling the shoes. He was. I asked him, "You're sure they don't belong to one of the members?"

"Oh, they do," he said. "But he's left the country, and I doubt he'll be returning." He smiled wryly. "These are the shoes of Jacobo Arbenz."

I didn't buy the shoes. They certainly fit well, but somehow I didn't believe I would be really comfortable walking around the golf courses of Latin America wearing the golf shoes of the deposed President.

Indeed I had played a personal role in toppling the Arbenz regime, and I thought about that at length, wondering whether I was pleased with myself or not. One night at a dinner party I sat next to a British diplomat. After I commented casually about the unexpected victory of Castillo Armas and his army, the Briton said: "The soldiers had nothing to do with it. The war was won by that radio station."

The clandestine broadcasts of the Voice of Liberation were just one segment of the complex operation which led to the downfall of Arbenz. Armas and his motley band, few as they were and as untested in battle, did invade Guatemala and their presence was the catalyst for the revolt. Other vital contributions were the daring low-level raids of the rebel air force; the stirring of political action pots by Hector and Peter; and Ambassador Puerifoy, speeding through the narrow streets of Guatemala City in his jeep to meetings with influential government leaders to tell them, bluntly, of official Washington concern about Arbenz's alliance with Moscow. But Mario, Pepe, and the psychological campaign of the

52

Voice of Liberation handled the single element of the conflict which was decisive. Arbenz would not have resigned had he not been manipulated into what he conceived as an impossible situation by the rebel radio, especially in creating a climate in which he would not allow his pilots to fly or permit the colonel from St.-Cyr to commit his troops.

During those quiet days after the revolution I thought a great deal about my participation in it. It was clear that the Guatemalan operation of CIA was brazen intervention. After reviewing the documents left behind by Arbenz and his collaborators, I was more inclined to agree with those who saw the endeavor as a justifiable act of American foreign policy. The documents revealed a paradigm of Soviet Cold War expansionism, a program clearly intended to establish a power base in the Western Hemisphere. Certainly President Eisenhower had reached that conclusion. He considered Guatemala as a CIA success, and did not have, I am sure, any moral qualms about sponsoring it.

Two aspects of the Guatemala operation on the negative side of the ledger stand out. The first was born from the very success of the endeavor: it had been so easy, there had been so little blood spilled, everyone was so pleased with the outcome—Eisenhower, Allen Dulles and his brother, Richard Bissell, Tracy Barnes, Howard Hunt. And Dave Phillips. So many of us who were involved, up and down the line, were subsequently to participate in the planning of another operation seven years later: the Bay of Pigs.

A second negative aspect was to be found within Guatemala in the decade to come. Carlos Castillo Armas, after serving briefly in a three-man junta, selected himself as president. This was possible because one facet of CIA planning had gone awry in a development beyond control—the moderate civilian who had been groomed to become the interim President contracted a fatal illness. Armas was a bad President, tolerating corruption throughout his government and kowtowing to the United Fruit Company more than to his own people. The United States could have prevented this with the vigorous exercise of diplomatic pressure on Castillo Armas to assure that he pursued social reform for the many rather than venal satisfaction for a few. Instead, Washington breathed a collective sigh of relief and turned to other international problems.

After 1954 Guatemala was a typical Latin American banana republic with polarized political forces spawning personal violation. Castro-supported rebels murdered politicians and diplomats; Guatemalan security officials sponsored death squads which eliminated opposition leaders. The Guatemalans I had known best did not survive. Pepe, leaving his home one morning for work, was gunned down in front of his family by assassins. Mario, too, was assassinated, dying outside a downtown supermarket in a hail of machine gun slugs. Castillo Armas was killed by a member of his palace guard, whose motives have never been explained. Arbenz wandered in exile, finally settling into obscurity in Cuba.

Perhaps Arbenz, already a Soviet sycophant, would have become a Soviet hireling. He was a vain and weak man and would have undoubtedly succumbed to the political flattery and pressures of his advisers. Principal among them were his wife, a dedicated Salvadoran Marxist poetess, and a coterie of foreign Marxists.

One of those foreign advisers came to my attention while I was sorting and sifting documents in Guatemala City after the revolt. A CIA analyst approached me and showed me a piece of paper. "Should we start a file on this one?" she asked.

I read the paper. It contained biographical information on a twenty-five-year-old Argentine physician who had gone into asylum in the Mexican embassy; later he was to meet and scheme with Fidel Castro in Mexico.

"I guess we'd better have a file on him," I said. Although the name meant little to me at the time, the file on Ernesto Guevara, known as "Che," eventually became one of the thickest to be maintained by the CIA.

3

WASHINGTON, CUBA, LEBANON, CUBA 1955–1959

In Washington Tracy Barnes escorted me to the office of Frank Wisner, the DDP—Deputy Director of Plans—who wanted to look me over before approving Tracy's recommendation that I become a CIA staff officer, that is, a professional with tenure. I certainly preferred that in lieu of the tenuous contract status I held in Chile and during the Guatemalan operation, although I was far from making the decision that intelligence would be my career occupation.

Frank G. Wisner was Chief of CIA's Clandestine Service, the worldwide network of intelligence operations. "Wiz," as he was affectionately known in the Agency, had been a scholar and athlete at the University of Virginia and went on from there to develop a lucrative law practice in Manhattan. A veteran of O.S.S. and, at the time, a Deputy Assistant Secretary of State, he was selected by General George Marshall to organize and head the Office of Policy Coordination, the first covert action component of CIA. Control of Wisner's "dirty tricks" department however was shared by the Director of Central Intelligence (DCI) with Defense and State departments—a type of compartmentation for espionage often proposed today. But hyphenated responsibility did not work well with both a "dirty tricks" chief of station and an espionage chief of station operating independently in the same capital abroad and competing for the services of the same agent. In 1950, a merger with espionage operations brought covert action completely under the DCI's direction, and Wisner became head of all CIA's clandestine operations and the second DDP, succeeding Allen Dulles who held the post briefly before becoming DCI.

Wisner, a native of the small town of Laurel, Mississippi, had quietly become one of the most potent men in the U.S. government. If Allen Dulles was the master spy, his protégé Frank Wisner was the master of Cold Warriors. He deployed his former O.S.S. colleagues around the globe in a skirmish line against Soviet agents who were quite successfully taking advantage of every opportunity to expand Communist influence. Wisner, a ruggedly handsome man of incredible energy, drove his associates relentlessly. He could be alternately charming and, as one of his subordinates put it, "iron-assed." He did not have the patience for organization, but saw to it that tasks were accomplished by assigning the same job to two or three officers and then immediately hounding them for results. He disliked bureaucracy, administration, or planning. He pondered purpose and then reveled in action. His office door was guarded by a special assistant known throughout CIA as "the Ozzard of Wiz." ("The Ozzard" graduated second in their law class at the University of Virginia; Wisner was third.)

During our interview, Wisner told me he was pleased with the progress of the seven-year-old Agency, which he felt had come of age. He said that John Foster Dulles, the Secretary of State and brother of the DCI, had recently attended an international conference, and when he sat down at the table with delegates from fourteen nations he knew, from CIA, the negotiating positions of nine of them. "Not bad," Wisner said. "We're earning our pay."

"Why are we so involved in covert action?" I asked. "Now that Stalin's dead won't Khrushchev ease up on repression at home and subversion elsewhere?"

"Don't count on it," Wisner said. "He'll be ruthless when he has to. Witness how he smashed the strike in East Berlin. So, we will be in the business of covert action for a long time. Don't forget this: 'Peace' to the Soviets simply signifies a cessation of armed conflict, but they'll use every other means they can muster to win out. It's our job to see that they don't succeed, and covert action, like in Guatemala, is the way now."

After we chatted for fifteen minutes, Wisner looked at the clock. I was beginning to detect a pattern in meetings between senior CIA officials and their subordinates: ten minutes for routine matters, twenty for serious ones. Then: "Tracy tells me he is convinced you have a future in the Agency. Certainly you did well in Guatemala, and we do plan to give you a decoration. What about coming aboard? In deference to your four years' experience, area knowledge, and good Spanish, I'll bring you in as a staffer on very favorable terms. What about it?"

"What are the terms?" I asked.

"GS-13," Wisner said.

I thought a moment. Tracy had told me, when discussing another officer's brashness in demanding a double promotion from Allen Dulles, that overweening ambition was tolerated in CIA only when being hired. I decided to test Tracy's thesis. I would ask for a better grade than the one being offered.

But I couldn't remember! Which was higher, a GS-12 or a GS-14? (The State Department grade scale works in reverse from CIA's with the highest rank being an FSO-1.) My contracts with CIA had not been based on the GS (Government Schedule) system, so I couldn't recall— did one strive for a small number, as in golf, or for a high one, as in baseball? Dammit, was Tracy a GS-1 or a GS-18? Should I ask for a GS-14 and gain, or for a GS-12, show my ignorance and perhaps be taken up on the suggestion? I took a chance and plunged.

"Mr. Wisner, I really feel I must be a GS-14."

I chose the right way to go. Wisner's face stiffened. He turned and glared at Tracy, not at all amused. Tracy squirmed, eyeing me with a "why did you do that to me?" expression.

Wisner then faced me. He appeared to be angry. Well, I thought, I blew that one. But then Wisner smiled. A bit thin, but a smile. "Okay," he said. "Welcome aboard."*

Through 1955, I worked at CIA headquarters, taking leave without pay to give several dozen lectures for which I had obligated myself before leaving Chile. CIA encouraged this as useful in building cover as a Latin American specialist.

I signed the Secrecy Oath, a covenant required of all CIA personnel; it bound one not to reveal, even after resignation or retirement, classified information learned while working for United States intelligence. I submitted to a lie-detector test—"boxed" we called it—a routine which is repeated over the years by CIA as part of a continuing security review of its people. I had been warned that I would be asked questions about my political, social, and even sexual life. I recounted for the examiner each detail of my past, from adolescence to the lurid fleshpots of New York. I hoped I wouldn't shock him. He must have heard it all before because, after I was unstrapped and disconnected from the machine, the operator only opened his mouth to emit a long, bored yawn.

I shared an office with "Len," a large, nervous man with an artificial leg. He had been an infantry major in Germany during the war and he was proud of the Silver Star won in an action that cost him his limb. Len was articulate and conscientious, but a bit uptight in some respects. He

---

* The years of strenuous work took their toll on Frank Wisner. He became chronically ill, never fully recovering from a bout with hepatitis contracted in the Mideast. Depression followed. He retired from CIA and in 1958 killed himself with a single bullet—the only CIA officer I knew who committed suicide.

was sensitive about the fact that he was from a small town and out of a state university, while most of our colleagues in adjoining offices were scions of wealthy families with Ivy League and O.S.S. credentials. He seemed relieved, even cheered, when I told him I didn't have a college degree. Under stress, Len had the habit of nervously scratching his underwrists—on bad days to the point of bringing blood.

One of my first supervisors, a woman intelligence officer, also had an artificial leg. Len told me she had to remove the limb and strap it to her body when O.S.S. parachuted her behind German lines in France. I was skeptical but Tracy, who had worked with her, assured me the story was true.

Frank Wisner's Cold Warriors worked in I, J, K, and L buildings, collectively known as Cockroach Alley. The reflecting pool harbored even older navy buildings across the way, "temporary" from World War I. One of my companions later wrote to me, "I was slaving. Summer time. The aroma emanating from the 'Kafteria' and the sewage was something that even Chanel could not have imagined. The cockroaches were having an orgy. There I was, all alone, plotting the downfall of the Soviet Union and its nefarious undertakings, when the door opened and in marched A. W. Dulles. 'Good morning,' he said and then stood looking and sniffing. 'Good God,' Dulles added, 'this is a damned pig sty,' and marched out. I feared he might have been referring to me, but he meant the working quarters."*

Morale among CIA's Cold Warriors was surprisingly good in late 1954 after the bleak months of irresponsible attacks by Senator Joseph McCarthy. One of the principal targets of McCarthy's infamous witchhunt was the State Department. The level of sensational accusations then, as now in the case of CIA, had risen to the point where the man on the street was prepared to believe almost anything—particularly that the State Department was riddled with Communists and Russian spies. An unrelenting and vicious attack against Far Eastern diplomat-scholars emasculated State's China cadre, and those experts who might have helped us understand and cope with the critical problems of Southeast Asia were disgraced and, in some cases, cashiered. The CIA was not overlooked by Senator McCarthy in his barrages of innuendo and outright lies, but it came out somewhat better when Allen Dulles stood firm against the allegations of the Wisconsin Senator. Individual CIA officers who were caught up in this political maelstrom survived. William Bundy, an early McCarthy target, later became an Assistant Secretary

---

* Dulles was lobbying even then for funds to construct a permanent CIA headquarters outside Washington, a dream not realized until 1962 at a lovely countryside site near Langley, Virginia.

of Defense under Johnson and is today editor of *Foreign Affairs*. Another senior CIA officer, publicly known as a liberal and one of the founders of the World Federalist Movement, was vilified; he was suspended from CIA until he finally cleared himself in a long legal process with the assistance of attorney Abe Fortas. Morale was completely restored in December of 1954 when the Senate censured McCarthy. In the aftermath of this *cause célèbre*, CIA people admired Allen Dulles even more than before; he had defied McCarthy while his brother at the Department of State vacillated.

Len and I shared responsibility for reviewing and commenting on proposals from CIA overseas stations involved in psychological warfare operations. Down the corridor from our office were men and women with experience in printing and publishing, radio broadcasting, and political action. The names of some were known to the public, but they had now become silent manipulators who could derive only private satisfaction from whatever professional successes they realized. In the next office a former screenwriter worked alongside a man from one of America's most renowned publishing families. It was a colorful crew, bursting with talent, ideas, and enthusiasm. And, they enjoyed life and their job.

Life and job in K Building were not always dull, and certainly not always serious. One day I was treading carefully down the hall, wary of stepping too hard and splintering the older floorboards, when a man frantically waved me to a stop. He was clutching a memorandum in one hand.

"I've got it! I've got it!" he shouted, thrusting the paper in my face. "The greatest psychological warfare operation in history! The Soviets will never recover. Russian morale will plummet, never to be restored. The Communist system will totter!"

I read the title of the memorandum: OPERATION PENIS ENVY.

With fantastic ardor, he explained his scheme. "First, we make millions of contraceptives! Condoms!"

I was aghast. "CIA will manufacture condoms?"

"Yes," he said, eyes gleaming. "Rubbers. Millions and millions. Not just ordinary ones, but giant-sized. Immense!" He spread his hands in the gesture fishermen use to describe the one that got away.

"Rubbers four feet long?" I stammered.

"Exactly. Then we drop them all over the Soviet Union. Planes flying everywhere, from St. Petersburg to Vladivostok! We'll drop them by the millions!"

"You are totally demented," I said. "What possible good will that do?"

"Oh, it's not the rubbers." He leaned toward me, his eyes wide with enthusiasm. "It's the propaganda—it's what we will say. You see, on each one will be printed in Russian: 'MADE IN USA. MEDIUM SIZE!'"

Shaken, I returned to the office. I spoke to Len. "That man is crazy. Is there really a chance the taxpayers' money will be spent on that ridiculous scheme?"

Len laughed. "He's kidding. It's his standard performance for new-comers. He's really a brilliant guy, just a little bored. He has a lot of fun with that act. Come on, let's have some lunch at Napoleon's."

We lunched at the Connecticut Avenue restaurant which was a favorite of the covert action specialists and, after a martini, I had a good laugh at Operation Penis Envy.

That afternoon Colonel J. C. King called me to say it was time for an overseas assignment. I had a difficult time keeping a straight face while the Division Chief talked to me. King, a West Point graduate, joined the CIA after making a fortune in Latin America. Disregarding the advice of friends he constructed the first condom factory in Brazil. All the pundits told him the Roman Catholic population would be a poor market, but the Colonel knew better. He eventually sold out to Johnson & Johnson not for money but for shares, and he grew rich as the pharmaceutical firm prospered. I couldn't help thinking how valuable he would be as a consultant on Operation Penis Envy.

The assignment was in Havana, Cuba, under deep cover. I couldn't have been more pleased—Havana in those days was a choice post.

The first tourist to visit Cuba wrote in his journal: "This is the most beautiful land that eyes have ever seen." The traveler was Christopher Columbus, and he had sailed into one of the many mangrove-fringed bays on the northern coast. Columbus was the earliest but not the last visitor impressed by the lovely country. One enthusiastic admirer wrote that the sea washing Cuban shores was "the color of melted peacocks."

Havana, when we arrived in 1955, was an exciting city—truly the Paris of the Caribbean. We moved into a furnished house and awaited our furniture. Maria, six, entered school. For $60 a month we were able to hire a cook-housekeeper and a nursemaid to take care of David, Jr., three, and Atlee, two. Cool trade winds tempered the tropical climate. We liked the capital from the day we arrived and soon had many friends, Cuban and foreign.

We began to learn the lessons of leading the double life demanded by deep cover. Other than CIA officers in the station, only the Cubans on the CIA payroll working for me knew I was an intelligence officer, and with most of them I used an alias. Helen and I joined the little theater group of the English-speaking community, which I was again

60

able to use as a secure way to meet some agents. We had several friends at the American embassy, including Dick and Nancy Cushing, whom we had known in Chile. Few of these acquaintances realized I was an intelligence officer and maintaining the deception was important. Overseas, American diplomats and businessmen constantly play a guessing game, the purpose of which is to identify the spooks* among the foreign community. A thin cover is likely to be seen through sooner or later. My cover as lecturer on Latin American affairs held up nicely; being true, it was solid. My residence in Cuba was logical: I told the curious that my lecture agent had advised me it would be difficult to promote my talks unless I resided in Latin America and could be billed as an authority with more than commuting experience and contacts in the area. In fact, he had said that.

Any hopes I entertained that lecture fees would augment my CIA salary were soon shattered. When deep-cover personnel earn income from their ostensible occupation, or profits from a cover business, the money gained is subject to an "off-set" arrangement against their CIA salary. Thus, in effect, lecture fees were turned over to the United States Treasury. (For the record, I was never asked to insert propaganda in my lectures; indeed, CIA didn't even look at the texts.)

In the business of deceiving relatives, neighbors, and close friends to protect cover, the CIA wife must play as important a part as her husband. She must learn to lie automatically and convincingly so that her spouse can be effective overseas and, in many cases, to insure his survival. A false step by the wife can result in the arrest of her husband. CIA officers working under light cover, identified as American officials and attached to an embassy, enjoy the protection of a diplomatic or official passport. If discovered they are declared *persona non grata* and deported. In most countries the deep-cover officer must expect to go to jail, or worse, if his cover is blown. Highly valued spies or deep-cover officers in prison are sometimes exchanged for counterparts of opposition services after long periods of negotiation. For example, Colonel Rudolf Abel, the Russian master agent jailed in New York, was swapped for Gary Powers, the U-2 pilot.

My cover was buttressed financially because I could mention casually to friends, or inquisitive local authorities, my modest, independent income from *The South Pacific Mail*, which Rick was profitably running in Santiago. That and my CIA salary were deposited to my Fort Worth bank account.

Cover considerations create peculiar problems. After a lecture

* "Spook" is the term often used by Foreign Service people in referring to CIA colleagues—sometimes pejoratively, sometimes affectionately. CIA officers have learned to live with the term, and occasionally refer to themselves as spooks.

in Chicago I was telephoned by a man who, to my surprise, identified himself as a CIA employee. He asked me to lunch. I accepted,
and he explained that he was from the Chicago field office of CIA,
an "open" installation with a telephone number in the local directory
(as is the case in a number of major cities in the United States). He
showed me a CIA identification card, something I didn't know existed.
His interest, he explained, was in hearing about any developments in
Latin America which might be useful to government analysts. It was
my first contact with CIA domestic operations, and I was nervous
throughout the lunch. I knew there was a regulation which prohibited a
CIA officer from claiming entertainment expenses involving another
government employee, and yet I did not feel free to tell my host that I
was a CIA colleague. Later in my career I would have been quite frank
about it, but then I let it go.

A lecture in West Palm Beach, Florida, led to my being the personal
guest of a Central American president. In discussing a political development in Costa Rica, I praised, deservedly I think, the country and
its administration of the time. A pretty blonde in the rear of the hall
stood and applauded. She introduced herself after the speech: she was
Karen Figueres, the American-born wife of José "Pepe" Figueres, President of that pleasant, democratic country.

Two weeks later in Havana I received an invitation from President
Figueres to visit San José as a guest of the Costa Rican government.
CIA told me to accept; it is always a good idea to cultivate influential
friends, especially presidents. In San José I stayed with Allen and Marian
Stewart, friends from Chile days when Allen was press attaché in the
American embassy at Santiago. For the first time Allen learned I was
with CIA. Since he was chargé of our embassy in San José and acting in
the absence of the Ambassador, I was obligated by CIA–Department of
State ground rules to tell him about my dealings with the Costa Rican
President.

It was a fine three-day visit. In the Costa Rican Congress I observed
deliberations while sitting in a red plush chair with a name tag on it:
EXCELENTISIMO DAVID PHILLIPS. Pepe and Karen Figueres gave a dinner
for me in the National Palace, really a ramshackle wooden structure
somewhat reminiscent of CIA headquarters in Washington. During
dessert I remarked to Karen Figueres, "You have a fascinating situation here. The American wife of a Latin president. It certainly would
make a great book."

"Unfortunately," Karen Figueres said, "Pepe's first wife has already
written it." I had not been aware that Figueres's first wife, too, had been
an American.

Now, for the first time, Pepe and Karen will know that their guest in 1955 was a CIA spook. They still live in San José where as ex-President Pepe remains active politically as well as, I understand, economically in a business endeavor with Robert Vesco, the American fugitive—who, contrary to some rumors, is not in any way connected with CIA. There was no ulterior motive for my acceptance of the invitation to visit San José other than to get to know the Figueres in the hope of some future political dividend. They were both charming hosts, and meeting the mercurial, MIT-educated Pepe was a stimulating experience.*

Pleasant as the assignment to Havana was in many aspects, 1955 and 1956 taught us the grim lessons of living in a rightist dictatorship. An ex-sergeant named Fulgencio Batista ran the country ruthlessly, concerned to some degree with the public welfare but at the same time accumulating a personal fortune of three hundred million dollars. American corporations, protected by Batista, prospered. Labor problems were resolved by getting the word to the National Palace that something was awry, and the dictator would fix things. It occurred to me at the time that American businesses would have to pay for this indulgence, sooner or later. Two very conservative American ambassadors in succession fueled latent anti-American fires.

I learned from friends and, especially from agent reports, that internal opposition to Batista was growing steadily. One prominent political opponent made a radio speech against the regime which should have been dramatic because the man planned to commit suicide while on the air. He killed himself all right, but due to an error in timing pulled the trigger seconds after the broadcast was terminated. Other less dramatic developments indicated that the middle class in Havana, weary of the rampant corruption in government, was conspiring against Batista.

One morning I took Maria to the front door to wait for the school bus. Before she could get out the door, I grabbed her quickly and escorted her through the kitchen, the back door, and the yard to wait for the bus on another corner. I didn't want her to see the body hanging from a tree in the front yard.

I was concerned that the murder had something to do with me. Perhaps someone had discovered that I was with CIA and the swinging corpse was a warning. But after a thorough investigation the CIA station in Havana found it had nothing to do with me or my work. The tree in front of my house was simply a convenient place for the regime to dispose of a political enemy.

In December of 1955 Cuban air force planes strafed eighty-three

* In fact, nothing came of the visit. I never saw Karen Figueres again, and only observed Pepe on one occasion, from a distance, when he visited Havana in 1959.

exiles who had sailed from Mexico with the intention of invading the southern coast of Cuba. The boat foundered and several invaders were drowned; two days later a dozen men survived an ambush to escape into the Sierra Maestra Mountains. With Fidel Castro were his brother, Raul, and the Argentine doctor, Che Guevara.

The landing created little stir in official Havana. The CIA Station Chief told me, in one of our infrequent meetings, that the Ambassador was unconcerned. He himself was concerned however and had suggested that the United States discreetly sponsor the creation of a third political force in Cuba, a moderate group between Castro on the left and Batista on the right. The Ambassador had vetoed the proposal, insisting that Cuban officials had assured him Castro would never get out of the mountains alive.

But word that Castro was in the hills galvanized the student and middle-class opposition to Batista in Havana.

Late one afternoon I was walking down a narrow street in the old section of the capital. The sound of a burst of machine gun fire ripped through the noise of evening traffic. Then another, longer burst prompted pedestrians to duck into doorways and taxi drivers to abandon their cabs. The blast of a grenade shook shop windows. A man ran by, shouting: "Students have just attacked the National Palace! They're after Batista!"

I headed for the firefight, two blocks away. If a serious attempt to topple Batista was under way the CIA station would expect an eyewitness account from someone. I dodged into a shop near the National Palace. The shopowner was peering over his window ledge; I joined him. He told me a group of student Catholic activists, supporters of Fidel Castro, had stormed the Palace in an attempt to capture Batista.

The students were inside the Palace, controlling part of it and shooting from the windows. Cuban army trucks and black police cars converged on the scene. Soldiers and policemen began to return the fire, raking windows of the building with rifle and machine gun bullets. I used the shop's telephone to call my case officer. I described the action, pretending for the benefit of the shopowner that I was a newsman reporting to my office. A bullet drilled through the plate glass of the store's display window, leaving a symmetrical pattern like a giant snowflake, and lodged in the wall behind us. The shopowner said, calmly and politely, "*Adiós*," and slipped out the rear entrance. I continued reporting to my CIA case officer, now without pretense.

Forty minutes later it was over. A dozen students were dead, and many injured. The bold attack had failed. Batista was not even in the Palace.

As I watched the captured students being carted away in buses, the shopowner returned through his rear door. We surveyed the battle's aftermath.

"It's over," I said.

"No," the shopkeeper said. "It's not. It's just the beginning. It won't be over until Fidel Castro is dead, or until he comes down from the mountains."

Life was comfortable for the Phillips family despite the growing political tension in Havana. My work was routine, leaving time for golf and the beach. Sometimes Helen and I thought our lifestyle was too good, and the children would be spoiled by the soft living and cheap servants. Once Atlee, age three, was in her crib and wanted attention. "Mommy!" she shouted. No answer. "Daddy?" Again, no answer. Finally Atlee screamed, "Maids!"

My favorite luncheon place was the Floridita restaurant in colonial Havana, largely because of the renowned daiquiris served at the bar (the Cuban rum drink was named for the mining city of Daiquirí, where it was first concocted by an American engineer). I was enjoying one of the frozen cocktails with a friend when I remarked, "This place really has atmosphere. That man at the other end of the bar looks just like Ernest Hemingway." He replied, "The atmosphere is authentic, all right. That man *is* Ernest Hemingway." As we watched, Hemingway downed a dozen daiquiris—yes, twelve—and, when he departed, he carried a quart-sized ice cream container filled with the delicious mixture of rum and lime juice for the ride back to his villa. Later I learned that he was a friend of the Havana Chief of Station—whether personal or professional I do not know.

In October of 1956 the Soviet Union smashed the uprising in Hungary, and I recalled Frank Wisner's warning that Khrushchev would be brutal if events demanded it. A few days later newspapers headlined the British and French bombing of Egypt, and the invasion of the Sinai Peninsula by the Israelis. In Havana, Batista's police chief violated the most inviolate diplomatic norm and led an attack on the Haitian embassy, slaughtering the Cubans in asylum there.

Helen and I celebrated New Year's Eve in the hospital. In her room we greeted 1957 with champagne as she was recuperating from the birth of our fourth child, Christopher. After midnight I was evicted by the nurse and went to Dick and Nancy Cushing's home to join a party. A CIA colleague was there: Dick Helms was vacationing in Cuba with his friends from USIA. It was my first social evening with the CIA veteran who was then Chief of Operations for the DDP. Of course we pretended not to know each other.

In his office in Washington Helms was civil but businesslike. In Havana, away from the pressures of worldwide responsibility, he was a different person, relaxed and gregarious. A moderate drinker, Helms had been celebrating with a few extra glasses of champagne and was having a thoroughly good time. He was neatly groomed, lithe and talkative. The women at the party glanced at him frequently; he favored them occasionally with his slightly twisted smile.

Someone had described for Helms the versatile Spanish word, *arriba*. It means "up" or "over." It also means "onward," in the sense of moving ahead decisively, or charging in a military action. It is often used by Latins, particularly Cubans, in the same way "Excelsior!" is employed as an exhortation in English. Helms was fascinated by the word, especially in the latter meaning. He repeated it over and over again as the party went on into the early hours.

It was after three in the morning when he turned to Dick Cushing and asked, "Where's the action in Havana now?"

"Clubs downtown will be open until dawn," Cushing said.

"No," said Helms. "Let's find another party."

Cushing laughed. "The only one I know is too exclusive for us. There's always a blast at the Country Club, but for members only." He looked around at the half dozen guests. "None of us qualify."

"*Arriba*," Helms said. "Let's go. They'll let us in."

Despite protests from those resident in Havana, who knew how rigid and snobbish the rules of this establishment were, Helms insisted we pile into a car and drive to the Country Club. He led the way—*arriba*—as we marched from the parking lot to the main entrance. We followed him through the door.

"One moment." The maître spoke fluent English. "I'm afraid that only members are allowed."

Helms cocked his head haughtily. "But I am a member."

"You are?" The custodian of the portal was dubious. "Your name, please?"

"Oliver Cromwell," replied Helms.

"Cromwell?" The maître opened a huge black book of the club's membership, flipping the pages to the C's. "Cromwell?" He ran his finger down the page. "Ah, yes. Mr. Cromwell. Of course. Go right in, sir."

"*Arriba*," said Helms, and beckoned us to follow him into the crowded ballroom.

Perhaps Dick Helms ran some sort of operation that New Year's morning. But I know there was no bribe, no money changing hands, when we arrived. Anyway, it was a good party.

Arriba!

66

A few days into the New Year of 1957 I went home early from my cover office to discuss a cable from CIA headquarters with Helen. We had recently moved into a new house after a search for just the right one. Being on deep-cover assignment, I had expected at least a five-year tour in Havana. Helen was standing on a chair putting up new drapes when I told her that Washington had canceled the remainder of our tour. Events in the Middle East had shifted CIA priorities. We were being reassigned, as soon as Helen's doctor approved her travel, to Beirut, Lebanon.

Six members of the Phillips family boarded the Pan Am Constellation for the flight to Beirut from New York. Helen and I, and the three youngest, were able to sit together but Maria, age eight, sat alone several seats ahead preoccupied with her coloring book. The plane taxied for takeoff but stopped short of the runway, engines idling. The stewardess told us the radio tower had instructed the pilot to wait for a last-minute VIP passenger. The passengers were impressed when a black sedan sped out on the tarmac. A tall, handsome, elderly man carrying a small black bag boarded, and we were finally off for Lebanon. After the long flight from Havana, and the wait in the New York airport, we had an additional twelve hours of flying before us. The passengers seated near us eyed David, Jr., five, Atlee, four, and Christopher, just a few weeks old, with some apprehension.

During the first hour I briefed Helen on our cover situation. The assignment to Beirut had been an unexpected one, and there had been no time to prepare an elaborate cover scenario. In Lebanon I was to pretend to be a business consultant seeking investment opportunities. For whom was yet to be decided. The first priority was to build the cover, somehow. We were to rent an apartment, purchase secondhand furniture, and settle the kids in school. Then, and only then, was I to report to the station for duty. I had a telephone number to trigger the contact, which would occur in a safe house. I was not to visit the American embassy except on routine consular business. "Your cover is to be deep, deep, deep," I had been instructed. "Your contact with the CIA station can wait until you and the family are settled."

I went up the aisle to check on Maria. The distinguished-looking passenger who had boarded the plane at the last minute sat next to her. He and Maria were chatting as she colored her pictures, Maria selecting crayons from the box he held. Maria's companion introduced himself as Dr. Paul Dudley White. I recognized the name as the eminent heart surgeon who had recently been in the news while treating President Eisenhower's serious heart condition. He was flying to Beirut at the request of the Department of State to advise Lebanese doctors on the treatment of a massive heart attack suffered by the Lebanese foreign minister. Our plane had been delayed at the urgent request of the Lebanese government.

Dr. White and Maria seemed to be compatible, but I suggested to the physician that Maria and I exchange seats, and I could promise him some quiet. He would have none of it. Later he met and talked with David, Jr., and Atlee, and chucked Christopher under the chin. The children were captivated by the genial surgeon, especially when he opened his black bag to display his instruments.

Before we landed in Beirut Dr. White spoke with Helen, predicting that after the long flight she would be exhausted and need rest. He volunteered to babysit in our hotel with the three oldest children during lunch the next day.

The following morning Helen was dunking a squirming Christopher in the tub at our hotel when the telephone rang (there are telephone extensions in Lebanese hotel bathrooms).

"Mrs. Phillips?"

"Yes?"

"This is the American Ambassador."

Ambassador Donald Heath had a problem. He had invited a score of Lebanon's most distinguished citizens to a luncheon in honor of Dr. White. The good doctor had thanked the Ambassador but declined, explaining that he had a previous engagement with three children he had met on the plane.

"I really will have protocol problems canceling the luncheon on such short notice," the Ambassador said. "Perhaps Dr. White will come to the embassy luncheon if we invite your children as well. How old are the children, Mrs. Phillips?"

By this time I had picked up the telephone in the room. I could picture the Ambassador blanching when Helen told him the oldest of the trio was eight. We made it clear to the diplomat that he should go ahead with his luncheon without worrying about any disruptions from our brood. Ambassador Heath was grateful, and graceful in suggesting the kiddies visit the embassy some other time.

The telephone rang again in a half an hour. This time I answered. "Mr. Phillips," the Ambassador said, somewhat desperately, "Dr. White has agreed to postpone his luncheon with your children. But he insists that you and Mrs. Phillips attend. I realize an hour is short notice, but please be my guests for lunch."

I recalled my instructions: deep, deep, deep cover and don't even visit the embassy. I told the Ambassador we could not accept.

"Mr. Phillips"—the Ambassador's voice conveyed authority—"this embassy will do everything it can to assist you while you are in this

68

country. Meanwhile, as the President's senior representative in Lebanon, I must insist. Dr. White says you must be at the luncheon. I will expect you at noon."

I tried several times to reach someone at the telephone number to be used for my contact with the station. No answer. I wanted to alert the station to explain why I thought it politic that the Ambassador's invitation be accepted.

The luncheon was pleasant. Among the guests were a few embassy officers and visiting American luminaries. On my left at the table was A. J. Liebling, the *New Yorker* writer. After a conversation with him, I turned to chat with the American embassy officer on my right. He introduced himself.

I turned cold. The man was my new boss.

"And what do you do, Mr. Phillips?" the Chief of Station asked affably.

I had to swallow before I could get out the words. "Just arrived last night. Going into business here." Then, "My name is David Phillips." I repeated it. "David Phillips."

"I see," said the COS, without interest. But then his eyes widened. "Did you say David Phillips?"

I nodded.

"And did you just come from Havana?"

"Yes," I said, hurriedly adding, "sir."

It had finally gotten through to the Chief of Station. His newest deep-cover agent, the one who was going to be deep, deep, deep, and who was not to visit the American embassy under any circumstances, was his luncheon partner. His neck reddened, and I thought for a minute he was going to have some sort of convulsion.

Finally he recovered. "Well, Mr. Phillips, I must say you're quite an operator. Wasn't it kind of the Ambassador to bring us together?" His eyes narrowed. "I'm certainly looking forward to talking to you again."

Dr. White lunched with the children at the hotel the next day, and we saw him several times before he returned to the United States. He and Maria exchanged letters for several years, and he never failed to send each of the children a Christmas card. I remember Dr. Paul Dudley White fondly, a friend of the family, and a man who knew all about the human heart.

Our cover problems had just begun. We rented an apartment facing the Mediterranean. I ran across a furniture advertisement inserted in a local newspaper by an American businessman leaving the country. I purchased his furniture and we moved into our flat. The same day we met an English couple living in the building and invited them over for an apartment-warming drink that night. When they arrived the British woman looked around, smiled pleasantly, and said, "I see you are with the CIA."

I almost choked. I attempted a chuckle. "Why...why, whatever makes you think that?"

"The furniture," she said. "Everyone knows it belonged to a CIA fellow who had to leave Beirut in a hurry."

I laughed off the coincidence, saying I had bought the furnishings from a man I had never seen before. But she was right. I had unwittingly purchased the furniture of another CIA agent whose cover had been blown, forcing him to decamp hurriedly. There is such a thing, I began to realize, as too much secrecy in government.

Lebanon, in 1957, was a lovely country. The popular image of a Middle Eastern environment is that of searing wind, heat, and sand. Beirut is a seaport on the blue Mediterranean, with a backdrop of mountains where the celebrated cedars grow and Lebanese and foreigners have enjoyed skiing in winter months. An equal balance of Christian and Moslem Arabs contributed to political stability. The country prospered due to the cleverness of its businessmen serving as middlemen between the Arab states and the rest of the world. The French heritage was evident everywhere, especially in the fine restaurants; for less than two American dollars we dined on snails, filet of sole, white wine, and chocolate soufflé. The children were happy in good schools, although Maria and Atlee had to struggle with French and Italian. We frequented a beach club just below our apartment building or the vaster uncluttered beaches a few miles from the city. We made innumerable friends of many nationalities.

Professionally, I had problems building a cover sufficiently viable to explain my presence in Lebanon. Not the least of my difficulties was that of deceiving the sharp Lebanese businessman from whom I rented office space. I realized that I would have to improvise something solid to convince him and his office staff.

It is CIA policy that its officers, even those who specialize in a single area (as I had in Latin America) have at least one rotational tour in another region. The Agency goal is at least partial immunization against parochialism, omniscience, and staleness—a real danger after years in the same operational environment. Arabs, I learned quickly, were not the same as Latins.

I asked the office boy to run an errand for me and mail several letters at the post office. I gave him the letters and some money. I explained—carefully, because he did not seem too bright—that he should go to the post office, buy stamps, put them on the letters, and then insert the correspondence in the slot. To emphasize, I repeated my instructions.

Half an hour later the office boy returned and, with a satisfied grin, gave me back my money—all of it.

"But how did you buy the stamps?" I asked.

"No problem," he beamingly assured me. "I was able to save you money. At the post office the authorities paid no attention to me. So, when no one was looking, I *sneaked* the letters into the slot." He was quite proud of saving money which otherwise would have been wasted on stamps.

We had become friendly with a young Arab prince who retained an apartment in our building for use two or three days a month on visits from Saudi Arabia. He was rich. *Really* rich. Even when he was not in Beirut, which was most of the time, there were three cars parked in his garage: a long Cadillac, a black Buick, and a sporty Thunderbird. One day another car was added to the fleet, the most ostentatious Lincoln Continental I had ever seen. I mentioned his latest acquisition when I next saw the prince. "Oh, you like it," he said, in Oxford-polished English. "So do I. I bought it last week in New York."

"Last week?" I asked. "How did you get it to Beirut so quickly?"

"Oh, I liked it so much," the potentate explained, "that I had it airfreighted."

Beirut, with its comfortable living conditions and easy air travel to other countries, was a base of operations for foreign correspondents. The British chap in our apartment complex was the correspondent for London's *Daily Telegraph*, and through him we met other newsmen. I often visited the bar at the St. George's Hotel, a journalists' gathering place on the waterfront.

The newsmen at the St. George's bar regaled each other with entertaining, often hilarious yarns—some stretching even a CIA pilgrim's credulity. My favorite was recounted by an American correspondent and concerned his difficulty in crossing the frontier between Lebanon and Syria.

The Syrian border guards on the road between Beirut and Damascus were often confronted with bribes by motorists carrying contraband between the two capitals. Since the guards were miserably paid soldiers, they often succumbed to the temptation. Understandably, the government adopted the practice of frequently changing the guards before the provincial recruits' style of life could become too dependent upon corruption. When soldiers reported for duty they were briefed on the hiding places smugglers used in automobiles and were given strict instructions to search the trunk of each car.

The American newsman told us about the time he was stopped at the border in his Volkswagen by a Syrian soldier recently posted and unfamiliar with the car.

"Open the rear of your car," he instructed the American. After inspecting the back of the Volkswagen the guard returned to the driver. "You are under arrest," he said.

"Why?" asked the newsman.

"For smuggling a motor."

The American's Arabic was basic. He attempted to explain that in a Volkswagen the motor was in the rear of the vehicle and the inspector should have looked in the front, empty except for the spare tire. But his Arabic was not sufficient to the situation.

"This is my first day on the job," the soldier said. "I was told to inspect the rear of every car. Yours has a motor in it. Either I must arrest you or collect duty on the motor."

The American persuaded the soldier to allow him to turn around and head back down the road into Lebanon. A few minutes later he again approached the customs post, but this time he was backing up. "Now," he said to the Syrian, "you can check the rear of the car."

The guard went to the back (the front) of the Volkswagen and opened the hood.

"That's better," said the guard. "Now you may enter the country."

So—the American newsman claimed—he backed through the border and down the highway toward Damascus.

One evening at the St. George's bar I started chatting with an American woman who obviously was waiting for someone. After her escort arrived we continued our conversation for another half an hour. He was English. It was only after we had been talking for some time that a bell clanged in my head. The name had seemed familiar when he was introduced—Kim Philby. He was working as a newsman in Beirut, after "retiring" from MI-6, the British foreign intelligence service. A double-agent, working for Soviet intelligence, Philby had toiled diligently as a British intelligence officer until he achieved the eminent position of chief of MI-6's Soviet department. He was one of the most successful spies in history. A public defense by British Prime Minister Harold Macmillan, who attested in Parliament to Philby's integrity, enabled Philby to escape prosecution. But I had been told by CIA counter-intelligence people that he was guilty of treason. I finished my drink quickly, and excused myself.*

My intention to participate in amateur theatricals was thwarted by the smoldering Lebanese resentment against British and French bombing of Egypt in 1956. Leaders of the English-speaking community had

* In 1958 Philby married an American woman—I believe but am not positive that she was the woman who introduced me to him—and they both disappeared from Beirut to turn up in Moscow.

decided, prudently, to suspend any group activity which might invite Arab incidents. More disappointed than I was a young officer from the United States Information Service. Unable to engage in his avocation of acting and directing, he turned to writing. On several occasions, we discussed a book he was drafting. William Peter Blatty had genuine talent and shortly resigned from the Foreign Service to take his chances in Hollywood. *The Exorcist*—both book and film—was among his most successful works.

The problem of cover was fortuitously resolved when I made a connection with a rich Texan on a flight from Ankara to Paris. He had asked for a bourbon before takeoff and was visibly offended when the stewardess told him it could not be served until we were airborne. This was at nine in the morning. The Texan turned to me. "Suppose you think it's too early for booze? In fact," he said, "I never drink before five in the afternoon."

He guffawed, showing me his wristwatch. All the numerals were fives. "From Neiman-Marcus," he assured me. "Promised my wife I'd never drink until after five, and now I can always tell her I don't."

I became the Texan's informal and unpaid representative in the Middle East, a cover which I adopted informally and promoted in conversations with local contacts. It was not too thin because he traveled from Dallas to Beirut several times. And, I helped him in his attempt to purchase a controlling share in a Middle Eastern petroleum company, a task complicated by the fact that control was held—tightly—by Aristotle Onassis. My Lebanese office associates were impressed, especially when the Texan arrived in a private plane furnished with a double bed. My cover was finally established.*

During our year and a half in Lebanon I traveled throughout the Middle East and Europe on CIA business, sometimes being away from the family for several weeks. There were periods of intense activity, when I felt like James Bond at the barricades, followed by weeks of inaction and boredom, when I had a good deal in common with the military officer manning a radar screen in the Aleutians waiting for a Soviet missile to fly over.

I still followed events in Cuba with keen interest. Fidel Castro had been in the Sierra Maestra Mountains for more than a year, and his

---

* I wish, however, that the wealthy Texan had reimbursed me for several hundred dollars in expenses, mostly telephone calls to Texas, which I incurred on his behalf. Neither he nor CIA ever paid me. In fact I was later berated by an officer from CIA's cover section when he learned of my ad hoc cover arrangement. He pointed out the problems which could have ensued if my cover were blown and damaged the Texan's business interests.

guerrilla forces had eluded the Cuban soldiers giving chase. Middle-class opposition to Batista in Havana continued and grew. I decided that eventually Castro would depose Batista. I had a long talk with Helen.

It was time, I said, for us to make that million dollars. It was not difficult to predict that the Cuban political pendulum would swing far to the left should Castro become the new leader in Havana. Only a few of the American industries in Cuba bothered to have public-relations programs. Doing business with Batista required nothing more than finding a way to get a message to Batista. There was only one American public-relations firm in Havana; its major client was the Cuban government, so it would not long survive a Castro victory. American businesses would have an urgent need for employee- and, especially, government-relations programs. Ergo, I should resign from CIA, return to Havana, and open a public-relations office. We would enjoy Cuba, avoiding contracts with any political taint, until the bearded revolutionaries came down from the mountains. It was simple. The million dollars was practically in the bank.

So, leisurely, we began to plan. I gave CIA notice that I would resign and leave Lebanon in the summer.

Meanwhile, there was trouble in Beirut. A tremendous bomb blast woke us in the early morning hours, shattering every window glass in the apartment. We were almost thrown from bed. I went outside in bedroom slippers to inspect the damage and was relieved to find no evidence that the terrorists were acting against our apartment alone. I assumed they were protesting against the foreign presence so evident in our building.

Walking through the debris, I stepped on a shard of glass and embedded it in my heel. The wound was deep, so Helen drove me to the American University Hospital. A surgeon dug the sliver of glass from my foot.

"I'm afraid I've bothered you for something not very serious," I said to the surgeon.

"The wound is not serious," the doctor said. "But I fear you are the first foreign casualty of a very serious war among my people. Your foot is all right. I hope my country will be."

The surgeon's prophecy wasn't long in being borne out. Booming explosions and the sharp crack of rifle fire soon made sleeping in Beirut a series of catnaps. Moslem and Christian Arabs drew a thin red line between their sectors, and fighting erupted when one or the other crossed the boundary. Civil discord disrupted the booming economy. In the evenings, apartment dwellers were captives in their abodes, and social life was as restrictive as that on an ocean liner.

I nevertheless continued to travel on CIA business. One of my

74

trips was to Baghdad, capital of Iraq. I stayed for several days in a hotel on the banks of the Tigris. A nearby theater was showing an Arabic film: *Aladdin and His Lamp.*

My purpose there was to persuade a local official to sign a contract. Finally, late one afternoon, he did. Mission accomplished, I boarded the first plane for Beirut the next morning. Aloft, the pilot came into the cabin to talk with the passengers. He told us, "You were all fortunate to get on this flight. There was a revolt after we left Baghdad. Quite a few people have been killed."

Later, I learned that during the revolt the man who had signed the contract the previous afternoon had lost his head. Literally. A mob burst into his office and decapitated him.

Night fighting continued in Beirut streets. I was growing more and more concerned about leaving Helen and the children when I traveled. Toward the middle of 1958 the civil war became so serious that the American embassy ordered all American families to leave the country. Helen and the children flew to Vienna and found temporary lodging in a hotel.

Shortly thereafter, it was time for me to return to Washington, resign from CIA, and move the family to Cuba. The afternoon I was to leave our British friends bought me a farewell drink at the restaurant across the street from our building. The British woman told me, "You know, when you first came here, we really did think you were a cover boy."

"A cover boy?"

"The furniture," she explained. "It was some months before we realized you were not really an intelligence fellow."

My cover, so thin in the beginning, had held up in the end.

On the way to the airport I had the taxi stop at a local store where I owed a bill. The proprietor, a Christian Arab with whom I was friendly, asked me to do him a favor before leaving. My cover had held with him too; he thought I was a businessman.

"You must go now to see the American Ambassador," the shopowner said. "You must tell him that the only thing which can save this poor country is to send in the Marines."

I said that I must get to the airport.

"But you must do this for me," implored the Lebanese. "If I go to your embassy your Ambassador will be too busy; he will not see me. But if you, an American, go he must talk to you. You must convince him that he must save us by calling in American troops."

Finally, in order to appease the distraught shopowner, I let him think I would do as he asked. I didn't. The cab took me straight to the airport.

Mine was the last commercial flight to take off from Beirut for a long time. Near the island of Cyprus, only a few minutes' flight time from Lebanon, I looked out of the window. Below was a vast flotilla of American naval craft, steaming toward Lebanese beaches. President Eisenhower had sent in the Marines. They landed in the pre-dawn darkness of the fifteenth of July.

Four months later, in Cuba, I received a postcard from my Lebanese shopkeeper friend. It had been forwarded to my cover address in New York, to Texas, and then to Havana. It was limp and torn. The message read: "Dear Mr. Phillips. Thank you very much."*

The family was reunited in Rome. We sailed for the United States on one of the last voyages of the *Ile de France*. Foreign Service regulations insist that CIA officers travel on "American bottoms," so that the fare will benefit an American company. The only exception is where there is no United States transportation available, either in terms of general service or bookings for a specific time. The latter was our case, and we enjoyed the crossing on the French luxury liner. (Recently all sea travel has been proscribed; United States government employees traveling to and from assignments abroad must fly.)

In Washington I resigned from CIA. Colonel J. C. King, the head of the Western Hemisphere Division, asked me to reconsider the decision and to return to Cuba as a staff officer. I declined, explaining that I could not in good conscience stay on the payroll because of my intention to go my own way in private business—and if I were fortunate enough to make money I didn't want my income subject to an off-set clause. I did agree to sign a contract for a small monthly stipend and be available to the Chief of Station in Havana on a compatible part-time basis.

"Part-time?" Helen was again skeptical. "Isn't this where we came in?"

I assured Helen that I was serious this time. We were going to make a bundle of money and settle in one place so the children would have an uninterrupted education.

We had been in Havana exactly one month when a cable from CIA asked if I would undertake a temporary duty assignment for several weeks in South America. It was such an intriguing mission I could not refuse. Anyway, I was in no hurry to become active in the public-relations business since Castro and his guerrillas were still holed up in the mountains.

Returning to Havana, I hired one employee and opened my public-

* The reader will have noted that this description of my Lebanese interlude is more travelogue than an account of CIA duties. A more detailed explanation would violate my Secrecy Oath with CIA.

relations office. With only two of us it was perhaps presumptuous when I put a sign on the door: DAVID A. PHILLIPS ASSOCIATES. No one rushed the door in any event, nor did I solicit clients. Acquaintances in the American business community chuckled at my ingenuousness when I explained that I was waiting for a change in government.

Stage One of my three-part plan went pretty much according to schedule. I was the first American intelligence source in Cuba to report the departure of Batista. It was not a very sophisticated operation. Helen and I had been at a New Year's Eve party, bidding *adiós* to 1958, and, returning home, we had a final glass of champagne while relaxing in lawn chairs outside. A large airplane flew over the house about 4 A.M. I telephoned my case officer.

"Batista just flew into exile," I said.

"Are you drunk?" he asked.

"Feeling okay." I admitted. "But I know there are no scheduled air flights in Cuba at four in the morning. And a commercial airliner just took off and headed out over the ocean. If Batista's not aboard I'll eat your sombrero."

No hat-eating was necessary. Batista and a planeload of cronies had decamped, encumbered by a vast array of suitcases stuffed not with clothes but money. The revolution was over.

Several days later I stood on a street corner as Fidel Castro marched into Havana. The crowds went wild. I applauded and cheered along with them. Following Castro were his guerrillas, known because of their beards as *barbudos*, an impressive group of brave men who had outfought and outwitted Batista's army. Like so many Cubans, I was glad to see them.

Stage Two of the plan went as scheduled: for six months David A. Phillips Associates was the fastest growing public-relations business in the world. The American firm which had the Batista account closed its Havana office, leaving the field to me. Foreign industrialists sought my advice on dealing with the new, alarmingly Socialist Castro government. The pendulum was swinging to the left, and I did well.

It was in Stage Three that the plan went awry. I had not considered the possibility that the political pendulum would swing so far to the left that public relations would become a government monopoly, jealously guarded and vigorously enforced. Castro conducted a series of circus-atmosphere trials of former Batista officials in a giant sports stadium. Many were executed before television cameras. The bearded soldiers who fought with Castro in the hills began to defect, and nearly all of his original cabinet members resigned or were dismissed. The support of middle-class adherents in Havana—without which Castro, his brother Raul, and Che Guevara could not have entered the capital

77

totally unscathed and unopposed—evaporated. Disillusioned students complained in the coffee houses. Soviet advisers appeared on the streets of Havana, and revolutionary militants from other countries in Latin America swarmed into Cuba.

My former host in Costa Rica, and now an ex-president, José Figueres, flew to Havana to address a mass rally. As he sat on the speakers' platform he was appalled at the Marxist ranting and rhetoric of the speakers who preceded him. The man who introduced Figueres, a labor leader named David Salvador, castigated him for his moderate political stance before he even had a chance to speak. Fidel Castro stroked his beard and nodded his head frequently to emphasize Salvador's diatribe.

I was in the crowd as the diminutive, feisty Costa Rican faced the mass of chanting peasants and soldiers. He abandoned his prepared text and launched into a vigorous rebuttal, warning Cubans that their revolution would be betrayed if it took the course advocated by David Salvador, and that Communism in Cuba would be the inevitable result. It was a gutsy performance, ending only when Fidel Castro snatched the microphone from Figueres.*

The first of Castro's senior officials to defect was Pedro Díaz Lanz, the chief of his air force. He flew to Miami, rented an airplane, and promptly flew back to Havana, dropping anti-Castro leaflets over the capital. They fluttered down into the streets by the hundreds, a harbinger of the conflict that was to develop between Castro and Cuban exiles in Miami.

Stage Four of my plan—the million dollars—never materialized. Suddenly there were no public relations to conduct. Ironically, the way to get something done in Havana was to have a line into the National Palace, where Fidel Castro, ensconced in Batista's former office, would or would not take care of the matter. My dream faded.

Although still on a part-time contract, I began to put in a full day for CIA. Some of the work was what is known in the profession as "hairy": delicate or dangerous. It was in this situation that I received a notice that a parcel for me had arrived from the United States and could be retrieved at the central post office.

The post office clerk handed me a brown package the size of a briefcase. I took it to a table in the center of the room and opened it. The first item I found was a large photograph of me shaking hands with Allen Dulles. The photograph, with suitable inscription, had been taken when I was awarded the Intelligence Medal of Merit, five years earlier. Then a paperweight-size medallion in a fancy leather box emerged. Finally, I uncovered the citation read during the Washington ceremony

* David Salvador later was jailed by Castro. He remains a political prisoner in Cuba today, fifteen years later.

when Dulles presented the medal. The words *Central Intelligence Agency* were emblazoned across the top of the citation.

My god! What had happened?

What had happened was that the Awards people at CIA had seen my resignation papers. Thus I was qualified to have personal possession of the medal that I was not allowed to keep while still active in CIA. It had been forwarded, not too thoughtfully but with good intentions, to my new address in Havana. (Decorations awarded to officers in the Clandestine Service are sometimes referred to as "jock strap medals," that reputedly being the only article of apparel on which they can be worn. In fact, they cannot be displayed even on an athletic supporter, but are retained in a safe at CIA headquarters until the officer so honored retires or resigns. In some cases, to protect a cover mechanism, the medal is never turned over to the officer.)

As I prepared to leave the post office I noticed a sign over the exit: ALL PACKAGES MUST BE INSPECTED BEFORE LEAVING THE BUILDING. That prospect was not appealing. So I rewrapped the package, addressing it to my home in Havana. I had been fortunate to escape the spot check conducted on all arriving international mail—which could have meant my parcel would be delivered by a Cuban policeman—but I knew there was no postal inspection at that time on domestic mail. I didn't have enough cash to buy the postage stamps though. After a three-hour wait I finally saw a familiar face, a Cuban I had met socially. I borrowed money from him and mailed the package. (And, later, passed the medal to my case officer to be returned by diplomatic pouch to CIA headquarters, where it was re-buried in a safe for the next sixteen years.)

In the final days of 1959 I realized how precarious my situation had become, and how I would surely be jailed should Castro's new intelligence service discover I was an intelligence officer working for CIA. I had spotted another American, also a businessman in Havana, whom I suspected was cooperating with CIA. I wasn't certain at the time, and there was obviously no need for me to know. I was shocked when he was arrested by Cuban authorities and, without ceremony or trial, executed.

My case officer, at the end of a routine safe house meeting, told me to review my security practices. He gave me a new set of rules for our meetings, which involved increased vigilance and complicated contact instructions.

"Is it because of ... ?" I named my friend, so recently dead.

"I didn't say that," the case officer said, evasively.

"You don't have to," I replied.*

---

* Eight years later, when I became CIA's Chief of Cuban Operations, I was able to check. My suspicion that the executed American provided information to CIA was confirmed.

Hairy. I said nothing to Helen, but exercised extreme caution in meeting my case officer and the agents I handled. Before an encounter with an agent for instance, I spent as much as an hour ducking in and out of the narrow streets of colonial Havana to be sure I was not being followed, and adopted the same precautions after a clandestine rendezvous.

My public-relations cover was now in shreds, but it still provided some plausible access to government officials on the pretext that I was helping a client salvage his investment. I was amused by the sign Fidel Castro decreed must hang in every government bureaucrat's office: WE MUST LEARN TO BE HONEST. Castro was determined to eradicate the corruption which had been a shibboleth in Batista's time. In meetings with Cuban officials I found some disillusioned with the drift toward Communism and recruited them as intelligence sources for CIA.

One encounter with a leader of the revolution I will never forget. At the end of a long evening entertaining a visitor from New York, I took him to a popular Cuban coffee house where Cuban intellectuals once plotted by candlelight against Batista; now the converted basement was a favorite of Castro's followers. We were about to leave when there was a stir at the entrance. A *barbudo* wearing a beret came in, followed by an entourage of a dozen men in the green uniforms of those who had fought with Castro in the mountains. The owner skipped about excitedly. The waiters deserted other clients and clustered around the newcomer.

He was Che Guevara.

Guevara was not a large man, but his presence filled the room. Within minutes the corner where he sat with his companions became the stage of a small arena as chairs made of kegs were drawn in close. Che (an Argentine term used affectionately like the English "pal") was a hero of the revolution, second in popularity only to Castro himself, and the coffee house crowd's admiration for him was almost palpable. From down the street came the muted music of a guitar; the air was thick with the smoke of Havana cigars; giant shadows cast by the candles flickered on the hundred-year-old walls. The waiters served *anejo*, the distilled rum sipped with coffee in Cuba, much as brandy is drunk elsewhere. Soon there were questions. Guevara answered them in a soft voice, speaking slowly, sometimes pausing to catch his breath, his shoulders heaving slightly as he controlled the asthma which had plagued him since childhood.

Guevara talked for an hour, then another. It was four in the morning: a moving levee.

I had been an actor of modest talent in New York, but I retained some sense of the dramatic and, after CIA service, of history. I decided

I could not pass up the chance to meet the famous revolutionary.

Introducing myself as an American, I asked Guevara what he planned to do in the future.

Guevara turned, squinting at me in the semi-darkness. Then he smiled, and shrugged his shoulders.

"First, I plan to get out of the sugar business," Che said. This drew a laugh, as it was widely known that Guevara was neither comfortable nor proficient as the chief of Cuba's Ministry of Industries which managed Cuba's sugar and tobacco exports, a position to which Fidel Castro had inexplicably appointed him. "Then," he said, looking directly at me, "I will travel and take the revolution with me."

Che Guevara launched into a ten-minute lecture on the plight of the underprivileged of the world and on the inevitable triumph of Marxism which would unshackle them from their misery. He said nothing memorable or even new; his speech was a litany of clichés which I had heard from many Latins before. But Guevara's measured tone was mesmerizing, and his charisma held the coffee house crowd in thrall. In the eerie light, the locks of curly hair hanging over his forehead along with the panache of a single star—insignia of a *comandante* in Castro's army—glittering on his beret gave him the dash and romantic aura of a Latin American Robin Hood. That didn't keep his eyes from challenging me while he ticked off a list of the abuses of American imperialism and exulted in his prediction that it was doomed. In all this he was pleasant, speaking without rancor. Once he interrupted his lecture to instruct the waiter to refill my glass with *anejo*.

It was quiet when he finished. Guevara turned away from me and soothed his asthma by breathing deeply from an inhalator.

It was almost dawn when we left the coffee house. Guevara and his friends sped off in two jeeps.

Che Guevara was quite a guy. He had the charisma and charm—he was *simpático*—which are essential qualities for Latin Americans who aspire to greatness in any field of endeavor. I predicted to my friend that he would become the most successful revolutionary of our time. It was a forecast that turned out to be half right: Guevara achieved the image he sought, even with young people in the United States, but lost the guerrilla skirmishes he fought in Africa and Bolivia. In any event, I admired him. That early morning encounter in the coffee house helped me understand the aspirations and convictions of men with whom I disagreed and, on occasions in the future, would treat as adversaries.

My case officer asked me to undertake what he called a "special" mission. A group of anti-Castro Cubans in Havana was planning the first coup attempt against the new regime. He gave me the names of several conspirators, with the proposal that I approach one of them as an American anxious to assist anyone plotting against Castro. "There is little chance this group will be successful," the case officer said, "but we want to know what they are up to."

The case officer was nervous. "Think about it. It might be hairy. For this one, we would like you to volunteer."

That made me think, all right. It would be tricky. I could approach and cultivate one of the conspirators using a false identity, perhaps in disguise. But if one of the plotters already knew me, or recognized me from photographs which had appeared in a local paper after an amateur theatrical performance, the others would soon know who I was. It would not be difficult for Castro's secret police to track me down if there were an informant in the cabal, or if one of them should be arrested and reveal the participation of an American.

To my astonishment, I heard myself saying, "I'll do it."

Later, I mulled over more carefully the risks involved. It could be downright dangerous. That realization led to another decision; I talked with Helen about our future. We agreed that we should consider a long-standing job offer of a friend in New York—since there was no longer a chance of making our fortune in Havana, it was time to seek the pot of gold elsewhere.

After approaching and cultivating one of the conspirators, I attended a secret conclave in the home of another. I was dismayed to find many more Cubans there than I had expected. There were several hours of courageous talk, but it was soon apparent that they possessed neither sufficient organization nor resolve to carry out a successful coup against Castro. I wrote a report for my case officer. The final sentence suggested that in such a large group there might be a Castro informant, or someone who would become one.

A cable instructed me to fly to Washington to discuss the conspiracy. The people on our Cuban desk decided I should sever contact with the group because the risk factor was unacceptable. I agreed, happy to know that someone cared. Further, I was told to begin planning my departure from Cuba since my cover—now gossamer thin—could no longer explain in Havana the presence of a businessman without a business. It was suggested that I return to CIA once more as a staff officer. I replied that I planned to accept a job in a public-relations firm which I would be discussing in New York that very day, prior to returning to Havana.

The job offer was confirmed in New York. As I was getting ready to leave for the airport, the telephone rang in my hotel room.

"You were right about the informant," I was told by the caller from CIA headquarters. "Several of those who attended the meeting with you have been arrested."

I said nothing. There was a tingling at the back of my neck.

"If none of the Cubans knew your true name," the Cuba desk officer continued, "there probably won't be a problem. But if someone did . . ." Then, "Do you think it better not to go back?"

"I have to go back," I said. "Remember, I have a business to dismantle, not to mention a wife and four kids to get out of the country."

"Okay. But call me from Miami before you take off for Havana."

Standing in a telephone booth at the airport in Miami, I heard more disturbing news when I called the Cuba desk officer. An additional two Cubans involved in the meeting had been arrested. "We could have some of our people help your family pack out."

Of course I had to return. Without the protection of diplomatic passports, Helen and the children were potential hostages of Castro's police who were, by now, pretty ruthless and efficient.

The flight from Miami was about an hour. I was petrified. My stomach churned during the flight, and it jumped as I stood in the immigration line at the Havana airport.

One more passenger between me and the immigration official. The official checked his big, black book of undesirables with thoroughness. Then I stood before him. He was not an attractive man—he used his finger alternately to pick his nose and run down the list of P's—but I felt like kissing him when he stamped my entry paper, and nodded me past the barrier.

We packed. I told Helen about our predicament. I made reservations for the ferry which plied between Havana and Key West. My case officer, in our final meeting, passed me a Washington telephone number which I was to call from Key West. He was glassy-eyed with fatigue—the CIA officers in Havana were toiling long hours under the tension of constant police surveillance.

Again I waited in line, this time among the passengers boarding the ferry for Key West. The queue was slow, and again I was scared. My case officer pretended to read a newspaper in the lobby of the ferry terminal; although there was nothing he could do, he would at least know if I were arrested. Helen sat on a bench, shepherding the four children who were restive in the intense tropical heat. I nodded at Helen, trying to be reassuring. She smiled gamely.

This time it would have been easier to kiss the customs official when the permission to depart Cuba was stamped in our passports: she was a pretty Cuban woman. She smiled pleasantly as she wished us *adiós*.

The ferry chugged out of Havana harbor through a splendid sunset. The golden light adumbrated the Morro Castle and its lighthouse, and burnished the windows of the modern skyscrapers in the city. For the first time in a long while it seemed easy to breathe.

From the motel in Key West I telephoned the Washington number given me in Havana. I was connected with my friend Len.

"Welcome," Len said. I assured him it was good to be back.

Len asked me to stop by Washington; they wanted to talk with me. I said I would be glad to say hello, but that would be followed by good-bye. I would *not* work again for CIA. Not a chance. I was going to New York to begin a new career.

"Not a chance," I repeated with emphasis. "Len, you can take your cloak and dispose of it you know where." After I hung up I added, for my own satisfaction, "And your dagger, too."

4

WASHINGTON–THE BAY
OF PIGS 1960–1961

There was an interim of quiet in the back of the car as the four children dozed, stretched out on the seat and the beds improvised from the half dozen pieces of luggage which we had carried out of Cuba. Maria was nine, David, Jr., eight, Atlee seven, and Christopher four. After a morning of rest in a Key West motel, we were driving up the Florida Keys on the way to Miami, New York, and a new life. I was thirty-seven. High time for me to have a new job and a permanent career.

"Now," Helen said, "tell me about the telephone call."

From Key West I had called the Washington number passed to me in Havana. After the recognition conversation with a secretary, Len answered. "It won't be in our old office in K Building, but we can work together again," Len said. "Can't tell you about it on the phone. Stop by Washington and chat with us. We have a new thing going, and we need your help."

"Not a chance," I told Len. "I'm broke and have a job lined up in New York. Don't count on me this time."

"This is important," Len said. "At least come by and see us."

"So," I assured Helen, "I'll just chat with them, and explain that I'm not available."

Helen made a skeptical noise.

"I'm not kidding," I said, and I meant it.

Leaving Helen and the children in a Washington hotel, I drove to Quarters Eye, a former WAVE barracks off Ohio Drive and adjacent to Barton Hall and the shabby CIA buildings on the reflecting pool, across from the Lincoln Memorial. There was a routine security check at the front door, where I waited for Len to be called. My former office mate came out to meet me with a temporary pass, then escorted me through a second security barrier at which a sign announced OFF LIMITS TO UNAUTHORIZED PERSONNEL. Len winced at each step as we went into interior offices; his artificial leg was bothering him.

In his office "Cliff" poured coffee. I had met Cliff several times. He was a veteran in Western Hemisphere operations, out of the University of Pennsylvania and O.S.S. operations in Burma. Cliff was a husky man with a resonant voice, trained in his youth when he aspired to be a singer. He came to the point: "We have a new project. Len is my deputy, and we're pulling together the team now. I'll give you three guesses."

"Cuba," I said. "Cuba and Cuba."

"That's why we need you. In fact we've asked for all officers who have served recently in Havana. The Cuba project will require people with area knowledge. There are only ten of us so far, but we will have a task force of about forty officers within the next few weeks. Eisenhower approved the operation last week, and we have someone in Miami now looking for a secure base area."

"What's the plan?" I asked.

"The Guatemala scenario," Len said. I noticed he still had the habit of scratching his underwrists, as he had five years earlier when we worked together in K Building. "The propaganda shop will be yours. You can pick your own staff officers from any now in Washington and draw up your own program."

"How long is all this to take?"

"November, maybe early December," Cliff said. It was then the third week of March 1960.

"The papers are ready for you to sign, to come aboard again as a staffer." Cliff acted as if there was no doubt I would again become a full-time CIA officer. Of course he was right. "We have our first organizational meeting this afternoon. Come on, we have time for lunch at Napoleon's."

Allen Dulles chaired the meeting in Quarters Eye that afternoon. The genial DCI—Director of Central Intelligence—had just begun his opening remarks when he was summoned to Cliff's office to answer a call from the President. We chatted in his absence. General Charles P. Cabell, the DDCI—Deputy Director, Central Intelligence—slouched in the chair to the right of Dulles's; I had never seen the Texan, a craggy man who looked like he might be the mayor of Dallas (a job held by his brother in November of 1963). Dick Bissell, who had become DDP succeeding Wisner, sat across from him, a head taller than anyone else in the room, leafing through a stack of cables, reading rapidly. Dick Helms, Chief of Operations of the Directorate of Plans, chatted with Tracy Barnes about a Georgetown party of the night before. I wondered why

Colonel King, Chief of the Western Hemisphere Division, was not there.

Below the salt sat the working-level officers. Cliff, as the Task Force Chief, would be responsible for day-to-day decisions which fell short of policy determinations. His deputy, Len, shifted uncomfortably in his chair and scratched his wrists. There were several others, some of whom I had never seen. Sitting against the wall behind Bissell was a slender man with an American Gothic face, freckles, and bifocals, not at all like the other men in the room.

"Who's the fellow behind Bissell?" I asked Len. He told me his name was "Abe," Bissell's staff aide.

"Who's the political action officer?" I asked.

"There will be two," Len said. "One is out of Europe Division..." He identified the man I—and a great many more people—would know as "Mr. Bender." "He'll be joining us next week. And so will his sidekick, Howard Hunt."

Allen Dulles returned and resumed the meeting. The Director was ebullient as he recounted an anecdote he had related to the President. Dulles was a great storyteller, and he seldom missed an opportunity to enliven a meeting, no matter how small, with an historical excerpt from his long association with United States intelligence. His favorite recollection was of the time in Switzerland after World War I when he opted to play tennis instead of returning to his office to see a man who wanted to talk to him. Dulles told this story many times to students in CIA training courses as an example of an opportunity lost—the man who wanted to see him, but never returned, was a Russian named Vladimir Ilich Lenin.

Dulles provided the overview. Eisenhower had approved on March 17 the proposal that CIA unseat Fidel Castro and replace him with a regime that was neither extreme left nor right. The plan was to be devised within coming weeks. Guerrillas and aviators were to be recruited from the increasingly large community of Cuban exiles in Miami and elsewhere. The President of Guatemala had agreed to provide a training area, and Nicaragua an airfield and port facilities. Once the recruits were trained, a government-in-exile formed, and the populace of Cuba influenced by a sustained propaganda effort, Eisenhower would authorize a landing of guerrilla forces.

Dick Bissell elaborated and refined, being understandably pedantic in his presentation. The former economics professor was to be the architect of the Cuba project, a role he also played in the U-2 operation and Guatemala. Cabell asked a number of questions which made it clear he knew little of the Cuban situation, and Barnes spoke frequently. Dick Helms listened carefully, often inspecting his carefully manicured fingernails, but said nothing. It was the first time I had seen the usually articulate Chief of Operations so reserved.

That evening I went back to the hotel to tell Helen that we would not be going to New York. That was unnecessary; she told me she had looked at three houses and one, off Massachusetts Avenue near the Wood Acres school, seemed to be fine.

"Hello, Chico." I looked up from my desk and found Howard Hunt his hand outstretched and a pleasant smile on his face. "Good to be working with you again."*

"Welcome aboard." I was genuinely glad to see Hunt again. He had just flown in from Uruguay, his first COS tour (and, it turned out, his final command assignment).

"Tracy wants me to visit Havana," Howard said. "I'll soak up atmosphere at the Floridita bar, and think of you when I have a few *mulatas*. Do you have time for a briefing?"

I filled Howard in on the Cuban political picture and gave him a number of names and addresses which might be useful in Cuba. As he left my office he grinned and pulled at the brim of his stylish hat, as a golf professional will touch the bill of his cap in acknowledging the applause of the gallery. Howard was happy to be back.

A few days later I visited Bissell and his aide in K Building to outline my plans for the propaganda operation. I intended to organize exile groups of women, workers, professionals, and students to act as propaganda fronts. I would support a number of exile publications Radio broadcasts and, eventually, leaflet drops would be the vital operations. I would need my own airplane for the leaflet drops just before and on the day of the invasion, and a large medium-wave radio station in the Florida Keys under commercial cover—with the overwater path only ninety miles from Key West, a radio signal could fry an egg in Havana.

"A station in Florida or anywhere on the United States mainland

---

* Howard Hunt describes this encounter and our subsequent association during the Bay of Pigs operation in his book *Give Us This Day*. "I called on Knight, the Propaganda Chief, an officer who had worked for me brilliantly on the Guatemala Project. We greeted each other warmly and remarked that the old crowd was rallying to the new cause. Knight was a tall, almost theatrically handsome man who had spent most of his CIA career on the outside, i.e. under cover. He spoke fluent Spanish and at one time had owned and edited a Spanish newspaper. For the three preceding years he had served under cover in Havana, and was well versed in current Cuban politics and personalities. Knight was imaginative, enthusiastic, and a tireless worker." In this effusive passage Howard was protecting my identity. He knew, for instance, that my paper had been an English-language one. Bestowing the name of Knight was the ultimate accolade—people who have worked in CIA will recall that pseudonym belonged to one of the Agency's most senior officers, a man Howard idolized.

is out," Bissell said. "State Department would never agree. You'll have to find another location and we will give you everything you need."

I told Bissell that in view of that restriction I would need a powerful transmitter, perhaps fifty kilowatts, to broadcast on medium-wave. Cuban listeners, unlike Guatemalans, were not accustomed to short-wave. Further, we would be competing with Fidel Castro, a master performer who appeared frequently on Cuban television.

"Do the necessary," Bissell said. "Abe will work with you. How long will it take to create the proper psychological climate?"

"In Guatemala it was only six weeks," I said, "but in Cuba it will be nearer six months."

"Can you start broadcasting in a month?" Bissell asked.

"Absolutely impossible. A short-wave transmitter can be loaded into a truck. Medium-wave of the power we need will fill three box cars."

"I'm sure you and Abe can do it," Bissell said, smiling tautly.

Abe and I lunched in the K Building cafeteria, which was, with its warped floor and deteriorating clapboard walls, more like a prison camp than a government lunchroom. It was good to have Bissell's personal assistant working with me but I was dubious about Abe's qualifications. The twinkle in his eyes seemed too innocent for the tough job ahead; Abe certainly did not fit the picture of CIA officers I had imagined at the time to be typical. During lunch I learned that Abe was a fellow Texan. He was addicted to picturesque speech, and his humor was wry. Soon I realized that his droll stories were never told unless he had a point to make and that he was gifted with insight, intuition, and consistent good judgment.*

"Helms seemed to be very quiet at the meeting," I said to Abe, "That disturbs me. Has he decided this operation is not going to work?"

"Don't think so," Abe said. "As Chief of Operations under Wisner, Helms ran operations his own way. Bissell doesn't really use a deputy. When he became DDP he asked that all incoming cables be sent to him early in the morning; previously Helms had selected only a few for Wis-

---

* Cliff later told me of his background. As an infantry captain in World War II he landed on Utah Beach and fought with his company across Europe. At a headquarters in the Sudetenland section of Czechoslovakia, Abe's office was swept by a young German girl. After American occupation troops had been withdrawn, he visited the area and heard she and other single German girls were about to be shipped away as factory workers. He offered to smuggle her into West Germany dressed as a G.I. They passed muster with the Czech border guards, but the American sergeant logging them through the checkpoint a half mile downroad allowed that was "a mighty fine-looking G.I. you have there, Captain." They were married in the wake of much red tape. Abe then joined the CIA as a logistics officer after studying at the Foreign Service School at Georgetown and a stint as aide to a Texas Congressman.

ner to see. So I think Helms is just becoming accustomed to having less clout than he used to, and has decided he'll be happier running the rest of the world while Bissell manages Cuba and the U-2."

"If Bissell doesn't delegate," I asked, "what about Tracy Barnes? Isn't he Bissell's deputy?"

"Sort of, for some things," Abe said.

The "sort of" made me think of Howard. "What about Howard Hunt? What do you think of him?"

"Howard," Abe said, spearing a piece of tomato from his salad, "is a fine guy. Unfortunately he lacks certain essential elements of greatness."

"Judgment?" I asked, recalling Howard's decision that it would be all right to entertain Guatemalans in a Miami nightclub before the Guatemalan operation.

"Oh, he's absolutely consistent in the judgment department," Abe said, his eyes twinkling as he peered at me over his bifocals.

Abe and I began the business of locating, shipping, and erecting a fifty-kilowatt radio station, a task roughly the same as establishing an enterprise as large as most commercial stations today. Problems did pop up as we tried to meet the thirty-day deadline set by Bissell. A number of potential sites had to be abandoned because of political considerations, and we finally settled on Swan Island, a dot on the map of the Caribbean between Cuba and Central America. A small complication was evident when we learned, after the fact, that in addition to the New England businessman who said he owned the tiny island another party claimed ownership—the country of Honduras. (And, in 1971 the United States did acknowledge Honduran sovereignty and gave the island to the banana republic.)

In all the Western world we could locate only one available fifty-kilowatt transmitter; the property of the U.S. Army, it was on a train in Germany about to be turned over to Voice of America. A few telephone calls and it was CIA's. Abe and I visited the Pentagon and asked for help from an admiral who didn't even blink when we said we needed the equipment shipped to a small island in the Caribbean and in operation within a month. The admiral did blink, however, when I found out after a flying visit to Swan that the island had no port or even a beach where the heavy transmitter could be off-loaded. The admiral sent a detachment of Seabees to construct a pier before the arrival of the radio gear. Radio Swan was not to be a clandestine station, but one which would operate under commercial guise with a production unit in Miami that was already recruiting technicians, writers, and announcers on a crash basis. The enterprise required corporate cover, and the only corporation available in CIA's secret portfolio was known as the Gulf Steamship Company. I winced when signing the paper which would catapult that firm into the broadcasting business. The first program from Radio Swan was broadcast exactly thirty days after Bissell's ukase.

Howard Hunt returned from his excursion to Havana, where he had pretended to be one of the hundreds of tourists who visited Cuba during 1960, bringing news from a number of people he had talked to on my recommendation.* He also brought back four recommendations, which he did not mention to me until after the Cuban operation had failed—the first being that Fidel Castro should be assassinated prior to an invasion. In writing of this later in another book, he claimed that Bissell and Barnes answered his repeated queries about the proposal by saying it was being handled by a "special group." It was only when Howard wrote of this years later that I knew of it.

I did learn, about that time, from one of the officers in Quarters Eye, of the bizarre scheme to use a depilatory chemical to make Fidel Castro's body hair and beard disappear. Fidel Castro was visiting the United States, not as an official guest, but invited to be on a television talk show in New York. He and his entourage camped out in a nest of feathers where they were slaughtering and cooking their own chickens in the Theresa Hotel in Harlem. The plan was to pass him a box of cigars impregnated with the chemical. Someone told me of the proposal, asking if it were not true that Castro's macho image would suffer if he became hairless. I agreed that it would and asked how the cigars could be given to the Cuban revolutionary with the assurance that he and not others—perhaps David Susskind—would not actually smoke the stogie. That was the last I heard of the scheme.

After his television appearance, Castro traveled to Washington where he met Vice President Nixon, the interpreter being a multilingual colonel named Vernon Walters, later to become Deputy Director of CIA in the Watergate era. It is my guess that Nixon did not warm to the Cuban visitor, and that Castro probably felt the same way about Nixon.**

A CIA officer who used the alias Frank Bender joined the task force at Quarters Eye. He and Howard Hunt began "putting in the

* In his book Howard described an evening in Havana: "That night I dined with a girl whose name had been given me by Knight. Attractive and in her twenties, Violeta was the mother of a small child whose father had been killed in the mountains with Castro. In Batista days she had been a television dancer and entertainer...." I do not recall Violeta. Howard always appreciated pretty women, and I suspect he picked up this contact on his own.

** Subsequently Howard Hunt was to write that he lunched during that period with Robert Cushman, the Marine Corps general who ultimately became DDCI, and that Cushman said Nixon was the "action officer" for the Cuba project at the White House. This may have been true before the election of President Kennedy but I was never aware of it.

plumbing," as the phrase goes in CIA jargon, for the political action program of the Cuba project.* Their task was to oversee the formation of an exile coalition free of Batista taint, the group of anti-Castro politicians who would fly into Cuba as a "government-in-arms" after the guerrillas consolidated a landing position. The exiles bickered among themselves from the beginning, and Bender and Hunt were constantly flying between Washington, New York, Miami, and Mexico City to act as referees in the squabbles and to cajole the exiles into some form of cooperative endeavor. Relations between Hunt and Bender were about the same as between the rival Cubans: fragile and strained. Hunt and Bender could not have been more different. Bender was, like Peter (the experienced professional who had taught me to remove laundry marks from clothing before foreign travel), a German who had fought against Hitler, achieving renown for his O.S.S. work behind the lines in France as an organizer of resistance groups. He was a political liberal whose ideas clashed with Hunt's adamant conservative views. Bender was slight, balding, and careless in dress. He chain-smoked cigars and Camels, often finishing an entire cigarette without removing it from his lips while the ash lengthened, drooped, and finally fell on his jacket. Sometimes he would brush away the ashes. Bender was loquacious, his conversation alternating between long anecdotes and abbreviated speech. Hunt, with his writer's vocabulary and Brown University–polished conversation, would cringe when Bender answered his questions with "Yo," his term for "Yes and No." When Bender referred to Howard as "Popsy," which he frequently did, Hunt could scarcely conceal a shudder.

During a trip to Mexico City in the early summer of 1960 Howard either lost, or was involved in the loss of, a briefcase containing classified documents. Hunt's version—the accurate one, I believe—was that an agent working for him had been responsible, but Bender and others hinted that Hunt himself had pulled the worst of tradecraft blunders. Then it was Bender's turn. For a meeting with one of his Cuban politicians in Miami, Bender rented a motel room with too-thin walls. The occupant of the adjoining room was a stenographer whose brother worked for the FBI. She was bothered by the acrid smoke from Bender's cheap cigar, which drifted under the door between the two rooms. Suspicious of Bender's German accent, she listened and took shorthand notes of the secret encounter, later turning them in to her brother. The Washington FBI recognized the nature of the conversation and passed the notes to the CIA, to the chagrin of Bender. Howard Hunt chortled with glee as

* The White House "plumbers" were so called because they attempted to plug leaks to the press. In CIA parlance "the plumbing" refers to the operational support capabilities which must be installed prior to any significant operation.

he repeated the story of Bender's embarrassment up and down the halls of Quarters Eye.

Others were working on paramilitary planning. The principal task was to supervise the recruiting and training of a thousand irregulars. Occasionally I would skim through the files of the exiles who were being sent to the training camp in Guatemala. Many of the names were familiar, young men from the activist Catholic student group which had been among the first to oppose Castro. Some of them had been recruited for the invasion force on my recommendation. The FI (foreign intelligence) officers set up shop as did the CI (counter-intelligence) fellows. The number of people working on the Cuba project swelled as support and communications teams went to work—from Quarters Eye Cliff could send and receive cables to and from stations anywhere in the world without checking with Colonel King, head of the Western Hemisphere Division in nearby Barton Hall.

There were familiar faces among the officers working on the task force, but most were new to me. There was a colonel with whom I worked on several matters who appeared a bit strange. He walked with a limp and had a glass eye which he once removed unexpectedly while we were talking.

"Is the colonel all right?" I asked Abe.

"Yup," Abe said, seriously. "He was on Utah Beach. That's where he got shot up. He also got the Medal of Honor."*

I agreed with Abe that the colonel had some credit in the bank.

The tenseness generated by the complicated planning for the Cuba operation was lightened by relaxed moments at home with the family, and by occasional reunions with friends we had first met abroad.

The Phillips family moved into a bare house off Massachusetts Avenue thanks to the generosity of the manager of the Alban Towers Hotel, who loaned us kitchenware, plates and saucers, and bedding. We rented beds and used old crates for tables and chairs until our furniture would arrive from Havana. We knew that might be a long time since while our household effects had been waiting on the docks for shipment, the Cuban government had decreed that electrical equipment belonging to foreigners would no longer be allowed to leave the country. A letter from Havana customs advised us that our refrigerator, television, stereo, and all lamps and small appliances had been removed from the lift van and were in storage in Havana "until your return to Cuba." (Each month for the next year I received a bill from the customs office

---

* John Wayne later played the role of the battered colonel in the film *The Longest Day*.

until a final invoice said the equipment had been confiscated by the Cuban government because storage charges had surpassed its value.)

May is a beautiful month in Washington, and the former tenant of the house had predicted that our spring would be exceptional because of the dozens of tulips he had planted before his unexpected transfer. He was a Dutch diplomat, and he had buried bulbs everywhere in the front yard. They bloomed in a blaze of color.

Christopher, age four, took his plastic baseball bat into the front yard one Sunday morning while Helen and I still slept and, with a really admirable 1.000 batting average, methodically knocked the blooms off each of the tulip plants. Helen and I were dismayed; the spartan living conditions of our house had been alleviated by the cascade of color in front. Helen gathered all the blooms and floated them in a large wash pan in the living room.

Dick and Nancy Cushing, our friends from Chile and Cuba, telephoned. We told them of our floral loss and invited them to lunch. Shortly thereafter the telephone rang again. The voice was guttural and European-accented: "Mr. Phillips, this is the secretary of the Dutch Ambassador. I wanted to tell you that the Ambassador is on his way to your home. I'm sure you won't mind if he gets out of the car just long enough to take a photograph of the tulips."

"Oh, no!" I protested. "He can't!"

"Why, Mr. Phillips?"

"Well, he just can't," I stuttered. "I mean he really can't."

"Mr. Phillips, you must know that the tulips in your yard were shipped from The Hague at the expense of the Dutch government. Certainly you will allow the Ambassador to take a picture of them. In any event, I'm afraid he's already on the way."

Dick and Nancy arrived as I put down the telephone, a gift bottle in hand. Helen and I explained what had happened, and that they should be prepared for the appearance of an unhappy Ambassador. Dick and Nancy clucked sympathetically. I looked down at the wash pan with its floating tulip blooms.

Eureka! "Scotch tape!" I shouted. "The blooms are still all right. We can tape them back on the stems!"

Helen was skeptical. "You're crazy!"

"Not at all," I said. "At least the Ambassador can take his goddamned picture."

So the Cushings watched as Helen and I ran about the front yard, hastily taping blossoms to stems. Then we changed clothes rapidly, I from my old sports shirt and golf shorts, Helen to a Sunday frock. We waited nervously for half an hour, often looking out front to see if the Ambassador had arrived and if the blooms were still taped in place. Finally I said, "Wonder what's happened to the Ambassador?"

The Cushings couldn't hold it any longer and began howling with laughter, admitting all. After our telephone conversation, they had persuaded a German friend to impersonate the Ambassador's Dutch secretary.

That's the nearest the United States Information Service ever came to having one of their senior officials done in by a CIA assassin.

Washington's lovely spring turned to Washington's humid and uncomfortable summer and then to its resplendent fall. In Quarters Eye the members of the Cuba project continued to lay in the plumbing, by now a maze of secret and not-so-secret pipes. Howard Hunt shuttled between Miami and Washington to negotiate with exile politicians. Bender conspired with others. Recruitment prospered and training continued at the military camp in Guatemala, but the Cubans there were no longer referred to as guerrillas or irregulars, but as members of the Brigade.

A chief of operations for the task force joined Cliff and Len in the front office. He was a slight, wiry man with a feisty manner and an inexhaustible supply of epigrams. "Bill" had the habit, disconcerting to his CIA superiors, of describing as "horseshit" any plan or proposal which he considered dubious. A lawyer out of Yale, Bill had been a tank commander under Patton. In mid-September a Pentagon guerrilla warfare expert joined us to take charge of the military phase of the operations. "Colonel Alcott" was an intense, dour officer who sought perfection in planning. He had a reputation as a brilliant guerrilla strategist in the Philippines during World War II, and we were impressed—somehow we didn't pause to question why a guerrilla expert was coming aboard to help us with the Brigade.

Trinidad, a small town on Cuba's south coast, was selected as the invasion site for Brigade 2506. (Each soldier training in Guatemala was assigned a number, beginning with 2000. The Cubans honored soldier 2506, who fell to his death in a mountain training accident, by using his number in the name of the Brigade.) Trinidad had been chosen because of its proximity to mountains where anti-Castro guerrillas were already encamped. In the event that landing forces could not hold on to a military position in the town they could easily fade into the mountains and be supplied indefinitely by airdrop. The Trinidad Plan was approved by the Pentagon and the White House.

An increasing amount of intelligence was flowing from Cuba as new agents were recruited in Miami and infiltrated back into Cuba. There the neophyte spies contacted friends and relatives to work with them. Usually their reports were useful, but often these enthusiastic agents would report the wildest of rumors. In Quarters Eye there were regular morning meetings where Cliff and his officers would review the messages which had arrived during the night. The purpose was to decide which reports were valid and to sift from them the doubtful ones which might originate with agents captured by Castro or simply from new spies anxious to please.

One morning there was a particularly dubious report from a new source. The agent reported that a network of powerful new guns had been established throughout Cuba. The cannon were remarkable, the agent said, because they could fire throughout 360 degrees, that is, in any direction.

"Doesn't sound right," Cliff said. "We would have known of them from photography. Where are these guns supposed to be located?"

Bill laughed. "The agent explains that. He says the guns are hidden in caves."

"Cannon that shoot in any direction from a cave?" Cliff flicked the ash from his cigar. "Sounds to me as if that agent doesn't know his azimuth from a hole in the ground."

Intelligence reports from Cuba—when the information was accurate—were valuable to me in planning the propaganda program. A bright young bilingual officer was now working for me in Miami, supervising the activities of the various front groups. A team of civilian contract technicians and a single CIA security officer manned Swan Island. News analysis and entertainment programs were taped in the Miami office of the Gulf Steamship Company. Selected anti-Castro exile groups prepared their own programs for which they purchased time with CIA funds passed to them by Bender and Hunt. Exile leaders not so supported soon learned the trick of traveling to Washington to meet with congressional and White House officials: more than once the word came down to me from on high suggesting that such and such a group be accommodated.

Radio Swan was reaching the intended audience in Cuba and bothering the Cuban government. We knew this from interviews with refugees and because Castro began to jam the broadcasts. I decided, however, that a single station was not sufficient for the task of convincing Cubans they should join the exile winners after a landing. We soon created a second capability independent of Radio Swan and the exile political groups by having CIA agents buy space on existing radio stations around the perimeter of the Caribbean. These broadcasts were low-key and not recognizable as anti-Castro. Only after D-Day would they become activist voices, to influence Cubans when they faced the decision of who would win and who would lose.*

Abe and I briefed Bissell on the propaganda effort, and provided the details of the new radio outlets on a dozen stations in several countries. The DDP got out of his chair and paced back and forth, as he always did when concerned. "Almost too good," he said. "Too American, too professional. Go back and put some rough edges on it, make it more Cuban."

I agreed. Then I reminded Bissell of the need to use leaflet drops to create a climate of anxiety in Cuba, describing the stir and confusion in Havana when Castro's first air force chief, a week after defecting to Miami, dropped hundreds of leaflets on the capital. Bissell said he would authorize a few isolated drops in the interior, since this could be explained in Washington as necessary to cover actual supply drops to agents. But leaflet drops on Havana and major cities would have to wait, he said, as Foggy Bottom would consider them too provocative. Again I asked that for D-Day and the first days after a plane to be controlled by me be reserved for leaflet drops.

A meeting to review the Trinidad Plan was held in the office of the Deputy Director, General Charles P. Cabell. A sense of urgency prevailed as CIA had just received intelligence reports that the Soviet Union would be sending MIG fighters to Cuba and that they would be operational early in the summer of 1961, by which time Cuban pilots would return from training in the Bloc. The final agenda item was to obtain Cabell's permission for a supply drop to a CIA infiltration team; Dulles had delegated this authority to his air force general.

Cliff described the difficulties encountered in the use of former airline pilots to make drops within Cuba; the flyers had no experience in combat situations. Through a relay station near Cuba, CIA headquarters was in communication with the infiltrators, who complained consistently that supplies were landing far from the drop zones.

Cliff's air officer had explained the new mission and was rolling up his charts to leave when Cabell stopped him.

"Just a minute," The general pulled at his pursed lips. "How much of your cargo space is needed for the arms you are dropping?"

"About a tenth of the space," the officer replied.

---

* There is a durable myth that a CIA estimate anticipated a general uprising of the Cuban population against Castro and convinced Kennedy this would occur. This was not true. Certainly all of us hoped such a bonus would occur, but the propaganda plan was to influence Cubans after the fact of a successful military landing. I never saw or heard of such an estimate. As Chief of Propaganda it is inconceivable to me that such a sanguine forecast would not have reached my desk.

"In that case," said the general, "fill the plane with sacks of rice and beans and drop them to the team."

Bill, the Operations Chief, was startled. "General, we're dropping specific items requested by the team by radio. Only a few men will be at the DZ. They can't carry many sacks."

"Let's be forward leaning," Cabell said. "Let 'em know we're behind them all the way."

I could see that Cliff's neck was turning red. "General," I interjected, "I've spent four of the past six years in Cuba. Rice and beans is the national dish in Cuba. I can assure you there's no shortage."

Cabell turned to me. "Son, I don't want to have to explain to an appropriations committee why we're flying nearly empty planes over Cuba." He turned to Cliff. "Drop the rice and beans."

The former Cuban airline pilots were becoming more proficient in low-level airdrop missions because that night their cargo, including the sacks of rice and beans, fell directly in the drop zone. The team leader sent a radio message, in English rather than the customary Spanish: YOU SON OF BITCH. WE NEARLY KILLED BY RICE BAGS. YOU CRAZY?

I wondered whether the incoming agent message would reach Cabell. Just to be sure, I enclosed a copy in an envelope marked *Eyes Only For DDCI* and forwarded it anonymously to the office of the Deputy Director. Later I found that my ploy was unnecessary—Allen Dulles did the same thing. There were no more requests for deliveries of food in future drops, and Cabell became known to some in CIA as "Old Rice and Beans."

On a Sunday morning I had just returned to the house when the task force duty officer telephoned. A cable had come in from the CIA security officer on Swan Island. He had heard a radio broadcast from Tegucigalpa announcing that a boatload of Honduran students was sailing to Swan Island to occupy it and to proclaim Honduran sovereignty. The CIA officer and the civilian technicians had only a few hand guns to defend the island. What should he do when the invaders arrived? I told the duty officer I would return to the office at once; meanwhile he should contact the Pentagon to find out if any United States naval craft was in the area of Swan Island. By the time I reached Quarters Eye the navy had confirmed the presence of a destroyer not too far from the island. I asked that it be diverted and ordered to steam for Swan Island and be prepared for the launching of a landing party.

I flashed a message to the CIA man on Swan Island, instructing him to welcome the students graciously, to do everything possible to soothe nationalistic fervor, and to brandish his gun only if the students threatened to damage the radio equipment or attempted to enter the radio communication shack, where CIA cipher pads were kept. I advised him that the Marines were on the way, but could not reach the island before the Honduran students. A series of flash messages rocketed to and from the island as the CIA man requested detailed instructions. I cabled: YOU ARE IN COMMAND. GIVE THEM PLENTY OF BEER AND PROTECT THE FAMILY JEWELS.

During the next several hours a series of cables came in from Swan, as the security officer on the island found time to jot them down and slip them to the communicator. None needed a reply.

SWAN TO HQS. HONDURAN SHIP ON HORIZON. BEER ON ICE.

SWAN TO HQS. TALKED TO STUDENTS. THEY CONFABING. HAVE ACCEPTED BEER.

SWAN TO HQS. STUDENTS MIXING CEMENT IN WHICH THEY INTEND WRITE "THIS ISLAND BELONGS TO HONDURAS." ONE GROUP MALINGERING, LISTENING TO EARTHA KITT RECORDS AND DRINKING FIFTH BEER.

The telephone rang in Quarters Eye. The Pentagon duty officer told me the destroyer was approaching Swan Island. I asked him to instruct the captain to heave to and wait just under the horizon with his Marines at the ready.

SWAN TO HQS. STUDENTS HAVE JUST RAISED HONDURAN FLAG. I SALUTED.

SWAN TO HQS. BEER SUPPLY RUNNING LOW. NOW BREAKING OUT THE RUM. THESE KIDS ARE GREAT.

SWAN TO HQS. STUDENTS HAVE EMBARKED FOR HONDURAS. LIQUOR SUPPLY EXHAUSTED. FAMILY JEWELS INTACT.

I telephoned the Pentagon and told the duty officer his destroyer could resume its normal course. Then: HQS. TO SWAN. WELL DONE. PLEASE TAKE TWO ASPIRIN BEFORE BED.

Fidel Castro delivered one of his famous four-hour television harangues, announcing that the diplomatic representation of the United States in Havana must be reduced to eleven officers. President Eisenhower's reaction was to pull out the entire mission and break relations with the Cuban regime. Only deep-cover CIA officers remained in Cuba to handle agents and provide intelligence. "Douglas," my former COS in Havana, joined the task force at Quarters Eye, to work with Bender and Hunt in political action operations.

The men of Brigade 2506 in Guatemala were becoming restive, some of them correctly believing they were being overtrained. Dulles advised Eisenhower. Bender and Hunt reported that exile political leaders were becoming unmanageable; they were especially upset that CIA would not tell them what date had been chosen for the invasion.

We were told by Bissell and Barnes, who often visited the White House, that President Eisenhower was concerned. He believed more time was needed to complete military planning, and that it would be unfair to President-elect Kennedy to saddle his new administration with the incubus of an unsuccessful Cuban operation. So, late in 1960, *Eisenhower decided to postpone the invasion until the new President would have the opportunity to review and approve it.**

The period between an American President's election and his inauguration vitiates United States government planning, perhaps more in covert action programs than in others. On the one hand Eisenhower had the moral responsibility of allowing his successor a vote on the Cuba plan. On the other the President's decision not to go through with the invasion during his tenure had the inevitable result of interregnum doldrums, when top planners and senior policy makers concerned with survival under a new administration consider indecision a virtue. Responsibility for Cuban affairs was delegated to less and less senior officers in the Department of State and the Pentagon. Frictions among the Cuban exile leaders festered and unrest grew at the camp where the Brigade was training in Guatemala.

In Cuba Fidel Castro took advantage of the reprieve. His security forces became more efficient. Guerrillas in the hills were captured, middle-class opponents in Havana were ferreted out and jailed.

The euphoria of a new era was in the cold air when John Kennedy was inaugurated on January 20. Heavy snow fell on the capital causing, as it always does, traffic jams and confusion. Bill lived near me, and we left Quarters Eye late in the afternoon of the inaugural ball. We were stranded for two hours behind stalled cars on MacArthur Boulevard. That noon I had purchased liquor during the lunch hour, and we sat in the car warmed by brandy. The radio announced the festive tribulations of foreign dignitaries and Hollywood film stars similarly beset with traffic problems as they tried to reach the ball. I had voted for Kennedy, and all seemed right with the world. It was Camelot Eve. How could anything go wrong?

Allen Dulles and Dick Bissell briefed President Kennedy on the Trinidad Plan. The new chief executive asked for a further review by Pentagon experts, in what was to become a series of feasibility studies. A Joint Chiefs mission went to the Guatemalan training camp and returned with a report that the Brigade was ready and the odds on a military success acceptable. The military endorsement satisfied Kennedy, and he initialed the plan of landing in Trinidad, after strikes against

---

* "Why did it fail?" is the question most frequently asked about the Bay of Pigs. Obviously my recollections are suspect and my opinions biased, but I will try to be objective in italicizing the key decisions and actions which, I believe, contributed to the fiasco.

Castro's air force. The President made it clear, however, that he reserved the right to call off the operation at any time.

D-Day was selected: March 1. Although Castro continued to bolster his security services, there was an upswing of resistance among the middle class in Havana where there were nightly protest bombings, and the capital's largest department store was burned by saboteurs. Although leaflet drops over Cuban cities were still proscribed, the tempo of radio propaganda broadcasts from Radio Swan was accelerated.

The base of the exile political front was broadened by the addition of left-of-center politicians. The new political mix disturbed Howard Hunt and led to increased friction between him and Bender, now supported by Douglas, who backed the participation of the new liberals. Bissell and Barnes resolved the conflict by calling a meeting in which they were unequivocal in saying they did not intend to be responsible for a right-wing government in a post-Castro Cuba. Howard Hunt was relieved of his political action responsibilities. Tracy Barnes sought a new job for him outside the Cuban task force, but CIA division chiefs said they had no openings. Finally I was told that henceforth Howard would work with me in the propaganda shop. I was able to use his writing talents, as the half dozen of us responsible for propaganda were working eighteen hours a day, often sleeping in Quarters Eye on army cots set up barracks-style in an office a few doors from mine. Howard was assigned to work with Lem Jones Associates, a New York public-relations firm—a firm responsive to CIA—which was now handling the public pronouncements of the exile coalition.

The invasion date slipped. Colonel Alcott and his military advisers decided that the Brigade would have to be increased by four hundred men; they were recruited and flown to Guatemala. April 17 was selected as the new invasion date.

The offices at Quarters Eye hummed with activity. Now the Cuban task force was indeed "forward leaning," to use the phrase admired by General Cabell and adopted by some in CIA for many years. President Kennedy approved the new D-Day, but reiterated his right to cancel the operation at any time.

"April is the cruellest month," wrote T. S. Eliot. April of 1961 in Washington was the worst month of my life.

At the very beginning of April I thought I was victim of an April Fool trick of the meanest kind. Cliff told me to talk with Colonel Alcott concerning a change in military plans about which I needed to know in developing propaganda gambits. I went to the War Room of the para-military officers, an inner sanctum within the inner sanctum of the Cuba task force in Quarters Eye. Several men studied maps and charts. I walked to the largest map. Someone had scrawled a large red cross over the site of the town of Trinidad.

"There's been a change in the plan," Colonel Alcott said. "Trinidad is out. Now we are going to land here." The colonel touched an area on the coast one hundred miles west of Trinidad. I squinted to read the fine type. Despite years in Cuba, I had never heard of the place.

"*Bahía de Cochinos?*" I laughed. This really must be April Fool. "How can we have a victorious landing force wading ashore at a place with that name? How can propagandists persuade Cubans to join the Brigade at the 'Bay of Pigs'?"

The colonel was not concerned with the exigencies of psychological warfare. "That's the new plan," he repeated.

"But it's too far from the mountains." Even with my limited ability in map reading I knew those little symbols resembling clumps of grass denoted swamps. "How will the Brigade take the beach, and hold it?"

"The first ships to land will carry tanks."

"Tanks!" I was stunned. "We're going to mount a secret operation in the Caribbean with tanks?"

"That's right," said the colonel. "A company. Three platoons of five each, and two command tanks."

Something had gone crazy. I left the War Room and burst into Cliff's office, where he was talking with Len and Bill. They confirmed the madness.* What had been conceived as a classic guerrilla warfare operation with individual fighters carrying their own weapons had been converted, only a few weeks before D-Day, into an amphibious landing of tanks on Cuban beaches. *Dean Rusk had persuaded President Kennedy that political risks made unacceptable the plan of landing near a town where women and children might be hurt and where there was no airstrip which could explain the flights of exile B-26 planes.* The Bay of Pigs was the alternate site chosen by the military planners and approved by Rusk and the President.

On April 4 the section chiefs of the task force waited anxiously in Cliff's office while a portentous meeting was held at the White House. Kennedy's approval of the April 17 invasion date was being sought because, to meet that timing, the ships which would transport the Brigade would have to embark soon on the voyage from Central America to Cuba. Dulles and Bissell briefed the President. When they were done Kennedy took a poll of his advisers. With various degrees of enthusiasm, a "yes" recommendation came from Rusk, McNamara, Dillon, Lemnitzer, Mann,

* Cliff did not tell me at the time, but I learned much later that he and Colonel Alcott wanted to resign when told of this switch in plans, but were dissuaded.

Berle, Arthur Schlesinger, Jr., and Richard Goodwin. Only Senator William Fulbright urged Kennedy to abandon the project. Kennedy approved —again warning that he might cancel the landing even after the exile troops were at sea.

One of the President's principal advisers was not present: Adlai Stevenson, the United States Ambassador at the United Nations in New York. *Stevenson should have been at the meeting, despite the vote he may have proffered, so he would have been aware of details of an operation liable to provoke a furor in the U.N.*

During the next few days there were several indications of the political caution and hesitation which now marked each decision of the policy makers, especially the recommendations of the Department of State to limit operations which might be "noisy" and cause adverse reaction abroad. The first was an instruction that despite one of the key elements of the military plan being a series of air strikes before and on D-Day to destroy Castro's air force, only two forays were now being approved. One just before D-Day, and one that morning. The restriction was discussed by the CIA officers in Quarters Eye. Never mind. Two air strikes should accomplish the objective, with the first strike followed by photography to guide the second, and the Brigade would be able to land under skies dominated by the exile B-26 bombers.

A second limitation affected my propaganda plans. While the radio broadcasts were the essential element of the campaign, a second and significant one was dropping leaflets on the days preceding the invasion. I had already dispatched an officer to Central America to supervise the effort. At the air base in Nicaragua, along with the bombs and rockets, were stored eleven million leaflets of different texts. Some appealed to soldiers and others to peasants, workers, women, and, especially, the middle class in Havana. I had envisaged several drops in the two weeks prior to the invasion, recalling the impact of the similar effort in Guatemala. Again I asked that a plane be allocated to the sole task of dropping leaflets.

On April 10 the cherry blossoms were beginning to bloom in Washington. On the same day the old freighters transporting Brigade 2506 steamed out of Central America.

Chester Bowles became one of the circle of advisers around Kennedy to know of the invasion plans. He joined Fulbright in recommending against it. By now, Adlai Stevenson in New York knew of the operation, but only in general terms. His concern was relayed to the President. In one aspect, then another, the Cuba project became alarmingly truncated.

I was told that leaflet drops would not be allowed until the morning of D-Day. I protested, pointing out that propaganda must work before as well as after the fact since the Cuban populace could not be expected to make an instant decision on who would be the winner. While this argument was to no avail, I did extract the promise that each B-26 to fly on D-Day would carry a load of leaflets, to be dropped after the strike and before their return to Nicaragua.

On the penultimate Sunday before D-Day Bissell called a meeting of Quarters Eye section chiefs in Cliff's office. We were assembled when a telephone call came from Bissell's secretary indicating the DDP would be delayed and that we should all stand by for a 3 P.M. meeting. "Come on," Cliff said, "let's get out of here and have some lunch." A dozen of us drove to Napoleon's. Over before-lunch martinis we discussed the shrinking options which were threatening the operation. Someone ordered a round of brandies after we had eaten. When the waiter had withdrawn Bill demanded the floor.

"You gentlemen are masquerading as experts in overthrowing a government," Bill said caustically. "Have any of you entertained the notion that this damned thing might not work?"

We were all uncomfortable. Bill, with his customary candor, had broached what many of us had contemplated but all of us left unsaid. Cliff clamped his cigar in his teeth. Len squirmed in his chair, adjusting his artificial leg. Colonel Alcott appeared to be offended. Abe removed his bifocals and cleaned them thoughtfully with his napkin.

"What can we do?" I asked Bill.

"Not go back," Bill said. "We cannot go back to Quarters Eye. We can stay right here and drink brandy, and when Bissell shows up in Cliff's office there will be no one to run the show. Without us, it won't go."

It was quiet for a long time. Finally Cliff finished his brandy. "Come on," he said, "let's go back."

"Why?" someone asked.

"You know why," the task force chief said. *"Because we're good soldiers, that's why."*

In Quarters Eye I stood in the hall outside Cliff's office with Abe while we waited for Bissell to arrive. We drank black coffee. "This is becoming tricky," I said. "The restrictions and techniques of what used to be a secret guerrilla operation are now being used for what has turned into a conventional military operation. Bill may be right. It might not work."

"The important thing," Abe said, "is that all of Castro's planes are destroyed. That way it can work."

We were all living at Quarters Eye. On occasion we would sleep for a few hours on the army cots in the makeshift dormitory down the hall. I once instructed my secretary, who had been working long hours with the rest of us, to take a nap. She returned after a while, saying there was a long, tall man sleeping next to her, a man she did not recognize. I checked.

The tall man asleep on the cot was Dick Bissell, whom the secretary had never seen.

On April 12 President Kennedy, in a speech to the American Association of Newspaper Editors, volunteered that the United States would not under any circumstances intervene militarily in Cuba. This probably bothered me more than anyone else in the United States government—the assertion was repeated widely in Cuban media to the people I was trying to convince that the exiles would, one way or another, assume power.

Four days before the invasion. The first air strike was scheduled for April 15, D-Day minus two. Abruptly, I became involved in the air action. As another of the last-minute efforts to mask United States involvement, and to make the external aspects of the exile attack appear to be "internal," it was decided the first air strike must seem to originate in Cuba. Three Cuban airfields were to be bombarded, but in a manner which would make it appear that defecting Castro pilots had done it, rather than exile planes from Central America. It was my assignment during the next twenty-four hours to stage-manage the incredible charade.

"How in the hell can we make that story stick?" I asked Cliff.

"That's your department," Cliff said. He was busy with other problems.

I worked desperately to work out the scenario to be followed by the "defecting" pilots and crews; one plane was to land in Key West, another in Miami. They would claim to airport authorities—and to American newsmen—that they had attacked Castro's aircraft after a decision to defect with their planes. It occurred to me that this would be a difficult story to sell in Florida—and an impossible one in Cuba, where Castro could quickly ascertain the truth. I sent a series of cables to the airbase in Nicaragua so that the crews selected for the deception would be prepared: what they should wear, what they should say, and that at least minor damage should be done to the aircraft before takeoff to create the illusion they had been in combat.

The actual strikes were carried out by exile planes which returned to their base in Central America. It was successful. I had attended enough post-mission briefings in Italy during the war to know that the destruction of more than half of Castro's airfleet of B-26's, Sea Furies, and T-33 jet trainers at three airfields was as effective as could be expected. In fact it was highly encouraging: the air strike scheduled for D-Day, two days later, would have an excellent chance of knocking out the remainder of the Cuban air force, unless Castro was clever enough to disperse his planes quickly to other bases.

The two exile B-26 planes carrying flying actors landed in Key West and Miami, their wild claims made more credible as a bona fide defector had landed just previously in Tampa with his Cuban plane. There was a bad moment when a Miami newsman noted that one of the planes had machine guns with tape—to keep the barrels clean from Nicaraguan dust—still over the muzzles. But the first wire stories out of Florida generally accepted the deception in reporting that Castro pilots had blasted their own air force as a final blow for freedom before defecting.

The Cubans, of course, knew otherwise. I watched on television as Raul Roa, the Cuban Foreign Minister, denounced the fraud at the United Nations in New York. Adlai Stevenson took the podium to refute the Cuban. The former presidential candidate was eloquent and emotional in countering Roa. He held before the television cameras front-page photographs of the exile plane in Miami, proof that the defection was authentic. Adlai Stevenson, I said to myself, is quite an actor—he can lie along with the best.

As I watched Stevenson defend the deceitful scheme a chill moved through my body. What had we done? *Adlai Stevenson had been taken in by the hoax!* Had no one bothered to tell our Ambassador at the United Nations of the deception involved in the air strike? I asked Abe. Was it possible that Stevenson had not been briefed?

"It's possible, I guess." Abe grimaced. "Tracy Barnes and Arthur Schlesinger went to New York last week to fill him in. But you know Tracy. He can be charming and urbane and talk around a subject until you don't know what he means to say. *Maybe he and Schlesinger gave Stevenson the flavor but not the facts.*"*

President Kennedy asked CIA when it would be too late to turn on a red light to cancel the invasion. He was told noon on Sunday, April 16, when the ships carrying the exile troops would be nearing the Cuban coast for the April 17 dawn landing. On that Sunday Allen Dulles was in Puerto Rico. It had been decided that too clear a signal of the impending invasion would be given to Castro if the DCI canceled a long-standing speech engagement there. President Kennedy was at Glen Ora, his new rural retreat in Virginia. About noon the President gave the green light: the invasion was approved.

The officers in the War Room at Quarters Eye were jubilant that the long months of planning were over and the decisive hour was near. And there was a sudden belief that it would work: U-2 photographs revealed that instead of dispersing his now shattered air force, Castro had assembled

* Schlesinger, in his account of the Bay of Pigs in *A Thousand Days*, tells it this way: "In preparation for the [United Nations] debate, Tracy Barnes and I had held a long talk with Stevenson on April 8. But our briefing, which probably was unduly vague, left Stevenson with the impression that no action would take place during the UN discussion on the Cuban item."

all his military aircraft at one airfield near Havana. They were lined up in a neat row. (Not far away on the same base Castro had brought together most of his tanks.) It should be an easy target for the exile B-26's the next morning, and the Brigade could expect skies free of opposition. It appeared a pledge could be honored: the exiles had been told, "The sky will be yours."

The ships of Brigade 2506 slipped through the green and blue shallows south of Cuba. Bombs and rockets were loaded on the exile B-26's in Nicaragua. The propaganda officer there cabled that each plane had stacks of leaflets to be dropped after the combat runs. The Brigade pilots prepared for a midnight takeoff.

I do not know exactly what happened during those hours of Sunday afternoon and early evening at the White House, the Department of State, the United Nations, and at Glen Ora. One story is that Adlai Stevenson, understandably indignant after his embarrassment at the United Nations, insisted that President Kennedy reverse his decision. Another is that Dean Rusk told the President that air strikes which could not be described as taking off from a Cuban airfield were not acceptable. Whatever the case, Bissell was staggered by a telephone call from McGeorge Bundy at the White House, coming only a few hours after Kennedy had given the green light to the invasion. *The President had decided to cancel the D-Day air strike!* Dean Rusk, at the Department of State, was in charge during Kennedy's absence in Virginia.

Bissell advised General Cabell, and he and the Acting Director of CIA hurried to the State Department to convince Rusk that an air attack against Castro's remaining planes was essential. Dean Rusk did not agree, but said he would talk to the President again. The Secretary of State telephoned Kennedy at Glen Ora. Rusk explained that the CIA men were in his office asking that the presidential order be reversed and presented their reasons. He added that he remained unconvinced. Then Rusk turned to Cabell, while the President waited, and asked him if he wanted to speak with Kennedy. Cabell hesitated. The Acting Chief of the CIA, a four-star air force general, was perhaps the man in the United States most qualified to assert to his commander-in-chief that air power was essential to victory at the Bay of Pigs. *Cabell said no, he would not speak with the President.*

When Bissell and Cabell returned to Quarters Eye and walked into Cliff's office Cabell's first statement was, "There's been a little change in our marching orders." Cliff and his officers were speechless. Barnes drafted the flash cable to the airbase in Nicaragua: the air strike was off. The paratroopers who would drop behind the beach had already departed when the message arrived. The B-26's were on the tarmac, warming up for takeoff. The Brigade landing parties and the paratroopers would be on the beach alone. And, of course, there were to be no leaflet drops, not even on the morning of the invasion.

From my propaganda shop a series of cables was flashed to the Radio Swan broadcasters to change all program schedules. Prerecorded martial speeches were no longer appropriate.

It was just after four in the morning when I next returned to Cliff's office. I stood in the doorway and listened while Cabell and Bissell spoke insistently on the telephone, often exchanging the instrument. They were trying to convince Rusk that landing craft of the Brigade must have air cover over the beach, a task impossible for the Brigade B-26's several hours away in Nicaragua. Cabell asked that navy fighters of the U.S.S. *Boxer*, about fifty miles from the beach, be authorized to protect the invasion force. Rusk would not agree.

This time Cabell decided he must talk to President Kennedy. We waited for the call to go through to Glen Ora and for the President to be awakened.

Cabell talked to Kennedy. The conversation lasted for some time. Obviously the President was asking a number of questions, which Cabell answered in detail. He presented his case for air cover from the *Boxer* but as he did so I thought to myself: if only Dulles were here to sell this one. Cabell's voice dropped lower and lower; it was mostly, Yes, yes, sir, now. The conversation ended. Cabell put the telephone into its cradle.

"The President says no deal," Cabell said, looking at Bissell. Then he turned to the rest of us. "I guess," Cabell said, "we'll just have to be headsy-headsy about this."

Headsy-headsy?

The first exiles of the landing party arrived on the beach at dawn. The paratroopers landed safely and headed inland to secure the approaches leading through the swamps. The first of Castro's soldiers they met threw down their arms and raised their hands in surrender. A Brigade bulldozer began to clear the abandoned runway.

Castro's aircraft took off from their base on the few minutes' flight to the Bay of Pigs. There were B-26's and the four remaining jet trainers, which had been hastily equipped with rockets. Two Brigade transports were sunk immediately, one of them carrying the bulk of the ammunition for the men on the beach. Another carried the radio broadcast equipment I had scrounged hastily when Trinidad was scrapped. Defeat had set in.

All day Monday the news was bad. Kennedy authorized the flight of B-26 planes of the Brigade on Tuesday morning. Low clouds shrouded the beach, frustrating the strike. Some planes returned during the day. Three Brigade B-26's were shot down, others damaged. The pilots and crews were stiff with fatigue.

Tuesday night the President hosted a White House dinner for Congressmen. Bissell sent word that he must see Kennedy. Between midnight and 2 A.M. the DDP argued that air cover from the *Boxer* was now essential if the members of Brigade 2506 were to survive. Kennedy and his aides were still dressed in evening clothes. Rusk voted no, as did civilian White House aides. The military advisers were for it. *Kennedy chose to compromise.* The navy jets, the President said, could fly over the beach the next morning for one hour, to protect landing craft and to permit the Brigade B-26's to strike again at Castro's air force and the Cuban ground forces which were converging on the beach.

There was a tragic and fatal error in timing on Wednesday morning. The Brigade B-26's arrived half an hour ahead of the scheduled time; the navy fighters on the *Boxer* were still on the flight deck. When they did finally arrive the fighters were at 20,000 feet, without instructions to descend and engage Castro's forces. Two Brigade planes were destroyed. The air battle was over.

And the ground fighting was finished that afternoon.

I was holding back nausea as I hurriedly composed cables for Swan Island to begin broadcasting cryptic messages of the type beamed to resistance fighters by the BBC in World War II: "Look well to the rainbow. The fish will rise very soon. Chico is in the house...." It was nonsense. But something, however desperate, had to be said during the broadcasts which had been programmed to trumpet the victorious landing and to give the signal for action to infiltration and sabotage teams.

I went downstairs to the War Room. The task force officers in Quarters Eye were in direct communication with the Brigade commander on the beach. Cliff, who had known the commander and many of the Brigade officers, was white with remorse and fatigue. Colonel Alcott held one hand across his face, as if hiding. Len scratched his wrists viciously; blood stained his cuffs and darkened his fingernails. Bill left the War Room; later he said he had vomited in a wastebasket.

The Brigade commander radioed that he was standing in the shallows. "I have nothing left to fight with.... Am headed for the swamp." He cursed. The radio was dead.

It was over.

Two dreadful days passed in a slow-motion nightmare. I remember Robert Kennedy arriving and going into Cliff's office, his countenance grim. His brother had sent him to find out what went wrong. The task force officers who had walked so briskly through the halls before now moved like zombies. The dapper Howard Hunt was disheveled. Tracy Barnes attempted to cheer us up; his smiles were thin. Cliff sat at a typewriter, a bottle of whiskey at his elbow, and wrote out his resignation several times. Bill tore them up as soon as they were typed.

The next night, I went to Cliff's office. Only Abe was there.

"Abe, go home and get some sleep," I said.

"Can't," Abe said. "The others are at Bissell's house. I'm in charge." There were still messages to be sent, and sad remnants of the dreary episode to be pulled together.

I went home. I peeled off my socks like dirty layers of skin—I realized I hadn't changed them for a week. Helen tried to feed me, but I couldn't eat. I bathed, then fell into bed to sleep for several hours. On awakening I tried to eat again, but couldn't. Outside, the day was sheer spring beauty. I carried a portable radio to the yard at the rear of the house and listened to the gloomy newscasts about Cuba as I sat on the ground, my back against a tree.

Helen came out from the house and handed me a martini, a large one. I was half drunk when I finished. I went to the house for the gin bottle, the vermouth, and ice and sat again with my back to the tree. I could look up and see a clear blue sky above the foliage. Suddenly my stomach churned. I was sick. My body heaved.

Then I began to cry.

Helen came out of the house and pleaded with me to come in.

"Get the hell away," I sobbed.

It was growing dark. Helen came out of the house again with a blanket, which she draped around my shoulders.

I wept for two hours. I was sick again, then drunk again. I kept thinking of other tears, in another place, of a colonel from St.-Cyr whom I had made weep.

Oh shit! Shit!

How did it go so wrong? In the accretion of institutional error there was plenty of blame to go around, as President Kennedy said when he resolutely accepted the ultimate responsibility. Two mistakes eclipsed all others. The first was the decision to cancel the air strike on D-Day. The blame here was not just Kennedy's, but Cabell's, the air force general who allowed "headsy-headsy" instead of action.*

The second, and to me equally egregious, error was CIA's. Dulles's fault, Bissell's fault, a fault shared by all of us. At some time we should have cried "enough." When told the plan was to be changed from a classic guerrilla landing at Trinidad to a military operation we should have protested individually to the point of refusing to go along. We should have

---

* Several years later in Boston, professor Ernst Halperin, who was among the first Americans to visit Havana after the Bay of Pigs, told me he was present when a newsman asked Fidel Castro, "Why did the Americans fail?" Castro replied, simply, "They had no air support."

been more astute in recognizing the realities of CIA's operational situation in contrast to the inhibiting political realities.

Later I talked to Abe about it. I had come to realize the sagacity of the man who had been so unimpressive when first we met. "Abe," I asked, "how could we have been so dumb?"

Abe was philosophical. "I don't know. Even after the change from the Trinidad Plan I believed it still had a pretty good chance of working. Probably would have worked, if we had been able to knock out the rest of Castro's planes when they were lined up like sitting ducks."

Abe removed his glasses and cleaned them. He was more sober than I'd ever seen him.

"But you know, it was inevitable." Abe blew softly on the lenses of his bifocals. "The fiasco, I mean. The disaster. If it hadn't been the Bay of Pigs it would have been something else, some time in the future. In 1953 Kermit and a few fellows manipulated that crowd which toppled Mossadegh without any trouble at all. Then in 1954 we took care of Eisenhower's little problem in Guatemala. So easy, it seemed. All those successes just had to lead to a failure eventually, because the system kept calling on us for more and more even when it should have been obvious that secret shenanigans couldn't do what armies are supposed to do."

Abe pushed his glasses onto the bridge of his nose.

"If it hadn't been this time at the Bay of Pigs, it would have been somewhere else, at some other time."

5

MEXICO 1962–1964

Depressing weeks of picking up sad pieces followed the disaster at the Bay of Pigs. The training camp in Guatemala and the airbase in Nicaragua were dismantled, and the CIA officers in Miami came back to Washington or were assigned overseas. The exile newspapers I had supported folded, the radio programs in the Caribbean littoral were suspended. Radio Swan continued to broadcast, purposelessly. Most members of the Cuba project checked out of Quarters Eye and returned to their regular jobs in the four wooden buildings on the reflecting pool.

There were a number of post-mortem investigations, within and from outside of CIA. Kennedy appointed his own commission. I went to the Pentagon to be questioned by General Maxwell Taylor, who headed the presidential probe. The multilingual general shook his head slowly from side to side as I described the frustrated propaganda plans, the eleven million leaflets not dropped. Robert Kennedy, in shirtsleeves, delved into the inner workings of the Agency; in the end he did not shake it up as his brother had wanted, but fell in love with CIA and the concept of clandestine operations. Colonel J. C. King regained leadership of the Western Hemisphere Division, obviously pleased that he had been on the periphery of the abortive operation, and that his authority had been re-established. The few officers remaining in Quarters Eye moved up and down the halls like attendants at a sepulcher. There were long lunches after too many martinis at Napoleon's. "The Agency is finished," said some.

A former CIA colleague in business in New York telephoned offering me a job concerned with Latin America at $25,000 a year, much more than I was making with CIA. I grasped at the opportunity, at the chance to escape the depressing corridors of Quarters Eye. I went to Richard Bissell and told him I intended to resign.

The tall economist rose from his chair and paced, hands clasped behind his back. He rang for his secretary and dictated. He finished, saying, "Mr. Phillips has a promising potential for operations and leadership." He looked at the secretary, and not at me. "Should he remain with CIA he can expect promotion and, eventually, assignment as a Division Chief. Thus I have asked him today to reconsider his decision to resign."

The secretary left to type the short memorandum, the most tangible incentive a Deputy Director for Plans could offer a relatively young officer. The prediction that I would become a Division Chief would weigh heavily with promotion panels, or with those considering senior assignments. Bissell asked me to talk with Winston Scott, COS in Mexico City, who was visiting Washington to find a new covert action officer; the job was the number-three position in the Mexico City station, and one which would be an excellent first official cover assignment in preparation for future managerial posts, perhaps as a COS. When the secretary returned Bissell signed the memorandum, marking it for my personnel file. He went to the window and looked out at the reflecting pool for several minutes, without speaking. He turned. "Don't go to New York. Some of us will *have* to leave. The others must stay. See Scott."

I talked with Win Scott. He asked me to join him in Mexico City, in the job Howard Hunt had held in the early fifties and in which Hunt had handled, among others, an American contract agent named William F. Buckley.

After discussing our future again with Helen, I called my friend in New York to say I would not be taking him up on his offer. We packed for Mexico. We both knew, then, that I would never make that personal fortune I had sought. Actor, writer, lecturer, editor. Now my career was set. I had become a professional intelligence officer.

The CIA station in Mexico is one of the most important in the world. This status does not derive from any special interest in Mexico and Mexicans as intelligence targets as Mexico doesn't have much in the way of secrets except for the identity of the man selected each six years by the ruling political party as the next candidate for President, and, perhaps, a few foreign ministry intentions. The reason for a large CIA contingent in Mexico City is to conduct what are known as "third country operations." That is, using Mexico for access to the nationals of other countries.

Traditionally, Mexico City has been the main outpost of Soviet intelligence for its activities throughout Latin America and, since 1959, for the support of Cuban skulduggery in the Western Hemisphere. The mainland Chinese have an embassy there, as do all the other Socialist countries. Even Mongolia recently opened an office in Mexico City, presumably to issue visas to all those Mexicans who travel around the Gobi desert. The Mexico City airport is the hub of international travel for revolutionary motleys, especially to Havana. Mexico is an exile haven for Latin Americans of whatever conviction who are waiting, and often trying to abet, a change of government in their countries. The FBI has had a keen interest in Mexico City since the McCarthy era, when several hundred American Communists transplanted themselves there, and also because the Soviet embassy is a base for Russian intelligence operations into the United States. All of this has spawned a conglomeration of intelligence officers, agents, spies, provocateurs, and the shadowy figures of those who manage financial and communication nets to support international intrigue. Each intelligence service in Mexico City plays the cat-and-mouse game of attempting to penetrate the other's organization. In short, the Mexican capital is a huggermugger metropolis of cloak-and-dagger conspirators.

The Mexican government observes these international shenanigans with bemused tolerance. The Mexicans do not find it amusing however when they uncover an operation aimed against Mexico, and occasionally send Soviet or Cuban "diplomats" packing when they are caught in flagrant espionage excesses.

I reported for work at the Mexico City station to take over the covert action desk. Most of my work involved support to CIA projects in third countries and was relatively routine, allowing me some leisure to observe other CIA officers working against the "hard targets"—the Soviets, Cubans, Czechs, and other Communist countries—and "soft targets," the Mexican and Latin American Communist parties. It was new to me, and a valuable learning period.

Much of my time was spent on anti-Castro propaganda operations. This called for many hours of coordination with the station officer whose job it was to know what was going on in and around the Cuban embassy. The head of the Cuba section was "Wally," whom we had first met at the University of Chile in Santiago. He, too, had been hired by the CIA as an intelligence officer.

Wally's job was to maintain "total coverage" of the Cuban embassy. Ideally, blanketing a hostile foreign installation for intelligence purposes would include: at least one spy within, reporting on his own government; the ability to read the mail to and from the embassy; being able to listen to telephone calls; at least one microphone broadcasting secrets from within; the capability of obtaining photographs of everyone working in the embassy and nearly everyone who visited it; and access to its trash. Confidential papers in an embassy are supposed to be disposed of in an incinerator. People are forgetful, especially in fledgling intelligence services, and classified papers or typewriter ribbons are dropped in a waste-basket. An agent of mine in Mexico City once found copies of the Cuban foreign service's most secret cables in a garbage heap.

It would be inappropriate for me to say just how total a coverage of the Cuban embassy Wally had achieved when I arrived in Mexico in 1961, but it was thorough. He undoubtedly knew as much about the Cubans who worked there as the Cubans themselves did about their own colleagues and, in the case of many intelligence officers, a great deal more.

"That doesn't seem to be very glamorous work for an Ivy League graduate," I kidded an officer in the CIA station one day when I found him sifting through papers purloined from the trash of a foreign embassy. "Well, it's better than one of my first overseas assignments," he replied dryly, "which was to obtain a urine sample from a foreign minister."

Intelligence work is not all fun and games but more often plodding perseverance in collecting what might appear to be trivia. Laboring to put together the whole picture in intelligence is usually like assembling a jigsaw puzzle from an almost infinite number of tiny pieces with the hope that enough of the final mosaic will emerge to mean something. Obtaining and storing mundane shards of information—on 3-by-5 cards, or in files where they can be retrieved quickly—is a monotonous business. (One of our veterans once suggested truth would be better served if the symbolic cloak-and-dagger of the intelligence operative were replaced by six 3-by-5 cards and a typewriter.) Does it matter that a local Communist sometimes uses the alias "Carlos"? Yes, it does if he someday goes to Europe and becomes a terrorist. Is it really important if a young Latin woman is having an affair with an intelligence officer from a Bloc embassy? It might be, if she later applied for a maid's job at the home of the CIA Station Chief, or, gets involved with an American or Mexican official. Why bother to keep tabs on the international travel of a student radical; or will it be significant, years later, when his absence coincides with the period when a local guerrilla group has trained in Cuba? Is it notable if a political crackpot has a second apartment his wife doesn't know about? Probably not—unless an American ambassador has been kidnapped and the CIA is trying to assist local authorities in finding him. The list of trivia which might become vital in an unknown future goes on endlessly, and it must be recorded and made retrievable on demand, sometimes years later. I know of a case where a Soviet "sleeper"—a deep-cover agent who had spent years living under a false name using a false nationality—was uncovered and arrested because a CIA analyst had noted for the record a decade before a defector's recollection that the agent's pseudonym began with the letter C. That apparently trivial observation was the key unlocking the mystery of the Russian's clandestine existence, ten years later.

The routine work of intelligence people abroad sometimes is so dull that it invites frustration. Checking lists of names for security purposes is a random example—perhaps thirty guests the Ambassador has invited to a reception. Or, as was the case in Mexico, vetting, one by one, each applicant for a visa at the American embassy to be sure the would-be traveler was not ineligible on security or other grounds. Sheer boredom—except for the time the check resulted in the arrest of a drug-peddler in Laredo who had stuffed his anus with a million dollars worth of heroin.

And, being in my first "official cover" assignment, I could observe a COS at work for the first time.

Winston Scott, the CIA Chief, had become an almost legendary figure in the organization before I went to work for him. Born in a small Southern town, he was fullback on the football team at the University of Alabama and spurned a big-league baseball offer in favor of continuing his studies. He was a mathematics professor at Alabama by age nineteen and went on to the University of Michigan for his Ph.D. in matrix theory mathematics. During World War II he served brief stints in the FBI and the navy. He was once assigned to Cuba early in the war, where he put his actuarial skills to work breaking German code messages to the Caribbean. In CIA he combined long work hours with mental agility and rapidly rose to senior positions. He was Chief of Station in London. In Washington he was in charge of the section which conducted liaison with other intelligence services—he once remarked on his uneasiness at being asked by Kim Philby to describe CIA's operations division. Later, he headed the Agency's European Division. Weary of the routine of Washington, he asked for assignment as COS in Mexico in 1958. When packing out, he told a colleague he intended to stay in Mexico until he died. His tenure as COS, Mexico City, a full decade, was with one exception the longest ever for a CIA Station Chief.

When I arrived, Win Scott worked long hours but, I was told, shorter days than in previous years. He found time to play golf—a sport he took up and mastered in Mexico—with his lovely Irish wife. They met in London, when she was a postulant for one of the Catholic orders. Win became a Roman Catholic convert so they might wed. Not long after I was in Mexico she died. Win returned to his heavy work schedule, leaving the office at night carrying a bulging satchel of books and abstruse mathematical journals which had arrived in the day's mail. He suffered from insomnia. At night he would play bridge with himself but without cards —mentally dealing and playing hands until sleep came.

Win had a near-photographic memory. He would scrawl file numbers —sometimes three or four different ones—on intelligence reports and retrieve the file numbers by memory months later when he needed a specific report. The unique filing system he established for the station became the despair of management experts in Washington, who winced at the mountains of paper Scott accumulated in defiance of Agency practice. I pointed out to one visitor that the system worked very well—as long as you had a photographic memory.

Win captivated people, when he wanted to. Mexicans are cautious about developing friendships with Americans, especially any gringo named Win Scott (General Winfield Scott invaded Mexico and took Mexico City in 1847). But the Mexicans, notably high-ranking government officials, were charmed by Win Scott. His appearance had something to do with it: he was a large, handsome man with a shock of gray-white hair. And, it was partly his disarming professionalism and his fluent Spanish, but mostly it was the result of a calculated charm which Win could apply in a low-key yet relentless way—if the subject of his attention was worth cultivating.

When dealing with me, Win was relaxed and pleasant and kind, devoting long hours to indoctrinating me on the operation of a CIA station—a tutorial course I certainly needed from the old master after eleven years at the end of the line in deep-cover assignments.

In addition to Win's schooling, I was given a particularly memorable bit of advice by a senior CIA officer and veteran Latin American hand, passing through Mexico City.

"Now that you are under official cover," he told me, "you're in the business of management as well as operations. You'll spend less time on the street and more at your desk, sniffing out the winds of political change and the smell of smoke from hidden operational fires. An important part of intelligence reporting is sensing that a critical development will occur before all the facts are in and you can actually prove it with hard intelligence. Professional intuition. The conviction that a number of pieces, when eventually assembled into enough of the entire puzzle, will constitute a revelation that is vital. I always try to think of it in terms of being aware of when grandmother is on the roof."

"Of *what*?" I asked.

He then launched into a story which he identified as Brazilian folklore. Immigration from Portugal, the mother country to Brazil, has been fairly constant over the years. Brazilians, bright and alert, always joke about the newly arrived Portuguese, whom they consider to be slow and even less than bright. They delight in telling "Portuguese" stories somewhat on the order of yesterday's Irish and today's Polish jokes in the United States.

"A Portuguese living in Brazil," my friend said, "received a cable from his cousin in Portugal, announcing the death of the family cat, a pet the immigrant had been especially fond of. 'Our beloved cat,' the message said, 'fell to her death in the courtyard.' "

The immigrant wrote to his cousin in Lisbon: "Do not send such a message again. I am a sensitive person; I can't stand shocks. Should such a thing happen again consider my temperament and let me know gently, in stages. For example, you should have sent a message saying, 'The cat went up on the roof.' Then, a few days later another, saying, 'The cat went to the edge of the roof.' Then, finally, a letter with the bad news: 'The cat fell off the roof and died.' "

Some months later the immigrant in Brazil received another cable from his cousin. It read: "Grandmother just went up on the roof."

"So that's what I look for," said my friend. "That one new piece of information, perhaps a single line in a report, some awareness which gives you a funny feeling at the back of the neck—the suspicion which suddenly is a conviction that something important is in motion, that grandmother is on the roof."

In late November of 1961 the word reached Mexico that CIA had a new director. Allen Dulles was asked to leave in the wake of the Bay of Pigs. President Kennedy is reputed to have said to the retiring DCI, "In a parliamentary form of government, I would be leaving office. In our government, you must go."

I was sorry to see Dulles go. He was a professional, and his relish for the intelligence trade was infectious. His image as an avuncular, teddy-bear kind of Director somehow made espionage and covert action seem to be good clean fun.*

John McCone, the wealthy shipbuilder, became our new Director. He was highly respected in business and political circles for being a tough administrator who knew how to get things done, as he had demonstrated when producing assembly-line freighters during World War II and in several important government positions in Washington. The people of CIA were dubious. Could an outsider, without experience in clandestine operations, manage our intelligence agency? In his first appearances at Langley he left an impression of austerity, remoteness, and implacability.

McCone wasted no time on amenities. While awaiting congressional confirmation, he traveled to Europe with Allen Dulles to inspect CIA stations. Later the COS at one of the major European stations told me a story that pinpointed the basic difference we would see between Dulles and McCone as personalities and managers of CIA. A security officer

* Dulles's long-cherished new CIA building at Langley was in its final stages of construction. One office was completely furnished, however, so that Dulles could work during his last days—almost alone amid the workmen—at Langley.

traveled with McCone and Dulles. He had the primary responsibility of protecting Dulles as long as he remained DCI, but obviously he had some obligation to be concerned with the next Director's security as well. The security officer approached this Chief of Station, saying he had a problem.

"McCone just told me he's flying to Germany tomorrow morning. He hasn't even mentioned it to Dulles, who will be staying here. McCone told me I was to travel with him, but, by the book, I should stay with Dulles as long as he's DCI."

"Speak to Dulles," advised the Chief of Station.

"I just can't do that."

"Then I will," said the Chief of Station, and he later told Dulles that McCone would be leaving the next day with the only security escort available.

"Extraordinary." Dulles stroked his ample mustache. "Of course. Of course. He must go with him." But then he added: "*Extra*ordinary!"

It would never have occurred to Dulles to expect protection from the Director's security escort until he was officially DCI. McCone, who liked to get on with the job, probably never entertained the notion that the old school thing to do was to leave the security man with Dulles, even if he was a lame duck.

Dulles retired and wrote his *The Craft of Intelligence*, which remains a standard reference work for those who wish to study the history of American intelligence. In February of 1962 Richard Bissell, another casualty of the Bay of Pigs, resigned to become eventually a vice president of United Aircraft at a much larger salary than government could afford. His Chief of Operations, Dick Helms, who had remained distant from the Cuba project, replaced Bissell as the Deputy Director of Plans.

While the high-level shuffle went on in Washington, I continued to learn in Mexico how a CIA field station functions and, for the first time, had a chance to observe CIA people at work in a normal situation. While serving "outside" under deep cover my association with "inside" case officers had been limited to operational meetings once or twice a week. I saw senior officers even less frequently. In both the Guatemala and Bay of Pigs operations the frenetic pressures precluded a valid appreciation of what my colleagues were like as persons under ordinary working conditions. I had been inclined to be overimpressed, perceiving CIA officers as a very special breed, a band of brothers, Robin Hoods of the clandestine netherworld.

Working with them day by day, I soon found that my colleagues were simply people. Like most State Department officers, CIA people usually had two qualities which set them apart from other government bureaucrats: impressive talents and unswerving dedication. In other aspects, CIA officers were about the same as anyone else working in the embassy. Some were clever and others less than astute, but they were interesting human beings and working with them was stimulating.

In Latin America at Christmas indigenous friends of American diplomats tend to expect scotch whiskey as a Christmas gift. This is fine for the State Department diplomat who can import scotch duty-free from Europe or buy it cheaply in an embassy commissary. But it poses a problem for CIA personnel, because their local contacts are confidential, if not clandestine. It would be poor tradecraft to give them the scotch bottles sans the local tax stamps. A duty-free bottle, spotted in a home or office, would be too easily recognized as the gift of an embassy official. Thus CIA yule funds are spent on very expensive scotch from local stores because it has the proper United Kingdom and, in this case, Mexican tax stamps. This is costly, as scotch in most countries of the world is priced at least three times higher than in the embassy commissary.

One CIA officer in Mexico City pondered the problem, concerned that the extra expense was a waste of the American taxpayers' money. He pointed out that the station was paying perhaps five hundred dollars a year more than it need have due to the excessive local cost of scotch. He had an idea. "Why not have those printers at headquarters make the tax stamps for us? They print false documents all the time." He sent a dispatch to CIA in Washington with the suggestion. The reply was rather tart, explaining that it was not the policy of CIA to counterfeit tax stamps, and certainly not in this case, which could hardly please Her Majesty's government or the Mexicans, should it become known. Further, the dispatch said, to save Mexico City station five hundred dollars, it should be recognized that engraving plates, matching paper, and finally printing the tax stamps would cost CIA around $12,000.

The frugal fellow was disappointed. He didn't understand why we virtually collapsed in laughter when in a station staff meeting he complained, "Somehow we just have to lick this stamp problem."

One officer in the station, while a fine fellow, was a bit pompous. He was considered by some of his colleagues as too measured and conservative in his conduct of operations which, to be successful, must be approached and managed with vigor. He kept a 3-by-5 card under the glass covering his desk. It read, *If I can't do great things in a great way, let me do small things in a commendable way.* One night the card disappeared. It was replaced by another which announced, *If I can't do vast things in a vast way, let me do half-vast things in a half-vast way.*

During the Cold War of the fifties, intelligence cowboys from the CIA and the Soviet KGB engaged in pranks and dirty tricks, which were sometimes infantile. One CIA practice was to disrupt Communist meetings and rallies by having agents set off stink bombs fabricated in a CIA laboratory. They were of such pungency that the stench literally drove an audience from a lecture hall or meeting place. The stink bombs were known in CIA as "Who, Me?"

By the time I arrived in Mexico this type of harassment activity had ceased, but several ampules of the "Who, Me?" liquid remained on the shelves of the station storeroom. One of the station people cleaning out old supplies decided to get rid of the stink bombs. He was a grown man and should have known better, but he decided the easiest thing to do would be to crack the ampules and pour the offending mixture down the drain of the station darkroom. At that time the American embassy was situated on the top floors of a tall building which housed, on the first floor, a department store and restaurant, and in succeeding floors, offices of businessmen and professionals.

Holding his nose, the CIA officer disposed of the liquid. The smelly mixture went down the pipes to the basement of the building. There it somehow escaped the plumbing which should have drained it away. The aroma slowly ascended through the air-conditioning system of the building, floor by floor. The technicians who had developed the putrid essence would have been proud: the unbearable stench drove diners from the restaurant and customers from the store. Patients bolted from dentists' chairs; stockbrokers fled. Then, full circle, the miasma reached the offices of the CIA and the embassy. Hardy diplomats served their country by remaining on post. But the Ambassador, briefed by Win Scott on the origin of the problem, was not amused at all by the incident.

Aside from wars, riots, or sustained terrorist attacks, there is nothing that disrupts an American embassy abroad more thoroughly than a presidential visit. Routine diplomatic work is for all practical purposes suspended. The planning begins months ahead, and the weeks preceding the arrival of an American President are hectic with preparations. The visits usually go smoothly, racing along on a timetable which has been intricately rehearsed.

An advance unit of the United States Secret Service arrives early to work with the embassy and local security officials. Among a number of other special duties, the CIA must watch the travel of political crackpots around the world who might be en route to the scene of the presidential visit. A list of local subversives and otherwise suspicious characters is passed to the Secret Service. Local authorities sometimes round them up before the arrival of the foreign visitor, offering the hospitality of local detention facilities for the duration. In some countries on such occasions citizens with police records have learned to show up at the jail without being asked. In the embassy, everyone from the file clerks to the Ambassador has his series of tasks to perform.

In the summer of 1962 the Kennedys visited Mexico City. Jackie captivated Mexicans with a brief speech in careful, school-polished Spanish and the President's open and friendly manner with Mexican crowds was equally successful. One newspaper headlined a story about his acceptance: APOTHEOSIS!

As the number-three officer in the CIA station, my standing in protocol terms did not merit an invitation to several exclusive functions in honor of the visiting President. But Helen and I did attend a not-very-restricted Foreign Minister's reception, a gala for two thousand guests. Jackie was queenlike, lovely in a turquoise evening gown. Jack Kennedy was a king that night and acted like one. To the regal he added a touch of the politician, striding around the great hall to meet and shake hands with the guests. That caused a problem for me.

As Kennedy made his triumphant round of the ballroom he was chased by a pack of reporters and photographers. Some forty members of the international and Mexican press stayed as close as they could to the handsome young visitor as he stopped to introduce himself and chat, with a pretty woman here, a portly diplomat there, another pretty woman elsewhere.

Suddenly the President headed straight for me. He put out his hand.

"Hi," said the President of the United States, "I'm Jack Kennedy." I was surprised that, at close range, he was a much larger man than I had imagined from photographs, and that his face was not only ruddy, but downright red.

"Sir." I shook hands. "My name is David Phillips."

"What do you do here, Mr. Phillips, in Mexico?"

The forty newspeople behind the President were jostling for a place near him, those winning out jotting down notes on their pads.

"I work for you, Mr. President. In the embassy."

"I see." Obviously Kennedy preferred more definite answers to his straightforward questions. "What do you do in the embassy, Mr. Phillips?"

"I work in the Political Section, sir." Flashbulbs popped, reporters' pencils scribbled. Mr. President, I thought to myself, please stop asking questions. Would I be the first intelligence officer in history to have his cover blown by his own President?

Kennedy was persistent. He wanted a straight answer. "Mr. Phillips," he said, a tinge of the imperial in his voice, "what do you do? Precisely."

Precisely? God! Would I be forced to lie to my commander-in-chief?

"I write reports, Mr. President." Kennedy's face hardened, reddened even more. I continued, lamely, "Reports which I hope will be useful..."

"Mr. Phillips, I—" The President stopped abruptly. His jaw dropped. He finally realized my dilemma. He touched his lips momentarily with the tips of his fingers, as a little girl might do when caught out. Then, in clear tones, "I see. Well, good luck to you, Mr. Phillips."

Then the President looked at me, his eyes softening in apology. Soundlessly, he mouthed an "I'm sorry." Then Jack Kennedy continued his royal rounds. The reporters swept after him.

Desmond FitzGerald visited Mexico City. It was my first meeting with one of the most colorful and dynamic members of that small circle of well-bred, highly educated adventurers who were known to some in the CIA as the "Knights Templar"—Allen Dulles, Frank Wisner, Kermit Roosevelt, Tracy Barnes, Dick Bissell, and kindred spirits. FitzGerald shared their common background of family wealth, Ivy League education, and derring-do in O.S.S. In his case the path to senior positions in the Clandestine Service began at Groton (he married the headmaster's daughter), Harvard, and O.S.S., where he marched with Stilwell through Southeast Asia in World War II. In CIA he began in Far East operations, rising to the head spot in that division. Shortly before I met him in Mexico, he was appointed CIA Chief of Cuban Operations by John McCone. FitzGerald visited Mexico to review the station's Cuban efforts and to discuss with Win Scott a replacement for Wally, who would soon transfer to the Dominican Republic.

FitzGerald entered my office. I couldn't understand why he was so ebullient even when sitting, until later I found it to be a normal condition for him. His Irish face was part pixie, some leprechaun; he was not a handsome man but had an engaging smile not unlike that of Jack Kennedy, to whom he was related from the Boston, FitzGerald side. He and Win had decided that I should change jobs and replace Wally as chief of the station's Cuban operations. He explained there was interest on the part of McCone and "higher authority" in beefing up CIA capabilities to thwart the Cuban drive to increase their influence throughout Latin America.

"What about dinner?" FitzGerald asked. "I'll fill in the background for you."

"Fine," I said. "Shall we eat at Sears and Roebuck?"

FitzGerald laughed. "Perhaps something a bit more typical."

He was amused because shortly before, in his trip around South America, he had suggested dinner to a Chief of Station who was a bachelor and a hard-working man who often stayed late at the office and cared not a whit about social life, or when and where he ate. This Chief of Station had asked FitzGerald where he wanted to eat. The urbane Chief of Cuban Operations, who relished the finest in clothes, companions, and good food, had been gracious enough to say, "Why don't we go to your favorite place?" So the elegant FitzGerald dined that night at the cafeteria of the local Sears and Roebuck store.

I took Desmond FitzGerald to a suitable restaurant; he was pleased when the waiter used an atomizer to add vermouth to a martini. During dinner he spoke of John McCone, who had now been our Director for a year.

The skeptics at CIA had changed their opinion about McCone; he had turned out to be an excellent DCI. He was admired for his tough, practical mind and his capacity for hard work. His demands on his subordinates were enormous. When he came to CIA he brought with him a personal assistant, who worked so hard that some CIA people referred to him as "the slave." The aide at one point was allowed to take a three-week vacation in Greece, which seemed to be very generous on the part of McCone, until it was learned that the leave was his first in eleven years! While a hard taskmaster, McCone himself worked as diligently as his employees—Mrs. McCone once told an Agency officer his hours were so long and exhausting while he was mobilizing ship construction during World War II that he couldn't fall asleep at night unless she read to him. Despite his crisp, driving style, those who worked closely with McCone found him to be an entertaining and stimulating luncheon companion who thoroughly recognized the value of a dry martini and a wry anecdote.

McCone remained unpredictable to most of our high officials even after some months of association. A senior CIA officer once found himself in profound disagreement with a position taken by McCone, and refused to back down, after a serious confrontation on the matter. The official went home to warn his wife that his adamant stance might well lead to his being transferred or even dismissed. The wife was not concerned: shortly before her husband came home John McCone had sent her a gift—a *quart* of fine French perfume.

McCone's performance during the Cuban missile crisis of 1962 erased any vestige of doubt about his ability as an intelligence chief. FitzGerald glowed as he recounted the story over an after-dinner brandy.

The early fragmentary reports that Fidel Castro had agreed to Soviet missiles being installed secretly in Cuba began to arrive in Washington in late 1961. The very first, I believe, came across my desk before I left Washington for Mexico: a vague assertion that someone's brother-in-law had heard in Havana such a plan had been approved. Other bits and pieces filtering in from diverse sources were vague and unconvincing but they continued to accumulate over the next year. John McCone began to suspect that grandmother was on the roof. He went to see President Kennedy in August of 1962 and told the President it was his belief that the Soviets were in the process of establishing missile bases in Cuba. He admitted that his estimate was not supported by hard intelligence. Nonetheless, he persisted. In late September McCone reviewed our U-2 photographic reconnaissance of Cuba and decided it was inadequate: he arranged for the air force Strategic Air Command to take responsibility for U-2 overflights. On October 14 a SAC photograph revealed a medium-range ballistic missile site at San Cristóbal, Cuba. The photography was passed to the top policy makers in Washington.

That first photograph—the hard evidence which had eluded McCone and his staff for so long—was the felicitous result of a marriage of two kinds of espionage, technical and human. The U-2 flew directly to the target site in Cuba because a CIA agent had said it could be found there. The analysts who identified the missile had an easier job because another spy, from the Soviet Union, had provided highly classified manuals on Russian missile systems—Colonel Oleg Penkovsky.

From October 17 to 22 President Kennedy met daily with his security advisers. They were divided: those on the one hand who suggested that Kennedy prepare for an air strike and an all-out invasion of Cuba and, on the other, the group which recommended a more cautious course based on negotiation with Khrushchev. On October 19 the Board of National Estimates—after mulling over the reports from all intelligence sources—produced the critical judgment that the Soviet Union would not risk a war over the issue of removing its missiles from Cuba. The blockade of Cuba and the removal of the missiles followed, when Khrushchev blinked.

It was as near to Armageddon as the United States had been since World War II.

After the October crisis, John McCone had another canny premonition. He was concerned that the agreement with Khrushchev—a pledge by Kennedy that the United States would stay out of Cuba—would leave Fidel Castro in a strengthened position to pursue subversion in the other countries of Latin America. McCone readied CIA for the period when it must fight Castro's surge to export the Cuban revolution. That, Fitz-Gerald explained over a second brandy, was the reason he had been pulled away from his Far East duties to head Cuban operations and why I among others was being asked to change jobs in midtour. My task would be to monitor the Cuban embassy in Mexico City and any nexus it might have with pro-Castro groups in the hemisphere.

Before leaving Mexico City, FitzGerald asked who I thought should take over my covert action desk in the station. I suggested that Abe, who had been assigned to another Latin American country after we had worked together so closely on the Bay of Pigs, would be just right. He agreed, saying that he had worked with the ex-infantry captain in the Far East and admired him and his work.

Des FitzGerald returned to Washington. Wally and his wife went off to the Dominican Republic; and Abe and his family arrived in Mexico.

During this period I learned that CIA people sometimes practice even their avocations in secrecy. One morning Win Scott came into my office, shutting the door behind him. He appeared to be unusually sober.

"I'm going to tell you something," the Chief of Station said, "which you must never tell anyone."

"All right," I said.

"I mean it," Win said. "This is to be between you and me and no one else."

"You have my word," I promised.

"If you do tell anyone," he said, "I'll kill you."

I had been curious before, but now I was frightened. Was I about to be told some dark and chilling secret, something I didn't want to know? Win was serious.

"All right," I gulped. "I'll never say a word."

"You see," Win said, "I read a while back about a poetry competition in the States. There's a national prize for the best new volume of..." Win stammered, his face flushing under the strain of getting the words out. "...of love poems."

Now I understood why he had threatened to kill me if I revealed his secret to CIA colleagues.

Win threw his manuscript on my desk. "Do me the favor of reading these and telling me whether they are worth submitting."

That night I read Win Scott's love poems. The next morning I recommended that he enter the competition.

The CIA is not authorized to watch American citizens abroad unless they are clearly engaged in the espionage game. Some are and bear watching. Others, a rather large number, visit the embassies of unfriendly foreign powers for one innocuous reason or another; when they do they appear as blips on the CIA radar screen. It would be imprudent not to observe them long enough to find out what they are up to in contacting Russians, Cubans, and the Chinese. If an American legislator wearing a big hat, for instance, should visit the North Korean embassy in Paris, it should be no great surprise that the CIA notes the fact for the record. In Mexico City a number of such contacts were made by American citizens.

On the American embassy local staff in Mexico there were a number of young Mexican delivery boys. One of them sought me out, saying that he had been accosted on the street the night before by a man who spoke broken Spanish and appeared to be an American. The stranger had asked the Mexican youth—whom he obviously did not suspect of being a local

employee of the American embassy—to perform an errand. He gave him
an envelope and a ten-dollar bill, asking that he deliver the note to the
Cuban embassy. "I'll wait here," the stranger said, "and I'll give you
another ten dollars when you return after delivering the note."

The young Mexican accepted the offer but carefully weighed the
implications of the proposal as he walked toward the guardhouse at the
gate of the Cuban embassy. He chatted for a moment with the gatekeeper,
then returned to collect the additional ten dollars from the American
stranger, who had been the victim of really monumental bad luck.

"I didn't really hand over the message," the delivery boy explained
to me. He produced an envelope. "Here it is."

The letter was written in English, apparently American idiom, and
advised the Cuban embassy that the writer was prepared, for a price, to
pass it important information on United States military matters. He
provided his room and telephone number at a local hotel and asked for
a private meeting to discuss the proposal.

I discussed the case with Clark Anderson, the affable and capable
FBI chief in Mexico City. Before assuming responsibility for the case he
wanted to be sure the man was an American. He asked if I had an agent
who could contact him under the guise of a Cuban intelligence officer
responding to the message and find out more about the stranger's proposal.

I had just such an agent, "Enrique," who spoke fluent English and
could pass for a Cuban intelligence type. I briefed Enrique. Later that
day he called to tell me he would be meeting the stranger at a local
restaurant. Helen and I decided to dine there too, so that I could get
a look at the man who wanted to sell secrets to the Cubans. When we
arrived that night the owner of the restaurant, harassed by the good
fortune of having an overflow crowd, led us to the only available table.

The would-be traitor was having a streak of really bad luck. Helen
and I were seated at the next table, not four feet from where he sat with
my agent. Although surprised to find his case officer so close at hand,
Enrique behaved admirably. He spoke to his dinner partner in feigned,
heavily accented English: "I'm sorry, but you must speak more loudly.
My hearing is not too good. Stop whispering."

The American facing Enrique surely would have preferred to speak
softly, but, after a nervous glance at Helen and me—both obviously
American—he went on with his conversation.

The next hour was almost surrealistic. With Enrique prompting the
American to speak louder, I listened as the novice spy explained why he
was ready to betray his country. He was a middle-grade United States
military officer, and he needed money. He was, he told Enrique, locked
into a marriage to a woman he hated from whom he could not extricate
himself. He would provide information to the Cubans—"and you can

pass it on to the Russians"—for one year to accumulate enough to allow him to flee from the marriage he could no longer countenance. It was a motive for treason which I did not expect then, but in later years would not find surprising.

I reported to Clark Anderson the next day. He asked me to have Enrique meet again with the American, tell him that his offer had been accepted by Havana, and instruct him to return to his home in the United States to await contact. I don't know how the case turned out, but it must have been a surprise and shock to the disloyal military man when, eventually, there was a knock on his door. He would be expecting a case officer from the Cuban intelligence service, but the caller would have been one of Clark's colleagues from the FBI.

The systematic recruitment of agents—spies—is the most practical way to obtain new sources, for CIA or any intelligence service. My first recruitment, of Juan in Chile in the early fifties, is an example. The task is not easy or quick and normally involves the identification and development, sometimes over a period of months, of a person with access to a particular target on which intelligence is needed. It might involve a Communist Party, a terrorist band, a political party, or, more and more these days, economic or scientific areas.

More often than is generally realized, potential spies become aware that they have something of value to offer a foreign intelligence service and make a calculated decision to seek out an intelligence contact and volunteer their services. These people are called, in espionage parlance, "walk-ins." Throughout history they have been important sources of information. Penkovsky was a walk-in.

Walk-ins are driven to treason by a variety of motives. Penkovsky, the Soviet intelligence officer who became a CIA spy, envisaged the Western system as better than the Soviet and saw a way to combat the Communist ethic by cooperating with the Americans and British. Most walk-ins accept money—but not all, some considering themselves above the crass practice of selling their loyalty. Some spy to satisfy basic passions such as revenge; they are getting even with a person or system they don't like, or with a supervisor who has not promoted them. The American I had turned over to the FBI sought a new life away from a nagging wife.

Basically, most spies work because they want or need money. They turn to espionage because they know, as Willie Sutton the bank robber knew about banks, "that's where the money is." Most espionage candidates, however, have an unrealistic view of the value of their services. I remember a member of a Communist Party in a Latin American country who walked into an American embassy and blithely allowed that he would be willing to work for the CIA for $3,000 a month. He was stunned when told that the going rate, in that particular republic, was $60.00 to $100.00. Despite the disappointment of walk-ins when they learn that spying is not as lucrative as they had expected, I have known only a few cases in which walk-ins retracted their offer and walked out.

Walk-ins are usually viewed with suspicion due to the number of provocations mounted over the years by the Soviets to flush out intelligence officers from among the embassy staff. If the initial determination is that the walk-in has significant intelligence potential, a message is flashed to Washington. Representatives of various government agencies convene there to decide just how valuable he or she might be. In rare cases the individual will be flown to the United States to be debriefed. The Director of CIA has the authority to bring into the country without immigration red tape a very limited number of persons each year. A Central Committee member of a Communist Party would not receive this preferential treatment, unless from a really major country. A Soviet nuclear physicist would.

The rubric "walk-in" describes all volunteers, even those like my American who do not actually come near an embassy. They might wait to make contact at the home of an embassy official; some telephone and arrange a meeting in a dark alley; wives have walked in for their husbands. There have been several cases in espionage history of "write-ins," where the would-be spy establishes contact and provides his intelligence by mail without identifying himself. In such cases, he receives his payment the same way at a general delivery address, or by retrieving the money surreptitiously from a cache, say, in a public park.

When the bona fides of a defector or potential agent are established, the first CIA officer who meets him has the responsibility of trying to persuade him to return to his office or home before his absence is noted so his superiors will not know he has become a traitor. A foreign code clerk, for instance, is immensely valuable if he is willing to report intelligence from his embassy over a period of time, but as a defector can only contribute perishable or dated intelligence. At the very least he should be cajoled into returning long enough to obtain code books and other valuable documents.

This course is not always easy. Even after the crackpots and professional fabricators have been weeded out, the good prospects are in a confused mental state. "You must remember," Win Scott told me, "that every defector has just committed emotional suicide." Regardless of his motives and rationalization, the potential spy or defector has just slashed the ties binding him to family and country. He is, in effect, a temporary mental patient, and must be handled by a CIA officer with the same caution which a doctor would use when confronted with an unknown psychopath.

One reason CIA maintains light cover for some officers in embassies overseas is to provide a lightning rod for those who want to know where they can establish contact with United States intelligence. Walk-ins often insist on proof that they are actually dealing with CIA, a precaution the American who wanted to work for Cuba would have done well to take. Once I met a man on a street corner who wanted to spy for CIA. The contact had been set up by telephone. He insisted on some visible sign that I was really an intelligence officer and that the United States government would stand behind any commitment I made.

"What is your favorite American cigarette?" I asked.

"Kent," he said.

"Tomorrow morning walk by the embassy at ten A.M. There'll be a carton of Kents leaning against the sill of the window in the Ambassador's office."

The next morning I went into the office of the Ambassador, who was busy revising a speech he was to give that day. "I won't keep you, sir. I'd like to put this carton of cigarettes in your window for a while, if I might. There's a potential agent who asked for my bona fides and he'll be watching for the signal."

"Go ahead." The Ambassador didn't even look up from his papers as I tilted the cigarette carton against the window sill.

The second walk-in, following the American military officer who detested his wife, I was to handle was an important case, a young Cuban intelligence officer, and I bungled the job thoroughly. Earle Perez Friman was a DGI (General Directorate of Intelligence, the Cuban intelligence service) man stationed in Montevideo, Uruguay. He came through Mexico City on his way to Havana. Just after dark one evening he walked into the American embassy where he talked to the military attaché, who had been summoned by the Marine guard. "John," a CIA officer who worked with me on Cuban operations, waited with me in an outer office until the attaché reported. He said that there was no question that Perez was authentic because he had documents to prove he was a Cuban intelligence officer.

John and I talked with the defector. He said he had decided to break with Fidel Castro and his Soviet-dominated regime. He refused any enticement to remain in place, that is, to stay in the DGI and report as a penetration of the Cuban service. He only wanted to join his family in Miami. To achieve that he would tell us everything he knew about the DGI. A secondary consideration, he said, was that he wanted $100,000 to get a start on a new life.

After several flash cables to and from CIA headquarters and extended negotiation with Perez, we settled on a much smaller sum, which we promised would be paid the next day on his arrival in the United States.

Perez was unhappy with the offer, but reluctantly agreed. John and I escorted him to a safe house where the Cuban gulped down several sandwiches and a quarter of a bottle of bourbon, an unsual preference for a Latin.

Earle Perez Friman was not an attractive person. Although he was in his early twenties, his stomach already spilled over a low-slung belt; his plump face was pocked with unhealthy pustules. But we were not in the market for charm contest winners. Perez could provide new and vital information about the Cuban intelligence apparatus and the people who worked in it. John and I extracted some interesting details that night before Perez fell asleep, snoring heavily.

I left John with the defector. There were several things to be done before dawn: advise Win of developments, send cables to headquarters, arrange for an early morning flight from the Mexico City airport. I called John at the safe house at 5 A.M. He said Perez was still sleeping. I instructed him to meet me at the airport at 7 A.M. "I'll go ahead," I said, "to be sure the flight is ready, and that our DGI friends from the Cuban embassy aren't planning some Terry and the Pirates foolishness. They might be, if they've noted Perez's absence. You drive him to the airport."

That was a case of bad judgment. I should have returned to the safe house to accompany John and the defector to the airport. One person is not an adequate escort for a man who has just committed emotional suicide.

John and Perez were in the early morning crush of Mexico City traffic when the Cuban changed his mind. He told John that he had decided he could not betray his country and service. John attempted to dissuade him, pointing out that the DGI would never trust him again after his contact with the Americans. But Perez was confused and emotionally distraught, and he insisted that there would be no danger in returning to his own people. He insisted that John stop the car so he could get out, and disappeared into the heavy traffic in such haste that he left behind his large suitcase. John considered physically detaining Perez but decided, correctly, that a possible charge of diplomatic kidnapping could cause a flap of some magnitude.

We learned very soon about subsequent developments from our excellent sources within the Cuban embassy. Perez returned to the embassy and, instead of telling a plausible story to explain his overnight absence, strained the credulity of the DGI by claiming that he had been kidnapped by the CIA, but had managed to escape. The DGI Chief of Center did not buy that fiction. Perez was told he would be returning to Havana on the next flight, two days hence. John, Win, and I discussed Perez's predicament. He was headed for trouble in Havana, and we decided to contact him again to persuade him that was so.

Perez wanted to leave the embassy to buy a new suitcase to replace the one he had lost to his "abductors." He was not allowed to leave, but another DGI man went out to purchase luggage for him, asking that the suitcase be delivered next day to the embassy. That was poor tradecraft, as was the DGI man's failure to observe the CIA surveillance team following him to the store.

In the suitcase destined for Earle Perez Friman, an envelope marked *Instructions* contained a message for Perez signed with the false names John and I had used in meeting him. We warned about the dangers awaiting him in Cuba and assured him that arrangements for his reception and safety would be made at the airport should he decide to bolt before boarding the plane. I don't know that he ever received the note; I suspect the DGI intercepted it, since there was a phalanx of DGI heavies escorting Perez when he arrived at the airport for the Havana flight. And, the Cuban Ambassador was with them, ready to throw his diplomatic weight around should there be any attempt to keep Perez from boarding the flight.

I waited at the entrance of the passenger lounge as Perez and his entourage approached. The faces were all familiar to me, not because I knew the individuals personally but because I remembered them from the photographs in the station mugbook. The Cuban intelligence officers undoubtedly recognized me as well.

Perez may not have known me. Although I stared straight at him as he approached the gate, there was no hint that he remembered me. I drew my finger across my neck, warning Perez of the danger which lurked in Havana. His eyes were wide, pupils dilated. He was in a stupor, obviously having been drugged. One of the DGI officers cursed at me as he passed.

The defector who had come out of the cold and gone back so quickly flew to Cuba. Later he realized how uncertain his future was, and found asylum in a Latin American embassy in Havana. He panicked, and ran away from the embassy, as he had from John. Once again he found himself in the traffic of a large city, this time running through the Almendares tunnel, which connects downtown Havana with the Miramar residential section. Perez died in the tunnel, gunned down by "unidentified" assailants. Cuban newspapers treated his death as a criminal matter.

Earle Perez Friman had consummated the suicide attempt that began when he walked into the American embassy in Mexico City.

In retrospect, I should have been with John in the car taking Perez to the airport in Mexico City. Perhaps two of us could have persuaded him to go on to Miami, rather than to return to a predictable death in Havana. In any event, it was my responsibility, on my watch, and I had botched the operation badly. "Egg on your vest," the Division Chief of Operations told me when he flew to Mexico City to determine what had happened.

My future looked bleak, and Dick Bissell's prediction that I would become a Division Chief seemed unjustified. Promotion and senior assignments are not given to CIA officers with operational egg stains on their vests.

From Washington came word that Colonel J. C. King, approaching mandatory retirement age of sixty years and his health faltering, was stepping down as head of the Western Hemisphere Division after a tenure of a decade. Desmond FitzGerald was to be the new chief.

Working on the Cuban problem in Mexico City kept me occupied as we monitored, and when we could, obstructed Cuban attempts to promote a Latin American revolution with substantive clandestine support to local pro-Castro groups—particularly in Guatemala, Venezuela, Bolivia, Brazil, Colombia, Peru, and Uruguay. Again I participated in amateur theatricals, combining business with pleasure and playing the lead roles in Mexico City productions of *Mr. Roberts* and *Stalag 17*. Part-time histrionics still served as useful cover for meetings with several of my agents, who "volunteered" to work backstage.

It was great fun working again with Abe in Mexico City. His office in the CIA station was distant from mine, and we often met halfway in the hall, each hurrying to see the other. It was as though our minds were working on the same track; we were like two comedians testing a routine as we put our operational schemes together. Much of Abe's propaganda work was in support of Cuban operations, so we worked in tandem against the Cubans.

We also worked together on some dirty tricks.

One of our endeavors was aimed at a "cultural officer" in the Cuban embassy. He was energetic and bright, despised Americans, and had hatched a number of schemes designed to embarrass the United States as well as several Cuban dirty tricks aimed at CIA. While we admired our adversary's guile, some of his operations stung. Abe and I often remarked that it would be useful if we could arrange for his departure from Mexico City, so that we could spend more time getting about our own jobs, rather than reacting defensively to his operations against us.

One morning Abe and I became aware of a personal peccadillo in the private life of our Cuban nemesis at just the same time, and we recognized simultaneously what should be done. We met in the hall, halfway between our offices.

"Antique jewelry!" I shouted.

"Exactly," said Abe, waving his finger on high. "We help him sell it!"

Abe and I learned that our cultural officer had smuggled into Mexico, in the diplomatic pouch, a trove of antique jewelry, purchased at bargain

prices from Cuban upper-class families desperate to sell personal posses-
sions—paintings, gems, stamp collections—in order to have a financial
stake when they succeeded in leaving Cuba. He intended to sell the
jewels in Mexico for his own personal profit. This type of chicanery was
not tolerated by Fidel Castro; those signs I had seen in government
offices were having their effect, and personal dishonesty was ample cause
for immediate dismissal from a government job.

Abe and I requisitioned the services of Enrique, who placed an advertisement for us in a local newspaper. *Bargains in antique jewelry! Fantastic supply. Private collector. For information telephone ...* The number
listed was for the private telephone of the cultural officer at his residence.
We also asked Enrique to phone the Cuban Ambassador, complaining
that the prices being asked by his employee were too high—indeed,
gouging the Mexican public.

The Cuban cultural officer—really a DGI man—received a number
of inquiries about the jewelry he wanted to sell. One of the questions
came from his Ambassador. A week later he was back in Havana. As far
as I know, he never worked overseas again for the Cubans.

After the mail had been delivered one morning, Win Scott came
into my office. He dropped, almost defiantly, a thin volume on my desk.
"I won that competition," he grunted. "Thanks."

When the Station Chief left I thumbed through the book of love
poems, published under a pseudonym. The dust jacket revealed that
the poet, an unknown, had won one of America's most prestigious literary
competitions. I kept my word to Win, and did not reveal that the laureate
was a CIA Station Chief.

A popular notion exists that intelligence officers spend much of their
time bugging other people, listening to their conversations on telephones
and eavesdropping with all manner of hidden microphones and audio
devices. It is done frequently, but not to the extent fiction writers would
have one believe. Telephone taps are used routinely against targets of
specific interest, such as foreign embassies, opposition intelligence officers,
drug traffickers, or terrorists. But the inordinate expense and demands
on case-officer time are such that telephone tap operations are undertaken
on a highly selective basis. Listening to another's telephone conversation,
directly or in collaboration with a local security service, is relatively easy.
Processing the "take"—the tedious review of tapes, the preparation of
transcripts in foreign languages, interpreting and following up on the
hodgepodge of trivia—is expensive and difficult.

Bugging, the concealing of listening devices where confidential conversations might be held, is a fundamental technique in espionage. The

amount of intelligence obtained in this type of technical operation is almost infinitesimal compared with other means of gathering information. Much of the "take" from a surreptitiously placed microphone is useless and often consists more of grunts and groans and belches than anything else. But the tiny percentage of useful intelligence obtained can be vital—such as when the ambassador of a Communist country in, say, Mexico returns to his post and briefs his staff on the latest political development at home in a room infested with CIA bugs.

Ian Fleming's fictional James Bond had success with ingenious, tiny microphones, but the real-life intelligence officer has to work harder. That apocryphal olive which transmits from a martini just doesn't exist, or, if it does, won't work. A bugging job requires hours of access to a room, or an object which will be in the room, in order to install and mask microphones, batteries, and electrical connections, if effective coverage over a worthwhile period is to be expected. There are some devices which can be slapped under a desk or a chair bottom, but despite the most modern glues they tend to drop off with a great clatter at inauspicious times. In most cases intelligence officers abandon plans to use hidden microphones and take the more reliable course of recruiting an agent who can hear and relay his reports without distractive chit-chat and other audibles.

The Soviets love bugs and place them everywhere. A Western traveler to Moscow must assume his hotel room is auditory. Western diplomats in the Soviet Union and the Bloc must live with the certainty that their offices are bugged (as the Great Seal of the United States was in the American Ambassador's office in Moscow) as well as their private quarters—diplomatic couples simply have to learn to accept that a KGB voyeur, or better said *écouteur*, somewhere down the street is listening to their most intimate family episodes. The cleverest audio device—of those known to the public—was found not many years ago in the rubber heel of an American diplomat's shoe in Poland. His Polish maid, an agent of the local intelligence service, checked and, if required, changed the tiny battery each morning she shined the American's shoes.

Finally, audio operations are fraught with the possibility that, when a device is discovered, the operation will be turned against its master and used to feed spurious, confusing information to those who own it. It hardly seems worthwhile sometimes. The intelligence services of the world might do well to sign a secret covenant—an Audio Device Limitations Agreement—which would save everyone time and money. But until that is achieved, all major powers are concerned enough that teams of specialists travel about the world sniffing out hostile bugs, and most embassies are subjected to the constant hum of technical equipment attempting to neutralize hidden michrophones or, better yet, to locate them in hidden nooks and crannies. Some embassies even have special enclaves or rooms especially protected against electronic eavesdropping so that diplomats will have a haven where they can chat safely.

It is difficult to write about the esoteric techniques of audio operations without violating security rules, especially those concerning methods. But let me relate one story that happened in Mexico, fuzzing and fictionalizing a bit.

John and I suddenly found ourselves with the opportunity to have access for a few hours to an armchair which we knew was to be delivered to a Communist embassy. It was a fine, expensive piece of furniture and we decided to bug the chair on the long-shot chance such a luxurious item would be for the Ambassador's personal use. Should it go into his office the intelligence take might be useful, and we could expect a few redemption points from that Division Chief of Operations—and we needed some credit because of the residue of egg still on our vests after the bungled Earle Perez Friman defection case.

The armchair was large enough that we were able to insert in its interior not only a microphone, but a battery of sufficient power to guarantee an operating life of several months. John and I were up all night doing the carpenter work. The next morning we returned the chair, through an agent cut-out, to the firm which was to deliver it to the embassy. We waited in the listening post—there must be a secure receiving station near any listening device—when the armchair was scheduled to enter the embassy. After the long night's work converting the armchair into a broadcasting station we were understandably tense with anticipation. Would the chair be placed in the Ambassador's office? Or would it be shunted off to some reception room where we would hear nothing more stimulating than cocktail party chatter? In the Ambassador's office we could expect an immediate payoff, since we knew from other sources that on that very morning the Ambassador had scheduled a conference with the chief of the local Communist Party, recently returned from his capital; his report might contain valuable intelligence information.

From our observation post we saw the truck arrive to deliver the armchair, the upholstery of which we had so tenderly altered the night before. John switched on the microphone by remote control. (Like a flashlight, a hidden microphone powered by a battery will not last long if continually in operation. Some sort of thrifty on-and-off switch is as useful in a bug as in a flashlight.)

We heard the grunts and groans of the delivery men as they hoisted the heavy armchair from their truck and up the stairs into the front hall of the embassy.

Then a voice: "Ah, yes. Please take it into the Ambassador's office."

Further movement. Then a new authoritarian voice, dashing our hopes: "No, no. That chair is not for my office. Put it in the library."

Our scheme had failed, our work was for naught. The Ambassador had spurned our chair. Would the microphone relay nothing but the whisk of pages being turned as someone read Socialist tomes in the embassy library?

Despondent, we flipped off the switch and prepared to go home for some sleep. Just then a cab arrived in front of the embassy: it was the leader of the local Communist Party, calling on the Ambassador, as our agent said he would. John switched the microphone into operation again. Soon there were sounds. Feet scuffling. A pause. Then, the voice of the Ambassador's secretary, "Please make yourself comfortable. The Ambassador will be with you in a moment."

Five minutes of nothing as the visitor waited, alone, in the library. The sound of pages being turned. A creak of springs as the visitor shifted his weight in the chair. Quiet.

Then there was a cautious little ziplike sound.

John chuckled. Didn't seem very funny to me. We had stayed up all night to hear flatulence.

But then the visitor really ripped one off—a solid, reverberating proletarian fart. Then a relieved sigh of satisfaction.

John roared with laughter; he thought it was hysterical. I thought he was acting like an idiot. Altogether, the technical equipment and our time had probably cost the United States taxpayer hundreds of dollars. This hardly seemed a suitable reward.

"Will you please stop laughing?" I asked John.

"Sorry," John said, as he continued to chortle.

Soon, we heard the sound of approaching footsteps. Greetings, in a familiar voice—the Ambassador had entered the room. He added: "No, don't get up. We'll talk in here. I'm afraid the Americans might have my office bugged, so I hold all my really important meetings here in the library."

John cast his eyes heavenward, in appreciation. I reached over and shook his hand.

We listened to the Ambassador that morning. And for many, many mornings after. But only, of course, to his really important conversations.

On a consultation trip to Washington I visited the new CIA headquarters at Langley, Virginia, for the first time. Agency personnel were delighted with the fruition of Allen Dulles's dream, especially the vast parking areas surrounding the functional building. All Washington bureaucrats yearn for a parking space and they are hard to come by in downtown Washington. Veteran CIA officers quip that, should an

Agency officer be captured and interrogated by hostile forces, he is authorized to answer only three questions for the enemy; he may give his name, grade, and parking space number.

John McCone, after a most successful tenure as Director of Central Intelligence, was getting ready to leave government service. I was told that he missed the close relationship he had with John Kennedy and was uncomfortable with Lyndon Johnson, quite aside from the fact that the new President was not as accessible as McCone felt he should be. So he was preparing to resign in early 1965 and return to his business in California. Dick Helms moved up to the number-two job—DDCI—and most CIA people fervently hoped Johnson would appoint him the new DCI. Des FitzGerald, after only a year as chief of the Western Hemisphere Division, took over from Helms as the DDP, chief of the operations side of the Agency.

A young officer drove me to the airport upon the conclusion of my business at Langley. On the way he told me he would soon be assigned to the Cuban operations group in the Western Hemisphere Division. I said that should be a good assignment where he could expect action.

"Yes," he said. "I understand the Kennedy's told CIA, to put it in their words, to get off its ass and do something about getting rid of Castro. And that the marching orders haven't changed much under Johnson."

"We tried that at the Bay of Pigs," I reminded him. "And Kennedy promised Khrushchev we would stay out of Cuba."

"I know," responded the young officer. "But we're still supposed to do anything we can short of invasion."

After a few minutes there was another, disturbing question. "Do you think we're trying to assassinate Fidel Castro?"

"I certainly do not," I answered. "Why do you ask?"

"Just some rumors I've heard," he said. "I wouldn't want to be involved in anything like that." Then, "If we were would you know about it?"

"Not necessarily," I said. "But that would be dumb. It couldn't change anything in Cuba, except maybe to put power in the hands of people even more pro-Soviet and less predictable than Fidel."

"Yeah." The young officer shrugged. "Probably just rumors."

The conversation was unsettling. After returning to Mexico I didn't think of it again until I heard a vignette concerning Des FitzGerald from a traveler. It involved a party in Chevy Chase, a Washington suburb, a short time before FitzGerald became the DDP. Several Agency employees were there as well as people from other agencies and outside government; about twenty guests in all. The host had brought in a palmist to read the guests' past and future. Of all the guests only Des FitzGerald refused to extend his palm to be read.

That was strange, I thought when hearing of the incident. Of all the people I had met in the CIA the ebullient and fun-loving Fitz-Gerald was at the top of the list of those most likely, under such circumstances, to go along with the crowd.*

The most crucial development during my four-year assignment in Mexico City occurred slightly past midtour, in the fall of 1963. Just another blip on the station's radar screen. It did not seem important when we first noticed it.

The slight, sallow man boarded a bus in Laredo, Texas. He arrived the next morning in Mexico City, after the grueling twenty-hour trip, and registered at a cheap hotel—less than $2.00 a day—not far from the bus station. He was one of the many faceless tourists who visit Mexico from the United States; on any given day there may be five thousand of them in Mexico City. Most visit the Aztec ruins, the art galleries, the marvelous anthropological museum, and frequently the capital's restaurants and nightclubs. The CIA has neither the inclination nor the time to observe them.

A few American tourists stop by foreign embassies. At some, especially the Soviet and Cuban embassies, these travelers appear as blips on the CIA radar screen. This particular tourist, tired as he must have been after the all-night bus ride, immediately began to contact the Cuban and Soviet missions.

None of the CIA personnel in Mexico City knew anything about Lee Harvey Oswald; that he had previously lived in the Soviet Union and married a Russian wife. He was just another blip. How much attention should be paid to him?

"Craig," the case officer in charge of Soviet operations, was the first to become aware of Oswald on the basis of the latter's contact with the Soviet embassy. The circumstances were such—Oswald wished to return to the Soviet Union via Cuba—that a cable to headquarters asking for a Washington file check on Oswald was in order. Craig procrastinated as he was busy with other things. One of his assistants prodded Craig several times; his aide was his own wife, working part-time for the station because of her extensive knowledge of Russian and Soviet matters, garnered when she was a CIA staff officer prior to their marriage. Finally Craig's wife typed out the cable herself, dropping it

* When the Senate Church Committee released its report on assassination plots against foreign leaders in 1975, it revealed that on the day President Kennedy was killed in Dallas FitzGerald had offered a poison-pen device to a CIA agent identified as AM/LASH. This was inaccurate, as FitzGerald was not in Paris on November 22, 1973, but he had met the agent in the French capital previously to encourage him to get rid of Fidel Castro.

on her husband's desk for his review before it went to Win Scott for release. Who, the cable asked Washington, is Lee Henry Oswald?

It was seven weeks later, early afternoon on the twenty-second of November 1963, that I was called from my desk by a secretary who said that someone from the defense attaché's office wanted to speak to the CIA duty officer. I went out to see the sergeant who waited at the Dutch door.

"My wife just telephoned to say she heard on the radio that President Kennedy has been shot in Dallas. Have you people heard anything about it?"

We had not. As CIA officers picked up the story during the lunch hour—the news swept through Mexico City—they returned to the station. We gathered in Win's office to listen to the radio and monitor television reports on the tragedy.

The death of the president was finally confirmed, and, then came the news that the assassin had been apprehended: Lee Harvey Oswald.

"That's the man we sent the cable about," Win said quietly, and called his secretary. From memory he gave her several file numbers, and she went off to fetch them.*

For the next several weeks the station was occupied with reviewing all available intelligence concerning Oswald's visit to Mexico City and the events in the Cuban and Soviet embassies then and afterward. There were, and still are, some missing pieces in the puzzle, but the final accumulation and interpretation provided a reasonably clear picture. Some knowledge was gained while Oswald was in Mexico, some after he left, and even more after Kennedy's death gave the matter top priority among our activities. The tedious collection and storage of trivia paid off.

In the United States there seems to be a compulsive tendency to suspect conspiracy in the face of facts not easily explained. As some of the details of the CIA coverage of Oswald in Mexico have been, at least until recently, confidential, the swarm of skeptics who have found a lucrative profession in conning lecture audiences and writing ludicrous books with bizarre explanations of conspiracy have, of course, combined the true with the false in coming up with conspiracy theories on the "Mexico City connection" of Oswald. Some of these *may* seem plausible. In fact, I know of no evidence to suggest that Oswald acted as an agent for the Cubans or Russians, that he was a CIA agent, or that any aspect

---

* Author Tad Szulc, in his book about Howard Hunt, *Compulsive Spy*, writes that Hunt was the Acting Chief of Station in Mexico City when Lee Harvey Oswald visited there. He refers to this as "an extraordinary coincidence." In fact, Hunt was not even in Mexico, but Win Scott was, and in charge. He retired in Mexico and lived there until his death from a heart attack.

of his Mexico City trip was any more ominous than reported by the Warren Commission.

Some of those who do so well financially lecturing before college groups on this subject claim that a "mystery man" was in Mexico City, pretending to be Lee Harvey Oswald. They are right in that there was a mysterious person, with the physical appearance of an American, who was in Mexico City and in contact with the Soviet embassy at the same time Oswald was there.

In writing that first cable from Mexico City about Oswald, Craig's wife described Lee "Henry" Oswald as "approximately 35 years old, with an athletic build, about six feet tall, with a receding hairline." She had put together two pieces of a jigsaw puzzle which appeared compatible but which did not, in fact, fit together. We had learned of a contact Oswald made with the Soviet embassy, asking the Russians if they had any news on his application to return to the Soviet Union. Craig's wife, incorrectly, surmised that the contact was made by another person, photographed as an individual of interest because he had frequented the Soviet embassy. She was describing the mysterious stranger and not, as found later, the person making the contact. She had put one (Oswald, seeking a visa from the Soviets) and one (an unknown visitor to the Russian embassy) together and come up with an incorrect two: the assumption that the two men were the same. If that second person, the hefty fellow with an athletic build, would present himself today, like a Rip Van Winkle, it would be useful to all of us. Meantime he remains a mystery figure, who could be, from his appearance, an American—or could be a Soviet or Nordic seaman from any ship docked in a Mexican port.

Why did that first cable identify Lee "Henry" Oswald? Because Craig's wife did not *read* about Oswald, but *heard* about him. It was her phonetic observation. In any event, it became apparent to the CIA before the assassination of Kennedy that a mistake had been made: a message from CIA in Washington to the U.S. Navy requested photographs of the real Lee Harvey Oswald "to determine if the Lee Oswald in Mexico City and subject are the same individual."

Another speculative assertion of the conspiracy buffs was that Oswald made a secret air flight to Havana. There is not a single piece of evidence to support this allegation, and much to prove it untrue.

Several skeptics have said Oswald returned with several thousand dollars from Mexico. I think I know where that came from.

After President Kennedy was assassinated there was a walk-in to the American embassy in Mexico City. He was a young Nicaraguan, who said that he had been inside the Cuban embassy when Oswald visited there, and that he saw a red-haired black pay Oswald $6,500 in American money, an advance payment presumably for his role as the hired gun in killing Kennedy. I was surprised when, in response to a cable we sent to Managua, capital of Nicaragua, our station said that the Nicaraguan intelligence service had identified the walk-in as a prominent Nicaraguan Communist. It seemed strange as we had no information on the man in our 3-by-5 cards. John and I were assigned to interrogate him. It soon was apparent that he was lying, and not very well. A lie-detector test—a specialist was flown down from Washington—soon confirmed that he was a fabricator. The Mexican government talked seriously with him. He finally claimed, after four days, that he had made up the story because he hated Fidel Castro and hoped that his story would provoke the United States into taking action against Castro. (I have a theory, almost a conviction, that in fact this man was dispatched to Mexico City by the Somoza brothers, the authoritarian but pro-American rulers of Nicaragua, in what they considered a covert action to influence the American government to move against Cuba. If so, it was a nice try, but a transparent operation.)*

Finally, there has been much talk of photographs taken of Oswald by the CIA in Mexico City. There were none. A capability for such photographic coverage existed, but it was not a twenty-four-hour-a-day, Saturday and Sunday capability. John and I spent several days studying literally hundreds of photographs available to the CIA before and during Oswald's trip to Mexico City. He did not appear in any of them.

The facts about Oswald's Mexico City visit, obvious to me and anyone who knew all the details, were simple. Oswald tried to return to the Soviet Union by way of Cuba. The Cubans and the Soviets rebuffed him. They thought he was a kook. Oswald went back to Dallas, alone, on another bus.

I know a great deal about Oswald's stay in Mexico, much of it learned by questioning agents, reviewing the record, and coming to a conclusion based on many disparate items of information. While I certainly can't be sure Oswald was not involved in some sort of conspiracy back in Dallas, I am confident that he was not recruited in Mexico City by the Soviets or the Cubans to assassinate Jack Kennedy.**

* The Warren Commission Report describes this man as "a young Latin American secret agent."

** It was revealed in 1975 that Oswald wrote a letter to the FBI in Dallas threatening to blow up the Dallas police station. This was several days before the assassination. Foreign intelligence services do not have their assassins bring such attention upon themselves just before the hit. Also, in 1975, a poll showed that 85 percent of the American people believed that Oswald was somehow a part of a conspiracy in Dallas. I am one of the 15 percent which believes that he acted alone, and that the Warren Commission was right. Despite the motivation Fidel Castro might have had after learning of plots against his life, I am convinced he did not select Oswald as an instrument in an attempt against Kennedy. To date there is no

The CIA information about the nondescript visitor to Mexico City was passed to a number of other United States government agencies—before the assassination. With a little luck, it might have reached the Secret Service, and it might have prevented the assassination of Jack Kennedy.

Good news from Langley in February 1965. I had been promoted to GS-15, the highest of the middle-grade ranks of CIA officers.

We had kidded Wally and his wife when he was assigned as DCOS in Santo Domingo, an unimportant, backwater post. It did not seem so amusing when, in March 1965, a cable arrived advising me that I was to have my first Chief of Station assignment—COS, Santo Domingo. The stimulating four years in Mexico were at an end. I was to report to Washington at once, to attend a two-week course of training for first-time Chiefs of Station.

The Dominican Republic? While I was pleased to be appointed a COS and to have a chance to move up the management ladder, I was distressed at the prospect of a tour on the Caribbean island. Santo Domingo, I feared, would be a dull post.

---

evidence that the Cuban dictator tried to kill the American president. In 1976 Senator Richard Schweiker, who has become an assassination buff, was primarily responsible for a report which raised all sorts of doubts about the Kennedy assassination but no evidence. I testified in executive session before Senator Schweiker and his staff about the circumstances of Oswald's visit to Mexico City and the investigation by me and "John" following the assassination. I was surprised and disappointed when I read the published Senate report, which I felt was not completely objective. Certainly it did not make the Warren Commission Report "collapse like a house of cards" as Senator Schweiker had predicted it would.

6

THE DOMINICAN
REPUBLIC 1965-1967

Believing that gunboat diplomacy was a thing of the past in Latin America, I was surprised in late April of 1965 when United States Marines landed on the outskirts of Santo Domingo to protect and evacuate the American citizens gathered at the Hotel Embajador. That trauma—Marines who had occupied the country in 1906 and 1916 were once again on Dominican soil—was enough of a shock. Now I was stunned to hear Lyndon Johnson announcing that the army's 82nd Airborne Division would join the Marines.

The President of the United States, I told myself, has lost his mind. What would the reaction be throughout Latin America when the headlines erupted the next day? How could American prestige ever be recovered in the hemisphere? But Lyndon Johnson saw the Dominican Republic and the revolt that broke out there in late April of 1965 as a part of a larger problem which included a Communist Cuba ninety miles from Florida and an escalating American involvement in Southeast Asia.

I was in Washington to attend the training course for first-time Chiefs of Station preparatory to transferring to Santo Domingo to relieve our Chief who had a serious medical problem with a bad back. Desmond FitzGerald had chosen me because he foresaw a situation where a political action program in support of the shaky incumbent regime might be needed.

The history of the Dominican Republic was dreary. Achieving independence from Spain in 1844, things went so poorly for the larger half of the island of Hispaniola (Haiti shares it) that the Dominicans went back to Madrid, sombrero in hand, pleading to be readmitted to the Spanish empire. The Spanish declined. Then the Dominicans sought to become one of the United States—a proposal that the island be annexed was approved by the Dominicans, but the United States Senate vetoed the move by the narrowest of votes; otherwise the Dominican Republic might be part of the United States today. After being spurned by the mother country and the Colossus of the North, numerous governments in Santo Domingo expired in corruption and lethargy—from 1844 to 1930 there were forty-three presidents and fifty-six revolutions! Then an officer of the Dominican National Guard, Rafael Leonidas Trujillo, took over. He became one of the worst tyrants in the history of Latin America, where there has been a long succession of some pretty seamy and despicable types.

It was well known to us that Trujillo, over a period of thirty years, disposed of thousands of political enemies by tossing them into an inlet near Santo Domingo—known as "the swimming pool"—where they were devoured by sharks. Other enemies Trujillo hung from meathooks in a private cold storage vault, leaving them hanging until dead, a process which sometimes took several days. Trujillo's despotism ended only with his assassination by a dozen Dominicans. Two of them, Antonio Imbert and Luís Amiama Tío survive; both are considered national heroes by a grateful Dominican people.

Juan Bosch, a quixotic poet and politician, won the first election in thirty-eight years in 1962. His purposes were noble, but he was a hopeless failure as a president and administrator. Having become a professional exile during the last twenty-one years of Trujillo's reign, Bosch was an inept manager and his government, even with strong United States support, came apart at the seams. In a coup in 1963 the military dumped Bosch and a three-man junta, eventually civilian, tried to run things. Its leader was Donald Reid, an affable and attractive Austin Motors distributor, who was Dominican-born despite his English name and heritage. He was neither effective nor popular. Since no better alternative to him was apparent, it was United States policy to support him and to try to keep the country on a steady course. (After the fall of Trujillo, John Kennedy had sponsored a program to make the Dominican Republic "the showcase of the Caribbean" to counter the attraction of Castro's nearby Cuba, already alluring in the eyes of many Latin Americans. Perhaps it was this intense concern with the threat from Cuba which led President Kennedy to make the unfortunate decision to support the Eisenhower and CIA proposal to launch the Bay of Pigs.)

But the Dominican Republic under Donny Reid was hardly a showcase. The economy was in a shambles, integrity in public servants was almost unknown, highways were impossibly potholed, downtown Santo

Domingo was scabrous, and there was little faith in the current regime's competence or intentions.

"I selected you as COS, Santo Domingo," Des told me, "because the country is sick, Reid is ailing politically, and we need a doctor."

Each day after the training course—different from others I had attended, as it concentrated on management rather than operations—I read files on the Dominican Republic and talked with officers at Langley who had served in Santo Domingo.

On a Friday afternoon I stopped by FitzGerald's office on my way out.

"I've been reading files," I told him. "I'm afraid you don't need a doctor in Santo Domingo. You need an undertaker."

Des gave me a pixie smile and shrugged.

On Sunday I left the apartment in Southwest Washington I was using while the CIA tenant was on temporary duty abroad. It was a lovely April morning; I bought a Washington *Post* and prepared to relax on a park bench.

The front-page headline read: US TO INCREASE VIET STRENGTH BY 5000 IN MONTH. There was another story:

DOMINICAN COUP BALKED

REBELS GIVEN ULTIMATUM

SANTO DOMINGO. April 24 (AP). Supporters of exiled former President Juan P. Bosch rebelled today against the ruling civilian junta of the Dominican Republic, which is headed by Donald Reid Cabral.

By nightfall the military-backed regime declared that the coup had collapsed. But Reid said in a nation-wide television address that two military bases were still in revolt and he had given them until 5 a.m. (EST) to surrender.

I was concerned about my future post and decided to drop in at Langley. Coups which have collapsed except for two military bases had frequently proven not to have collapsed at all. I recalled several revolts in Latin America, apparently abortive, which eventually succeeded simply because the rebels controlled a single radio station.

The parking lots at CIA headquarters were empty except for the section set aside for communicators and Sunday intelligence watch staff plus a number of cars in the area reserved for Western Hemisphere Division personnel. I went into the building, not to emerge, literally, for three and a half weeks. Once inside I learned that Dominicans were killing each other in the streets of Santo Domingo.

Ever since the Dominican Crisis, CIA headquarters has maintained a twenty-four-hour operations center to handle crisis situations whenever they occur around the world. In 1965 an area division blessed with its own crisis would establish a separate operations center or "war room" where the headquarters team responsible would assemble in order to monitor developments away from the routine of everyday operations. In this case the windowless center was dubbed "The Pit" on the first day.

The Pit was frenetic. We stumbled over loops of electric wire on the floor as technicians installed half a dozen teletype machines. One for the cables from the station; others for information copies of Department of State traffic and messages from the military attachés. Another from FBIS (the Foreign Broadcast Information Service, an overt radio monitoring activity administered by CIA) was spewing out worldwide radio and press comments. There were other machines, some disgorging reams of sensitive and esoteric information. Telephones of various colors were being installed. The room was relatively small and there were too many people trying to be helpful but often managing to be in the way.

Lyndon Johnson's aides at the White House telephoned The Pit a dozen times the first day. What was happening? Were the wire service dispatches accurate? Was there really fighting in downtown Santo Domingo?

President Johnson, having decided on what in Caribbean terms was a massive military intervention, wanted to know what was happening. His interest never waned throughout the crisis and continued through the next year. Johnson always wanted to know *now*.

I was leaning over one of the teletypes, making notes on the station's cables as they rolled in. Someone touched me on the shoulder. A second time, as I was absorbed in the reports.

It was Dick Helms, DDCI, Deputy Director of CIA and our number-two man. We had all been hoping that he would become Director after John McCone's resignation, but that was not to be for another two years.

Helms said, "Dave, meet our new Director. Admiral, Mr. Phillips will soon be our chief in Santo Domingo."

Admiral Raborn grunted. Then he stalked about the hectic room, fascinated by the clattering machines and the paraphernalia of an intelligence agency operations center. Then he came back.

"What's going on in the countryside?"

"Quiet," I told him.

Raborn asked, "Do you have people out there?"

"One officer in the consulate in Santiago." Santiago de los Caballeros is the Dominican Republic's second largest city. "But we know the boondocks are quiet. Fighting is confined to one section of the capital."

"If you don't have people how can you be sure?"

I said, "Because we have liaison contacts, even some agents at the receiving end of the Dominican government communications in Santo Domingo. We know about developments reported from the interior as soon as the government does." I elaborated briefly on other methods of a technical nature available to us which indicated the state of countryside affairs.

Raborn snorted, obviously skeptical. He had been on the job about fourteen hours. In charge of the navy's Polaris missile development program, he had by all accounts done a remarkable job in lobbying in Congress to muster support for the program. It was this achievement which prompted Lyndon Johnson to appoint him as our Director. He knew little about the intelligence business and apparently nothing about foreign affairs. Politically, he was naïve. But he did know that he was new on the job and that the Dominican crisis was on the front burner at CIA and in the Oval Office on Pennsylvania Avenue.

"Send the reports to my office the minute they come in," the Admiral instructed.

"I'll tube them," I said. I explained briefly the pneumatic system which rocketed documents from one office to another throughout the building.

Raborn fixed me with a two-feet-firmly-on-the-bridge stare. He was short, stocky. His face was veined with red lines across a white skin and his eyes were crowed from years of squinting across sun-glazed seas. Helms stood behind him, relaxed, smiling, saying nothing. I wondered what Helms's impression was of the man who had just been appointed to the job he must have coveted for years. Across the room Des Fitz-Gerald was on the phone to the White House situation room, but his eyes were on the Admiral.

"Don't tube the reports," Raborn barked. "Send people." He strode out, stepping over and around the spirals of electrical wire without looking at his feet.

Now blood was staining the twisted streets of Santo Domingo. Department dispatches from our embassy recounted tales of violence. Station reports indicated that the Communists, who had absolutely nothing to do with the revolt originally, were beginning to assume a disquieting degree of control. The coup had been sparked by a small group of Dominican army officers attempting to arrest another group of officers; the latter resisted and another palace coup was in motion, a routine affair which normally would not have been unusual in Santo Domingo and would hardly have been noticed abroad. But suddenly Dominicans trained in Havana, Moscow, and Peking were passing out arms to the young people in downtown Santo Domingo. An obscure lieutenant colonel, Francisco Caamaño, soon emerged as the military leader of the revolt. Not a Marxist, he was brave and not unduly clever; soon he began to welcome the counsel of hard-core Marxists from various groups.

There was a shooting incident at the Embajador Hotel where American citizens had congregated that prompted President Johnson to send in the first Marines. Once he did that his appetite for information was insatiable.

We started putting out situation reports every hour, twenty-four hours a day. These were compiled in The Pit, everything the teletypes were spewing out from State, Defense, and our station. For the first time CIA officers from DDI (Directorate of Intelligence, the analysis group who were overt employees) worked directly with officers of the clandestine DDP. It was like a busy newsroom. I sat at a desk with a DDI officer across from me and together we prepared the hourly situation reports which were flashed to the White House, State, Defense, USIA, and a half a dozen other agencies. The DDI officers rotated each eight hours. I stayed for a twenty- to twenty-two-hour stretch, bunking down briefly on a cot in the office of the medical staff and occasionally showering in a boxlike stall in the makeshift gymnasium in the bowels of the building. A week passed. Two. Three. I didn't leave the building.

Apparently my assurances to Admiral Raborn that we knew what was going on in the Dominican countryside were not satisfactory. He instructed us to establish bases throughout the rural areas to augment our base in Santiago. It was a ridiculous order. Our people in Santo Domingo hadn't slept in days, certainly none could be spared to wander through the interior. I called Des and told him he had to convince Raborn that establishing bases would be a fruitless and expensive endeavor.

"The Admiral is new," Des said. In CIA our chief has always been known as the Director, except for Raborn, always the Admiral. "He feels the pressure from the White House, and he wants to be able to say to Johnson that his people are reporting from the interior. Go ahead."

That was a Sunday, one week after the coup. Between ten and eleven that morning I telephoned Western Hemisphere officers whom I knew to have fluent Spanish. The message was brief. "A plane is leaving for the D.R. this afternoon. Be at Andrews Air Force Base at fifteen thirty. Bring one small suitcase, light clothes and, if you have one, a pistol."

Not one of the nine officers asked questions; all were at Andrews on time and ready.

The Office of Communications made similar calls to communicators. That afternoon our operations officers and the communicators left for the D.R. Within hours after landing, teams of one operations officer and

a radio operator were fanning out throughout the Dominican countryside. The first message we received was from COO, Dajabón (Chief
of Outpost, Dajabón, a hamlet on the Haitian-Dominican border). The
cable read: THE MOSQUITOES ARE KILLING US. During subsequent weeks we
never received a message of import from any of these bases, but the
Admiral was content with the negative situation reports.

By now the death toll in downtown Santo Domingo was staggering.
We had one report of a mass burial of 350. The International Red Cross
estimated that perhaps 3,000 died eventually.

Lyndon Johnson continued to demand more information. Our station, less than a dozen people including secretaries and communicators
before the revolt, was now approaching half a hundred with nine bases
and constantly increasing temporary personnel. There were eighty-two
military intelligence officers—not CIA—and staff people billeted next
door to the embassy. Nonetheless, Johnson ordered the FBI into Santo
Domingo. Twenty-four Spanish-speaking agents from FBI field offices
in the United States and abroad flew into a country where they had not
operated since 1947 and were instructed to recruit agents and begin
turning out intelligence reports. They didn't even have 3-by-5 file cards,
a basic tool of an intelligence organization, or more than cursory knowledge of the local situation.

There has been much conjecture on Johnson's rationale for sending
the FBI into the Dominican Republic. At Langley we decided that he
wanted to be able to explain to Congress and the American public, in the
event of a fiasco, that it had occurred despite the fact that he had committed his "first team"—not only the CIA, State, and U.S. military, but
the then highly respected FBI as well.

Only CIA was able to provide intelligence from the rebel zone.
Despite the chaos the local telephone system seldom failed during the
crisis. Our agents were reporting regularly by calling a sterile number
and double-talking their information. One agent in particular provided
significant and extremely useful information. He had been recruited a
few months ago by Wally, the young scholar I first knew in Chile and
later worked with in Mexico, after the two of them had developed a
friendship following a contrived encounter in a Santo Domingo bookstore.

This agent telephoned Wally late one night. He was desperate. He
and fellow rebel leaders had been listening to a broadcast of the Voice
of America describing events in Santo Domingo. There was a report on
a meeting of a dozen or so persons, all Communist activists, and VOA
had broadcast a verbatim account of the intelligence the agent had given
Wally shortly before. But one name was missing from the account—the

agent's. He told Wally that he would be suspect because of the omission. Do *something*, he pleaded, to be sure that VOA identified him too, as a Marxist rebel. Wally flashed a cable to Washington.

I checked quickly. Our intelligence reports were being distributed to USIA as well as other agencies for the information of the top officials there. Not, of course, to be broadcast on VOA. By some incredible snafu the report in question had gone to the VOA newsroom. The editor on duty at midnight had aired our secret intelligence report to a Latin American audience in twenty countries. Among avid listeners were the rebels in downtown Santo Domingo, who depended on VOA for up-to-date news.

It was four in the morning. I thought of calling Des or Dick Helms, but decided that would be a waste of valuable time. Instead I telephoned the home of Carl Rowan, then Director of USIA.

I doubt that Rowan, a longtime newspaperman, often receives telephone calls at four in the morning from an unknown voice which wakes him with: "My name is Phillips, from CIA. By mistake VOA has just broadcast one of our secret reports from Santo Domingo. Our agent is literally in danger of losing his life if we don't correct the situation on your six a.m. broadcast."

There was a long pause. Then Rowan said, "The odds have to be that you are some kind of nut, yet somehow I believe you. Give me ten minutes, then call this number and tell them what you want."

I spoke to a puzzled news director ten minutes later. He said, "I'm damned if I know what's going on, but our Director just told me to jump when someone named Phillips called. How high?"

I dictated a new, slightly embroidered report to the VOA night shift man. It concerned the same people mentioned in the original broadcast—plus the name of our agent as one of the conspiring group. This was broadcast at six A.M.

Shortly thereafter Wally sent an immediate message to The Pit from Santo Domingo. "The agent and his friends heard the broadcast. All have been speculating on who the traitor might be. Our man, because he was named along with the others this time, has been able to brazen it out. He sends his thanks."

Often, these many years later, I watch Carl Rowan on the Martin Agronsky show. I've never met him, but I recall that early morning call and his unbureaucratic acceptance of what must have been a strange request, and I, too, say "thanks" to Rowan.

I lived and worked in The Pit. Sandwiches from a machine or an occasional hot meal someone would bring on a paper plate; there never seemed to be time to eat in the CIA cafeteria. Day and night was one in the windowless room.

In Santo Domingo the fighting continued. The rebels controlled Radio Santo Domingo, the powerful government station established by Trujillo. The propaganda from the rebel enclave was potent and increasingly Marxist as the Caamaño spokesmen called for popular support; Radio Havana contributed short-wave exhortations. Ambassador Tapley Bennett sent in disturbing cables describing bearded agitators shouting Communist slogans. An American citizen, sympathetic to the rebels, renounced his citizenship in an emotional harangue (some months later he sheepishly approached the embassy and asked how he could regain citizenship; he was told that he had never lost it, not having the right to resign from being an American so informally).

The country was now a Caribbean Gaul, divided into three parts. In the old section of Santo Domingo the rebels—now known as the Constitutionalists—ran their own government and paramilitary forces, naming their own civilian President and confirming Caamaño as leader of the military. The newer section, largely consisting of upper- and middle-class homes and foreign embassies, was an international zone, policed by U.S. forces and, later, the Brazilian, Costa Rican, Nicaraguan, and Paraguayan troops which arrived as members of the OAS contingent. The interior of the country was controlled by the right-wing Dominican military, with the power resting in the commander of the tank corps, General Elías Wessin y Wessin, a hard-rock conservative with an intense hatred of Communists. Wessin was of Lebanese extraction; he was both respected and feared by Dominicans who had observed him in recent years. He had become a potent political force; a simple instruction to his tank commanders could unseat a president. One public figure had drifted apart from the ruling military in recent years: General "Tony" Imbert, one of the two surviving assassins of Trujillo and now a national hero. In a remarkably casual manner he became President of the "Loyalist" Government of Reconstruction when former Ambassador John Barlow Martin, visiting Santo Domingo after the coup, requested that he take over from Donny Reid and the junta. One version has it that Martin asked Imbert, "Tony, will you be President if I ask you?" And Imbert replied, "Yeah."

The radio and television broadcasts continued, exhorting the populace to attack the foreign troops and the new Imbert-led government. An agent who had worked for me in South America—I'll call him Pedro—was in Santo Domingo at the time of the revolt. Before returning to his country he flew to Washington, contacting a mutual friend to find me. Pedro said it was an emergency and that he must talk to me. I couldn't leave The Pit, but had the number of a sterile phone at Langley passed to Pedro. (A sterile telephone is one which cannot be located even by checking with the telephone company; a secure phone is the same, but is safer in that a conversation cannot be intercepted, as it can be on a sterile line.) When Pedro called he told me, "The difference in Santo Domingo lies in that radio station. If the rebels continue their propaganda they will take over the entire country. The radio must be silenced! I tell you this because I know your people can do it. Can you deliver that message to your Dominican office?"

I told Pedro I could pass the message, but that I saw little prospect of silencing a radio station in the sanctity of the rebel zone. Finally, in order to assuage Pedro and to be able to get back to work, I muttered something about doing the best I could.

One hour later the Dominican air force bombed the radio station. The reverberations shattered the delicate crystals of the radio and television transmitters and the rebel propaganda capability was effectively silenced for the duration. Neither CIA nor the U.S. government had anything to do with this; indeed, the bombing and strafing of the station was a surprise to all of us. But Pedro will never believe that.

The wire services carried the story immediately. My sterile phone rang. It was Pedro. "*Increíble!*" he exclaimed. He was speaking in Spanish, and the word is perfect with its rolling "r" to express amazement and admiration. "I always knew CIA was good. But so quickly! So thoroughly! My congratulations!" I've seen Pedro several times since, and he is still convinced that I arranged—within an hour—for Radio Santo Domingo to be bombed.

The Pit became less hectic. During the day there was bustle and activity, with Raborn, Helms, and FitzGerald visiting several times a day to be briefed on the situation in Santo Domingo. Staffers from the White House continued to call, insisting on instant replies to queries from the President; but during the evenings, especially after midnight, the noise of the machines would subside for long periods and we were able to reduce the situation reports from an hourly to a several-times-a-day schedule. This allowed some of our exhausted people in the embassy to get some sleep. Even so our Station Chief there, "Laird," still lived in his office, just as I lived in the headquarters building at Langley.

Laird and I "talked" occasionally on the teletypes in the small hours. At the keyboard in the communications room in Santo Domingo he would peck out a sentence, much as an unskilled typist will operate a typewriter.

"That message about such and such today was pretty silly," Laird would strike on his keyboard, the sentence appearing simultaneously on

153

the unrolling paper of my teletype in The Pit. It was enciphered, of course, so that foreign monitors would not be able to read it. Nor could anyone else in CIA headquarters.

"Sorry," I would peck back slowly to Laird, "but the Admiral insisted. How's the back?"

"Aching. When will you come down to take over?"

I said, "I'm not sure...."

And I wasn't sure. It was now mid-June. I had been in The Pit for three weeks, and no one had mentioned when I might be leaving.

When designated as Chief in Santo Domingo, I was a very new GS-15. The station was not an important one, but the abrupt developments in Santo Domingo had changed that. I could glance at a chart on the wall of The Pit and see that there were now eighty-three CIA people in the Dominican Republic—the boondocks teams, extra communicators, liaison officers working with the FBI and the 82nd Airborne, temporary operations officers, technicians, and secretaries—making it one of the largest stations in the world. Politically it was vitally important, second only to Saigon. Lyndon Johnson and U.S. policy makers already had to juggle the political hot potato of a Communist Cuba in the Caribbean; the specter of a second Cuba so near to Florida was disturbing. Santo Domingo was, in short, the kind of station where it would be reasonable to assign one of the most senior and experienced officers available, perhaps a GS-17 or GS-18. Would the Admiral, schooled in military discipline, approve the assignment of a relatively junior GS-15 on his first Chief's tour to the country where Lyndon Johnson had invested so many political credits? Would Des FitzGerald? Originally I was selected because "a doctor" was needed in a small country which meant little to the Agency. Now our Station Chief would have to deal directly with Ambassador Ellsworth Bunker, the OAS senior ambassador and Johnson's personal representative, as well as with resident Ambassador Tapley Bennett. Then there was three-star General Bruce Palmer, the contingent of FBI officers, and a steady stream of VIP visitors. I decided to brace Des.

I asked him, "How many officers senior to me want to be COS, Santo Domingo?"

Des smiled. "I believe eleven."

"Am I going? I want to."

FitzGerald scraped his pipe, then tested it thoughtfully. "If you go, what is the first thing you will do?"

"Send a cable asking that Abe be my deputy."

Des smiled. Again, it was the second time I had recommended Abe to him.

"I'll speak to Helms and the Admiral today."

I was not concerned about Helms, but the Admiral was something else.

I don't know what legerdemain Des practiced, or what reasoning he employed, but shortly he called. "Send a message to Laird, telling him you will take over in early June."

May passed. Twice Des came by The Pit on his way out of the building and took me with him. First to his home in Georgetown for dinner and to meet his vivacious second wife Barbara, a former British movie actress I remembered as Barbara Rollins in *The Moonlight Sonata*; then on a budbursting spring Sunday afternoon we drove to the two-hundred-year-old FitzGerald country home in Virginia. I sipped a gin and tonic while Des played tennis with Barbara on the court where he was to suffer a fatal heart attack two years later. Frances, his daughter, talked to me about a trip she was about to make to Mexico, and I gave her the name of friends in San Miguel Allende.*

It was time to return to Mexico to turn over my agents and operations, some of them to Abe. Or at least I thought it was to be to Abe. But Des had cabled Mexico advising Abe that he would be my deputy in Santo Domingo.

Before leaving I chatted with Dick Helms. This was traditional. As DDCI (and later when he was DCI), Helms would meet with outgoing Station Chiefs to give them marching orders. A few minutes of laconic conversation and then Helms would deliver one of his famous one-liners. Often it would be, "Ring the gong for me"—meaning that he wanted to know in advance of a coup or other rapid change of government. Or it might be, "Teach those people how to run their intelligence service." Or, "See what you can do to swing the Ambassador around," meaning that he wanted good relations restored where a Station Chief and an Ambassador had been feuding.

What would my instruction be from Helms? Certainly this time the marching orders would be detailed, the demands clearly enumerated. People were still killing each other in Santo Domingo, and the President was observing developments there with keen interest, mindful of the equities he had invested domestically and abroad by sending in twenty-two thousand American soldiers. But my instruction was a one-liner too.

Helms said, "Get along with the FBI."

Was Helms joking? He was not. "Get along with the FBI. It is very important!"

At the time I was not aware of the severity of the strain on relations between J. Edgar Hoover and Helms. While Hoover and the Admiral held many common views and were in frequent contact, that rapport

* Later I would remember that lovely afternoon when reading *The Fire in the Lake*, Frances's superb prize-winning book on Vietnam.

155

was not shared by Helms and others in the Agency. The schism with Hoover was sharp, with overtones that affected Agency activities for years and had ramifications in the allegations of CIA "domestic" spying in early 1975.

Helms was relieved when I told him I had been working in Mexico City for the past four years with Clark Anderson, who was now heading the FBI unit in Santo Domingo. I added that Clark was a personal friend and a fine guy.

I returned to Mexico City for a few days. After putting my operational affairs in order for my successor I packed a single suitcase with light clothing for the flight to Santo Domingo. Once again a long separation from the family was about to begin; no dependents were being sent to the Dominican Republic. Indeed, the families of embassy officers in Santo Domingo had been evacuated to Puerto Rico.

On the plane I read a batch of newspaper clippings concerning the Dominican strife that disturbed me. Journalist Dan Kurzman reported, ". . . innumerable conversations with individuals and groups in many parts of this nation have strongly indicated overwhelming popular support for the rebel regime of Francisco Caamaño and a corresponding anti-American sentiment arising from antagonism towards the United States. . . ." Reports from Tad Szulc in the *New York Times* and from journalist Bernard Collier were equally disturbing. If these experienced reporters were to be believed, the situation was much grimmer than I had realized. Did the United States face decades of resentment, perhaps the prospect of prolonged civil war, on the island of Hispaniola?

Was it possible? Had I been wrong in insisting to the Admiral that all was quiet in the countryside? Were the CIA officers in the nine bases more preoccupied with mosquitoes than any potential threat? If so the task ahead might be impossible.

I fell into fretful sleep. I awoke when the June heat of Santo Domingo began to buffet the airliner on its approach to the airport. A tower of black smoke spiraled from a plaza in the rebel zone—a street gang burning a pile of old tires. I could see U.S. Navy ships offshore and several helicopters parked on the polo field next to the Hotel Embajador. My pulse was pounding when I stepped out of the plane into a blast of tropical heat.

After a sixteen-mile drive from the airport, the approach into Santo Domingo proper is over a bridge. From the bridge a tall smokestack caught the eye because of a neat hole drilled into it by an American tankgunner who had thus checked out his 105 mm. recoilless gun before crossing into the city. I drove through the corridor which separated the rebels from government troops; sentries guarded checkpoints at intervals and, in some cases, civilians were in evidence, several of whom I recognized as colleagues from Langley. For a period of some weeks these colleagues reported to our station from the perimeter of the rebel zone despite being under fire often.

The embassy was bedlam. Military couriers arrived in a screech of jeep tires; half-a-hundred correspondents interviewed anything that could walk and talk; there were temporary duty people from State, USIA, and a dozen other agencies. Cases of C rations were stacked in hallways. Our own station office was separated from the others by a waist-high Dutch door guarded by "Adele," our reports officer, who over a period of weeks retained her sang-froid while simultaneously clicking out reports on her electric typewriter and fielding questions from reporters. Occasionally she would call on "Bryan," her husband of less than a month, to eject an eager newsman who tried to enter the station in search of a typewriter, or at least a desk where he could write his dispatch in longhand. Adele and Bryan had been married in the embassy during the height of the fighting—rumbling explosions from the rebel zone, only a few blocks away, punctuated the wedding ceremony. Their honeymoon had been one afternoon at the Hotel Embajador.

I talked with Laird in his office where wooden shutters were closed as protection against spent bullets which occasionally dropped into the embassy grounds. Laird's face was tight from the pain of his ailing back. I expected that he would ask me to take over on the spot after what had now been seven weeks of nights with little sleep and C ration snacks, but he had a suggestion.

"There is no way to understand this country," Laird said, "unless you know the interior. Once you take over here I doubt you'll be able to travel for months. So visit the boondocks before you relieve me."

I admitted that I was concerned about the countryside, especially after reading on the flight to Santo Domingo Kurzman's story about the unrest there.

Laird said, "Kurzman is wrong. See for yourself."

So my first three days were spent touring the country—not difficult as it is one-third the size of Florida.

It didn't take long to verify how quiet it was. The *campesino* knew less about what was going on in Santo Domingo than a newspaper reader in Washington, and probably cared much less. I traveled to San Francisco de Macorís, considered to be the most politically active of the provincial towns. I sat in the plaza having my shoes shined and soon a cluster of local citizens were chatting politics with me. When I asked them about American troops they simply shrugged. On occasion I

157

baited them, but they would not rise to it. Where are the young people who oppose the government? I was told that, in the first days of the revolt, they had gone to Santo Domingo to join the rebels. Thus the firebrands and young activists had left the countryside and the towns to their elders, and now were fighting with Caamaño.

The problem of the Dominican crisis was in Santo Domingo, and that was where it must be resolved. And youth would be an important consideration.

Early on the morning of June 14 I took over from Laird. He had predicted that it might be an eventful day: the largest of the Marxist groups and one of the most active in the affairs of the downtown rebels was the 14th of June organization. The name commemorated an anti-Trujillo invasion attempt from Cuba in 1959, Fidel Castro's first fruitless effort to export his revolution only six months after toppling Batista.

Laird was right. Early in the morning a tremendous explosion, followed by a billowing cloud of black smoke, heralded a revival of fighting in the streets of Santo Domingo. During the next three days over a hundred people were killed, including several American soldiers. Mortar shells were lobbed from General Wessin's headquarters into the rebel area; rifle fire could be heard throughout the day and into the night. My tour as Chief of Station, Santo Domingo, began with a true baptism of fire.

Abe arrived from Mexico. Several days later I asked him why he continued to carry his in-box under his arm; he explained that he had no desk. Wally would disappear for a midnight rendezvous with his agent—previously featured on VOA—who had slipped through the corridor with a treasure-trove of rebel documents. Another station officer, "Willard," made regular morning trips into no-man's-land to debrief a key military informant, often under fire and in perilous circumstances where an American was not welcome (he later received a medal for valor).

On the second day of my tenure a planeload of TDY (temporary duty) personnel arrived. Somewhat stunned to find themselves in a small war when they had left Washington thinking the fighting was over, they squeezed into my office for an initial briefing. They were young and inexperienced. During the briefing an electrical circuit fused; there was a whish of acrid smoke and a crackling of electricity. The new arrivals turned to the noise, curious to see what was happening. When they turned back they found that Abe and I were flat on our bellies on the floor—only the two World War II types automatically hit the deck!

I met with Ambassador Bennett and his political officers. They explained that the first embassy priority was to assist Ambassador Bunker and the OAS mission to defuse the violence so that a provisional government acceptable to both sides could take over until elections could be held. The U.S. troops and the OAS Latin American contingents were to stand between the rebels and the government forces, restraining the latter and protecting the former. All agreed that some political and military leaders from each side would have to resign and even leave the country if tempers were to cool to the point of political reconciliation. Imbert and Wessin from the government side, and Caamaño and two or three of the rebels from the other, would certainly be among these.

A cable spelled it out. At a Washington inter-agency meeting, it had been decided that one of the rebel leaders must be persuaded to leave the Dominican Republic. The proposal, it was felt, could not at that early stage be put to him overtly, but was to be attempted covertly; that is, CIA was requested to contact the rebel commander and cajole, persuade, suborn, or otherwise convince him to leave. If necessary, the cable said, I could make a generous financial offer which would guarantee his future. First, however, I was instructed to discuss the operation with Ambassador Bunker.

Ellsworth Bunker was then—and is now—the most impressive American diplomat I have known. A political appointee, he began his diplomatic career at age fifty-six; when I met him on that first day on the job in Santo Domingo he was past seventy—tall, slender, back as straight as a cavalry officer. Immaculately dressed, his face was patrician. Even in the most hectic days in Santo Domingo he never failed to manage his twenty-minute morning walk around the grounds of the Hotel Embajador, where he had his headquarters.

Introducing myself, I explained the Washington proposal. I described it as a risky and dubious proposition, implying that I would be delighted if he would counsel me to forget it. His reaction was immediate and positive.

"As the President's representative," Bunker explained, "I approve of any action, even if irregular, which will calm tempers here enough to stop the killing and to hasten the establishment of a provisional government. As the senior OAS representative, I approve even more emphatically. If you can convince your friend to vacation on the Riviera, or elsewhere, it will be a positive step. Please try."

I said, "Mr. Ambassador, a large amount of money might be involved."

"Young man," Bunker peered over his glasses, "do you realize how many millions of dollars it costs the United States government each week that we keep twenty thousand troops here?"

I warned the Ambassador: "You may become personally involved. We have an agent with some influence who can contact the fellow. He can make the offer, but I'm not sure he will be trusted. Our prospect may insist that *you* satisfy him; that you confirm that the U.S. government stands behind our clandestine proposal."

"How's that?"

"Mr. Ambassador, when you make one of your daily trips down to the rebel zone, our prospect might demand a signal from you."

"What kind of signal?"

I said, "He might, for instance, insist that you wink at him three times, or something of the sort."

Bunker did not hesitate. "If that would do it, I'd be delighted."

The Ambassador and I discussed other matters for a few minutes. It was time to go and at the door I stopped and turned to Bunker.

"Are you sure, sir?"

"What's that?" the Ambassador asked.

"Are you really prepared for personal involvement in this? The business about winking three times?"

Ellsworth Bunker had had just about enough from a novice Chief of Station. "Young man," he said, dismissal evident in his voice, "will you please get about your business? If necessary I'll lift my left leg and break wind three times!"

Over the years my admiration for Ellsworth Bunker—a man of patience, wisdom, flinty integrity, and, may I say, guts—has never waned.

Clark Anderson and I discussed how we would work together. The FBI chief was candid.

"Here I am with twenty-four men. My instructions are to gather intelligence. None of us knows anything of the local political and security situation and our experience is in criminal, not political, investigation. J. Edgar has told us to start churning our reports. What do we do?"

Then and there Clark and I contrived a program. The important element was that we would keep from trying to recruit and handle the same agents by a frank review of our candidates. We met every morning. Clark would identify potential sources. I would tell him whether we had already recruited the agent, or if we had tried with dubious results. One does not often identify agents to another government agency, but in Santo Domingo Clark and I violated the rules. If one of his officers recruited a source, he would advise me. Thus over the period of more than a year while the FBI was in Santo Domingo, we avoided problems and were useful to each other. Unorthodox, but it was, I believe, a good way to handle American affairs in an unusual circumstance. Clark and his people were appreciative, and after a period of time, able to help us as we helped them. CIA "got along" with the FBI in the Dominican Republic.

The shooting, although sporadic, continued. A large contingent of

Brazilian troops was bivouacked only two blocks from the embassy. On occasion a nervous sentry would trigger a round and the entire encampment would wake and fill the night with the roar of gunfire. We kept the wooden shutters of the station offices closed and the short walk from the embassy to the Ambassador's residence sometimes was enlivened when a bullet clipped a branch from one of the trees.

One night I had dinner at the residence with Ambassador Bennett and General Bruce Palmer. Palmer had been sent to Santo Domingo after Lyndon Johnson had ordered that "the best general in the Pentagon be given the command."

Palmer, possessed of a political sensitivity unusual in field officers, was adroitly managing one of the toughest jobs in American military history: commanding troops who were being shot at—over a hundred American soldiers died in the streets of Santo Domingo—but who were not allowed to return the fire except in self-defense.

As we dined, a spent bullet whistled softly somewhere outside in the darkness.

"That's close," said Ambassador Bennett.

Palmer said, "Oh, no. That's not close." He sipped his soup.

Shortly, another round passed through the trees outside the dining room, leaving a strumming sound in its wake.

"What about that?" Bennett asked, peering at Palmer.

"No, that wasn't really near us," said the General.

Crack! A bullet smacked into the frame of the dining-room window; fragments of wood and paint fell to the floor.

Palmer hardly interrupted the movement of his spoon from bowl to mouth. "Now *that's* close," he said.

I often wondered where Laird, Wally, Willard, and the other officers found the stamina to survive the long days and nights with so little sleep and such a poor diet. In the early days the chancery had been under constant rebel sniper fire; several snipers were killed by the Marines guarding the building. The embassy staff—beginning with the Ambassador—worked around the clock and snatched two or three hours of sleep when they could. Bunker and his aide, Harry Shlaudeman, a former political counselor in Santo Domingo, maintained similar schedules at their Hotel Embajador suite. Often I would call Harry after midnight to tell him Bunker had received an important message from Washington that he should see first thing in the morning. Invariably Harry would say, "Come on over. We'll be up for a while."

I, too, was staying at the Hotel Embajador. After my first two months in Santo Domingo I realized that I had never had coffee there in the morning, as the coffee shop did not open until 7 A.M.; nor had I eaten there, as the kitchen closed at midnight. This schedule didn't fit with my office hours.

I promised myself to program a reasonable amount of exercise and recreation, despite the fact that fighting continued in the rebel zone. My first attempt was a round of golf. The first nine holes were great; I was the only player on the course. At the ninth hole turn, however, an officer from the station was waiting to tell me that I must return to the embassy at once. I finished the eighteen a year later.

Such were my recreational activities. Barton Connett, wife of the DCM, Deputy Chief of Mission, invited me to dinner, insisting on black tie. I borrowed Wally's for the evening. Ten of us sat at the candlelit table for an elegant French dinner, served by two white-gloved waiters. The women—all Dominicans except for Barton who, as wife of the chargé had not been evacuated—were slim and provocative in bright, long dresses. It was unreal. Barton pointed out the bullet holes which already existed in the dining room walls while we could even then hear distant gunfire outside. Most amusing was Barton's description of how she had managed to scrounge enough food to keep the animals alive in the nearby city zoo. They had been abandoned since the first day of the revolt and Barton's one-woman effort to sustain them was the subject of an amusing story on the wire services.

The evening was cut short when a blast of sustained gunfire erupted and the sky above the rebel zone flashed with tracers. Bill Connett, a Brazilian diplomat, and I excused ourselves and returned to our offices.

Twice during coming weeks I accepted dinner invitations and again each time, failed to make the dessert course. Back to the C rations at the embassy, with an occasional after-midnight trip to a nearby pizza restaurant.

Street fighting became less frequent, but there were still much tension and occasional deaths as untrained youths in the rebel zone and nervous soldiers of both the OAS contingent and the government fired at every shadow.

Bunker, Shlaudeman, and the Brazilian and Salvadoran ambassadors at the Embajador Hotel negotiated with both sides on establishing a provisional government. An obvious choice to head the interim government was Héctor García-Godoy, a Dominican respected by and acceptable to a large spread of people of both sides. Formerly the Dominican foreign minister as well as ambassador in London, García-Godoy was an experienced politician, known for his political acumen and integrity. He was the leader demanded by the times.

Before García-Godoy could assume power and hope to last until elections could be held, a number of people had to leave the country or at least resign from high positions. This was hardly a new phenomenon in the Dominican Republic, or for that matter in Latin America with its historical precedent of politicians and plotters shuttling back and forth from exile, some many times during their political careers.

Juan Bosch returned from exile in Puerto Rico. Our intelligence reports indicated that he was privately shocked to find that the rebel forces had been so effectively penetrated by Marxists, but publicly he accepted their support in a bitter anti-American harangue. Then Bosch disappeared into his home, not to leave except on two occasions—once to visit a son who had been accidentally shot in a downtown fracas, and once to vote in the elections. Bosch had good reason to be careful, but his retreat from public view was seen by some as a lack of machismo—in this instance, cowardice.

No one expected Tony Imbert to leave the country, as everyone realized that once outside the Dominican Republic, unprotected, without his bodyguard, he surely would be gunned down by Trujillo supporters who still vowed vengeance for the death of the dictator four years earlier.

General Wessin, it was conceded by all, had to leave the country. His implacable hatred of the Communists was such that he was incapable of reasonable negotiation and, commanding such a formidable tank force, he would be a constant source of friction if not new outbreaks of fighting.

It was also universally believed that Caamaño would leave, and his nomination as military attaché in London was proposed long before he finally accepted the post. Several other luminaries on both sides were marked for vacations as well.

Attempts to effect the necessary travel and resignations were made by Bunker and his OAS colleagues, by Ambassador Bennett and his embassy staff, and by General Palmer and his Brazilian colleague, General Alvim. The moderate elements of Dominican political society on both sides of the corridor supported these efforts. On some occasions these were semi-overt endeavors, with García-Godoy and other Dominicans bargaining with the persons involved in an attempt to persuade them to step down or step out.

When negotiations stalled and no solution was in sight, the CIA station was called on for the hard job of final persuasion—not by force or threat, but by enticement. "Uncle Dave's friendly travel agency" as one wag described it. There were four such instances.

The first involved a rebel leader and was unsuccessful. Bunker was not called on to wink even once. (Later, however, this person did leave the country, never to return to Santo Domingo.)

163

A second instance, which concerned a well-known Dominican, has never been revealed. But "Preston," a newly arrived officer, went out one evening and arranged for the official's departure.

As the weeks passed it boiled down to three cases which García-Godoy believed—quite rightly—must be resolved if he were to have a reasonable chance to complete his provisional tenure: Caamaño, now declared President of the Constitutionalists in the rebel zone, and his counterpart, Tony Imbert, President of the Government of National Reconstruction, and finally, General Wessin, the tank commander.

As the four months of civil war in Santo Domingo drew to a close, General Imbert sent word to the OAS ambassadors that he would resign to allow Héctor García-Godoy to take over as provisional president until elections could be held in June of 1966. Bunker and his Brazilian and Salvadoran colleagues were ecstatic. Imbert promised to resign before the end of August, so that García-Godoy could begin his term on the first of September. From Miami we had a report that Luis Conte Aguerro, an exiled Cuban radio personality, had received a copy of the resignation statement Imbert planned to make. Imbert had never met Conte, but had become a devoted listener to the anti-Castro commentator's eloquent radio broadcasts from Miami. He had sent a draft resignation statement to Conte, we were told, asking the Cuban's assistance in preparing the final version. I had known Conte in Cuba and could understand why Imbert sought his help. Conte was a word master and political wizard.

Expectedly, the plan became unglued as the end of August approached. After a series of disputes and acrimonious meetings, Imbert reneged on his promise to resign. He felt that the OAS was offering him nothing; certainly not guarantees for the future of his staff, and he believed that the negotiations would be a victory for the rebels downtown.

Bunker was distraught when I gave him a report from inside the Imbert camp. General Imbert was organizing a giant anti-Communist, anti-rebel rally. It was his intention to denounce the OAS as incapable of containing the rebels and to ask his followers to demand the withdrawal of the OAS mission so that he, Imbert, and his supporters could save the country. We all interpreted that to mean elimination of the rebels.

Efforts were made to meet with Imbert, but he refused to talk, even on the phone, with the OAS mission or with García-Godoy. Suddenly, only a few days before the provisional government was to be realized, the situation was at a stalemate. The OAS could not retreat, leaving the recalcitrant Imbert free to attack the rebels, but his refusal to engage in any dialogue created a tense situation. Imbert's plans for the giant rally continued.

Bunker asked if there was anything CIA could do. I told the Ambassador that this seemed doubtful since we were not in contact with

Imbert nor with any of his advisers. What was needed in this situation was an agent of influence, an advocate of U.S. policy and someone Imbert trusted and admired. We had no such agent in the Dominican Republic, and the only possibility was a Cuban exile in Miami, a man whom Imbert had never even seen. I said we would try.

I sent a message to Conte in Miami, reminding him of our acquaintance in Havana. Would it be possible for Conte to fly immediately to Santo Domingo to discuss with me a matter of importance?

Conte flew to Santo Domingo, ostensibly to offer his services to Imbert as an adviser in planning the giant rally, "modestly" offering to deliver the principal address himself. Imbert accepted the proposal; he disliked public appearances and, especially, speaking in public.

I met Conte. I asked him, as an old friend, to persuade Imbert to reconsider, to proceed with the rally but to make it the occasion for his resignation rather than a confrontation with the OAS. I solemnly described the role which would be ascribed to Conte by historians if he would be responsible for solving this Dominican dilemma. Conte was dubious. His role had been that of a political agitator in his anti-Castro campaign from Miami; he was uncomfortable in the role of peacemaker and negotiator. But he agreed to try. This was on the evening of August 28.

It was well past midnight—the morning of the twenty-ninth—when Conte called me.

Conte said, "I am speaking from the home of the President." His voice was emotional. "I have delivered your message. The General wishes to discuss the course of action he plans to pursue."

"Marvelous," I told Conte. I looked at my watch; it was almost 2 A.M. "I will arrange a meeting with Ambassador Bunker and the OAS representatives first thing tomorrow."

"*Momentito.*" There was a pause, then Conte returned to the phone. "The General says he does not wish to talk with Bunker, or the Brazilians, or anyone else. He will talk to you. Now."

I drove from the embassy to General Imbert's home. He lived in a large house hidden in palm trees behind a high wall. At the gate several heavily armed men inspected the car carefully. These men were a part of the contingent of bodyguards which a grateful government had provided Imbert for life after he helped assassinate Trujillo. Luís Amiama Tío, the other survivor, had a similar group and guarantee. Amiama, I am told, had a bust of Lincoln in the study of the fortress where he lived.

After a thorough frisking by the guards, I was met at the door by Conte. The Cuban exile was effusive as we embraced, the traditional Latin *abrazo*.

165

Conte is a big man; he was regally tall as he announced: "The President awaits." He escorted me to Imbert's study. The General rose from his chair as I entered, and shook my hand perfunctorily. We sat again, while Conte hovered about us. My eyes went to the machine gun on the floor beside Imbert. (An ordinary, black machine gun; the legend was that it was gold plated.) Nothing was said as an attendant with an enormous pistol stuck in his belt served coffee.

I had seen Imbert once before, when he sat a few rows in front of me at church. The General never missed a Sunday, but always changed the time and location of his worship to avoid establishing a pattern to be used by would-be gunmen sponsored by the sons of Trujillo, who had sworn to avenge the death of their father. In church I had noticed that Imbert had almost no neck, and that his head was continually thrust forward, turtlelike.

Now Imbert pushed his head toward me. Imbert was a small man, balding, with a compact paunch. It was quiet as we sipped the strong black coffee. He squinted at me for several minutes, as if inspecting a new recruit of doubtful potential. A tropical insect, of a kind which can inflict a nasty sting, buzzed around Imbert's almost petulant face; he brushed it away languidly. Several air-conditioners whirred. I was face to face with a tyrannicide.

Perhaps sensing my uneasiness, Imbert smiled and asked in English, "Whadda you want from me?" In Spanish I described the need for reconciliation, and the vital and patriotic role Imbert could play by resigning. Imbert reverted to English, which he spoke well, although his conversation was studded with slang of some vintage. He explained his concern, and why he felt he would be betraying the Dominican people if he resigned.

Conte could restrain himself no longer. He broke into an eloquent speech, praising the President and describing the niche in history he would achieve on this momentous occasion. He elaborated for half an hour.

Oh God, I thought, Conte is going to spoil everything with his incredibly flowery rhetoric. Imbert listened attentively. When Conte finished Imbert turned to me.

Imbert said, "I need guarantees."

I said, "I'm sure the OAS—"

Imbert stopped me, waving his hand impatiently. He said, "I don't give a big goddamn about the OAS. I don't care what the State Department says. I wanta two guarantees for *you*."

Here it comes, I told myself. What will it be? Money? Sanctuary in Miami? A promise of future political support?

Imbert said, "I'va decided to resign. But only if you will make me two promises. First, that you will not allow the Dominican military to be destroyed. Next, that you will not allow this country to becoma Communist."

I said, "*Mi General*, I give you my word of honor that neither of those two things will happen." Imbert stood, and we shook hands solemnly.

Driving away from Imbert's home I felt guilty about my quick assumption that he would seek some personal gain in exchange for his resignation. I decided that Tony Imbert was a gentleman and a patriot, and that I liked him very much.

When I reported back to the Hotel Embajador, Bunker was pleased when I told him Imbert would resign at the rally, on national television, on August 31, two days hence. Bunker was also businesslike. "We need to move faster," the Ambassador said. "Please arrange to have the rally one day sooner."

I phoned Conte at Imbert's home. Would it be at all possible to have the President step down one day sooner than planned?

"No problem," Conte said. "Patriotism reigns."

So Imbert resigned before a crowd of five thousand, the next day, in a nationally televised ceremony. The hour-long speech in his behalf was delivered by Conte—an emotional but conciliatory discourse by a Cuban exile whom Imbert had never seen until three days before, and whose face was completely unfamiliar to Dominicans.

Ambassador Bunker, Harry, and I watched the telecast in Bunker's suite at the Embajador. The Ambassador was bemused, as if it were perfectly natural for a President to leave office with the benediction of a foreign orator. Harry, despite his years of experience with the unreality of Dominican politics, shook his head in amazement.

Harry said, "I just don't believe this is happening."

But it did.

A major goal had been achieved. A provisional government headed by a skilled and respected politician now could begin to prepare for elections. Tensions eased, hatreds were less intense, there was less violence. Americans were amused when new graffiti began to appear on walls. One read: "Yankee go home—but take me with you!"

Another travel candidate was thrust upon the station. Within a week after becoming provisional President, García-Godoy told Bunker and the OAS ambassadors that he could not govern as long as General Wessin remained in the country. In the rebel zone the populace lived in fear of mortar shells which they believed were being lobbed into their sector

167

from the headquarters of Wessin's tank troops. The rebel leaders refused to negotiate with the provisional government until that threat was
removed.

García-Godoy, his military chiefs, and even the conservative political
leaders tried to persuade Wessin to depart voluntarily. He vacillated. On
one occasion he told Ambassador Bennett that his only worldly possession
was his house, which he would have to sell. Bennett allowed that might
be arranged; the embassy needed housing for its expanding personnel.
García-Godoy offered him the face-saving sinecure of consul-general in
Miami. Wessin came to the embassy to see Colonel Joe Weyrick, the
military attaché, carrying a cigar box filled with personal papers, including the deed to his house, and said that he was ready to go.

But then Wessin's position hardened. He announced that he would
not leave the country until the rebels downtown were eliminated; it was,
he declared, a matter of saving his country from Communism. He
sincerely believed that, I am sure.

His political adviser, an American, also believed it. (Just about
everyone in the Dominican crisis—including the Marxists downtown—
had an American political adviser at one time or another.) We did not
know it then, but Wessin was meeting secretly and regularly with Jules
DuBois, correspondent of the Chicago *Tribune*. I had known Jules for
many years; he was a good reporter and, as a specialist, knew Latin
America as well as any American except Jerry O'Leary of the Washington *Star*. But Jules's political convictions had swung to the extreme right
margin of the spectrum. DuBois was sincere in his belief that the United
States by supporting the provisional government and restraining Wessin
and his tanks was courting a second Cuba in the Caribbean.

Families returned from their evacuation points in Puerto Rico and
Florida, and Ambassador and Mrs. Bennett began to entertain again. I
was at a large formal dinner at the residence when Bunker arrived and
summoned Bennett, Shlaudeman, and me to the library.

Bunker said, "I've been meeting with my OAS colleagues and
García-Godoy. The President says he will resign because there is no way
he can continue as long as General Wessin is here. So Wessin must go."

I had an uneasy feeling that I knew what Bunker would say next.
He did.

"Dave, I want you to go to Wessin's headquarters. Convince him,
one way or another, to go. By noon tomorrow."

I reminded the Ambassador that we already had an officer in touch
with the General, an officer known to Wessin only in alias, the way we
like to do business. The Ambassador, perhaps remembering my negotiation with Imbert, said he understood; nevertheless he wanted me to see

Wessin. I asked if there was time for me to request approval from Langley, but Bunker said there was not.

With the thought that I might be near the end of the shortest Chief of Station tour in CIA history, I agreed, although I insisted that another United States government representative accompany me, suggesting that Joe Weyrick, known to and trusted by Wessin, was the right man. Joe was summoned and, reluctantly, agreed to join me for the Wessin visit.

We arrived at Wessin's suburban headquarters about midnight. His home was guarded by a small army of tank troopers; a number of sullen civilians lounged on the veranda.

I talked with Wessin for an hour. He understood that he would have a Dominican diplomatic appointment in Miami (or Madrid, if he preferred) and that he would be a welcome visitor to the military establishments in the Canal Zone and the United States. And, without naming a specific sum, I told him that I was a pretty fast man with a buck when it came to the real estate business. Our conversation was strained, but not unfriendly. But Wessin was adamant. He refused to leave.

A detailed account of my meeting with Wessin appeared the following day in the Chicago *Tribune*. Byline: Jules DuBois. The day after, the story was repeated on the front page of the *New York Times* and the Washington *Post* and was carried on all the international wire services.

I learned that Jules DuBois had been hiding behind a curtain—literally—when Weyrick and I talked with Wessin. His story was quite accurate. He took shorthand notes while I was attempting to persuade the recalcitrant General to travel.

Headquarters was not pleased. In those days Langley expected officers of the silent service to "keep a low profile." My friend Jules had really gone beyond the rules of the game. In those days newsmen did not identify CIA personnel by name, especially overseas, when writing about the Agency and its operations. According to convention (how things have changed!) I would have expected Jules to describe me as David Phillips, "an embassy political officer," or without naming me, "as the CIA Station Chief." Jules combined the two, using my true name and CIA title.

The headquarters cable was terse: please explain. Fortunately, it crossed with our cable describing the incident—and predicting a possible flap.

So the score in the CIA game of influencing sudden travel or abrupt resignation was two hits, one assist, and one strikeout. All of us failed on Wessin except the 82nd Airborne. An army general used his paratroopers to escort General Wessin to the airport. Under protest, the anti-Communist General was flown to Panama in a U.S. Air Force plane.

Reaction was predictable. Left-of-center Dominicans saw the United States in a new, noble role; the right-of-center predicted a Communist takeover.

A cable announced that the Chief of the Western Hemisphere Division, my immediate boss in headquarters, was arriving shortly for "consultations."

My chief arrived and departed. Although he never said so, he was undoubtedly an emissary of Des FitzGerald, who might have been harboring second thoughts about his Chief of Station, Santo Domingo. After a session with Bunker, however, the visitor appeared to be reassured.

García-Godoy began making key appointments in his provisional government. He was able to persuade a number of young Dominicans, many of them left-of-center, to join him. It was a necessary step, but there was uneasiness in Washington. J. Edgar Hoover and the Admiral were concerned and warned Lyndon Johnson, who continued in his role of senior desk officer on the Dominican Republic, that García-Godoy was installing "pinkos" in his administration.

The Admiral called me to Washington for consultation. Des Fitz-Gerald took me into the Director's office. The first question concerned reports that the rebels had large supplies of arms available to them.

I assured the Admiral that this was true.

"How do you know?"

I said, "From the reports of our agents."

"How can you be positive?" the Admiral asked.

"If you put enough reports together over a period of time, you can be pretty sure," I told the boss. "In one case we are positive. One of our best agents has two hundred rifles buried under the concrete floor of his cellar."

The Admiral leaped from his chair. He pointed a finger at me. "Have him arrested!"

My jaw dropped as I turned to Des. A muscle on the side of Des's neck began to jump.

"We can't have that," the Admiral shouted. "Is he a Commie?"

It was incredible: Des FitzGerald, of all people, speechless.

"He is a member of the Communist Party," I admitted. "He joined at our request and now works from within against Communist interests."

Des finally regained the power of speech, and patiently explained to the Director of Central Intelligence the concept of long-range penetration of opposition groups, and why it was best not to have our agent jailed. And I mollified the Admiral by promising to have the agent dig up the arms long enough to remove the firing pins (which was never done, of course).

Now the Admiral addressed the concern that had prompted my recall. He explained that J. Edgar Hoover had told him that he feared that some of García-Godoy's appointments were secret Communists.

I assured the Admiral that this was not accurate. Des and I explained the Dominican scenario: First the intervention, next the restoration of order to prevent further bloodshed and prolonged civil war, then the relaxation of tensions by arranging the departure or resignation of several leaders from both sides so that García-Godoy could form a provisional government; and finally achievement of sufficient stability to allow departure of foreign troops—a condition García-Godoy insisted on before calling elections. To accomplish this latter point, the President would need a base of political support in his provisional government broad enough to represent all but the extremes of right and left. Youth must be part of such a coalition. I told the Admiral of my visit to the plaza in San Francisco de Macorís, and my subsequent conviction that the Dominican problem could not be resolved if the young people of the country were ignored.

The Admiral was dubious, but accepted the argument, although he cautioned me to keep an eye on the García-Godoy appointments.

Between meetings I spent half an hour working out in the basement at Langley. Viewing the massive CIA building from the outside, it is easy to imagine that inside might be found a modern and well-equipped gymnasium, perhaps a swimming pool, where American spies exercise in order to maintain James Bond–type physical fitness. In fact, there is no pool, and the CIA gym is a makeshift one; jogging is performed in a dark hall under a maze of steampipes. As I was dressing Dick Helms came in for his daily exercise session. We chatted briefly. Although I knew he would be reading the cables from Santo Domingo, I was surprised that he asked nothing about the developments there. But just before trotting off into the hall he turned to me with one question.

"How are you getting along with the FBI?"

I assured the Deputy Director that everything was going well between the CIA and the FBI in the Dominican Republic.

"Good," Helms said. "Keep it that way."

Shortly after my return to Santo Domingo the embassy faced a problem. García-Godoy had requested some equipment from the Ambassador. When foreign presidents, even provisional ones, ask for something the diplomatic response should be as rapid as possible. This is not easy in Latin America, where presidents are prone to solicit rather rich gifts— helicopters, for instance. This time the request was simple. The provisional President of the Dominican Republic had asked the United States government if he could borrow a Thermo-Fax machine.

A Thermo-Fax was available in my office, and I was asked to deliver it to the President's home. That evening I drove to the modest residence where García-Godoy was living. A number of Dominicans sat on the terrace. It occurred to me that neither the President nor I would profit from the publicity which might well result if one of the loiterers was a newsman. It was black dark as I pushed through the tropical bushes at the side of the house and toward the rear entrance. Presuming that any president would have guards around his residence, I figured the odds were pretty close to fifty-fifty that I was about to be shot. In contrast to the armed camps around the homes of Bosch, Imbert, and other Dominican leaders, however, the back yard of García-Godoy's residence was unguarded. The President himself opened the door when I knocked. He held the screen door as I entered with the copying machine, which I deposited on a table before introducing myself.

"Phillips?" García-Godoy reflected. "You are the man I was reading about in connection with General Wessin's departure?"

"Yes, Mr. President."

"Mr. Phillips, what exactly do you do at the embassy? Other than deliver Thermo-Fax machines," the President added with a smile.

It did not seem the time to be evasive. I said, "I'm the Ambassador's principal adviser on intelligence matters."

García-Godoy's smile disappeared abruptly. Then he said, "I would like to talk with you. Come with me."

The President took me to a small bedroom which had no chairs. We faced each other while sitting on twin beds.

"You are the chief of the CIA?" His English, polished at the Court of Saint James, was fluent. I responded affirmatively in Spanish, in which the conversation continued.

"I am having real problems holding my government together," the President said. "It is essential that I broaden the political base of the provisional cabinet and my subministers. To do that I plan several new appointments. Some will not please your government. One will undoubtedly make *you* very unhappy." García-Godoy mentioned the name of a prominent Marxist. "I realize that I cannot keep this flimsy government together without American support, but I must have some young people of the left in my camp. Otherwise it will not work. I want you to tell this to Bunker and to Bennett."

"They will understand," I said. "They know that you need young people, including leftists, in your government. And I can assure them that the Marxist you mentioned has no foreign ties." While I was saying this I remembered my recent conversation in Washington, when the Admiral told me of J. Edgar Hoover's concern that García-Godoy was placing "secret Communists" in his government. It was not difficult to envisage very real problems should word reach Washington that García-Godoy was about to appoint politically suspect Dominicans.

"Perhaps I can help you," I told the President. "It is my office in the embassy that has knowledge of subversives. If you would like me to review your candidates—"

That was the wrong thing to say. The President was indignant. "Mr. Phillips"—the voice was hard and even—"this is *my* country. I am the President. I will not do it. To me you are nothing but a foreign spy!"

I winced at the "foreign spy." I explained that I was offering to help the President by being sure that no alarming reports went to Washington; that I would perhaps bend the rules in an effort to allow him to appoint those persons he needed in his government; that I would support the appointments unless the case was an extreme one.

"A strange proposal." García-Godoy hesitated for a long time. I guessed that he was calculating the risk of trusting a foreign spy.

Finally the President spoke. "Mr. Phillips, will you join me in a brandy?"

And, thus, the deal was sealed.

In the following weeks García-Godoy toiled around the clock, preparing for elections six months hence. Not the least of his problems was that few of his people were accustomed to making decisions. One evening I was with him—discussing political appointments—when an aide insisted that he personally resolve a vexing issue posed by a telephone call from Santiago, the second largest city of the country. The custodian at the local ballpark could not be found and an angry crowd was milling about the main gate, which was locked. What was to be done? García-Godoy suggested that it was perhaps not an appropriate problem for the President, that it should be taken care of in Santiago. A few minutes later another call: the crowd was becoming ugly; there was no one in authority, no keys could be found.

"In that case," said the President, "tell them to break down the gate with a truck, let the spectators enter, and start the ballgame."

Ambassador Bunker and Harry Shlaudeman were still spending long hours with the OAS mission at the Embajador Hotel. It was after midnight when, on one occasion, Bunker asked me to leave the room while he accepted a call from France. In the anteroom his secretary confided that Bunker frequently received calls from Paris, from an ex-actress who was a friend of the widowed Ambassador.

"Who is Madeleine Carroll?" the secretary asked.

Albeit shaky, García-Godoy's government held together. Among many problems, three occurred in the interior.

Several Marxist extremists disappeared from the rebel zone and, a few days later, attempted a midnight attack on the town of San Francisco de Macorís, where I had discussed politics while having my shoes shined in the plaza. Four were killed, the rest captured.

A more serious incident followed. Caamaño, heading a motorcade of one hundred followers, left the rebel zone and drove to Santiago, a conservative bastion, to attend the funeral mass of a comrade who had been killed in Santo Domingo, but was to be buried in Santiago. Harry Shlaudeman was convinced the provocative action would result in a violent reaction in Santiago which would threaten García-Godoy's provisional government; in Santo Domingo there were OAS troops to keep the peace, but none were in the interior. So, for the first time the Dominican military would be free to clash with Caamaño in Santiago. Every effort had been made to dissuade the rebel leader, but Caamaño, always brave if not always wise, insisted—perhaps seeing a chance to build popular support.

Harry was right. During the mass there was shooting—never really adequately explained—which sent Caamaño and his band scurrying to the nearby Hotel Matum. Soon a battle was under way between local Dominican troops and Caamaño and his men, barricaded in the lobby of the hotel. Tanks rolled up and fired into the building, where a number of guests were trapped—including eighteen American citizens, performers with a rural circus. A dozen Dominicans died, including one of Caamaño's top aides, in the first hour of the battle.

The situation was politically as well as literally explosive. García-Godoy made frantic telephone calls to the provisional government military chiefs, asking them to call for a cease-fire. The officer on duty at Dominican air force headquarters in Santo Domingo did just the opposite. Seeing an opportunity in Santiago which did not exist in Santo Domingo, he sent instructions (we learned later) to the air force in Santiago: bomb the Hotel Matum!

I had two officers in the consulate in Santiago. Lester, the Base Chief, spent much of his life in Latin America, managing the difficult trick of getting along well with military liaison types without the amenity most expected. He was a serious Christian Scientist and a teetotaler; indeed he served only fruit juice in his home or office. A gringo who doesn't offer scotch to his guests is considered rare indeed.

Lester was monitoring the air force frequency on the radio in his office at the consulate. He was stunned to hear the pilots at the airbase —only a few blocks away—preparing to take off with the clear intention of bombing the Hotel Matum. Simultaneously the Consul received a telephoned plea for protection from the manager of the American circus troupe which was under fire from the Dominican tanks around the hotel.

Lester was a quiet person, but resolute. He jumped into his Volkswagen and sped to the airport. He drove onto the runway and parked there just as the first of the Dominican fighters was revving for takeoff.

The commander at the airbase was furious. He jeeped to the runway, shouting imprecations at Lester. In essence, and in colorful language, he instructed him to get his car the hell off the runway. Lester refused. The colonel was apoplectic. He screamed at Lester, pointing out in vivid terms that Lester was interfering with his pilots, his air force base, and Dominican sovereignty. Lester explained that as a consular officer it was his duty to protect American citizens and that he would not move until all Americans were evacuated from the Hotel Matum.

By this time there were a number of guns being pointed at Lester. Lester always had a streak of stubborn righteousness. He opened his sports shirt so that the butt of his pistol was evident. He told the irate colonel that he would leave only if forced and warned the colonel of the ramifications of attacking an American diplomat.

Lester stood his ground and the fighters remained on the tarmac. He stayed there, while the colonel fumed, until he could hear the whir of five helicopters. A hastily dispatched flight of OAS troopers had just completed the short flight from Santo Domingo; peace was restored, and the tanks drew back from the hotel.

There was little doubt that Lester's action saved the lives of Caamaño and his colleagues, as well as some of the Dominican and American guests of the hotel—including the circus fat lady, who smothered Lester in an appreciative embrace when she next saw him at the Consulate. There is even less question that Lester's bold action saved the country from a political trauma which might have brought down the provisional government—perhaps, even, sparked a new civil war.

CIA bestows medals on its officers and agents for valor. In this case the State Department decorated Lester, an unusual gesture.

My family had arrived in September, except daughter Maria, who stayed behind for school. When Maria did arrive in December for Christmas I arranged with General Palmer to fly her into Santo Domingo from the airport by helicopter. Maria was terribly pleased, saying that she had no idea I was important enough to merit my own helicopter. What I didn't tell Maria until we were at the house was that there was no other way to make the trip—a flurry of renewed fighting near the bridge had closed the corridor through the rebel zone.

1966

Caamaño departed for London as military attaché in January, a month after his adventure at the Hotel Matum. Thus the last of the must-travel or must-resign leaders left the political scene, allowing García-Godoy the relative stability necessary for his provisional government. Relative stability in the Dominican Republic, however, is not really too tranquil, as events were to prove.

A few conservative extremists in Santiago continued to believe that the country was being sold out to Fidel Castro and that García-Godoy's provisional government must be replaced by one which would deal firmly with the Communist-supported rebels still holed up in downtown Santo Domingo. Lester began to send intelligence reports indicating that a small group of diehards were plotting against García-Godoy. Nothing indicated the group had the clout to achieve anything, and Harry and I concluded there was no serious problem. García-Godoy was from Santiago and highly respected there; therefore, the plotters would have little hope of recruiting the action cadre required for a coup unless they could enlist supporters from outside the city.

García-Godoy invited the three OAS ambassadors for a weekend cruise on the government yacht for a high seas working session. Bunker looked forward to the trip as a chance to relax away from the tensions of Santo Domingo and away from the Embajador Hotel, where he had been living for ten months. He was firm in his instructions on embarking, telling John Crimmins, who had now replaced Tap Bennett as ambassador, that he did not want to be disturbed unless the reason was compelling. In fact, he told Harry and me, "Don't call me back unless the government is about to fall."

The presidential yacht was only a day from port when the reports from Lester indicated that the rightist plotters in Santiago planned to make their move. Harry and I studied the messages carefully, but continued to agree that there was little potential for a serious coup attempt without some provincial support to the conspirators. Then Lester sent a cable predicting the plotters would move the next day. One sentence read: A NUMBER OF STRANGERS HAVE BEEN OBSERVED ON THE STREETS OF SANTIAGO. Grandmother was on the roof. Crimmins radioed the ship, asking that it return to Santo Domingo. Bunker was met at the dock by Harry, who apologized for cutting the trip short, but cited our report predicting that a coup attempt would be made in Santiago within the hour.

It was actually forty-five minutes later. A captured radio station announced a new government and a feeble minicoup was launched but quickly put down. Nevertheless the value of Lester's intelligence was evident. On the presidential yacht with Bunker and the other OAS ambassadors were García-Godoy, several of his cabinet members, and the chiefs of the three armed services. Had they all been at sea at the time of the coup the danger to the provisional government might have been serious.

Despite gloomy predictions that it would never happen, election time came to the Dominican Republic. Joaquín Balaguer returned to Santo Domingo from New York, where he had gone into exile nine months after Trujillo's assassination. Balaguer had been President of the Dominican Republic under the dictator but had adroitly distanced himself from the repressive image of Trujillo's more infamous minions. A diminutive, austere bachelor, he was to be the opposition candidate in the contest with Juan Bosch. Bosch, although he remained a virtual prisoner in his heavily guarded home, campaigned vigorously by radio. The electoral battle was joined.

Lyndon Johnson wanted to know who would win. The embassy prepared cables and dispatches analyzing electoral developments. As a part of the country team effort, CIA intelligence operations were diverted from traditional espionage to the less secret task of predicting the results of an election. Who will the women vote for? How will it go in the countryside? Most news reports reaching Washington predicted a Bosch landslide. Balaguer represented the political sector more acceptable to American interests, and most observers believed that plus the Trujillo taint would defeat him. How could the Dominican people vote for a man sympathetic to the United States after a massive military intervention which included the third landing of U.S. Marines?

Six months before the elections there was a meeting of the seven embassy officers most concerned with predicting the outcome. I was one. Before the meeting Abe and I pondered long and reviewed all available information, overt and covert. It was early in the game, but we decided that Balaguer's paternalistic image, which would invite support from the *campesinos*, would make the difference.

The seven of us ended our discussion with a poll. Six embassy officers predicted a Bosch victory. I was the exception.

Johnson sent his Vice President to visit Santo Domingo. As is traditional, an advance party of Secret Service agents arrived to establish security controls; also, traditionally, CIA was asked by the Secret Service to provide the names of extremists or fanatics who might make an attempt on the visitor's life. Preston and his officers came up with a list of seven very black hats, one of them a Venezuelan with a history of political terrorist activity.

I found Hubert Humphrey to be *simpático*. Certainly loquacious, he bubbled with enthusiasm and bounced with energy. During a security briefing he asked the right questions and displayed a keen interest in the upcoming elections—obviously his mission was to survey the election situation for President Johnson. What were the key issues? How would the polling booths be monitored to prevent election fraud? Were the predictions of the press corps that Bosch would certainly win accurate? The Vice President met with García-Godoy and candidate Balaguer in their Santo Domingo homes. While a knowledgeable observer would have little problem in discerning that Balaguer was the favorite of Lyndon Johnson, an attempt was made by the embassy to be as neutral as possible. A last-minute decision was made that the Vice President should visit Juan Bosch. Plans were prepared hastily, but canceled abruptly. When the chief of the Secret Service detail responsible for Humphrey's safety heard of the plan to visit Bosch he reacted strongly. Rufus Youngblood—the agent who sat on Lyndon Johnson to protect him from the assassin in Dallas in 1963—was a methodical man who shared with all Secret Service agents concern with any unexpected departure from a VIP schedule.

Youngblood asked me if we knew all the individuals who would be at the Bosch residence when the Vice President was to visit it. He was especially worried because of the large number of armed guards who surrounded Bosch. I told him we didn't have that information, but would get it. Only hours before the visit our agent in the Bosch camp reported. Of the seven persons we had listed as being most likely to attempt violence against the Vice President in the Dominican Republic, two were members of Bosch's personal bodyguard—one of them the Venezuelan terrorist! Youngblood told Humphrey he could not call on Bosch. The political fallout from a sudden cancellation bothered John Crimmins. Humphrey was sympathetic, but he deferred to Youngblood and suffered a diplomatic illness.

I decided that I, too, needed a guard for my home. This came after a sneak thief broke into the house and, to my chagrin, stole my .38 caliber revolver. It was quite embarrassing to have to report the loss; rather like a cowboy having his gun or horse stolen. I asked Abe what the other officers in the station were saying about the robbery.

"You really want to know?" Abe peered over his glasses.

"Sure," I said.

Abe said, "Well, I'm afraid you have a new nickname. 0038."

So I hired a night watchman. He tilted a chair against the house and slept soundly throughout the night except for one early morning when he decided to clean his gun. It fired accidentally, the bullet passing through his hand, through my bedroom window and into the wall above my head. The only hospital open at four in the morning was in the rebel zone. The trip down and back was unsettling. While the rebel sentries who stopped us from time to time waved us on promptly, seeing the guard's bloody and mutilated hand, I couldn't help thinking how uncomfortable it might be for me if any of them had known that the CIA chief in Santo Domingo was among them.

Shortly before elections the OAS approved a resolution that the foreign troops should depart over a ninety-day period, beginning before elections but, prudently, ending afterward. The first contingent of departing American soldiers left the country.

Speculation ran high on the elections. The foreign correspondents overwhelmingly predicted a Bosch victory, and their observations, especially in the *New York Times* and the Washington *Post*, spread gloom in the White House.

The seven-man team in the embassy met again. One officer in the political section joined me in predicting a Balaguer victory. We were a lonely pair then and until the elections were held two months later.

As elections neared, foreign correspondents converged on Santo Domingo until some sixty-five made the Happy Hour for evening cocktails at the Embajador Hotel the busiest spot in town. The embassy devoted itself to predicting the outcome. Everyone was engaged; Clark Anderson of the FBI muttered. I sent several teams of agents through the countryside to test opinion informally, risky because revelations of "polling" by the embassy would have made sensational headlines in the press at that time.

The night before the election the embassy drafted its final message, which forecast a Bosch victory. Of the seven-man team only two of us reiterated our conviction that Balaguer would win; because of this the embassy message noted that there were dissenting voices. Unquestionably those who believed so firmly that Bosch would win were influenced by the conclusions of the foreign correspondents. Early on pre-election eve each of the newsmen contributed five dollars to a pool, the winner to be the one who most accurately predicted the final tabulation. Only a few were betting on Balaguer. Jules DuBois, despite his lack of objectivity, was an experienced Latin American hand. He had just returned from five days in the interior where he had been talking with *campesinos*. He strode into the Embajador Hotel bar and proclaimed: "The sound of the cock can be heard throughout the land!" (The cock was Balaguer's campaign symbol.) Other correspondents jeered. One who didn't was Jerry O'Leary of the Washington *Star*, a veteran newsman who had visited and learned more—many newsmen just visit—about Latin America than any other American journalist. He, too, predicted a Balaguer victory and bet on it.

One visitor at the hotel knew more about elections than any of us; Richard Scammon, former Director of the Bureau of the Census and an eminent election authority, was the U.S. member of a special OAS supervisory commission for the elections. Scammon, a very large man, sat quietly—a wise Buddha—observing the bustle at the bar.

The Admiral had instructed his station to prepare its own election forecast the night before the elections. Abe and I convened station officers for a final review, then prepared the cable. We predicted that Balaguer would win handily, probably with 57 percent of the vote. This was heresy, as the embassy cable predicted Bosch the winner and likewise the press corps except for a few dissenters.

"What the hell," I said to Abe, "might as well be hung for a goose." So we added a note to our informal message suggesting that our prediction be sent to the White House.

When booths closed on election day we waited for the first returns from several electoral tables in downtown Santo Domingo, a Bosch fiefdom. When the results were announced on television the newsmen at the Embajador Hotel cheered: Bosch had over 70 percent of the urban vote!

Dick Scammon pushed his heavy frame from his chair. He turned to a newsman. "I'm going to bed. Balaguer's a shoo-in." He had predicted some days before that Bosch would need at least 80 percent of the vote in the rebel zone to offset the pro-Balaguer provinces; he had discerned the will of "the real majority."

At the embassy I bumped into the AID chief and his deputy. Both were ecstatic, as they had been emotionally pro-Bosch. "What do you think now?" the AID chief asked me. I told him I thought I was damned glad he wasn't the political counselor.

Balaguer's mandate was overwhelming. The final tabulation gave him a majority of 235,000 of the votes—56 percent of the total. CIA had called the shot within one percent. The Admiral would be pleased. And the tall Texan in the White House.

At the Embajador Hotel the raucous Happy Hour was glum as despondent correspondents realized how seriously they had misjudged the people of the Dominican Republic. DuBois was jubilant, of course. Jerry O'Leary won $200. His most precious possession (I've been told) a twenty-dollar check he kept a long time as a souvenir: the payoff from his private bet with Dan Kurzman.

The newsmen did not question the honesty of the elections. The 1966 Dominican elections were certainly devoid of the hanky-panky which often occurs in Latin American voting. This was because the election was probably the most closely observed in Latin American history—at each polling center there were representatives of each candidate, and, as well, of the provisional government, and of the OAS. Additionally, a large group of Americans was flown to the Dominican Republic by Norman Thomas's Socialist Party to be sure that there was no chicanery. It is almost inconceivable that anywhere in Latin America —before or since—American citizens have (or should) become involved in an election process. But then there has never been a situation like the Dominican crisis in Latin America—before or since.

In Washington there had been another election pool—at the White House. Des FitzGerald won. Headquarters had decided not to disseminate our estimate from Santo Domingo, believing that our limb was just a bit too long, but Des had enough confidence in our prediction to win the White House pool. Lyndon Johnson, a reliable source confirmed, was pleased. The Admiral cabled tersely: WELL DONE! In navy parlance, that's about the best you can say.

1967

Peace had been achieved, the provisional government had survived innumerable crises, the foreign troops had departed, and the elections had been held. Bunker and Shlaudeman returned to Washington, having spent over a year at the Embajador Hotel.

García-Godoy was also going to Washington, as the new Dominican Ambassador. He asked me to come to his house. We had a final brandy, and García-Godoy gestured toward a cardboard box on the floor. It was the Thermo-Fax I had given him eight months before. "Thank you for your assistance," he said. The ex-President glanced at the duplicating machine, but he was talking about something else. "Actually I needed it for my wife, for her charity work with poor children."

I asked him if he would keep the machine, a donation to a good cause.

García-Godoy said, "No, Mr. Phillips. I needed it, but now that job is done, it is best I return it."

There was time for relaxation. I finished the round of golf begun so many months before, and, frequently played badminton with my friend Ian Bell, the British Ambassador. His wife, Ruth, was really very good about the fact that our game was in the living room of their residence. It was quite large, and a blue carpet was just the right size to mark the "court." On several occasions Ian and our mutual good friend Count von Spretti, the German Ambassador, drove out of Santo Domingo for archeology digs. We found many shards and some whole pieces of pottery belonging to the Taina Indians, the indigenous Dominicans who perished a scant fifty years after the arrival of Columbus.

I even participated in an amateur theatrical. This too was in the home of Ian Bell. The makeshift stage pre-empted our badminton court and this really tested the good will of Ruth Bell, whose living room seemed to be serving every purpose except its primary one. The original play was written by the Israeli Ambassador Benjamin Varon and his wife Miriam, formerly a professional actress who spoke and acted in five languages. Entitled *A Letter to the Times* the play concerned a Latin exile living in New York who was kidnapped by agents of the dictator of his Latin American country. As this was a dramatized version of a true incident of Dominican history—the abduction and subsequent murder of Jesús Galindez by Trujillo—we drew standing-room-only audiences of Dominicans during several performances. Paul Hoffman from the *New York Times* flew to Santo Domingo to review the play. The Western Hemisphere Division chief sent an amusing cable on reading the review, asking me if I needed another, more challenging assignment.

But there was also serious work to do. After the elections CIA had more time to devote to clandestine operations. Our first project was to find a man we knew existed, but only that. A source from Cuba had confirmed that the Cuban intelligence service communicated with its Dominican agents through a clandestine radio operator in Santo Domingo. Over a period of months we narrowed our list of suspects to a very few. Finally we became reasonably sure that the agent was a bachelor living in what had been the rebel zone. Preston rented a nearby apartment and surreptitiously photographed the suspect and the antenna atop his apartment building. To be absolutely sure, we had a team of intercept technicians fly in from Washington. They soon were able to monitor the broadcasts to and from Havana, using direction finders to establish without question that the transmitter was in the apartment we had under surveillance. We saw to it that this information reached the Dominican intelligence service and they raided the apartment. At first all appeared to be normal. But a thorough search led to a trap door in the floor where the "illegal" had cached his radio equipment and, behind a light switch plate, his code book. No larger than a Scrabble piece, the compressed pages of the code book and other documents allowed us to read back-traffic which we had recorded over a period of time. Among other things, it revealed that the Cubans had provided instructions to a local extremist group to rob a factory payroll—a robbery which had indeed occurred and in which Havana had predicted the loot precisely!

A report came from our station in Caracas. A Dominican revolutionary had been apprehended in the airport just prior to boarding a plane for Santo Domingo. Sewed into the lining of his coat were a score of documents which he was carrying to the Dominican Republic after he and a comrade had visited Cuba, North Vietnam, and Korea. The papers included detailed notes of a meeting with the chief of Cuban intelligence, and messages for Santo Domingo from the central committees of the Communist parties in Hanoi and Pyongyang. The report also noted that the papers were copies. We surmised that the originals had already arrived in Santo Domingo or soon would.

Our agents were tasked. Soon we began to piece together the story, and we were aware of which Communist leaders in Santo Domingo had received the original documents. Then we learned of plans to send a courier out of the country to Cuba, North Vietnam, and North Korea with responses to the message. They were in the form of plans for future subversive activities, including rural guerrilla warfare, in the Dominican Republic and requests for funds to carry them out. We thought we had identified the courier and so we passed our information to the local security service, which had complementary information. The person and baggage of the agent—and all passengers on the flight—were searched thoroughly. But nothing was found and the courier was allowed to board the plane, accompanied by his eleven-year-old son. Preston was at the airport and watched as they ascended the ramp to the aircraft. He spotted an airport employee who, darting out on the tarmac at the last minute, handed a small black bag to the boy. Preston signaled one of his agents who promptly told Dominican intelligence officers about the uncleared luggage. Security officials in the airport control tower instructed the pilot to cut his engines. Then they boarded the plane, removed the suspect courier, his son, and the black bag. In a tube of toothpaste, in a can of toothpowder, and in the carved-out handle of a shaving brush, were microfilms. These were the responses of the local Communists to Havana, Hanoi, and Pyongyang. One roll of microfilm consisted entirely of aerial photographs of the mountain regions of the country.

The haul was invaluable. The plans of the extremists—to and from

Communist capitals—were detailed, and knowledge of them by Dominican authorities considerably reduced the Communist capability to create mischief against the new Balaguer government. Combined with the knowledge garnered from the arrest of the illegal Cuban radio operator, this development was a major factor in maintaining political stability which has now lasted more than a decade.

As our agents who provided the information leading to the airport arrest are still working, the rather sexy details of how this intelligence operation unrolled cannot be revealed. But it was the kind of work that only an intelligence service can perform. A scenario of the operation was used in CIA training courses for several years.

Though the political situation was stabilized, there were occasional acts of violence. One night Preston, I, and Frank Devine, who had replaced Bill Connett as the Deputy Chief of Mission, were finishing coffee after dinner with a Dominican official. There was a tremendous explosion a few blocks away. We hurried to the site. A young American teacher from the local school lay dead, his body punctured with scores of holes from metal fragments and glass. He had been seated at the dinner table when terrorists lobbed a grenade onto the porch of his apartment. Hearing the sound of the bouncing grenade, he had risen from his chair and walked toward the plate glass door leading to the terrace—the grenade exploded, the shards of glass and fragments of grenade killing him instantly. Preston and I went with Frank, who had the grisly chore of identifying the body, arranging for a funeral home, and telephoning the young teacher's family in the United States.

Later we learned that the apartment had previously been occupied by two of Clark Anderson's FBI agents, and the terrorists, who were apprehended, believed their target to be a U.S. federal agent, rather than a teacher of high school English.

Early on a March morning we heard the sound of automatic rifle fire near the embassy. Down the street, just in front of Ian Bell's home, five men had attacked the car in which Tony Imbert was riding, wounding the driver and a bodyguard. Imbert took three slugs in his shoulder and, when the shooting was finished, drove himself to the hospital. Once again he had survived Trujillo vengeance.

Caamaño disappeared from his military attaché post in London. A Cuban intelligence officer in Paris provided him with a disguise, and the ex-rebel commander fled to Cuba. He was to die in 1972 leading nine invaders in a pitiful and futile attempt to promote guerrilla warfare in the Dominican mountains. Wessin wandered in exile. He was later to return to Santo Domingo only to be exiled again, this time to Costa Rica, when he was discovered plotting against the Balaguer regime. News from Miami revealed that my Cuban friend, Conte, had become a prize-winning Cadillac salesman. García-Godoy was to die in 1971 in his bed of a heart attack.

Bunker and Shlaudeman deserved a rest. So Bunker became Ambassador to Saigon for five years; and Harry went to Chile as Deputy Chief of Mission for what was to be an eventful tour during the Chilean coup against Allende.

Ian Bell went off to a European posting. Count von Spretti, the German Ambassador, went to Guatemala, where he was to be kidnapped and murdered by Communist terrorists. Benjamin and Miriam Varon went to Paraguay, where the Ambassador narrowly escaped death when terrorists attacked his embassy, killing one of his employees.

And there was bad news from Langley. Des FitzGerald collapsed on his tennis court and died of a heart attack.

The Dominican Republic prospered, as it does today.

In August 1967 my Dominican tour was finished. I returned to Washington to take on a new job.

I received a call from Bill Bowdler at the White House. Bill, Johnson's Latin American adviser, asked me to come to the White House at 7 P.M. I asked why. He did not say, but commented that I might want to wear a clean shirt. I gathered from this that Bill was not intimating that I was customarily disheveled, but that I might be seeing the President.

Bill escorted me from his office in the old Executive Building across the private street to the White House proper. Despite the hour a number of people were clustered in the office just outside the President's quarters. Larry O'Brien was on the telephone. Lyndon Johnson stepped out of his office, nodding a just-a-minute to Bill. Lynda Johnson came in briefly and stood high on her toes so she could kiss her tall father before going on a date. A number of secretaries and aides scurried about.

Lyndon Johnson stopped for a moment. He stared through the door. His face darkened. Then he turned and, in stentorian tone, asked, "How many times do I have to say it? Will someone turn off those goddamned lights in the hall?"

Then the President turned to me. He asked, "Son, would you like a Dr Pepper?"

Perhaps Bill had told the President I was a fellow Texan and would be acquainted with the soft drink popular in the Southwest. In any event, that was the first Dr Pepper I had drunk in twenty years.

I followed Lyndon Johnson into a tiny office, no larger than a college dormitory room. He motioned me to sit, while he lowered his tall frame into a reclining chair. He touched a knob and the chair extended; his long legs reached past the end of the footstand.

The President of the United States smiled at me. "Mr. Phillips, I want to thank you. I want to thank you for getting along with the FBI."

In 1968 I received a letter from Dick Cushing, my friend from Chile and Cuba. Dick had become the Deputy Director of VOA.

Dear Dave,

I thought you would be pleased about a reference to you which came up in the course of a longish conversation last night with Hector García-Godoy, former President of the Dominican Republic and now Ambassador here, about the turbulent events in his country three years ago.

"You know," he said, "looking back over those months when things seemed pretty bleak, two names come immediately to mind as able and effective representatives of the United States. They are Ellsworth Bunker and David Phillips."

Cordially,
Dick

Secondhand flattery is always best. Being thought of as a colleague of Ellsworth Bunker was pleasing. Most gratifying of all was to know that a Latin American could make this comment about the man he once referred to as "a foreign spy."

7

WASHINGTON 1968-1969

My tour in the Dominican Republic—which had not turned out to be dull at all—ended in the late summer of 1967. Abe stayed behind to become the Chief of Station. My new assignment in Washington was as Chief of the Cuban Operations Group of the Western Hemisphere Division. Although I would report to the head of Latin American affairs, my responsibilities were worldwide: to keep tabs on Cuban preoccupations in Europe, Africa, Asia, and the Middle East and in more than twenty countries in Latin America and the Caribbean, as well as to manage CIA espionage operations in Cuba. Professionally, it was a prestigious but demanding assignment.

At home, things were very difficult for me and the family. I moved into a house near Potomac, Maryland, a few minutes' drive across the river from CIA headquarters in Langley, Virginia. The four children were with me, but Helen was not. Our marriage of nineteen years was finished.

It was no solace to me that the divorce rate in CIA families is higher than in most professions. A number of factors related to my job contributed to our divorce; high among them were the tensions of leading a double life overseas, lengthy family separations, and long hours on the job when I was at home. The basic problem, however, was one of those marital developments to which no couple is immune. The Mexican divorce was painful for all of us.

The heavy workload of my new assignment was accompanied by demanding domestic duties at home. I was father, cook, and, with the help of the children, housekeeper. After Maria left for her freshman year at Brown University, David, Jr., and Atlee shared the chores, and helped care for Christopher, then eleven. Three months passed before I was able to manage a visa for the gardener who had worked for us so faithfully in Santo Domingo. Pepe, known affectionately to all of us as Pepito, had been eighteen when he first entered our employ and at the time did not own a pair of shoes. Pepito arrived on Christmas Eve and became our babysitter, housekeeper, and factotum, relieving me of much work and untold concern. Even so my day was a full one beginning with preparation of a hot breakfast—despite his other talents Pepito was not a cook—and, after the day's work at Langley, cooking an evening meal and adjudicating a potpourri of household problems for which I had little or no preparation. Fridays were the longest days because I was a Scoutmaster in the troop Christopher was about to join.

The days tumbled by. For the first time I was in charge of espionage operations in a "hard target" country. I had to make decisions on the recruitment of agents in Havana, and supervise the administrative support without which they could not survive and the communications without which they would be useless. It was serious business. When an agent was apprehended by the Cuban authorities, as they sometimes were, he (or she) was fortunate to be jailed and not executed. And, in 1967 Fidel Castro was relentlessly pursuing a policy of exporting his revolution to most of Latin America. Che Guevara was in Bolivia; Cuban agents and money were being sent to a dozen countries to support insurgencies, both rural and urban. It was usually dark by the time I arrived home from the office to cook the evening meal, to see that the children were in bed at a reasonable hour, or, on Friday evenings, to don my Scoutmaster's uniform.

When all had settled down for the night, I would read for an hour or so to unwind enough for sleep. Often I studied the history of espionage and secret operations, and was surprised to learn how ancient a profession intelligence is.

In 500 B.C., I noted, a Chinese philosopher named Sun Tzu established some rules for spying and covert action: "Discredit everything good in your opponent's country. . . . Use the collaboration of the most vile and abominable creatures. . . . Weaken the will of the enemy's soldiers with songs and sensual music. . . . Send prostitutes to accomplish the work of destruction. . . . Be generous in your promises and with your gifts to buy information. Do not spare money; money spent in this way brings in rich profits. . . ." And, in summary: "The acme of excellence is not the winning of a hundred victories in a hundred battles but rather to subdue the Armies of the enemy without fighting."

"Dirty tricks," I discovered, were not exactly new.

In the Bible I found that Moses sent his agents "to spy out the land of Canaan." Espionage techniques were refined by the Greeks and Romans and, of course, the Byzantines. The British intelligence service was created by Sir Francis Walsingham, Queen Elizabeth's Secretary of State, and his fledgling spies proved their worth by penetrating the French and Spanish courts. One of his agents is said to have interrupted Sir Francis Drake's game of bowls to give him hard intelligence on the Spanish Armada approaching on the horizon. In France, Richelieu ran a proficient intelligence service. European bankers sponsored private espionage nets; the Rothschilds had one of the best. Every major European power conducted intelligence operations. Under Czar Nicholas I the Russians combined espionage with police repression but Nicholas's service was puny in comparison to those which succeeded it—with the ubiquitous Soviet KGB, formally known as the Committee for State Security, employing today more intelligence officers and spies than all the other services of the world combined.

The 1771 edition of the Encyclopaedia Britannica briefly depicted the secret agent in these terms: "SPY, a person hired to watch the actions, motions, etc. of another; particularly of what passes in a camp. When a spy is discovered he is hanged immediately." An early American agent, Nathan Hale, described intelligence as "a peculiar service." Most of the many definitions of "peculiar" in the dictionary mean funny, odd, or strange. Hale was employing a British definition: "A particular parish or church that is exempted from the jurisdiction of the ordinary or bishop in whose diocese it lies and is governed by another." Hale was a spy and was "hanged immediately" when his mission on Manhattan Island failed in 1776.

In an Agency replete with unusual people, none titillated my imagination and curiosity more than the legendary James Angleton. The counter-intelligence chief and his operational activities were shrouded in secrecy and mystery; few of us knew the details of his job. His basic responsibility was clear though: to prevent penetration of the Agency by other intelligence services and to conduct high-level liaison with several of the more competent friendly ones. Angleton was CIA's answer to the Delphic Oracle: seldom seen, but with an awesome reputation nurtured over the years by word of mouth and intermediaries padding out of his office with pronouncements which we seldom professed to understand fully but accepted on faith anyway. After all, who could argue with the whispers that he had ferreted out Kim Philby's role as a double agent working for the Soviets?

Strolling to the cafeteria at Langley one day I remarked to a friend that I had never met Angleton. He replied that he knew the spy-master only by sight and—"There he is!" He stopped and nodded his head toward a man walking down the hall toward us.

"That's him. That's Angleton."

The man he identified was short, thin, with stooped shoulders, and shuffled rather than walked. His head was down, as if in deep thought; his hands were clasped behind his back.

"So that's the fabulous Angleton," I said, reverently.

Several times during the next two years I saw the man, always walking alone, hands behind his back. And I would identify him to others. "There he is. That's Jim Angleton."

The image intelligence has acquired in fictional accounts of international intrigue undoubtedly accounts for a good share of the characters attracted by CIA. Just as ex-soldiers spin yarns about their past, CIA's old hands cherish stories of personal experiences that are dramatic or humorous to the point of straining credulity. CIA war stories, while sometimes embroidered for effect, generally contain elements of truth because, in CIA, colleagues instinctively are skeptical and over the years can, and do, come across confirming sources.

I once visited a CIA man I'll call "Al" in Latin America. He told me the damnedest story about a snake I ever heard—one which I simply could not believe.

"Some time ago a cattle rancher," Al said, "told me about a huge snake holed up in a cave. He said that snake was over ten meters long; it had eaten, at the very least, ten Indians. He said the snake came out of his hole every three months, threw himself in a big loop around a steer, drug him into the river, drowned him, and devoured him. Then the snake would slip back into the cave and sleep it off over another three or four months period. The rancher wanted that snake captured if possible and carted off to a zoo since it was certainly the largest snake in existence."

"For the next few months," Al went on, "that snake was the subject of conversation at every embassy cocktail party. But how do you capture a snake over thirty feet long? Finally someone came up with a scheme. We had quite a long cotton-picking sack made in Lima. We had giant zippers sewn into each end. Our plan was to use tear gas to drive that snake out of his hole into the sack and then zip it up. We appointed a Head Zipper Man and a Tail Zipper Man. I was to oversee the entire operation, and to carry a .357 Python pistol in case something went wrong.

"Well, we went to the ranch and got ready. We took a long pole along with the idea that when we got the snake inside the sack and zippered up we'd tie the sack to the pole and then, by placing the pole between two Jeeps, get the snake to the railroad."

"Just a minute, Al," I said.

"I'm telling you the God's honest truth," Al insisted. "Well, we got everything set and shot tear gas into the hole. The snake coughed and thrashed around in there and then came barreling out. He saw daylight at the end of the sack we were holding at the mouth of the cave and headed for it. The Zipper Men stood their ground and zippered that snake right up. The flaw in our scheming was that we made the sack too roomy. When the snake discovered it was trapped, it dashed its body against the side of the sack with such force that it split the sack almost from one end to the other. The next thing I knew it was out and headed towards me. I finally got off a shot into the snake's head when it was about twelve yards away. It made a big loop with its body, hit a hardwood tree about the size of a small telephone pole, and shattered the tree like matchwood. Then, the snake fell over into the jungle where I was able to put two more shots into its head. We measured this snake and found it was thirty-four feet, three inches in length!"

Despite the fact I knew Al had been a former national pistol shooting champion, I decided he had gone far enough.

"Al," I said. "You are a damned liar."

Al was hurt. He invited me to accompany him into his back yard. He entered the garage and came out with the biggest snake hide I have ever seen. It was, without question, more than thirty feet long.

Yet, I still refused to believe Al's wild story about how he acquired the hide. During the next several years I saw him again and again. And, the snake story remained in active contention until one evening in 1967 when I attended a party at Nancy and Dick Cushing's in Washington. I found myself chatting with the number-three man in the United States Department of Labor, an Assistant Secretary. He mentioned that he had once served in the Latin American country where Al claimed to have bagged the monstrous snake.

"Did you know a fellow named ... ?" I mentioned Al's true name.

"Certainly did. Knew Al well."

With a big grin, I recounted Al's yarn about the snake. And I ended, "To this day he claims they made a canvas sack with zippers at both ends. Now, did you ever hear anything about that?"

"Mr. Phillips." The Assistant Secretary looked directly into my eyes. "I certainly have heard about that. *I* was the Tail Zipper Man."

For the first time I had the opportunity to meet and work with the scholars of CIA's Directorate of Intelligence. The Deputy Director, Intelligence, known as the DDI, heads the Directorate and is one of the four line officials in the Agency reporting directly to the DCI. In the early days DDI's were commended by an Ivy League and O.S.S. background. Among others, Robert Amory, now with the National Gallery of Art in Washington, and Dr. Ray Cline of the Georgetown University Center for Strategic and International Studies, have held the position of DDI in years past. Their three counterparts were the DDP, the Deputy Director of Administration (the DDA), and the Deputy Director for Science and Technology (the DDS&T).

Nearly all the men and women working for the DDI had one or, more likely, several advanced degrees. Their job was to collate all available information on foreign developments—from overt publications, highly technical sources of intelligence, and secret reports of spies— and produce studies and estimates useful to policy makers. There is not a university in the world which would not be envious of the academic talents which have been mustered into the service of the DDI. These people are part of the overt side of the Agency and identify themselves as CIA employees to friends and neighbors. Their intelligence publications range from thick compendiums to a slim folder printed early each morning for the use of the President. Many DDI people go to work at midnight so the chief executive of the United States can absorb the intelligence highlights of the past twenty-four hours with breakfast if he wishes to do so.

Naturally most of my working colleagues were from the Clandestine Service, the DDP. As in Mexico I was impressed by the qualities they brought to the job—unique talents and unswerving dedication. I was awed by their language capabilities. Some had grown up in the Orient— often children of diplomatic or missionary families—and they chattered in Japanese or Chinese in the halls. Those of European extraction often spoke half a dozen tongues fluently, and almost all DDP officers commanded at least one language other than English. In my own division a fellow spoke Quechua and Aymara, Indian languages of the Andes which are among the most difficult in the world to learn. (A language incentive program was abandoned after several years at CIA, when the practice of paying an annual bonus for learning a language or maintaining fluency in one already known became inordinately expensive. One wizard was drawing extra pay for twelve foreign languages.)

The people of the Clandestine Service were a diverse lot, and I met many who worked in other parts of the world while we both were enduring our headquarters tour—which every CIA officer must expect after two or three stints abroad. Some encounters were at evening gatherings, others in the cafeteria at Langley, in the basement gymnasium at our headquarters building, or perhaps during trips to and from downtown Washington on a CIA shuttle bus, known as the Bluebird.

In the halls I often saw a man who tap-tapped carefully through the maze of corridors with his white cane. He had been totally blinded in the bomb explosion which killed one CIA secretary and wounded others at the American embassy in Saigon. Or the officer reputed to have gallantly saved a turkey but lost thousands of dollars in the Middle

East: he was leaving the embassy just before Thanksgiving with two brown paper parcels, one containing a frozen turkey and the other several kilos of local currency for an agent. He was struck by a taxi and, even though dazed, realized that he must get back to the station because all that money might be difficult to explain if the police asked questions. He grabbed one of the packages and limped through the traffic to his embassy haven—when he opened it he was dismayed to find that he had saved the turkey but lost the cash which, of course, was never recovered. I often lunched with a CIA officer who had been a captain in the army in Germany after World War II and told droll stories about his jeep driver, a man of German extraction named Henry Kissinger. I was properly impressed by a CIA officer known as one of the best recruiters in the business, a brash rascal who often approached his recruitment prospects in the guise of an international banker, Hollywood screenwriter, or professional smuggler. In an African country he was once in a traffic accident. The occupant of the other car was injured, and our rascal rode with him in the ambulance and, finding the victim to be a person of some interest, recruited him before they reached the hospital. On another occasion this inventive officer simply couldn't think of a way to approach a recruitment target until finally he decided on the audacious solution of renting a brass band and marching up to the fellow's front door where, with trumpets blaring, he talked himself into the target's confidence and, eventually, recruited him as an informant for CIA.

Many CIA officers I met had taken a course in picks and locks; they had little concern if, by chance, they found themselves locked out of their homes. One fellow was an expert in crates; he would study wooden boards stenciled with Cyrillic lettering and casually announce that they had once surrounded airplane engines from a specific factory in Russia. One man I met was a professional forger; another, a scholarly-looking type whose specialty was taking things apart and then putting them back together again so that all appeared untouched. Code books, for instance. Or a pack of cigarettes with secret messages concealed in the tobacco.

Of all the many CIA people with varied backgrounds and peculiar talents the most remarkable I met was Dick Welch. Certainly he was the only one-eyed officer entering CIA to pass his medical examination with the rating of 20–20 for each eye.

Richard Skeffington Welch had a glass eye, the result of a childhood temper tantrum thrown by his brother, who flung a pair of scissors at him. During his first CIA physical examination the medic handed Dick an eye chart on a racket-shaped board, much like a Ping-Pong paddle. "Cover one of your eyes," the examiner said, "and read this for me. Then change it to the other hand and read it with your other eye."

Dick covered his glass eye and read. The text was familiar for one who had studied Latin at Boston's Classical High School and recently graduated *magna cum laude* in Greek studies from Harvard:

THE PRINCIPAL CONQUESTS OF THE ROMANS WERE
Achieved Under The Republic; *And The Emperors*,
for the most part, were satisfied with preserving
. . . .

The examiner stopped Dick when he reached the 20-20 point. Dick covered his good eye and repeated the text verbatim. It was not that he had a photographic memory but he had memorized, long before, the opening sentences of Gibbon's *The Decline and Fall of the Roman Empire.*

Dick Welch wanted to work in Greek affairs from the moment he joined CIA. He was distressed that the system did not recognize his desire and background by assigning him to the Greek desk. To make matters worse, he was bored with the odd jobs he was being given. Finally a supervisor approached him.

"Are you the fellow who studied Greek?"

Dick acknowledged that he was.

"Then translate this, and we'll see how you do." The supervisor dropped a clipping from an Athens newspaper on the desk.

Dick Welch did not have the vaguest idea how to read the modern Greek, much less translate it. He knew only ancient Greek, almost an altogether different language. But he could discern that the news item was a wire service release; Dick hurried to the CIA library and, sure enough, found the English version of the article in the Paris *Herald Tribune*. He copied the English text and took his handiwork to the supervisor.

"Hey, that was pretty fast." The supervisor was impressed. He ran his eyes over the copy. "And it's a perfect translation. Okay. You're assigned to the Greek desk."

At his new job Dick set about the business of learning modern Greek before his colleagues discovered the deception. He was soon awarded with a choice first overseas assignment—Athens.

Dick had a puckish sense of humor. One of the first stories I heard about him concerned the routine of family physical examinations prior to his Athens tour. A request made by the doctors on the eve of his departure had given him the opportunity to lighten the humdrum of departure chores with a bit of drollery. "Imagine!" Dick complained, feigning complete disgust. "The medics want me to bring in a urine sample from my daughter. She's only three months old. How in the

name of God am I to obtain a specimen from a three-month-old girl?"
His good eye twinkled. "Why, it would be easier to get it from my basset
hound!" Everyone had heard of Dick's basset, named for one of Harvard's foremost Greek scholars.

Three days later a friend saw Dick in the hall. Dick waved as they
passed.

"See you! We're off to Athens."

"Everything set?"

"Oh, yes," Dick Welch said amiably. "My basset hound passed the
urine test."

Dick never overlooked an opportunity to indulge himself with a
sally, even in circumstances where others would have been reticent. He
arrived in Athens and entered the Chief of Station's office for that
initial interview with the new boss—a numbing experience for most
young officers on their first overseas assignment.

"Is it true," Dick asked the COS, "that you have to be a Greek to
get ahead in this station?"

Welch was bright enough, fortunately, to detect that a sense of
humor was an attribute of his new chief: Thomas Karamessines.

My Washington tour from mid-1967 through 1969 coincided with
the peak period of civil unrest in the United States. In the summer of
1967 American cities were in revolt; twenty-six were killed in the riots
in Newark, and forty died in Detroit's black ghetto.

On a flight from New York to Washington on April 4, 1968, I was
absorbed in reading a newspaper. As the plane approached Washington
to begin our descent into National Airport, I glanced up and was surprised to see most of the passengers looking out of the windows on one
side of the aircraft.

"What is everyone looking at?" I asked a stewardess.

"They're watching Washington burn," she replied.

I joined the other passengers. It was true, and I watched in horror
as the plane flew over Washington's Fourteenth Street area, where
dozens of buildings were in flames.

Martin Luther King had been assassinated that day.

In Los Angeles, three months later, Robert Kennedy was gunned
down.

Maria, off at college, had become a beautiful woman. David, Jr.,
I was astounded to find, had grown until I had to look up at him from
my own six-foot length. Atlee, too, was changing from a girl to a
woman, with long blond hair and classic features. She was fifteen and
lovely.

195

On Saturday nights I always waited for Atlee to come home before going to bed. One Saturday night I fell asleep over a book. I was awakened by the telephone; Atlee wanted me to know she would be arriving a few minutes past her regular midnight curfew. She was usually punctual and always considerate, letting me know if she might be late.

I returned to my book, nodded, fell asleep again.

The telephone rang again forty-five minutes later. A nurse was calling from the emergency room of a hospital a few miles away.

"Come quickly," the nurse told me. "Your daughter has been in an automobile accident."

"How bad is it?" was my first question.

"It's bad. Come now."

I was afraid to ask the second question. I sped to the hospital.

A policeman at the door of the hospital told me Atlee was dead. Her boyfriend had been drinking, and his car had swerved suddenly into the path of another. The impact had been on Atlee's side; despite the fact that her seat belt had been fastened she died instantly.

In the fall of 1968 I had been divorced for a year. When not at the office I was occupied with the children's problems. Pepito, by now nineteen, needed some guidance as well. He was a handsome young Dominican with, I learned, the same human desires as most American males that age.

A neighbor visited me, solemn and serious. He was a foreigner and had brought two female servants with him to Maryland. He needed to discuss a problem which had arisen between Pepito and one of them. Indeed it was serious. One of the servants was pregnant and she claimed Pepito was responsible.

I braced Pepito.

"Pepito," I asked, "have you been sleeping with one of the girls across the street?"

"No, *señor*," Pepito said.

I was surprised. I had assumed my neighbor knew what he was talking about when he identified Pepito as the culprit.

"You're not sleeping with one of the girls?"

"No, *señor*," Pepito repeated. But then he added, "I'm sleeping with both of them."

Well, such were the domestic problems to be resolved from time to time. And, occasionally it was necessary for me to travel and leave these problems.

In September of 1968 I made an excursion to academe as the CIA representative in a political-military game at the Massachusetts Institute of Technology in Boston. The MIT exercise was sponsored by the Arms Control Disarmament Agency and focused on the hypothetical question of how should the United States government react if a leftist-Communist coalition seriously threatened the overthrow of a friendly conservative regime in Guatemala. I had been asked by CIA to attend because of my Latin American experience, especially in Guatemala and the Dominican Republic. To intervene or not to intervene? There were several subplots in the game's scenario reminiscent of the circumstances in both the Guatemalan and Dominican interventions, but from the outset it was obvious they did not make the participants nearly so wary as did the possibility of an escalating American involvement leading to another Vietnam.

There were two United States teams. They were physically isolated from each other but functioned—under a television camera's eye—with the same intelligence and instructions. Retired General James Gavin was the president of the Blue Team, and an MIT professor, formerly with CIA, was the president of the Green Team. Each had a make-believe staff—cabinet members, defense officials, foreign service and intelligence officers—comprised of prominent people who had held similar positions in real life. The most interesting team to observe was the Red Team, the insurgent cadre which plotted against the imaginary Guatemalan government. There were only four on the Red Team. One was Ernst Halperin, an MIT scholar, who adroitly played the role of a Guatemalan Communist leader. The leader of the Red Team was Richard Bissell. It had been seven years since Bissell had persuaded me to stay with CIA in the wake of the Bay of Pigs. For most of that period Bissell had been a vice president of United Aircraft.

The television monitors following the activities of each of the three groups were in the office of the Control Team. I worked there, with several others expert in political science and Soviet affairs. My task was to provide Cuban and Latin American expertise to the Control scenario on which the Blue, Green, and Red Teams had to base their reactions and recommendations. And we also were tasked with the umpire's job of keeping the game within reason. We had to exercise this authority only once, when Marxist leader Bissell sent a message from Guatemala to his Paris representative claiming that he had five hundred guerrillas in the mountains. I replied to the message, advising Bissell that "I will use your figure of five hundred guerrillas for propaganda purposes, but for my personal information how many guerrillas do we really have?" I watched the television screen as the message was handed to Bissell. The former DDP glanced sternly at the camera, admonishing me for being a smart-ass, but he couldn't conceal a smile.

The games were exciting for me, as so much of the substance of the scenario had mnemonic roots in my own CIA past. It was like playing political God. Imagine, Dean Rusk sent a message to the American Ambassador in Guatemala seeking information, and I composed the reply, an estimate of the situation. Fidel Castro spoke for four hours at the dedication of an artificial insemination center in Cuba, and I wrote the UPI dispatch describing his reaction to developments in Guatemala City. The editor of *Pravda* demanded the Party line for his morning editorial, and one of my teammates drafted it. Student opinion, United Nations anxiety, OAS indifference, messages enciphered in guerrilla caves, the private and public musings of de Gaulle—we created them all. A game, but stimulating.

The Blue and Green teams reached identical conclusions. Both agreed that United States armed force would only be used in the event American citizens had to be evacuated from Guatemala. I was mildly surprised when both teams unabashedly called for covert action—dirty political tricks—to influence developments. Some of the liberals among the actors—there was a dovecote of them—seemed quite ready if need be to circumvent international conventions and abandon moral considerations in seeking a new government which would be compatible with their ideals. Each team was unequivocal on one point: its policy would be to allow an opposition regime, however dubious its political nature, to take over Guatemala rather than to permit United States military intervention.

When the two-day exercise drew to a close both the Blue and Green teams were smugly convinced they had won the game by having the United States endorse the coalition government and promise it aid. Each team had allowed only two Communists to become cabinet members in the new government. But Bissell's Red Team of insurgents was declared the winner—it had manipulated the two Communist cabinet members into the positions of chief of the new intelligence service and commander of the militia, which had taken over national security from an army in disarray.

Both the Blue and Green President of the United States had approved a consensus that two Communist countries in Latin America, Cuba and the new Guatemala, were preferable to another Dominican-style military adventure.

Returning to Langley, I submitted a report on my participation in the MIT exercise. The last sentence read: "I came away from two days in academe with the conviction that any of us called on to assist an American president in another military intervention will feel that we are a part of a very lonely crowd."

The memorandum was back at my desk a few days later. A blue buck-sheet was attached, indicating that Dick Helms had sent the report to Walt Rostow, head of President Johnson's National Security Council. Helms had written, *For Your Very Private Eye*. Rostow had noted, *Fascinating*.

The evenings at home became longer and the reading less interesting, a poor substitute for companionship. I was lonely.

On election day of 1968 I voted for Hubert Humphrey, then went to a watch-the-returns party at the home of a CIA couple I had worked with in Santo Domingo. I met another guest, an extremely attractive blonde some twenty years younger than I. At first our conversation was strained, as Gina somehow had the impression I was a priest; perhaps it was the black turtleneck shirt I was wearing. When that was straightened out, we found we had much in common. Gina had previously been married to a CIA officer. We were each taking care of three children while working. And we shared a mutual dismay as the television commentators began to confirm the election of Richard Nixon as our next President.

Gina was living with her parents in Potomac, Maryland, and I drove her home. The route passed near my house on the outskirts of Potomac.

"What about a nightcap at my place?" I suggested. "We can watch the California returns."

Gina looked at her watch. It was 3 A.M. "Thanks," she said dryly, "but I have to work in a few hours."

Oh, well. She was lovely, and I was lonely.

Two weeks later the telephone rang in my office. My secretary, not recognizing the name or voice, was wary. "May I ask where you are calling from?"

Gina was telephoning from work. "I'm calling from the National Conference of Catholic Charities."

"Then you *must* have the wrong Mr. Phillips," my secretary said.

But it wasn't the wrong number. Gina and I were married six months later. There was no way to keep the wedding crowd small—among the other guests were her children, Deborah, Bryan, and Wynne and my Maria, David, Jr., and Christopher.

Our honeymoon was a weekend in New York. During that time a Cuban intelligence officer defected from his post at a Cuban embassy in Europe, carrying with him, as a good defector should, a suitcase of secret documents. The CIA headquarters only telephoned me about twelve times during the two-day honeymoon.

I was summoned to the office of the Chief of the Western Hemisphere Division for a pleasant announcement. I had been promoted to GS-16.

As a super-grader I became eligible for membership in the exclusive club on the seventh floor of the CIA building—the Executive Dining Room. The company was stimulating and food good, but there was no bread. Admiral Raborn, before his departure from CIA, had decreed that soft white bread was unhealthy. Thus each table in the senior luncheon room had a basket of cellophane-wrapped rye-crisps and other dry crackers; even today, CIA friends confirm, there is no bread except when sandwiches are ordered.

Lunch in the CIA Executive Dining Room—only the midday meal is served—is business-oriented. There are lapses into the latest political or sports developments but inevitably the conversation reverts to espionage. Business is often conducted there with visitors from other agencies. No alcohol is served, that amenity being reserved for the more intimate and even more exclusive DCI Dining Room. Senior officers find the lunch hour valuable as a time when management successes or failures can be analyzed, or professional gossip exchanged.

Luncheon is brief in the Executive Dining Room. But not as short as the twelve minutes Colonel J. C. King once suggested as sufficient time for his subordinates to spend in the cafeteria at noon. (A skeptical employee surveilled Colonel King the day after he made the recommendation and clocked him in and out in precisely eleven minutes.)

Dick Helms had finally received a presidential nod, and became the new DCI. Clandestine Service officers were delighted that an experienced professional was in the top job—particularly after the tenure of Admiral Raborn who lacked, as Abe would have put it, the essential elements of greatness as chief intelligence officer of the United States government. Helms was almost universally admired.

Helms maintained the loyalty and devotion of his subordinates despite an element of aloofness in his personal relations with them. I believe it was a deliberate posture. When directors of Central Intelligence become personal buddies of one senior officer and not others there are sometimes recriminations when promotions or senior assignments are handed out; the less favored is tempted to grouse that it was the personal friendship which tipped the scales at decision time. But Helms was respected for his devotion to taking care of all employees—even junior ones he seldom or never met—when they had personal problems. If Helms heard, for instance, that a CIA officer or a member of his family needed special medical attention, he would hound the chief of his medical department until he was assured everything possible had been done to alleviate the problem.

Helms's concern for his people was nothing new. When he was Chief of Operations for the DDP much earlier in his career, he made a comment in my presence that seemed to encapsulate his management philosophy: "My job is to hold an umbrella over you fellows and catch the crap so you can get on with your operating." This concept of responsibility to, and for, his subordinates undoubtedly contributed to the problems he encountered in post-mortems on CIA's activities over the years.

I remember a private conference with Helms. We discussed an impending operation which, while necessary, entailed considerable risk. After reviewing the complexities of the endeavor, Helms told me to go ahead. I reiterated my concern. His decision having been made, Helms seemed to have no doubts and he reminded me that in espionage anything less than controlled boldness would minimize the chance of success. As I prepared to leave he stopped me at the door.

"Dave?"

"Sir?"

"*Arriba!*"

It had been several years since we had celebrated the New Year in Havana, but Dick Helms still liked the Spanish exhortation.

Vice Admiral Rufus Taylor was appointed as the DDCI, the first of three military officers to serve in the number-two CIA position. (Marine Lt. General Robert Cushman and army Lt. General Vernon Walters succeeded him.) Next in the line of command was the new DDP, Des Fitz-Gerald's replacement after his death on the tennis court. Tom Karamessines was the new DDP and the intelligence officer of Greek extraction who had welcomed Dick Welch to Athens. Karamessines could afford to chuckle at the stock characterization of all senior CIA people as WASPs. He had risen to the top of the Clandestine Service after important Chief of Station assignments in Europe. I had been told that he had been irked when one journalist referred to him pejoratively as a "flaps and seals" man—the term described those expert in opening and closing letters without the tampering being detectable. Perhaps he was not as flamboyant as Des FitzGerald, but he was energetic. Often during meetings he would rise and stride about his office, tamping his ever-present pipe furiously. He was a kind man and liked by the people he worked with. This was especially true of women and junior officers. Karamessines usually shunned the Executive Dining Room, preferring to stand in line in the cafeteria with the troops. He would always tell his secretary, just before going to lunch, where he would be sitting in the cafeteria so he could be summoned at once to answer a query from the seventh floor.

From time to time I saw Howard Hunt. The bounce and quick smile which had characterized him in previous years had faded. His career was not prospering. He worked at one mundane staff job after another and promotions eluded him. In Guatemala in 1954 he had been senior to me; now I outranked him. But he continued to express an interest in my career and never failed to remind me he was ready to assist, should I ever need his services.

Several times I saw the man a friend had identified as Jim Angleton. He was always alone, with his head down, engaged in deep and intricate thoughts, I was sure.

The majority of CIA people in the DDI and the DDS&T are overt employees who rarely serve overseas. Some of the DDA support personnel share the vicissitudes of foreign service and cover problems with the DDP officers.

Those who must depend on cover to conduct their business abroad are obliged to continue the cover at home. A routine life is not possible for them even when living in the Washington area. They must pretend to be somewhere else when a creditor or visitor from out of town telephones them at the office at Langley on an "outside" line (that is, not tied into the CIA switchboard). If troubled they may not select their own psychiatrist, but instead must visit one cleared and approved by CIA. They—and their families—must lie constantly. They cannot tell the truth to bankers, neighbors, lodge brothers, or delivery boys. I even lied to the Boy Scouts of America when filling out the application papers to be a Scoutmaster. They must lead a double life at home so that cover will be intact when next they are assigned overseas. It is a vexing existence.

An insurance salesman lived a few houses down the street. He owned an absolute clunker of an old car, which often failed to start on cold mornings. Like my other neighbors, he believed I worked for the Department of State in downtown Washington. His office was near the Department. Thus on several mornings during 1968 and 1969 he knocked on my door at seven in the morning, asking for a ride to work "since it's not out of your way." My office was, of course, at Langley, a pleasant drive of less than fifteen minutes without the hindrance of street lights or traffic. But there was nothing I could do. So I drove him, on half a dozen occasions, through forty-five minutes of heavy traffic to downtown Washington and then returned, late, to my own job at CIA.

CIA people on home tours in Washington are, understandably, clannish, and in the evening they tend to congregate socially with the same people they work with during the day. An early decision must be reached, for instance, in planning a dinner party for eight. Will it be a mixed group of CIA and non-CIA friends, or one to which only CIA or other witting government employees are invited? Usually the decision comes down on the side of a party for spooks. Only then can husbands and wives talk freely; otherwise they are likely to appear as dolts to outsiders because they must be evasive about their past or must equivocate whenever the conversation turns to them and their business.

An example: a deep-cover CIA officer returned from overseas might be asked what he was doing all that time in Africa, and he must reply wtih some bland cover story of working with the natives for some reason or another, and change the subject when he can.

In fact this man was in Africa assuming the role of an international bum, an opportunist, a black marketeer after a fast buck. He had been written about in *Time* magazine, described as a horrible example of those who prey on disaster. He was eager for cash in Africa—but for CIA stations and in the sterile (untraceable) currency they needed for their operations. To do that he had to have cover, contacts, and mobility. But he can't talk about that, or the nightclub he operated for a while in an African capital. One night in his club he had enlisted the aid of an unwitting BBC correspondent to get a young black drunk and disarm him before he could carry out his intention of assassinating one of the country's leaders.

Or, the case of another friend, a scholar who—prior to his CIA service—had been an attorney, civil engineer and assistant to the United States Attorney General. Now, after serving overseas as a CIA Station Chief, he would have to pretend at a Georgetown cocktail party that he was a foreign service officer and his jokes or stories would have to fit his cover status. Obviously he would be more relaxed at a CIA gathering. There he could relate one of his many amusing stories, such as the account of the time he had arranged for a rectal examination of an ex-president running again for office. The examination was conducted in strict clandestinety, because the physician was an American doctor flown into the country by the CIA and the patient certainly didn't want anyone to discover that (a) he might have a serious medical problem or (b) that he didn't trust local doctors to diagnose it if he did.

At the last minute the visiting doctor found that he had forgotten the rubber glove necessary for the rectal examination, especially of such a high-level bottom. So the CIA Station Chief found himself scurrying about a small capital city at midnight when all the pharmacies were closed, in desperate search for a rubber finger. Obtain one he did, under suitable pretense, so the examination could be conducted. The grateful politician was soon elected president of his country again. He remained an appreciative friend of the CIA Station Chief; in intelligence jargon he was called an agent of influence.

I recall one evening when I was the only CIA person at a small dinner in Chevy Chase. A woman sitting next to me asked, "What do you do, Mr. Phillips?"

"I'm in the foreign service," I replied. "Right now I'm on a home tour assignment."

"What do you people do all day in that big State Department building?" was the next question.

"Mostly shuffle papers," I lied.

"It must be dull." The woman shrugged and turned to talk with someone more interesting.

In fact my day had not been dull. I had attended with Dick Helms a meeting of the Forty Committee, the small exclusive group which met in the situation room at the White House to consider covert action proposals. Henry Kissinger's discussion with Helms, Attorney General John Mitchell, an Undersecretary of State and top Defense officials would have made stimulating dinner party persiflage, had I been able to mention it.

After I married Gina in 1969 life became pleasant at home. Gina would be pretty when I crossed the threshold after a busy day at Langley, and we would chat about her day and mine. Then Gina would practice culinary legerdemain in the kitchen; Pepito soon lost his trim figure and I began to have problems with my waistline. I quit and resumed smoking several times.

On Friday nights I went with Christopher to troop meetings and spent some weekends in the woods on overnight hikes. I remember not being able to sleep one night. In my pup tent I listened to a portable radio predict snow when in fact there was already two inches on the ground. The bottle of brandy Gina had stowed in my knapsack was comforting.

Work at the office continued to be interesting. My desk at Langley was the control center from which CIA monitored intelligence operations of the Cuban DGI—Directorate General of Intelligence—around the globe. DGI agents were busy in most of Latin America, especially in Venezuela and Guatemala, and Che Guevara in Bolivia had called on Latin American revolutionaries to join him in creating two, three, many Vietnams. Cuban advisers were active in the Middle East and, despite Guevara's failure in the Congo, in a number of African countries. Soviet intelligence experts were present in the DGI offices in Havana, supporting and manipulating the Cuban service which had become, in effect, a surrogate of the Russian KGB.

Cuba was a "hard target." CIA had to report on developments in Havana, which meant that spies had to risk their lives, and sometimes lose them, to obtain the information needed and to get it off the island and to Langley for the use of United States policy makers.

Each day I learned more about life-and-death espionage, the very serious and risky business of conducting intelligence operations inside a closed society.

I learned about double-agents. Khrushchev reputedly told Allen

Dulles that both their countries could save money if they would stop paying the same spies. An exaggeration, but with an element of truth. Intelligence supervisors constantly must be alert for information that may be tainted, the deception of a double-agent. Some spies adopt the double-agent role yet remain sources of dependable, vital information; that is, they pretend to be working for, say, the Soviets but in reality remain loyal to the CIA. Others pretend loyalty to each of two sides, and their only dedication is to the money they make from both. Sometimes greed consumes reason, and they become triple or quadruple agents by contacting other intelligence services. These opportunists play a dangerous game, and seldom survive. Intelligence managers cross-check and, like good investigative reports in journalism, soon spot the clinkers among their sources.

Good double-agents, like any vital intelligence source, must be protected. If their information is improperly used, or leaks into the public domain, their usefulness or even survival is threatened. An intelligence service will go to almost any extreme to protect and maintain a valuable source of information—as Winston Churchill did when he allowed German bombs to fall on Coventry rather than warn the inhabitants and risk exposure of the Allies' most carefully kept secret: that the British had broken the German military code. George Blake, like Kim Philby a Soviet penetration of the British service, is said to have revealed to the Soviets the ingenious tunnel dug by CIA under the Berlin Wall. But the Russians allowed valuable information to continue to flow from our East Berlin operation for over a year after that, fearing Blake's position in London would be jeopardized if the East Germans were told about the tunnel.

Intelligence services are unremitting in their efforts to penetrate hostile services, and this is usually most easily accomplished by recruiting "in place"—that is, on the job—an intelligence officer who is willing to become a double-agent. Efforts to thwart such endeavors are called counter-intelligence or counter-espionage. The CI-nicks, specialists in counter-intelligence, burrow like inquisitive moles through stacks of documents searching for the elusive clue which will indicate a traitor at work. Probably because of Jim Angleton, CIA has the best record of defending itself from foreign penetration; there is no known case of a successful penetration at the staff level. This remarkable record is blemished only by the realization that an undiscovered penetration—an American Philby or Blake—might well be going to work each morning at CIA. The possibility keeps counter-intelligence officers scratching through their papers for some indication that grandmother might be on the roof at Langley.

In hard target operations, communications with an agent are tricky.

In many countries of the world a CIA case officer and his source can hold leisurely conversations in an out-of-the-way bar or restaurant. In a "denied area"—a closed society such as Cuba, the Soviet Union, China, or the Bloc countries—internal security is so hermetic that personal meetings of reasonable duration are usually impractical. Under such circumstances, intelligence information is often conveyed in secret writing, or invisible writing, sophisticated versions of disappearing lemon juice (which emerges when exposed to heat). Some spies report to case officers hundreds of miles away by radio, but the development of modern direction finding equipment makes this increasingly hazardous.

The safest way to pass instructions to an agent, or to receive intelligence from him (or her), is to use a "dead drop," as I had first learned during my clandestine training course in New York in 1950.

Perhaps the most macabre example was related to me by a CIA woman case officer. She handled a man and wife spy team—infrequent but not rare—in a Socialist country where the risk of meeting with local people was high. She asked the couple to find a safe place where documents could be cached. It had to be in a public place where her presence or theirs could be explained. She also told them that such a location was known in espionage jargon as a dead drop.

The man and his wife conferred for a few minutes, then made their suggestion. The appropriate site for the dead drop was the grave of their son in the local cemetery.

For several months the CIA woman had the ghoulish task of hiding instructions in the plastic flower basket at the son's grave and collecting purloined documents in subsequent visits to the cemetery.

Most intelligence officers who set out to persuade someone to become a traitor have to reach an accommodation of some sort with the code of ethics and morality they have inherited or adopted. Sometimes dirty tricks are involved in the recruiting of spies. One technique used by intelligence services is known as the false-flag recruitment, when an unsuspecting person with access to intelligence of value is approached in contrived circumstances by a recruiter pretending to be someone he is not. A Russian-speaking officer from a Western service, for instance, might cultivate a Marxist anywhere in the world, to ask him to report on his government as a favor to the Kremlin. A Soviet KGB officer, on the other hand, might pose as a right-wing American in approaching a conservative U.S. government employee. He would attempt to persuade the American to report on the inner workings of his agency or department "to help my patriotic organization to be sure the Commies aren't infiltrating our institutions."

Devious and ingenious schemes of this type have worked. Today

206

there are unsuspecting zealots around the world who are managed and paid as spies; they sell their countries' secrets believing all the while they are helping "the good guys." Some scenarios in false-flag recruitments are so complex they would be poor material for fiction writers; the stories would not be believed.

Another new and interesting facet of my assignment as Chief of Cuban Operations was that I was able to learn more about other Western intelligence services.

The British Secret Intelligence Service—sometimes known as SIS but more frequently as MI-6—is the Queen's foreign espionage and, on occasion, covert-action agency. The British have been adroit intelligence operators since Sir Francis Walsingham employed bright, young, energetic Oxford and Cambridge graduates as spies, much as the CIA scouts for talented officers on college campuses in our country today. MI-5, the British version of our FBI, has a charter to operate overseas in Commonwealth countries. British intelligence has a commendable record except for the egg on the vests of the counter-intelligence people who permitted Philby, George Blake, and other Soviet recruits to thrive so long as successful double-agents. The problem has been primarily that an Englishman simply can't allow himself to believe that a fellow wearing his school tie could be a traitor. As far as I know, the British services don't use lie-detectors or similar personnel security devices.

The American CIA and the British services enjoy a symbiotic relationship. CIA and O.S.S. before it owe much of their professionalism to MI-6 tutors, who guided the reconstruction of United States intelligence after it was abandoned (when Henry Stimson allegedly declared "that gentlemen do not read each other's mail"). This type of association is unique in the intelligence world but is feasible because of compatible national ideologies and traits. Professional considerations aside, British intelligence men and women are fine people and steadfast friends.

When CIA officers discuss in bull sessions the foreign services they have worked with or against there is often debate as to which is the best. Attempts to compare and evaluate other services are fruitless except in specific areas of competence. Certainly the British are best at procuring economic intelligence, but their counter-intelligence history is poor. And so the debate will go.

I do know this: should I find myself attempting to evade a terrorist gang in a large and unfamiliar city and dependent on a foreign service to give me the intelligence and operational support I need to escape with my cloak and dagger intact, I would seek help from these foreign services in the following order:

First, the Israeli service, known as the Mossad. (They have a sense of purpose—survival—and have learned how to be tough enough to operate in pitch-black alleys.*)

Second, the CIA. (I would nominate my own former outfit as best in the world if I were a policy maker seeking the missing piece of an international puzzle; but in the dark alley situation would prefer the protection of a case officer out of Tel Aviv.)

Third, the British.

Fourth, the Soviet KGB. (The Soviets, in the past, were clumsy and inflexible, the only intelligence officers in the world who allowed themselves to be spotted in a crowd because their pants cuffs were so wide they flapped. But they are becoming sophisticated, and the cut of their clothes less identifiable.)

Fifth, the Cuban DGI. (With Soviet guidance this young service is improving. But they insist on carrying large guns and acting like footpads. More than once Cuban ambassadors have been embarrassed when their "cultural" attachés have been arrested packing .45 pistols.)

While the Israeli service deserves first ranking on my or any other list, it has a built-in advantage that all other intelligence operators envy. The first phases of recruiting a spy are the essential ones of approach and cultivation before the pitch is made. The Israelis have ready access in nearly every country in the world to persons prominent in political, scientific, and economic areas: the indigenous Jews who are unlikely to resent a proposal that they cooperate with their ethnic homeland.

In the summer of 1968 I was involved in an assassination plot against the life of Fidel Castro. At the time I did not know of the plans and even attempts which had been made earlier in the 1960's.** In this instance the attempt was contemplated by Cuban exiles in Florida who had no connection with the CIA: they planned to slip ashore into the United States naval base at Guantanamo, Cuba, and launch their attack against

---

* I am sure there is one group which would agree with me: the hostages who were rescued in the daring commando raid at Entebbe in 1976. The Israeli operation would not have been even remotely feasible without superb intelligence support.

** I have often been asked how it was possible that I did not know of the Castro assassination schemes. The question is usually predicated on the assumption that when I became Chief of Cuban Operations and then head of all Latin American affairs someone would have told me, or I would have read about the endeavors in documents in my safe. The fact is that those few CIA officers involved did not discuss their participation even with senior officers not in the chain of command at the time of the plots. And highly sensitive papers are not retained in a division chief's office, where they might be read by successive chiefs and their deputies, and by the several secretaries who would have access to the files over the years.

Castro from there. In the event of failure, which seemed very probable, the Cuban government could have and certainly would have castigated the United States.

I carried the hard intelligence about the assassination scheme to the policy echelons of the Department of State. They agreed something must be done to thwart the scheme and head off the problems which would ensue if the plan went forward. The Department of State sent a message to the Cuban government, through the Swiss embassy in Washington, warning the Castro regime of the conspiracy. It was ironical that —given subsequent revelations concerning CIA plotting against Castro— the information which may have helped quash this attempt came from CIA.

As the decade of the 1960's drew to a close, Cuban efforts to sustain existing subversive groups and stimulate new ones in Latin America became less successful. In one country after another local governments shored up their counter-insurgency programs until urban extremists could not operate and rural guerrillas became impotent. In nearly every case this was the result of United States assistance in training and technical support. The CIA played a major role.

The death of Che Guevara in Bolivia in 1967 was the turning point. The asthmatic revolutionary had been the victim of his own intelligence and propaganda when he predicted that the *campesinos* of Bolivia would rise up against their government; it was a peasant woman who told soldiers where the beret-clad guerrilla was hiding, exhausted and wounded.

Bolivian counter-insurgency teams probably would not have tracked down Guevara, or at least not so efficiently and soon, without the training and support they received from the United States military and the CIA. To that extent only was the United States involved in Guevara's death. In fact, when he was captured CIA attempted to persuade the Bolivians to spare Guevara's life. Moral considerations aside, there was always the possibility he might provide information we needed on Cuba and the certainty he would become an international martyr if executed. The Bolivians would have none of that. By their standards death was the inevitable penalty.

I heard a number of reports about the circumstances leading to Che Guevara's death. Some described his final days, hours, and even minutes. All the spectators—the hunters and curious alike—in the Bolivian mountain hamlet on October 8, 1967, agreed that the revolutionary, who had compared himself to a Don Quixote tilting against imperialistic windmills, died with dignity. When the end came he was wounded and ill. And brave.

The Bolivian authorities took numerous photographs after his execution by firing squad, to prove that Che was dead. His admirers saw in the grim photographs the picture of crucifixion.

During the period of my headquarters tour, which extended from the fall of 1967 through 1969, I often visited the CIA training establishment located in Virginia, some distance from Langley. I was a lecturer in the training course for young officers and attended seminars there with other headquarters managers. Once a year the Chiefs of Station from Latin America convened there for a conference.

For many years military cover which protected "the farm," as it was called, remained reasonably solid. Few realized that what appeared to be a military special operations training site was really an espionage university where young college graduates were schooled in the arcane arts of covert action, production of intelligence, physical survival and political science. One would have thought the bright young men and women would have been weary of studying, but they reveled in the post-graduate curriculum of tradecraft, derring-do, and intelligence esoterica.

In 1968 the violence of political extremists had escalated to such a degree in Latin America that it was decided in 1969 the Chiefs of Station in the area should have advanced training in defensive weapons and how to use them. Two days were allocated for that purpose prior to the Chiefs' conference at the training site. The weather was inordinately cold so the visitors were outfitted with arctic clothing for the outdoor exercises, which included night firing practice in the woods. Each of us was required to qualify in several types of hand guns, rifles, shotguns, and submachine guns. The training sessions were built around imaginary situations where we would be the victims of kidnap attempts or under fire from hostile terrorists. Most of the Chiefs of Station, despite their graying temples, shot exceptionally well. Dick Welch, in from his overseas post, shot as well as the rest and better than some.

One of our group did not have the appearance one would expect of a CIA Chief of Station. He was short, stocky, wore glasses, and always had a cigar jammed in his teeth. He was an able intelligence officer, but would never have been selected for the role by a casting director. His physical resemblance to former New York City Mayor La Guardia was so pronounced that we called him the Little Flower. We were amused when he first walked out on the firing range. Years of CIA service in the tropics had thinned the Little Flower's blood to the point that he chose to bundle up in several layers of the heavy arctic clothing. He looked like a rotund bear smoking a stogie.

Our final exercise simulated a terrorist attack against a man riding alone in a jeep. We all watched, chuckling, when the time came for the Little Flower to leap from his jeep and start shooting at the imaginary assailants. First he shot his pistol from the side of the jeep, then over the top, and finally, sprawled on his stomach under the vehicle. He never lost his cigar while blasting away.

When it was over we voted the Little Flower as the winner of the exercise. We agreed terrorists attacking him would have been dead—from laughter.

After dinner that night Dick Welch challenged me to a game of pool in the student club, wagering a glass of brandy on the outcome. That seemed a good, safe bet. I had spent considerable time—perhaps too much—lounging in a pool hall in Fort Worth during my youth and thought myself pretty sharp with a cue. Certainly I could win a snifter of brandy from a one-eyed Harvard man.

Several students gathered around the table as we played. After a few minutes I was chagrined as I waited helplessly while Dick plunked one ball after another into the pockets, calling his shots with precision. It was really quite embarrassing. On the rare occasions when I had an opportunity to shoot, Dick would regale the students with tales of how he made extra spending money at Harvard—by going into pool halls in the lower-class areas of Boston and fleecing the innocents who presumed, as I had, that an Ivy Leaguer would not know one end of a cue from the other.

Several students followed us to the bar, ordering beer while Dick Welch lingered over his selection of the expensive brandy I was to pay for. As we sipped our cognac he enthralled the young officers with yarns and anecdotes culled from his overseas tours in Athens, Nicosia, and Guatemala City. The students were wide-eyed. If things went well they could expect to be a Chief of Station some day, and they savored Dick's articulate descriptions of life in the netherlands of espionage.

A CIA instructor standing at the end of the bar also enjoyed Dick's monologue. He was drunk. He grunted with appreciation at the conclusion of each story Dick told to the students. Instructing the bartender to have another drink waiting, the man lurched off to the men's room. One of the students laughed, explaining that the instructor had been nicknamed the Sponge because of his ability to soak up bourbon.

"I know him," Dick said. He was not amused. He knew, as I did, that some of the instructors assigned to the isolated training school had been sent there out of compassion, as a respite after a tough tour overseas, or because of acute medical or family problems. "Don't laugh at him. He's been in some dark alleys and deserves better."

Shortly the Sponge returned and resumed his drinking.

Dick was enjoying his old hand role. He told the students several stories which illustrated the importance of tradecraft and how they could avoid wrecking an operation by slipshod practices. He was pleasantly and lucidly pedantic, and I thought how strange it was that this man had become a first-rate intelligence officer rather than a first-rate teacher.

One of Dick's stories concerned the necessity of using illegal tactics which in other professions would be considered highly questionable.

"Has it ever bothered you?" a student asked.

"Bothered me?"

"The dirty tricks side of the business," the student said.

"Not really," Dick said. "It goes with the job we're asked to do overseas. You should be prepared for that."

"That's right, Sonny," the Sponge interjected. "Don't get the idea you'll be Rebecca at Sunnybrook Farm."

The Sponge stood, preparing to leave. He swayed as he tried to insert his arm into the sleeve of his raincoat. He missed and tried again.

A student laughed.

"Shut up!" The Sponge glared at the young officer. "You think you're pretty hot, don't you? Think you're an intelligence man, don't you?"

Even the stolid CIA-cleared bartender was uncomfortable.

"You'll find out, Rebecca." The Sponge's eyes were red, his face cracked with operational mileage. "You'll find out when you get out there. You'll find out you didn't join the Boy Scouts. 'Cause you didn't. Wait till you get there. You'll see."

The Sponge lurched away from the bar.

Dick Welch inspected his brandy.

"What the hell was he trying to say?" the student asked.

"He's trying to warn you," Dick said quietly. "He's telling you that you're in a tough business. That it won't all be fun and games. That you're going to be standing the night watch."

Dick wet the tip of his finger, then ran it around the edge of his brandy glass until it produced a hum.

"He's trying to tell you that the night watch can be lonely, but that it must be stood."

8

BRAZIL, VENEZUELA
1970-1972

When that NO SMOKING sign lights up, I promised myself, I'll stop
the habit forever. A few minutes later it did, and I snuffed out what was
to be the last cigarette I would ever enjoy.

The Pan Am jet descended over Rio de Janeiro, one of the most
spectacularly beautiful cities of the world. It was the first time Gina had
seen the Brazilian metropolis. I pointed out the famous Sugar Loaf, a
rock mountain jutting up over the bay, and the towering statue of Christ,
paid for by pennies collected from Rio's poor, on another mountain. The
beaches—Copacabana, Ipanema, Leblon—stretched out toward the south.
Even in early January and at seven in the morning we could spot bikini-
clad figures decorating the sand.

In December of 1969 the Western Hemisphere Division Chief had
called me into his office to put to me the only foolish question I ever
heard him ask: How would you like to be Chief of Station, Rio de
Janeiro?

The question was an unnecessary courtesy. No foreign service officer
with all his faculties would turn down an assignment to the exciting
capital. Nor would any CIA officer not want to be Chief of Station in a
country of almost a hundred million people that borders ten of South
America's nations.

CIA people working in the Clandestine Service can usually burrow
out from under an undesirable foreign assignment once during a career.
Otherwise they are expected to be good soldiers. Challenging the wisdom
of the hierarchy a second time without truly valid medical or family
reasons tends to, as one supervisor put it, "stifle upward career mobility."
I had never tried to evade an overseas appointment, and I certainly
would not have started with Brazil.

Technically, Brasília was the capital, but to most Brazilians, especially federal employees, Rio remained the hub of government activity and influence. A serious suggestion to a Brazilian bureaucrat that he should work in Brasília—eight hundred miles inland, a new city surrounded by nothing—would bring a snort of derision. Lip service was paid to the concept though: important or ceremonial government transactions were supposed to bear a Brasília dateline. Complying with this requirement entailed a great deal of shuttling back and forth between Rio de Janeiro and Brasília. The British Ambassador told me, shortly after my arrival in Rio, about a meeting he had scheduled with the Brazilian Foreign Minister. The Ambassador took an early flight to Brasília from Rio, his residence, and was amused to find the Foreign Minister on the same plane. They conducted a forty-five-minute meeting in Brasília and the Ambassador flew back to Rio on the next flight. During the return trip he chatted at some length with another passenger—the Brazilian Foreign Minister.

My hectic two years as COS in Santo Domingo had not represented a typical tour. Now I had every expectation of serving as a member of the Ambassador's country team in a normal and routine atmosphere.

Most CIA personnel employed in a United States embassy abroad are more or less concealed by a veneer of diplomatic protection that is called "light cover." They carry official or diplomatic passports and identify themselves as American officials without elaborating. The fact that they are intelligence officers is a confidence reserved for the local security people with whom they conduct liaison. A few may have better official cover and work in some embassy office separated from the CIA center; they are generally known only to their immediate cover supervisor, and to the Ambassador and his senior officers.

American ambassadors always know—without exception—all the CIA personnel working on their staffs. The more senior CIA officers are known to everyone in the embassy, including many of the local employees, except in Socialist countries. In Brazil, for instance, the most junior State Department clerk in the most distant consulate knew I was Chief of Station.

There is a popular misconception that American ambassadors don't know what the intelligence people on their own staffs are up to, or cannot control them when they do. They know if they want to know. Any doubt about this was erased in 1961 when President Kennedy sent a letter to each of his ambassadors: "You are in charge of the entire United States Diplomatic Mission and I shall expect you to supervise all of its operations." Ambassadors generally do not know or want to know the identities of CIA sources in the local society unless they are high-level political types with whom the ambassador may be in contact—among

214

8: BRAZIL, VENEZUELA 1970–1972

other reasons, they would not want to have this information if kidnapped and tortured by terrorists. Some ambassadors, generally poor ones, want to be told as little as possible about CIA operations and push a Chief of Station away with, "That's your job; go ahead and do it." The great majority of ambassadors, however, know precisely what CIA is trying to accomplish, especially when it comes to covert action. When I arrived in Brazil in early 1970 I had never known of a covert action undertaking that was carried out by the CIA without the knowledge of the Department of State in Washington and its ambassador in the field. The ground rules of CIA–Department of State cooperation call for the ambassador being aware of a deep-cover officer with whom he has a relationship of any kind. On one occasion I exposed one of my "outside" officers to an ambassador because the two of them worked together frequently in a local charity. On another I advised the ambassador because my deep-cover man asked I do so: he said he simply couldn't relax on the golf course when he, the spook, won or lost the significant sums he and the ambassador wagered during weekend rounds of golf.

The composition and size of a country team depends on an ambassador's inclination. Some prefer very small groups, others convene all their senior officers. A typical country team might include the deputy chief of mission, the political counselor, the military attaché and, as the ambassador elects, the administrative counselor, economic counselor, USIS chief (United States Information Agency in Washington, but Service abroad), head of the AID mission (Agency for International Development), and others. Sometimes, the senior Peace Corps representative. During my first years as a Chief of Station I was nervous when the Peace Corps chief sat on the country team, believing he or she might not have the training or political sophistication necessary to discern that which should remain sacrosanct.

The CIA Chief of Station is invariably a member of the country team. When the ambassador is handing out assignments the COS does not expect glamorous diplomatic tasks; these can be and should be handled by the bona fide Foreign Service officers of the Department of State. The COS's job is to provide the embassy with intelligence and work on difficult assignments which might be embarrassing if revealed. Not all the tasks assigned a COS by an ambassador are connected with intelligence. While I was in Brazil one of my colleagues in another South American country was asked by his ambassador to go to the airport and do something about a deranged American hijacker who had landed there after a flight from another country. Armed with a six-pack of beer the COS did just that, persuading the skyjacker to surrender after hours of negotiation.

A Station Chief's popularity with his embassy colleagues often

215

depends on the degree to which he is willing to share his intelligence harvest with other members of the country team. Some Chiefs of Station hardly speak during the weekly or biweekly conferences, reserving their insights for subsequent briefings of the ambassador in private. These are generally CIA's least effective representatives abroad. To be useful, intelligence should reach as many customers as security permits. But even the most candid and forthright Chief of Station is forced into silence if one member of the country team proves that he cannot be discreet. Should that person persist in revealing classified matters—even the one who protests, "but I only told my wife"—the COS must keep his mouth shut.*

In 1970 terrorism directed against diplomats reached a peak in Brazil. American Ambassador Burke Elbrick had been kidnapped in late 1969 and released in exchange for the release of political prisoners. Then, in rapid succession, the German and Swiss ambassadors and the Japanese Consul in São Paulo were kidnapped. They were released after the Brazilian government freed a number of political prisoners and allowed them to be flown to Algeria and Cuba.

Dick Welch and I once pondered the incongruity of American ambassadors, consuls, and military attachés around the world being abducted, attacked, and even murdered while, somehow, CIA staff officers remained immune.

"Damned if I know why," Dick had said. But he predicted that one of us, probably a Chief of Station, would sooner or later die as the result of terrorist violence.

Shortly after I arrived in Brazil the CIA station received an intelligence report concerning a very recent conversation among Marxist activists. Our informant told us one man had informed the others that CIA had dispatched two thousand agents to Brazil to investigate the kidnapping of Ambassador Elbrick.

"That's not true," another of the group had countered. "They sent only five hundred."

At the time I was attempting to persuade Langley to increase my staff in Rio de Janeiro by one secretary. Not one additional CIA officer or agent was sent to Brazil to help us check out the circumstances of the kidnapping; not even a secretary, as it turned out.

I advanced a hypothesis, later to become a conviction, that CIA officers abroad had been spared by terrorists because of a myth: extremists of all stripes had decided that the CIA was so ubiquitous, powerful, and

---

* Having mentioned the Peace Corps, I should set the record straight: looking back over four tours as a Chief of Station, I realize now that only one category of Foreign Service officer had a perfect record for honoring caveats on intelligence I divulged in country team meetings—Peace Corps chiefs.

vengeful that retaliation against any group or person attacking it would be swift and certain. In other words, the political underworld around the globe believed CIA capabilities and resources were so unlimited that the risk of engaging the Agency in any sort of vendetta was too high to consider. If, in the mind of one Brazilian radical, the CIA sent "only five hundred" agents in the wake of an ambassadorial abduction, how many would CIA dispatch—seeking revenge—if one of CIA's own were harmed?

Unfortunately, State Department people and military attachés in Brazil were not protected by the myth. Thus, my station was obliged to devote much time and resources to gathering intelligence on the intentions of anti-American terrorists. They already had slain an American military officer in São Paulo.

My principal concern however was for the safety of the head of USIS in Brazil, John Mowinckle.

Many of the top officials of the American embassy in Rio de Janeiro had been tagged with nicknames, contrived and put into circulation by one of our senior colleagues and his wife, both of whom were blessed with a puckish sense of humor. One officer with a proclivity for late night visitations to Rio's clubs and an eye for pretty women was known as the Midnight Cowboy. Another swinger was dubbed Twinkle-toes. When William Rountree became the new ambassador he was tagged Square-Bush. John Mowinckle and I had more prosaic sobriquets: he was Big John and I was Big Dave.

Big John hardly fit the description of a conventional Foreign Service officer. He was handsome, dashing, and flamboyant—outrageously so at times. Multilingual, he had grown up in Europe, where his father had been an executive with Standard Oil. His service as a military intelligence officer during World War II left Mowinckle with a collection of colorful anecdotes which he was not shy about relating.* In Rio de Janeiro John was a highly visible member of the jet set, and his photograph appeared frequently in Brazilian newspapers. In a national magazine he was pictured wearing a white scarf around his neck. He seemed to be everywhere in Brazil, charming everyone with his fluent French and Portuguese. He was indefatigable.

Of course everyone in Rio de Janeiro believed John Mowinckle was really the CIA Chief of Station. John was crushed when, after months of waiting to become a member of an exclusive Ipanema beach club, he was blackballed by the membership committee. They didn't want a CIA

* For one, see *Is Paris Burning?* by Collins and Lapierre. Mowinckle, alone with 176 German prisoners in the Hôtel Crillon after the liberation of Paris, disarmed the horde like a gentleman, asking the Nazis to please check their arms in the cloakroom.

217

spook around the premises. The deliberations of the committee leaked to the social pages of Rio newspapers wherein John was labeled a CIA officer. Mowinckle's reaction was swift: he immediately changed apartments, the new one looming ten floors over the club that rebuffed him. He gave a marvelous party. The decor consisted of dozens of styrofoam balls hanging from the ceiling—all painted black. The cream of Brazilian society assembled, with Gina and I as interlopers, and applauded as John leaned out of his window and poured champagne on the club below.

It is true an energetic American official abroad who is highly mobile and meets a large cross-section of people is frequently assumed to be a CIA officer. Department of State political counselors are often suspect for this reason. In Latin America in recent years four American ambassadors have been miscast by the public as CIA Station Chiefs, despite the fact that CIA people never use the cover of chiefs or deputy chiefs of mission. Understandably, Foreign Service officers are not amused by this type of notoriety.

Big John Mowinckle loved it. He rather liked the idea of being identified as an intelligence officer. We had a conference at the end of each working day dedicated to testing the prohibition against liquor being consumed in U.S. government buildings. At one of these sessions, John told me he relished the idea of intrigue, and offered to help any way he could. He shrugged off my warnings that his public identification as CIA Chief might pose some security problems for him. He continued to pass information to me. His intelligence production was consistently dubious, but it made great listening.

The telephone rang early one morning, awakening Gina. She sleepily passed the instrument to me. It was Big John.

"Dave," Mowinckle said, "The French Ambassador is going to be kidnapped."

"My god, John," I said. "It's four in the morning. Where are you?"

"At a great party."

"And who at the party told you the Ambassador will be abducted?"

"The cook," Mowinckle said.

Big John Mowinckle was fun to work with, despite his poor sources and was not, I'm glad to say, the victim of violence.*

Brazilians, and the foreigners who live in Brazil, know how to enjoy life. The annual Carnival in Rio is the world's most spectacular party and everyone is drunk for several days—not on liquor but emotion.

* When I retired in 1975, the Washington *Post* reported: "At the [time of my COS tenure in Brazil] politically sophisticated, well-informed Brazilians were quite sure the station chief was John Mowinckle, a big, bluff man who was the public affairs officer. None suspected Phillips."

The Carnival season traditionally opens with a sybaritic fiesta at the Rio Yacht Club. The music and dancing do not stop until nine or ten in the morning. The men usually wear swimming trunks and the women bikinis and they frolic together in a sort of controlled orgy—cooling down occasionally by jumping into an olympic-sized pool.

An American tourist wearing a dark suit and tie somehow wandered into the first Yacht Club party Gina and I attended. He was bug-eyed. He drew a chair to the edge of the swimming pool to observe better the almost naked women splashing in the water. Within seconds the tourist, chair and all, was pushed into the water. He came up spluttering and furious.

"I want to see someone from the American embassy!" He was red-faced with anger. "Someone will apologize for this! I insist on seeing someone from the American embassy!"

"Relax, my friend," I told the tourist as I pulled him from the pool. "It was someone from the American embassy who pushed you in."

The culprit, in fact, was a CIA man.

Life was very pleasant. In August of 1970 Gina and I had our own child, Todd. Our hillside home looked out over a splendid panorama. Orchids bloomed in the yard. On Sunday afternoons I would swing leisurely in a hammock—to hell with it!—enjoying a cigarette. The snail was on our thorn, and all was well in our world.

In fact, it was pretty close to paradise. I was a Station Chief in a country where the pressures and demands of the job were not abnormal. Each day brought some new pleasure, or new and interesting friends. I played golf on a challenging course which ran along the Atlantic and up into the mountains. I forgot about dark alleys.

A message from Langley brought me back to reality. In September, our ninth month in Rio, CIA headquarters cabled: REPORT TO HQS ON NEXT AVAILABLE FLIGHT. TELL STATION AND EMBASSY ASSOCIATES YOU WILL BE SERVING FOR SOME WEEKS ON A PROMOTION PANEL. ADVISE ETA AND FLIGHT NUMBER.

Here we go again, I kept thinking to myself during the nine-hour flight from Rio. CIA Station Chiefs abroad are routinely brought back to Washington for several weeks on a committee which recommends candidates for promotion—but in that event they are not instructed to report on the next available flight. Something very special was in the wind.

At the Rio airport Gina had asked how long I would be gone, and I had to say that I had no idea. She would be staying behind with six children. Todd was only six weeks old.

I tried to sleep during the long night flight but only managed to doze. Why had I been asked to return? My first thought was it had something to do with Chile, but I dismissed that because Salvador Allende had just been elected President. I knew that CIA had provided massive support to Allende's opponent, Eduardo Frei, in the 1964 Chilean elections, but only opposed Allende without funding any candidate during the recent 1970 campaign. I ran mentally through the trouble spots in Latin America. In none could I imagine a situation which demanded that I be asked to absent myself from the management of the Rio de Janeiro station so precipitously.

On the morning of September 19 I arrived at Langley and, after retrieving my badge—the identification that every CIA employee must wear inside the headquarters building—I went to Abe's office. After a short stint as Chief of Cuban Operations, the third time he had succeeded me in a CIA job, Abe had become the Deputy of the Western Hemisphere Division. Now he was my superior.

Abe explained that I had been selected to head a Chile task force. The operation was to be so closely held that nobody from the embassy or Department of State and only a few officers in the Division were to know the true purpose of my temporary duty. CIA had been tasked to prevent Salvador Allende from assuming the presidency in Chile.

I couldn't believe it.

Allende, after three unsuccessful attempts to be elected President of Chile, had won 36 percent of the votes cast in the election just two weeks before. His plurality was razor-thin: the Conservative candidate, Jorge Alessandri, received 35 percent of the ballots, and the Christian Democrat, Radomiro Tomic, a few percentage points less. Since no candidate had received a majority, the Chilean constitution required that the Congress decide the election and custom decreed that the candidate with the highest tally in the general election, Allende, be ratified. The vote was scheduled for October 24.

"Why me?" I asked Abe.

"We're supposed to put the very best people we have on it," Abe said. He smiled, but his eyes did not have the twinkle I had grown accustomed to over the years.

"And we don't involve the embassy? Does that mean that Ambassador Korry and Harry Shlaudeman in Chile won't be told?" I had never known of a CIA covert action operation abroad being hidden from the American Ambassador.

"Yup," Abe said. "And Secretary of State Rogers won't be told either. That's what the man wants. Korry and Rogers will participate in diplomatic and economic efforts, which we are going to call Track I, but CIA is to try Track II, a second way, all by itself."

Abe explained that the Forty Committee, the small group of senior advisers to the President which approved covert action operations, had already passed on Track I. Two hundred and fifty thousand dollars had been allotted to bribe Chilean congressmen to vote against Allende's ratification. Other measures—designed to put pressure on the economy—were approved.

I told Abe, "You and I know that with two hundred and fifty thousand you can rent a majority of congressmen in some banana republics. But it won't work in Chile—not even with twenty-five million bucks."

Abe agreed. Then he explained that Track II, the effort to thwart Allende's inauguration by whatever means, had not gone to the Forty Committee. That was disturbing: a covert action scheme to be launched directly by a President and his intimates—in this case Kissinger and Haig—without being on the agenda of the Forty Committee and at least wafted by the Secretary of State and the Secretary of Defense.

"There is only one way," I told Abe. "A military coup."

"Yup," Abe said. "It'll probably come down to that in the end."

"And the odds against that working are very long indeed," I said. "What do you think?"

"I agree." Abe removed his glasses and cleaned them industriously. "Problem is, Helms has marching orders."

I spent most of the remainder of the day in meetings. I talked with Karamessines and, briefly, Helms. Then I installed myself in the cubicle from which I would direct the small task force.

I learned that DCI Richard Helms had been summoned to the White House on September 15. Richard Nixon had instructed the CIA Chief to do whatever was necessary to keep Allende out of office. I also read a memorandum Helms had composed after his return to Langley. Attached to the memorandum was a copy of Helms's handwritten notes jotted down at the White House.

> One in 10 chance, perhaps, but save Chile!
> worth spending
> not concerned risks involved
> no involvement of Embassy
> $10,000,000 available, more if necessary
> full-time job—best men we have
> game plan
> make the economy scream
> 48 hours for plan of action.

In the halls a number of my colleagues were surprised to find me in Washington rather than Rio. I lied to them saying that I had been asked to work temporarily on propaganda plans for Track I, which was known to senior people in the Division. Most of them believed me. Dick Welch, back from his overseas assignment, was skeptical. He listened to my cover story, nodding, but most uncharacteristically, said nothing.

That night I bedded down on the sofa in the Division Chief's office. I awakened frequently to smoke a cigarette and think about Track II. Salvador Allende had been the world's first avowed Marxist freely elected to the highest office of his country; given that historic fact it seemed to me that intervening in Chile to deny him office was a bad idea.

The first inner conflict I had about the personal ethics of being an intelligence officer was years before in Chile, when I had manipulated Juan's horoscope in order to recruit him as a spy. Doubts about that had long since been resolved as the value of his intelligence became apparent. In the case of Juan, I convinced myself, the end had justified the means. Looking back on the Bay of Pigs operation I had finally concluded that my remorse when it failed was because it had been ineptly managed, not because of personal moral qualms about my involvement. Then in 1965 I was shocked and disturbed when Lyndon Johnson sent more than 20,000 troops to the Dominican Republic. But then I remembered the front page of the Washington *Post* edition that reported the coup in Santo Domingo: the two-column wire service dispatch had been eclipsed by a banner headline announcing Johnson had just dispatched 5,000 more United States soldiers to Vietnam. The President's rationale could be appreciated—having involved the country in such an appalling investment of men and money in Southeast Asia, Johnson was not going to take even the slightest chance of another Cuba in the Caribbean.

Track II was harder to understand. Should I allow myself to be involved? Should the CIA, even responding to a President's ukase, encourage a military coup in one of the few countries in Latin America with a solid, functioning democratic tradition? I certainly realized, perhaps better than most, that Allende had been candid in his speeches for more than thirty years; he had never glossed over the fact that his goal was a Marxist Chile which automatically would mean an anti-American regime and nationalization of the important American-owned copper mines. But Allende also maintained that he would shape his Marxist state within the framework of the Chilean constitution. That was a forlorn hope to be sure, but not one, it seemed to me, that CIA should try to frustrate before it had been proven false. Should Allende falter and Chile become a Communist satellite with the constitution a mere facade, the wisdom of attempting to overthrow him might be considered. Meanwhile I was disturbed. I didn't really understand why—given Chile's circumstances, the risk, the odds—it was worth the candle right now.

"I don't understand," I told Abe, a few days later. "Why should we be doing this, especially when we believe it won't work?"

"Understand?" Abe removed his bifocals and polished them briskly; over the years I had learned that the action did not indicate the lenses were dirty, but that Abe was thinking long and hard.

"Some time ago," Abe said, "I returned with Dick Helms from a meeting downtown. On the way back the car was tied up in traffic for almost half an hour, and Helms and I talked about the assignment he had just been given. I ended by saying to Helms, 'I don't understand.'"

Abe replaced his glasses. "Well, you know what Helms said? He looked at me and said, 'Abe, there's something I've had to learn to understand. I've had to learn to understand Presidents.' So I guess you really don't need to understand as long as you understand what the President ordered."

For the next six weeks I worked twenty hours a day in the improvised office which housed the task force. Tom Karamessines would visit the White House and return with the word that we were to press on—the pressure was constant and heavy. Each evening I calculated the odds; at best they hovered around and sometimes below one chance in ten. Most nights I slept fitfully on the sofa in the Division Chief's office.

Early on the morning of October 22 a cable flashed into Langley from Santiago. General Rene Schneider, Allende's military chief and a strict constitutionalist, had been killed. I immediately assumed that CIA was involved somehow with the assassination, because the Santiago station had passed three machine guns the night before to a cabal of military officers who considered Schneider the principal stumbling block to their plans to block Allende's confirmation. Later reports indicated, however, that Schneider had been killed by men carrying hand guns; it had been their intention to kidnap him, but he died in the firefight which ensued when he drew his own gun to defend himself.

The Schneider assailants were later convicted for the crime. They had been contacted previously by CIA agents—then discouraged by CIA and contact severed. Thank God, I said to myself, for at least that small favor.

Those of us familiar with Chile and Chileans knew instantly that there were no more rails for Track II. The unexpected death of General Schneider made the odds of a successful military coup against Allende plunge to zero. Abe, Tom Karamessines, and I went to see Dick Helms. The DCI listened attentively as we explained that it was all over. Helms and Karamessines told the White House.

Track II was dismantled. Allende was confirmed by the Chilean Congress on October 24 and inaugurated as President on November 3.

I flew back to Rio de Janeiro. It was a long, long flight. During those hours I pondered as I had never before on means and ends, and on my own role in American secret operations.

223

Gina was at the airport with the children. They were disappointed; I had forgotten to bring them a present. But that night they had presents for me on my forty-eighth birthday.

Life was pleasant for the children in Rio de Janeiro and, as a bonus, the American school was good. I determined to do everything I could to ensure that we had a lengthy tour, and was prepared to expend to that end any political capital I had accumulated at headquarters.

Then they moved the damned capital to Brasília. Really moved it— it was no longer enough to make protocol visits: all of us had to move there.

A new Brazilian President established his own residence in Brasília, announcing that this time the change was serious and Brasília would become the center of government in fact as well as fancy. Foreign diplomats and Brazilian bureaucrats scoffed; they had heard it all before. The President had the local newspaper publish a daily box score on the number of days he, the President, had resided there. The message finally got through and, one by one, the government ministries and agencies reluctantly packed up and abandoned Rio de Janeiro. The American Ambassador became the first top-ranking diplomat to move permanently to Brasília. The country team had to move with him.

Eight hundred miles is not really very far, but the difference between the lively port of Rio and the sterile capital of Brasília was pronounced. Shortly after arriving I commiserated with a Brazilian diplomat who had been forced to Brasília. "There's not even anything to buy here," I complained.

"Oh, yes," he said. "Tickets to Rio."

The slow pace of professional and personal life did give me an opportunity to get to know more intimately the CIA people with whom I worked.

In earlier years there had been some validity to the popular notion that the Clandestine Service was a public service refuge for the scions of the East Coast, Ivy League establishment. This was no longer true. A composite of the average CIA officer working for me in Brazil showed that he (or she) was about thirty-three years of age, married and with perhaps two children. He held a graduate degree from a state university, spoke at least one foreign language and had worked in at least two foreign countries. Abroad he often performed two functions, his cover duties and, when that work day ended, his clandestine job. He claimed no pay for overtime (and didn't when working at Langley) and contributed 15 percent more time to the job than the ordinary nine to five worker. Since his government salary was about $20,000 a year, the United States was getting an additional $4,500 of uncompensated overtime from him annually. In his cover role, if he worked in the embassy or one of the consulates, he always ranked below his peers in the Department of State and other agencies, but he recognized that arrangement was absolutely necessary for him to operate.

A United States Senator, during a CIA briefing, was once surprised to hear a reference to a woman officer. "Do you have women working in CIA?" he asked.

Today one out of three CIA employees are women—32 percent to be exact. Many are secretaries, but their duties overseas often extend far beyond office routine; clerical service can be challenging when a young woman laboring at 13,000 feet plus in Bolivia is transferred next to the jungles of Southeast Asia. Other women in CIA are analysts and reports officers, the latter being responsible for assembling the assorted bits of intelligence into a meaningful report.

Women have always been case officers, but the number has increased in recent years. In some situations they perform better than men: they excel in role-playing situations; they can meet securely with male agents under the cover of mutual attraction; and two women or a woman and a man can be seen entering a safe house together without evoking neighborhood gossip of homosexuality (which sometimes occurs when two males see each other in an apartment). In Asian countries the American woman is considered emancipated, and an Oriental will work with her when he would lose face collaborating with a local woman. In the Middle East an Arab agent can rationalize his treason when working as a spy for a woman case officer, because a mere female cannot be taken seriously. Women intelligence officers can approach and cultivate a Latin American from his blind side, since few Latins really believe CIA would employ a woman for tasks of such delicacy and importance.

And women—sometimes co-opted wives—work as case officers in closed societies. One woman handled a male agent in an environment so risky that their meetings had to be "brush passes," contrived lightning-fast encounters which would appear as if two clumsy people were bumping into each other. On other occasions the agent dropped his intelligence production through the open window of a car driven by the woman as she passed him in nighttime traffic. In their final encounter the agent knew he would not see his case officer again, because she was being transferred to another country. He took the risk of thrusting into her hands a dozen red roses; attached to the stems of the bouquet was a canister of secret microfilms.

The worst mistake an intelligence officer can make while handling a spy is to "fall in love with his agent." Women officers are aware of this as well as men. They know too much confidence in a source can generate professional indifference and erode healthy skepticism—the best protection against becoming the victim of bad intelligence and performance or, worse, of a once valuable agent who has switched his loyalties. Although I am sure it must have happened, I never heard about a CIA woman literally falling in love with her agent.

Women spies sometimes do use sex but only up to a point as a technique in recruiting other spies, but I know of no case where a woman intelligence officer has allowed herself to lose the authority and control essential to managing an agent by sharing his bed.

The CIA women not actually on the payroll—wives and daughters—must share the tensions and dangers their husbands face. I know one teenaged CIA daughter who some years ago used her wits, courage and fluency in an African native dialect to save her mother and father from political assassins. She found a way to warn her parents so they could eventually escape—even though the terrorists, with a knife at her throat, had stripped her naked.

There has always been a sizeable contingent of ethnic groups in the CIA, especially Orientals and persons of Mexican-American background. In 1964 four CIA officers were killed in two separate helicopter crashes in Southeast Asia: one was a full-blooded American Indian who had been a sparring partner for Joe Louis; another was a black.

American blacks, understandably, do not seek employment in CIA's Clandestine Service if they want public recognition of a successful career. Nevertheless, a number of blacks have worked as intelligence officers; I served in only one station which did not employ at least one black case officer. One of my friends became the first black Chief of Station.

Once in Latin America I was entertaining a visiting newsman at a large restaurant, crowded with perhaps two hundred patrons. The visitor remarked on the apparent high degree of racial equality blacks enjoyed in that particular country. I tried to put his observation in perspective by noting that, while there certainly were a number of respects in which blacks were in a better position than in most countries, they still found definite limits on their economic and social mobility.

We were sitting at a corner table. I faced the wall. The newsman could look past me and see the people in the restaurant.

Without turning around I said, "I'll bet you the price of lunch that you don't see a single black in this upper-middle-class restaurant."

The visitor looked past me. "You lose," he said.

I turned to look at the crowd. There was one black—a CIA officer from my station.

Despite its near-perfect climate and spectacular sunsets, I did not rate Brasília high among my favorite posts. Thus I was not dismayed when a cable arrived, one year after we had moved from Rio de Janeiro, announcing that we were being transferred to Caracas, Venezuela.

There was another pleasant message from Langley. I had been promoted to GS-17, the penultimate grade to which a CIA officer can aspire, other than the presidentially appointed Director and Deputy Director.

Caracas is another of the world's more attractive cities, with modern skyscrapers jutting up in a narrow valley between mountains on one side and hills on the other. The smell of money permeates the capital, except in the shacktowns where the stench of poverty prevails. Nonetheless, unlike most Latin American countries, some Venezuelan petroleum profits have trickled down through the hands of the rich to the poor. The oil bounty is so great however that the loss is hardly noticeable; the people of Venezuela drink more scotch whiskey per capita than anywhere in the world, including Scotland. Venezuela has achieved political stability after surviving two lengthy dictatorships. Fidel Castro failed in his massive effort to disrupt the elective process in the 1960's and the country now ranks high among the few democratic republics in South America.

We enrolled the children in school again and rented a picturesque house which clung to a hillside. We encountered some difficulty in persuading the landlord to insert a diplomatic clause in the contract—which meant we could break the lease if the U.S. government moved us in the next two years—but I promised him that I would be in Caracas for a long, long time. There was an active little theater group in Caracas, and once again I was able to combine business with pleasure. I met some agents under that cover while I acted in the lead male role of *The Prisoner of Second Avenue.*

The Watergate break-in was not very big news in the Venezuelan press. I was surprised to read that Howard Hunt was involved: I didn't even know that he had retired from CIA two years before. Because of my association with Howard over the years, Gina and I followed the news accounts describing the break-in with intense interest, as we did the developments in the presidential campaign of 1972. In September, a few days short of the fourth anniversary of our first acquaintance, we mailed our absentee ballots, voting for George McGovern.

As Chief of Station in Caracas I retained the exasperation/admiration attitude I had developed for my communications personnel in other countries. Exasperation because I was frequently roused from sleep by after-hours calls from the communicators; this often meant I had to dress and drive to the embassy to read a cable requiring an immediate answer, as CIA messages can seldom be discussed on the telephone which intelligence officers must assume to be tapped. In very large stations a communicator is on duty around the clock, but in most the radio shack is closed down after office hours. In this case high precedence messages are heralded by the tinkling of a bell at the bedside of a communicator in his residence, summoning him to the embassy to open up and receive the cable. When he decides to call in the Station Chief, the two of them usually chat over a convivial cup of coffee after action has been taken. Once the sleep cleared from my eyes, I enjoyed this nocturnal dialogue and companionship when the embassy was quiet and, except for a Marine guard, empty.

CIA officers admire their communicators because they know CIA communications are, without question, the best in the world.

The Office of Communications, known as COMMO to oldtimers, was formed, like most of the Agency, around O.S.S. veterans. These people had served around the globe as communicators, some behind enemy lines, and they brought to CIA a vital expertise in supporting intelligence operations. As CIA expanded during the Cold War years, COMMO grew with it. It had two basic roles—to provide communications between CIA headquarters and its offices abroad, and between headquarters and sensitive agents abroad with whom regular contact was impracticable or a threat to their security. Commercial cable companies often close their doors for the duration of any political or natural disaster overseas. It is during such periods that communications self-sufficiency is essential for CIA, especially in terms of those messages conveying reports from CIA stations to Washington. An understandable pride in their work developed over the years as CIA communicators demonstrated an ability to keep their stations on the air despite earthquakes, floods, civil disorders—even when enduring gunfire or shelling.

The typical COMMO recruit comes into CIA in his twenties, not long after finishing his military commitment. He had been trained and seasoned in radio while in the military. Frequently he is also a ham operator with valuable experience in working with low-powered circuits over long distances under difficult circumstances. This sort of background closely matches the professional needs of CIA. Indeed, most of COMMO's original leaders had been hams. It was a classic case of doing well what one enjoys doing.

On numerous occasions I marveled at the skill and flexibility which marked the performance of CIA communicators. When I was working in The Pit at Langley during the first days of the Dominican crisis, the special telephone tied into the Pentagon rang. A distraught colonel told me that communications had been lost with the American troops that had just landed in Santo Domingo. For some time all instructions to the 82nd Airborne Division in the Dominican Republic went through CIA headquarters and the station.

During World War II and the five years which followed, encoded

228

manual Morse—an operator tapping out dit-dots on a telegraph key— was the primary method of electronic communications overseas for the U.S. government. As the U.S. presence expanded abroad, the demands for classified cable communications overtook the capability of manual Morse to provide the service. High-speed transmission and 60-word-per-minute teletype decoders became standard by the mid-fifties. Teletype decoding was increased to 100 words per minute by 1960. Then the computer came into play, with its useful ability to store messages and to switch circuits. The application of the computer to solve communications problems was a milestone, and made possible the handling of vastly greater volumes of traffic with fewer people needed to do the job.

By the end of the 1960's the satellite as a communications vehicle became a reality. Direct communication between Washington and any point on the earth's surface was now possible—a CIA agent huddled over a small radio in his attic somewhere abroad could literally bounce his message to Langley off a satellite. The need for large radio relay stations on foreign soil was largely canceled.

Progress in radio technology has been vital to individual agents who must report information and receive instructions by radio. Heavy emphasis was placed by CIA on research and development leading to speed in transmission. The shorter the period of time an agent must operate his set the better his chances of avoiding detection from ubiquitous monitoring devices. Survival may depend on speed. Spies around the world now use "burst" communications equipment, which emits the radio signal, even when it is a very long message, at uncanny speeds. The need for modern communications is as real for the Russian KGB as for the American CIA. Indeed, over the years there has been a striking correlation between the communications techniques and equipment of the world's intelligence services.

COMMO personnel have cover problems when they are assigned overseas, as do all CIA personnel. One of my good friends in the Agency was Director of the Office of Communications. He visited Caracas while I was there and related his own cover experience. He came from an army family; his younger brother entered the military service and became a two-star general. Once as he was preparing for one of his overseas tours, his mother asked what she could tell her friends he was doing abroad. He told her to say he was a civilian clerk with the army. The mother, widow of an old-line army colonel, was shocked and dismayed at the cover story. "No son of mine would ever be a civilian clerk!"

Some time later the Department of State asked my friend to take a leave of absence from CIA and head the Department's communications office. He did, for several years. And he was elated when he was able to tell his mother that this time she could tell her friends, truthfully, that her son was a Deputy Assistant Secretary of State.

Working in Venezuela was agreeable and relaxing. It is one of the handful of countries in Latin America with a truly democratic government, and CIA operations were confined to routine intelligence chores. In such an operational environment life for a CIA Chief of Station is sometimes easier because of the things he does not have to do.

For instance, in Caracas one of the officers in the CIA station needed emergency surgery. Had I been in command in another country where revelation of sensitive CIA operations would have caused local political reverberations it would have been necessary for me to decide whether there was time to have the CIA man evacuated to an American hospital in Panama or the U.S., or, if there was not time for that, to be personally present in the operating room during the surgery. This was because of the possibility, however remote, that the patient might inadvertently mutter secrets to the local hospital team during anesthesia. I could do nothing should that occur, of course, but it would be imperative for me to know what was revealed so as to be prepared for the consequences. On several occasions in other countries I had to find a way to persuade the surgeon to permit me to don gown and mask to observe an operation, not always easy while maintaining my own cover. In Venezuela, however, the CIA was not engaging in covert operations which would have embarrassed the American Ambassador or alarmed the Venezuelan government, so my responsibility was limited to being satisfied that the patient had adequate medical attention, abundant in Caracas.

Much of my working day was spent on routine management matters, keeping rein on energetic young officers whose imagination might get out of control, or in adjudicating minor personnel complaints. Part of each working day was spent in tutoring: a CIA Station Chief has the responsibility for on-the-job training until an officer working for him has reached the stage of maturity and experience when the caution required in conducting clandestine operations is ingrained. More often than not errors in tradecraft originate in misguided enthusiasm or an inclination toward personal convenience. An example: I had learned during my first CIA training in New York that when two intelligence people not previously acquainted meet clandestinely some sort of recognition signal is employed; sometimes this involves a newspaper or magazine prominently displayed as a signal. In Venezuela I observed a trend develop with one of my young officers which was poor tradecraft. The popular American magazine *Playboy* was exorbitantly expensive in Caracas, and this young man began sending recognition instructions in messages to colleagues expected to arrive from the U.S., which read,

"Meeting will be in such-an-such cocktail lounge. Please have a copy of *Playboy* in your left hand." That had to stop. A fresh-faced young headquarters type out of Ohio State University walking into a Venezuelan bar with a girlie magazine would look just too Yankee and out of place.

The use of recognition signals is known in intelligence parlance as "establishing bona fides." One CIA officer I knew owned a beagle hound to which he was devoted. He liked to use the hound instead of a magazine as his bona fides and would cable other CIA stations that a visitor could meet him on a certain street corner, where he could be identified by the beagle he would be walking. The response, on one occasion, acknowledged the fireplug locale of the meeting, adding, "Look forward to meeting your bono fido."

The quips and jokes which amuse CIA people, like most in-house humor, tend to be strained and sometimes corny. "Giles," one of the officers working for me in Caracas, once evoked laughter from his colleagues by a cabled query to headquarters. While serving in another country he had been involved in an ingenious scheme: from a distant observation post CIA had aimed a color motion picture camera at the courtyard of a Communist embassy. The operation was based on the premise that members of the embassy, suspicious of their offices being bugged, would stroll about the garden when they wanted to discuss something sensitive. The motion pictures of their conversations would permit CIA lip readers to gather the gist of their talks.

Giles was excited. The foreign minister of the country in question visited the embassy and the camera captured him talking with the ambassador in the garden. It was time for the lip-reading specialist. The film was flown to Washington. Several weeks passed, and there was no word from Langley about a transcript of the garden conversation.

Giles asked by cable why he hadn't heard. The response explained: to cope with the particular language involved the Agency had to have a team of two persons perform the job. The delay was due to the fact, the message said, that one member of the team was on a temporary duty assignment overseas, and the read-out would have to wait until the pair was together again at Langley.

Several days passed and Giles, exasperated, sent another cable to Washington. CAN'T STAND THE SUSPENSE ANY LONGER, it read. FOR THE RECORD, WHICH MEMBER OF THE TEAM IS OFF ON ASSIGNMENT? UPPER LIP OR LOWER LIP?

One young officer in Caracas was impatient with the paperwork duties which are an essential part of espionage, especially the extrication from a mass of material of apparently trivial bits of information which, when subsequently retrieved, might be useful. He resisted my instructions that he must note for the record what he disdainfully described as "chaff," the inconsequential details about people to be deposited in the station's information bank in the hope that some day they might be withdrawn with interest.

The young man was not convinced when I recounted the observation of the CIA veteran who had remarked that the truth would be better served if the CIA cloak-and-dagger symbol were replaced by one composed of half a dozen 3-by-5 cards and a typewriter.

"That's too dull," the young case officer said. "I didn't join CIA to be a file clerk. I want to handle agents, recruit sources, work against terrorists."

"Fine," I said. "Go right ahead and recruit informants in local terrorist groups. They will be invaluable if you can manage it. Meanwhile, pull file"—I glanced at the notes I had jotted down the previous week when reviewing Caracas station records of past years—"B-1507. When you've read it we'll talk more about 3-by-5 cards."

File B-1507 concerned the case of an American colonel kidnapped by terrorists in Caracas in the mid-sixties.* The Venezuelan security services and police launched a massive effort to locate and free the American colonel and to capture his abductors. However the Venezuelans had very little information on the members of the terrorist band which claimed credit for the kidnapping. They asked the embassy to provide information which might assist them in the investigation. The CIA station was tasked by the Ambassador to come up with intelligence.

But the CIA station had not been successful in penetrating that particular terrorist group. It had no agents even on the periphery of the subversive organization. It had nothing.

Except for several 3-by-5 cards.

The cards contained snippets of information on half a dozen individuals known to be members of the terrorist unit which had kidnapped the American officer: aliases used, restaurants frequented, names of friends or mistresses, meeting places, and some home addresses. The information was turned over to Venezuelan authorities. Within hours three terrorists were arrested and their detention led to more arrests. Soon some forty members of the group had been rounded up, several directly involved in the kidnapping. The police pressure grew until the terrorists were forced to release the colonel unharmed less than a week after his abduction. That terrorist cell never again played a significant role in Venezuelan subversion.

The young officer agreed, after reading the file on a kidnapped

* Phyllis Long, who with her husband I had known in Chile, was a captive of terrorists for a short time when Ted Long was assigned to the Caracas embassy. Allen Stewart, also a friend from Santiago, eventually became American Ambassador in Venezuela. While he was there his bathroom in the embassy was destroyed by a terrorist bomb blast.

American saved not by derring-do but by "chaff," that henceforth he would find time for tedious paperwork.

In Caracas I knew which diplomats in the Soviet embassy were really intelligence officers, as they were able to see through my own light cover. I had an encounter with one of them at a diplomatic party.

"Good evening, Igor," I said. "How's the cultural business these days?"

"Thriving," Igor replied with a smile, knowing that I knew he was a KGB officer. "And how is the petroleum business?" he asked.

"I'm keeping Washington fully informed," I told the Russian, knowing he knew I was from CIA.

Then we discussed an international development.

"Would you please explain to me," Igor asked, seriously, "what is this Watergate thing?"

By early 1973 Watergate had indeed become news around the world, and each edition of Caracas newspapers headlined a new revelation. CIA conspiracy was widely suspected; the suspicion was natural and shared even by some CIA people because of the earlier Agency mistake of writing a psychological profile on Daniel Ellsberg and outfitting Howard Hunt with exotic paraphernalia for his furtive expeditions (but not for the break-in). About this time there was a change in CIA management, not entirely unrelated to Watergate.

I visited Washington for a few days just after Richard Helms had become Ambassador to Iran, kicked downstairs—according to the in-house perception of the dismissal—by a vindictive Richard Nixon who believed Helms should have been more responsive to the cover-up scenario drafted at the White House. James Schlesinger became the new Director of Central Intelligence. William E. Colby, back from Vietnam, soon replaced Tom Karamessines as the DDP. Almost immediately Schlesinger and Colby changed the title from Deputy Director, Plans—which they considered a euphemism—to the more candid Deputy Director, Operations, or DDO.

With Helms's departure and Karamessines's voluntary retirement, CIA management—and management style—changed precipitously. I knew that when I returned to Caracas I would be pumped for information about the new hierarchy and its plans for changes, so I asked those at Langley who worked with him about Schlesinger.

The new Director, I was told, was a steel-bright and diamond-tough administrator. He charmed few personally, but impressed many professionally as he began to stir the pot at Langley. He decided to reduce personnel and went about it ruthlessly. Dismissal slips, effective COB—close of business that day—went out to some CIA veterans. (The reduction, despite the manner in which it was conducted, was necessary. I believe every federal bureaucracy in Washington would be healthier if slashed by 25 percent of its personnel; the trick is to get rid of the right 25 percent.)

Not long after his confirmation, Schlesinger traveled to London to meet with the chiefs of the British services. He let it be known in advance that he wished the weekend to be kept free. "No socializing," he instructed, "as I plan to do some bird-watching." There were all sorts of stories about the British reaction to "bird-watching." It was generally assumed that the American intelligence chief spent his weekend ogling pretty girls—attractive young women are known in England as "birds"—when in fact Schlesinger was in the fields outside London, with his binoculars, spotting feathered birds.

Shortly after my return to Venezuela an extraordinary instruction arrived in Caracas as well as in every other CIA station in the world. In Washington it went to all CIA employees, from the most senior managers to the men who constructed wooden crates in the warehouses. Schlesinger wanted to be informed about instances now or in the past when CIA had engaged in activities which might be considered questionable. It was a tricky question to put to intelligent people who had spent the better part of their adult lives in espionage and covert action, both illegal in every country of the world. The unusual survey made many of us ponder the fine line between acceptable and dubious illegalities. In the wake of Watergate, Schlesinger wanted to know if there were skeletons in the CIA closet, and of course there always are in any institution a quarter of a century old. The compendium which resulted was called, in fact, the Skeletons. Some in CIA referred to it as the Family Jewels. There are people in CIA who believe the self-catharsis was William Colby's idea, endorsed by Schlesinger. It was Schlesinger's. Certainly Colby approved the concept, because he continued to ferret out additions to the list after Schlesinger's departure.

Schlesinger, for all his toughness, was a devoted family man who could enjoy such gentle pursuits as bird-watching. When he became Secretary of Defense in the spring of 1973 he left behind a CIA seething with resentment and rancor. But there was also a residue of admiration which remains today. Despite his tactics, his goals were sound and the results beneficial.

A cable from Washington arrived in Caracas in May of 1973. It came to my desk in an envelope marked EYES ONLY FOR PHILLIPS FROM COLBY. The new Director of CIA wanted me to know he was considering my nomination as Chief, Western Hemisphere Division, and asked if there was any reason I could not accept the appointment.

234

8: BRAZIL, VENEZUELA 1970–1972

As a specialist in Latin American affairs the job of managing CIA's operations in some twenty countries of Latin America and the Caribbean was one I had coveted. The incumbent, after a short stint, was moving on to another position. It was the senior assignment I had not dared dream about.

Ten months to the day after arriving in Caracas we flew back to Washington.

The following year my income tax was audited. The Internal Revenue Service computers had coughed up a card indicating that I had claimed a moving expense deduction for a family of eight for four consecutive years. That the machines found suspicious.

9

WASHINGTON 1973–1974

Abe was already at the office when I went to Langley very early in the morning for my first day as Chief, Western Hemisphere Division. It was gratifying to be with my old friend again. For an hour Abe briefed me on the state of the Division, as usual interspersing his observations with pithy stories or droll witticisms. He told me of the unfortunate security violation record of the Division in recent months. Security violations are serious matters at CIA, and a sure indicator of the level of morale among employees. A paper fallen beneath a desk, a tape left in an electric typewriter, a desk calendar not put away, a burn-bag not locked up, or, worst of all, a safe drawer left open—all are security violations. One calls for a reprimand; two within a year calls for administrative warning; four over a two-year period means a loss of two weeks' pay. A fifth can mean dismissal. There were a number of reasons which might have explained the low morale of the WH Division and its poor record of security violations. Perhaps lingering doubts in younger officers about possible Agency connection with Watergate beyond the Howard Hunt wig and the Ellsberg psychological profile. Another explanation might have been the management style of my predecessor, which could fairly be described as authoritarian. Whatever the reason, I decided that the first item on my management agenda should be correcting the sorry record of six or seven violations per month, the worst in the DDO.

After talking with Abe I walked through the offices of the Division to meet each officer and secretary. Some opened their eyes in astonishment, surprised to see the Division Chief enter their offices, apparently an unusual event. In chatting with individuals and small groups, I indicated my concern about security violations and, several times, said something about promising a lollipop to anyone who could help in improving the poor record. This was said casually, but was stated in serious terms in subsequent conversations with each of my Branch Chiefs, the senior officers responsible for specific areas of Latin America. To them I made it clear that I would demand a better record in each of their sections and that they could expect something less sweet than a lollipop if improvement was not achieved.

After spending the morning on the tour of the Division, Abe gave me another briefing, this time going into some detail. The first concern, Abe said, was that a coup attempt, or some form of violent action against Salvador Allende in Chile seemed probable. The first Marxist anywhere freely elected as a President, Allende carried into office a shaky mandate—two-thirds of the popular vote had gone elsewhere. Opposition to Allende had increased markedly in recent months as the Chilean economy became a shambles. There had already been a number of strikes by copper miners and truckers and, in 1972, a "pots and pans" march of Chilean women in Santiago. When Latin American women muster to protest—as in the case of the market women in Guatemala—grandmother is at least contemplating a climb to the roof. Chilean moderates were increasingly concerned about the leftist drift of Allende's government; in the Allende coalition there were two parties farther left than the Communist Party; extremists of the left were taking over key government posts; and some ten thousand radical refugees from other Latin American countries had swarmed like revolutionary bees to Chile.

Abe explained Allende's dilemma. Despite the advice of Fidel Castro when he visited Chile in late 1971 that he must shed blood to institutionalize the revolution, Allende had elected to conduct a constitutional revolution, and this he did, except for questionable tactics of thwarting the will of the Congress when it impeached a government minister by immediately re-appointing the same man to another ministry, by allowing the opposition press to be bullied by government-controlled unions, and, most serious, by using presidential decree and government ministries as a political weapons to bring private business (which represented and funded most of his opposition) to its knees through selective tax, import and matériel control, and similar regulatory programs. But, on balance, Allende was a Marxist dedicated to carrying out his revolution within the framework of the constitution—a laudable goal unprecedented in history. It was the economy, Abe explained, that would be Allende's undoing unless he took Castro's advice and intimidated his opposition with violence. The national debt had swollen, the cost of living had skyrocketed, and two out of three Chilean mills had no wheat to grind. Strikes crippled the economy. "Are we helping the strikers?" I asked Abe. He said that we were not.

237

Abe described two cables sent to our Santiago station during the month of May. In a rather abrupt departure from CIA custom, these instructions pointed out the probability of an opposition move against Allende and the inevitability that CIA would be blamed as the instigator of any coup. The station response to the first message reminded headquarters that CIA continued to have the responsibility of predicting a coup—ringing the gong—and the station could hardly be expected to do that unless its agents penetrated all conspiracies. The second headquarters cable countered this valid argument saying that, this time, keeping CIA's record clean was more important than predicting a coup. In short, the CIA Station Chief was ordered to do the best he could on forecasting a coup from the margin of any plotting and to avoid contacts or actions which might later be construed as supporting or encouraging those who planned to overthrow Allende. (Only a few days following this conversation with Abe, tank units in Santiago attacked the National Palace, in a premature and quickly squelched coup attempt.)

Abe briefed me on a number of other new and particular problems, including the relatively new CIA responsibility for reporting on international drug-trafficking, tricky because sooner or later an American citizen would appear on the radar screen. Any coverage of an American would be subject to criticism and any information gathered from him or her would have to be provided to American courts in the event of prosecution. This could jeopardize our sources and operational methods.

But the basic problem I faced, Abe said, was the morale of the troops. CIA people were beginning to feel beleaguered. Sensational headlines were exposing Cold War endeavors which at the time were sponsored and applauded by American presidents but, after Watergate, were seen as irresponsible international forays by spooks without principles. There was renewed speculation that CIA was somehow involved in the assassination of John Kennedy. Victor Marchetti, who had worked for the CIA, and John Marks, who had not, were about to publish a sensational anti-CIA book. The kiss-and-tell authors were becoming folk heroes on college campuses while those within CIA saw their previously acceptable image deteriorating.

The most disturbing clinker, Abe continued, was in the person of Mr. Philip Agee, a former operations officer in the WH Division. Agee was living in Europe and writing a book in which he intended to expose —publicly identify—every CIA officer known to him, and each indigenous agent he had learned of in the three countries in Latin America where he had been stationed—Ecuador, Uruguay, and Mexico. A program of "cauterization" was already under way: the agents known to Agee were being terminated, and some relocated for their safety; and every operation which Agee might have been privy to was being terminated. This necessary exercise cost the United States some millions of dollars. CIA had had a remarkable record unique among intelligence services: there had never been a staff officer who had gone over to the other side; indeed, as far as I knew, CIA had never been penetrated at the staff level by a hostile service. Agee, who had been in frequent contact with Cuban intelligence officers for some time and had made several visits to Cuba, was a first in CIA's experience.

I attended my first DDO meeting, a weekly session at which area Division Chiefs conferred with Bill Nelson, successor to Wisner, Helms, Bissell, FitzGerald, Karamessines, and Colby. I anticipated the first opportunity to work with Jim Angleton, the enigmatic counterspy chief whom I had seen frequently in the halls over the years. While we were waiting for Nelson to arrive so the meeting could begin, I whispered to an associate, "Where is Angleton?"

"He'll be here," my colleague said. "He always sits on Nelson's right." He indicated an empty chair at the place of honor.

And then Angleton did enter the conference room and take the empty chair. Enigmatic indeed! That was not the man I had been observing all these years. The person who had identified him to me in 1954 had been mistaken—he thought someone else was Jim Angleton and foisted his error off on me. The real Jim Angleton was a head taller than the officer I had thought him to be, and I could not recall ever having seen him. (Later, I ascertained the identity of the other man; he was an authority on Communism who had the enviable task as an O.S.S. operative during World War II of helping Marlene Dietrich write lyrics for songs designed to affect German morale.) When the meeting ended Angleton spoke with me briefly. After a rather furtive look about, he asked me to see him in his office soon. As a Division Chief I should have The Briefing. The briefing? The Briefing, Angleton repeated slowly.

I watched Angleton as he shuffled down the hall, six feet tall, his shoulders stooped as if supporting an enormous incubus of secrets. He is extremely thin; he was once described as "A man who looks like his ectoplasm has run out." Dark-tinted bifocals shade a sallow and sensitive face. It is not difficult to conjure an image of the young Angleton blocking out an avant-garde poetry magazine with his literary colleagues Ezra Pound and E. E. Cummings. Angleton grew up in Italy, where his father later became a lieutenant colonel in the O.S.S. After Harvard and Yale, the son followed father into the espionage business, ultimately becoming the undisputed counter-intelligence and counter-espionage expert of American intelligence. In private life he savored fine food, bourbon and branch water, orchids, and fly-fishing. On the job, in measured and careful detail, Angleton described the pitfalls of the past and the perils of the future emanating from the Soviet KGB and its allied intelligence services. Pausing frequently to drag deeply from the filter tip cigarettes always between his fingers, Angleton attempted to warn skeptics against any relaxation of vigilance against the dark forces of Communism. He found it more difficult to sell his wares in the time of détente. One thing is certain: CIA has the best record of any intelligence service in history in defending itself against penetration by hostile services. Perhaps that will be Angleton's monument.

On a weekend in late July an unnerving cable arrived from Mexico City. A source had reported that a man presented himself to the Chilean embassy—walked in—in Mexico City. He told a Chilean envoy that he had just defected from CIA, because the Agency had been persecuting his family. As bona fides he offered Allende's ambassador "Plan Centaur," which he described as CIA's program to overthrow the Chilean government. He had a number of documents and microfilms in code which, he said, only he could decipher. He offered these secrets in return for safe haven in Santiago.

I went into the office on Sunday morning to read the cable. I was not concerned about the validity of Plan Centaur because I knew it did not exist; I was worried that a disaffected staff officer from my Division was using his general knowledge of our operations to enhance a fabrication. The unidentified walk-in, according to the Mexico City information, was an American black, about thirty-five and slim, who claimed to be an expert in codes and ciphers. I was immediately skeptical, as the black officers I knew were not the kind of people who would even contemplate treason. Two black officers who had worked in WH Division recently might fit the description. One was at his home when I telephoned on a pretext; another was not, the message being that he was away for the weekend and no one knew where he could be reached. I checked with other intelligence agencies on any blacks who could not be accounted for. One by one positive reports came in, the last verifying the presence of a black DIA (Defense Intelligence Agency) officer on Okinawa, and, to my relief, the second WH officer returned from his weekend. But I had an uneasy feeling that I hadn't heard the last of Plan Centaur.

On Monday morning Abe chastised me gently. Abe, who always described himself as "a lover, not a fighter," told me I must learn that I was now a manager, not an operator. An officer from our Mexico section should have spent Sunday on duty in the office on the Plan Centaur case. The Division Chief had to delegate even the most intriguing cases and allow others to enjoy the excitement of running operations.

Abe was right. I soon found that 95 percent of my time must be devoted to mundane management matters and only a precious few moments to the more interesting development and direction of operations. There was a budget of many millions of dollars to handle, and the affairs of several hundred people in Washington and the field to consider. There was a constant requirement for coordination with other agencies, especially the State Department and the National Security Council. There were meetings, meetings, meetings. I grumbled, but the meetings never stopped.

In my new role as a manager I found the average day might run something like this. I would arrive at Langley at 7:45 after a fifteen-minute drive from home in Maryland just across the Potomac River and read four cable boards for about an hour. Three were incoming: operational, support and administration, and the formal intelligence disseminations which described present situations and predicted future developments in twenty countries. The intelligence would also be on the desks of Latin Americanists in State, DIA, NSA, and other agencies. The fourth board contained all outgoing messages, most of which I would be seeing for the first time since they had been released by subordinates. There were also two small stacks of sealed envelopes, the first reserved for reports on very sensitive operations, such as the details of a Soviet case, and the second for eyes-only cables in the Division Chief's privacy channel, the only other copy going to my immediate boss, Bill Nelson, the DDO. This first hour's reading was the rough equivalent of scanning a book, and sometimes a thick one. Once done I was prepared to reply to calls from the Director's office, the Department of State, or elsewhere with clandestinely acquired details of the news behind the news of the day throughout Latin America. At 9:15 a Division staff meeting, usually lasting twenty minutes. Before lunch at least two meetings with other Agency components, and perhaps three times a week with other agencies, including a regular Friday morning meeting with my counterpart at State, the Assistant Secretary for Latin American Affairs and his two deputies and mine, Abe. The Assistant Secretary was Jack Kubisch, now Ambassador in Greece, who had such a ready smile that Abe dubbed him "Mr. Dentyne," and his deputies Harry Shlaudeman and Bill Bowdler, with whom I had worked during the Dominican crisis. Lunch, if not a sandwich at the desk, would be a business meeting; perhaps an ambassador at Langley for a briefing; perhaps with Bill Jorden, the Latin American man on Kissinger's NSC staff (Jorden is now Ambassador to Panama, one of the trickier Western Hemisphere assignments). Several times a week meetings with the DDO, the DDCI, or with Director Colby. And, between all the meetings, minisessions on personnel matters, including a visit from each member of the Division going to or returning from the field. Perhaps once a week I would appear as a speaker or panelist in one of the dozens of Agency training courses; the most pleasant chore being the veritable vacation of a flight to "the farm."

Albeit reluctantly, I became a manager of money and people, with an occasional lark into the decision-making process involving operations. And, it began to work. My management formula, which would not necessarily be approved at Harvard Business School but seems to work in a clandestine organization, consisted of four steps: (a) create respect for yourself, either by working harder or better or both than subordinates, (b) delegate, (c) kick asses when necessary, and (d) enjoy serendipity. Was it baseball manager Branch Rickey who said "Luck is the residue of design"?

In fact, after the first month we were lucky when the Division went thirty days without a security violation, the first unblemished month in years. Gina asked, "Didn't you promise a lollipop to everyone who helped?" I said that I had, but was sure that no one had taken that flip promise seriously. "I take it seriously," Gina said. So many lollipops only cost a few dollars, but it took Gina several hours to tie ribbons—the personal touch, she said—on each, and I spent three hours delivering a lollipop to each officer and secretary in the Division. There was some good-natured kidding from my colleagues in the Executive Dining Room about Operation Lollipop.

CIA had changed since 1969. The women, taking advantage of a relaxed dress code, almost universally wore slacks and blouses; there were many more blacks in the halls and offices, and some visiting dignitaries, especially foreign intelligence chiefs, remarked on the Afros on the blacks and shoulder-length hair on the younger whites. An Equal Employment Opportunity program had been implemented, and managers were called to task if women and minority groups did not receive enough attention. I got the EEO message and soon appointed the first female Chief of Station in CIA's history. She is working abroad now, and doing well I might add.

Director William Colby was changing the Agency, in some cases following the lead of James Schlesinger, who had abruptly dismissed so many of the old hands. But Colby was going much further. Perhaps sensing the impending storm, he began to change CIA into an "American" intelligence service; that is, the kind of service which could survive in today's domestic political climate, where any secret organization is suspect. In speeches to CIA personnel Colby reiterated the need to adjust to a changing American society. Some of the old hands were shaken by the new, more open Agency policy; others believed Colby was convinced

242

the new course was necessary if the Agency were to survive the stormy
seas in the wake of Watergate. In comparison to past practice, the Agency
was indeed wide open. Newsmen arrived for briefings; I told them what
was happening in Latin American countries they were about to visit.
We had hundreds of visitors to our building: college classes, high school
students, and businessmen. The last college group I saw in the halls was
from the Malcolm X College. I spoke on a dozen occasions to as many
as fifty businessmen at lunch at Langley, visiting in a program sponsored
by the Brookings Institute. Some old hands reiterated their conviction
that spying was a secret business to be conducted in absolute secrecy. But
an increasing number of the oldtimers defected to the ranks of younger
officers who endorsed Colby's "passive" public-relations program. The
rule was simple: public relations if asked. But passive public relations
has its shortcomings. An example had occurred some time before when a
Hollywood company requested exterior shots on the grounds of the
CIA for a film—a request granted, I've been told, when a California
legislator leaned on the Director. The Bell Telephone Company would
have insisted on the right to review the script, but CIA did not. The
result was *Scorpio*, with Burt Lancaster cast as the CIA agent who assassinated people at the drop of cloak.

I had met William E. Colby in the past, but only briefly. I lunched
with a friend from the Far East Division, who had worked with Colby
over the years. I asked him to explain the Director. He told me, "For
years in the Far East we referred to Colby as 'the soldier-priest.' The man
is difficult enough to understand in any case, without remembering that
you'll never fathom him." He mentioned a number of episodes in Colby's
past to illustrate the priest aspect of his character and described his devout
private life as a practicing Roman Catholic. A few days later the point
was brought home to me. A good friend and colleague from the Division died, and Gina and I went to the evening memorial service for him
at a huge Presbyterian church in Washington. When the minister went
up the stairs to the pulpit he turned out not to be a minister but the
soldier-priest, the Director of Central Intelligence. Colby delivered the
eulogy. I was astounded. I'm not aware that it has happened before or
since: it was a surreal happening—the chief of an intelligence service
speaking with measured ecclesiastical cadence, extolling the deceased
intelligence veteran, and providing a benediction for him and for his
years of service in espionage. I saw Colby at Langley the next day and
remarked that I found it unusual for the DCI to be a stand-in for a
minister, especially when his day at the office was such a full one. I
mentioned that I had not been aware that Colby had been close to my
deceased friend, and Colby said that, as a matter of fact, he had not

known him intimately. Then why did you deliver the eulogy? Colby said, "Oh, I had to. His widow telephoned me at the office and asked me to do it."

On another occasion I was visiting Colby's very modest home in Bethesda. We stood together at the window and looked out at the Catholic church which adjoins Colby's home and where the family worshiped. He said that he and Barbara had selected the home for its "convenience," obviously referring to the proximity of the church rather than his seventh-floor office at Langley, two miles away across the Potomac.

When reminiscing about Colby, my friend had also described the soldier side of the DCI. The credentials were in order: son of an army officer; childhood spent in army camps as far afield as China; O.S.S. officer who parachuted behind enemy lines as commanding officer of a sabotage team in Scandinavia at age twenty-four. Slight of build, with pale, dull eyes, Colby appeared to be almost anything rather than soldier or intelligence chief. His stamina and capacity for work is prodigious. "In the late forties," my friend said, "Des FitzGerald traveled through Europe, scouting for talent for the Far East Division. He had little regard for most of the officers he met there, with the exception of a young fellow named Colby working in covert action in Rome. Des promised Colby the job of Deputy Chief of Station in Saigon. When Colby came through headquarters for a two-week orientation visit I was chief of the Vietnam section. Colby asked what he should do for the two weeks. I was sort of busy, didn't want to bother, so I told Colby, 'Why don't you just read the files?' So he did—from seven thirty in the morning until eleven at night, for two solid weeks."

Demands on Colby the soldier were draconic when he was asked to assume command of the controversial Operation Phoenix in Vietnam. Rough business, in a rough war. It is generally assumed that Colby was the Chief of Station during this period; in fact he was given the rank of ambassador and reported to Ambassador Bunker in the embassy through the military command rather than the CIA Station. On numerous occasions Colby has testified about Operation Phoenix in Congress, and the program and Colby have been attacked frequently in the press. In several discussions with him on the operation, I have never detected any complaint or resentment that he had been saddled with the controversial endeavor, although Colby often acknowledged it as the greatest cross he had to bear in his effort to create a new personal image as the Mr. Clean of the intelligence community. During 1974 and until his retirement Colby has had the thankless chore of defending the Agency against allegations of improper conduct during the tenures of a number of previous directors. Operation Phoenix, however, was Colby's own albatross, and he knew it.

Colby the priest was concerned about people. He always found time, despite a hectic daily agenda, to listen to any CIA employee who had a grievance to discuss with the boss. "Bill," a senior colleague told me, "would stop his business to stroke any stray cat which wandered into his office." Colby lunched regularly with junior officers in the cafeteria, seeking their opinions and probing for early warning of morale problems.

Colby the soldier could be tough, even stubborn. In 1973 he conducted an informal poll among senior officers asking what they thought of his idea of publishing a daily newspaper at CIA. They unanimously considered it a poor idea, and told Colby so. The DCI mulled their recommendations then proceeded with his project.*

I met General Vernon Walters, the DDCI. Having served in Brazil, I knew that Walters was considered a folk hero there. He was the United States liaison officer with Brazilian troops in Italy during World War II and later served as military attaché in Rio de Janeiro. Walters is the finest linguist I've ever met: his Portuguese, Spanish, French, and German are flawless, and he is more than glib in half a dozen other languages. There are those who believe the General is perhaps too loquacious in all languages; it certainly requires initiative and alertness to find an opportunity to break into his lengthy monologues. I have heard him hold forth on perhaps fifty occasions—he was a spirited and entertaining host when foreign officials visited Washington—and I never tired of his stories, some of which I heard dozens of times. And he devoted an inordinate amount of time and energy helping me personally and the Division in a number of ways. I am indebted to him.

When the Director of Central Intelligence is a civilian, the DDCI—the number-two man—is traditionally from the military, and vice versa. Walters, a three-star general, was a Nixon man at the time of his appointment. When the Watergate cover-up began Walters, after initially agreeing to ask the FBI to go slow, abruptly turned his back to Nixon, and held fast against attempts by Haldeman, Ehrlichman, and Dean to use him as an agent of influence within CIA.

Vernon Walters is a large, heavy man. I'm surprised he is not even heavier as he consumes an impressive amount of food and wine. A bachelor, he spends his energy at work and at the dining table. He has been responsible for a marked change in the quality of food served in

* The NID—*National Intelligence Daily*—is an intriguing paper. It has only a few pages, no advertising, and the most limited circulation in the world, within CIA and to the heads of a few other agencies. It is much like other papers except that all of the stories are top secret.

the Director's dining room, where visitors often lunch. Before Walters the food was plain, nutritious, and inexpensive. Now when the General hosts a luncheon the cuisine is superb and the wines of the best French vintage (Colby is not much for serving wine; it is always California if he does). This is fine until the bill comes, as CIA officers attending must pay their own way when entertaining an American colleague—perhaps an ambassador or desk man from State—and the General's repasts always include French bread, which he picks up on the way to work, a selection of imported cheeses, and the French wine. The food is certainly tasty, if somewhat rich for a bureaucrat's budget.

I went to see Jim Angleton in his office, hoping that along with the business which sent me I might hear The Briefing. I have never seen so much paper. Each executive desk at CIA will have an in-box and an out-box—and some one or two extra. On Angleton's desk there were several. On a long table which was in effect an extension of his desk there were perhaps a dozen additional in-boxes, each spilling over with documents. Red *Priority* stickers were everywhere in the mass of papers, like poppies growing through a field of snow. In my own in-box more than one *Priority* sticker would make me nervous—Angleton ignored the array of red urgency indicators as we finished our business. On leaving I was tempted to ask about The Briefing, but decided not to appear too impatient, and Angleton didn't mention it.

Gina was waiting expectantly when I arrived home one night. "Well?" I told her that the second month of Operation Lollipop had been successful—the Division had now gone for sixty days without a security violation. This time we decided something other than a lollipop should be the reward. It takes several hours to polish so many red apples. The next morning I delivered them individually to each employee, having borrowed a cart customarily used for heavy files to push the load of three baskets of apples through the halls. My colleagues in the Executive Dining Room thought me to be a bit strange, but they did not joke this time.

In late August of 1973 it became increasingly evident that a coup was imminent in Chile. Following the abortive effort of the tank commanders in June, resentment and discontent festered among the military, and even the wives of the military officers protested in front of the home of the army chief of staff in Santiago. The Chilean Air Force conspired with the Chilean Navy, and both joined in anti-Allende cabals with the Chilean National Police. The missing element was the army, vital to any coup endeavor. There were several false starts and postponements. Then a report said that the army was about to join the other conspirators. Grandmother was on the roof. On the night of September 10, I phoned Jack Kubisch and Bill Jorden, saying that this time it looked real.

The first critical message announcing the coup arrived early in the morning at Langley as in other agencies in Washington. A state of siege was declared; the Chilean military, tutored in battle tactics by German instructors until World War II (Chilean cadets still goosestep in front of the National Palace each morning during flag-raising ceremonies), moved ruthlessly against Allende.

At 4 A.M. on the morning of the coup the CIA Station Chief called into the office a TDY reports officer billeted across the street from the embassy at a hotel. For several weeks the Chief of Station and this reports officer, a young and attractive woman, had carried on a debate, he insisting that a coup might occur at any time, she maintaining that it could not possibly occur before Christmas. When the bombs started dropping on the National Palace that September morning, a few hundred yards from the embassy, the young reports woman walked into the office of the Chief of Station, kissed him on both cheeks, and said, "Merry Christmas."

I have often been asked three questions about the Chilean coup. I can answer two.

Did Allende commit suicide, as claimed by the Chilean junta? I don't know. It could have gone either way in the interior of the National Palace that bloody morning. There was one report that Mrs. Allende had spoken on the phone with her husband shortly before his death and her immediate reaction upon word of his demise was that he had taken his own life. There were other conflicting reports. Obviously it was convenient for the Chilean military to propagate the death-by-his-own-hand legend, which would make Allende less of a martyr in Latin American eyes. Allende was, I am convinced, a brave man, and his death by whatever hand marks him as a military casualty.

How can the savage consolidation of power by the Chilean military, previously paragons of constitutionality among Latin American armed forces, be explained or justified? I certainly do not pretend to justify it, and it is difficult to comprehend how a country which was a Latin American model of the democratic process for so many years could erupt in violence—the last coup had been forty-three years before, and that one quick and bloodless. The answer, I believe, lies in the fact that Chilean officers planning the coup were convinced that they faced a minimum of two weeks of street fighting in Santiago and, perhaps, civil war throughout the countryside. In classes at the military academy Chilean cadets studied the last really significant coup, which had occurred in 1891. José Balmaceda, a liberal, anticlerical President much in the mold of Salvador Allende, was forced from office by rebelling Congressmen and their military allies. Balmaceda committed suicide rather than surrender for a trial. Thousands of Chileans died in the disastrous civil war which ensued. This political precedent might have been in Allende's mind when he was besieged in the National Palace.

Why didn't the United States warn Allende that the coup was imminent, if CIA had advance information? There are two sides to the coin of that query. On the one side, if the United States government were to warn the incumbent regime in Latin America each time there were reports of a coup it would soon become suspect, as most coups are planned but do not come off. Crying coup-wolf would soon result in a lack of credibility for the American embassy. The other side of the coin is what happens should the Americans warn a regime that it is about to be overthrown and it is. Relations with the new government, when its leaders learned that the gringos had attempted to thwart their plans, would be sticky indeed. However, in the case of the Chilean coup of 1973, both observations are irrelevant. A decision to advise Salvador Allende's Marxist government would have had to be made at the highest levels of the United States government. I'm not sure what Henry Kissinger's position would have been, although I can make an educated guess. There was never a doubt in my mind what Richard Nixon's decision would have been, had he been asked whether we should forewarn Allende, and thus allow the Marxist to defend himself. It never even occurred to me that Nixon would have done otherwise than scotch the proposal. And that is the real reason no United States official even considered the idea. It would have been a waste of time to ask.

The day following the coup a meeting of the WSAG (Washington Special Action Group) was held at the White House. This group convenes when there is an unexpected and significant world development, such as Mideast hostilities, a clash in Southeast Asia, or an abrupt change of government anywhere in a country vital to United States interests. The WSAG is an after-the-fact type of Forty Committee, with a slightly larger composition but with the same chairman—Henry Kissinger.* The meetings are held in the same conference room—which is below ground level and about the size of a two-car garage—where the Forty Committee meets. The Director of Central Intelligence is a member, and I went along as the CIA Latin America man. Each principal is normally accompanied by a specialist in the area under review. Under Secretary Kenneth Rush was on hand from State, Bill Simon from Treasury, Bill Jorden from NSC, and representatives from Defense and its Joints Chief of Staff, among others. After a few moments—very few—of light banter,

---

* Henry Kissinger is no longer chairman of the Forty Committee and the WSAG. An Executive Order in 1976 proscribed such multiple responsibilities, which is a good idea. Similarly, it would be wise in the future to insure that a director of Central Intelligence not be the brother of the Secretary of State, as was the case with Allen and John Foster Dulles.

Chairman Kissinger opened the discussion. Kissinger runs a tight meeting. Colby kicked off with a review of the developments in Santiago (fighting continued) and in the countryside (quiet). Then, and later during the meeting, I would on request slip him a note occasionally with a comment or statistic. There is an unwritten but inflexible rule at WSAG and Forty Committee meetings that the backup men, like good little children, do not speak unless called on by their principal to answer a question the more senior man cannot answer. (Colby speaks Italian and French, but no Spanish; it took him a while to learn to refer to A-yen-day rather than Ah-lend-eh.)

One of the military officers noted that a number of United States naval craft were approaching the northern Chile port of Arica for a fueling stop on the long trip around the Straits of Magellan. They were in southern waters as part of an annual exercise involving navies of most Latin American republics and the United States. Kissinger said simply, "Turn them around." There were remonstrances: very expensive, everyone would understand about the naval exercise; it would be a loss of face. Kissinger listened not very patiently and repeated, this time with a slightly metallic edge to his voice, the instruction. One of the backup men for Defense violated the time-honored rule that juniors did not volunteer opinions. Once a State Department officer, he began, "Mr. Secretary, as a former ambassador I believe..." His voice trailed off weakly under the heat of Kissinger's glare.

Then Kissinger became really businesslike in shutting off conversation about the political and military situation and concentrating on economics. He seemed to care little about the status of opposing forces, or who would be running the new government, or the chances of increased street fighting or civil war in the interior. He was interested in economics. He asked a number of questions for which no one had an answer. Indeed many of his questions were beyond my comprehension. About unencumbered gold reserves, for instance. Rush and Simon understood, but the rest of us were ignorant. I did jot down many of his esoteric questions on my pad.

I thought the meeting was ending when Kissinger excused himself to see President Nixon, who was working upstairs in the Oval Office. Then he returned and announced a number of decisions. I was surprised. I had always thought of Henry Kissinger as a man who made such decisions for the President. Obviously, in this instance at least, he checked them out with Nixon.

That was a Tuesday. Another WSAG meeting was scheduled for Friday morning. On returning to Langley, I consulted my reports chief, who was responsible for preparing intelligence requirements for our overseas stations, and asked what the chances were of providing answers to

Kissinger's arcane economic questions. "We have sources in Santiago," he replied, "but I don't see how the station can get to them. The case officers are sleeping in the embassy; there's a curfew and state of siege. But we'll try." The cable which went out that afternoon began with an apologetic WE REALIZE IT MAY BE IMPOSSIBLE...and posed some sixty questions, all in the economic sphere. Our station was lucky. It had the proper equipment, in working order, to communicate clandestinely and securely with a nonofficial cover officer, a "businessman" outside, and he in turn managed to contact the proper principal agent, who then found a way to contact his subagents and a number of nonwitting informants.

When the WSAG meeting reconvened on Friday morning Secretary Kissinger had the answers to his questions. If I recall correctly, no other American agency in Santiago could provide a single answer under the wartime conditions.

Plan Centaur, the fabricated CIA plan against Allende, raised its deceptive head. Mrs. Allende, arriving in Mexico City from Santiago, was the house guest of the gullible ex-envoy who had swallowed the wild story of the walk-in pretending to be a disaffected CIA staff officer. By now we knew the fabricator's name and that he was an American parole violator with a criminal history. He had flown to Cuba using a false Chilean passport supplied by the envoy. I have no doubt that the Cuban DGI was soon aware that this parole violator was an impostor; nevertheless he flew on to Chile on a Soviet airliner. Apparently the envoy told Mrs. Allende of the parole violator's Plan Centaur and apparently she believed him. Shortly after, in a Reuters interview in Havana, Mrs. Allende recounted the bizarre details of Plan Centaur as the basis of her conviction that CIA was behind the coup which overthrew her husband. I certainly understand why Mrs. Allende, whom I know to be a fine person, might readily accept the fabricator's story. But, I can assure her now, there was no truth to it, and the evidence provided by the envoy was spurious.

Another month passed without a security violation in the Division—three months, a really commendable record, certainly the best in the history of the Division if not in CIA for a component of similar size. I popped with pride, but this time decided that a more formal recognition was in order, and prepared laudatory citations for the personnel file of each officer, clerk, and secretary in the Division. For the first time I found real pleasure in a managerial rather than an operational accomplishment. (As I write, a paperweight sits on the desk, a gift from the Division on my retirement day—a miniature CIA safe, with gold numbers indicating 116 days without a violation; one of the original lollipops and its ribbon is attached.)

250

While Operation Lollipop indicated a satisfactory level of morale in the Division, morale generally in the Agency countinued to sag as 1974 drew to an end. The CIA was almost universally suspected of being behind the Chilean coup. Sensational stories, including allegations and innuendo concerning the Kennedy assassination and Agency involvement in Watergate, multiplied and festered. Some journalists became more and more fervid in uncovering and describing in detail CIA operations and, increasingly, identifying our officers overseas and in sensitive positions in headquarters. Marchetti and Marks, having published their book and discussed on talk shows their reminiscences to tatters, became shriller in their allegations. We learned that Philip Agee's book was nearing completion and that the publishers had agreed to his plan to identify even our foreign agents. Those consequences would be devastating.

So William Colby erected a statue of Nathan Hale just outside the main entrance to the CIA building. Hale, the first American spy, though a martyr, was a pretty poor intelligence operator: he hid his secret instructions in his shoe, where they were found on his capture by the British; he arrived too late to accomplish his task of reporting on the British order of battle from Manhattan; in short, he failed in his mission. But Nathan Hale did die for his country, regretting that it could be just once. It was in this spirit that the soldier-priest apparently decided that a stiff dash of patriotism was just what was needed for CIA. The unveiling of the Hale statue prompted considerable comment in the halls of CIA: older cynics thought it corny and some of the younger officers believed it to be camp. When inevitably some of the whispering reached Colby, he only smiled.

The CIA Nathan Hale statue, of a man who went to school at Yale, was erected by Colby, who was educated at Princeton. It has been claimed by at least one historian that Hale was betrayed to the British by his Tory first cousin, who as irony would have it went to Harvard. Be that as it may, there was some tittering among CIA Harvard alumni, and at least one complained that it was all unfair, that Harvard should have equal representation.

Dick Welch was walking out of the building with Abe when he saw the statue for the first time.

"What's this? A Yalie! Perhaps we should demand that a statue of a Harvard stand on the other side of the entrance."

"Who?" Abe asked.

Dick thought a minute, then grinned. "Alger Hiss?"

I believe that two newspaper revelations led to the present furor concerning CIA and were directly responsible for the multiple commission and congressional committee investigations of the Agency.

The first was the erroneous public charge of CIA "destabilization" of the Chilean government of Salvador Allende and subsequent allegations that CIA funded the strikes which were the ultimate catalyst for Allende's downfall. The covert action program of CIA in Chile began in 1962 under Kennedy and continued under Johnson and Nixon until the coup in September of 1973. During this period congressional committees were briefed a number of times, how thoroughly prior to 1973 I cannot say, but certainly frequently. In early 1974, we heard, Democratic Congressman Michael Harrington of Massachusetts began to pressure Chairman Lucien Nedzi of the House Armed Forces CIA subcommittee with demands for a detailed review of CIA operations in Chile over the years. Nedzi, I was told, assured Harrington that he and his committee had been thoroughly briefed but declined to give details to Harrington, who was not a member of the committee. Harrington persevered, so Nedzi called for a new briefing, on April 22, 1974. Special security precautions were taken because Colby planned to reveal all the details of a decade of CIA involvement in Chile. I was surprised to find that CIA technicians had "swept" the conference room before the testimony, searching for microphones that might have been placed by hostile services. I went with Colby to Congress where, after we were both sworn in, the Director provided a lengthy description of CIA's role in Chile over the years: how much money had been approved, spent, and for what, and how much had been approved, not spent, and why not. Occasionally I was asked by Colby to participate.

A transcript was made of the testimony by a congressional court reporter. As is customary, the transcript was held in the security of a CIA vault at Langley, subject, as always, to recall by the committee which had prepared it. On a Saturday morning in June 1974, a lawyer from the CIA's legislative liaison office called me. He said that Harrington was insisting on reviewing the transcript—the right any Congressman has to review testimony of any committee, but a privilege which had not been exercised previously in requests to CIA oversight committees. I told the lawyer that I was concerned about the prospect, because Harrington was known as a vocal, hostile critic of CIA. In any event, I said I would insist on two conditions: that I have the opportunity to review the transcript, to be sure it was an accurate version of what Colby and I had said, and, that Colby personally must approve the release of the document to Harrington, something I would wish to discuss with the Director before the fact. I also told the Agency lawyer to send the transcript to my office first thing on Monday morning.

On Monday I phoned the lawyer, asking why the transcript had not arrived. He explained that late on Saturday, after our conversation, the committee had again asked for the transcript and that he had checked with Colby. The DCI said that he could not refuse such a request by a member of the Congress and thus released it. It had been delivered over the weekend. I had a funny feeling grandmother was on the roof at Langley. When I did obtain the transcript for review, I found that the House committee had taken extreme precautions to emphasize the sensitivity of the document when providing it to Congressman Harrington. In fact a written statement signed by Harrington, in which he acknowledged his obligation to hold the contents closely, was attached to the transcript—the only congressional "secrecy agreement" I had ever seen.

Congressman Harrington, who reviewed the transcript on two occasions, wrote a letter summarizing its contents with the details of CIA funding in Chile over the years to Congressman Thomas E. Morgan, Chairman of the House Foreign Affairs Committee. This letter leaked simultaneously to the Washington *Post* and the *New York Times*. In the latter, under the byline of Seymour Hersh on September 8, 1974, the second paragraph read: "The goal of the clandestine CIA activities, the director, William E. Colby, testified at a top-secret hearing last April, was to 'destabilize' the Marxist Government of President Allende, who was elected in 1970." Twice again in the Hersh rendition of Harrington's letter, based on Colby's testimony, "destabilization" was mentioned, each time in quotation marks. The term was also used in the *Post* account.

Colby was visibly agitated when I spoke to him following the leak. First because it came smack in the middle of Solidarity With Chile Week, a vast worldwide propaganda activity sponsored by the Soviet Union. But, more importantly, Colby instinctively recognized that "destabilize" was just the sort of word which could quickly become a part of the international lexicon with a pejorative ring to the detriment of CIA. After World War II Colby had been one of those responsible in Europe for successfully countering an effort by Soviet propagandists to monopolize the word "peace."

A few days later Colby and Harrington met in a public encounter, which I heard on the radio. The DCI told Harrington, "I want you to know that I did not use the word 'destabilize' anywhere in my testimony. I've reviewed the transcript, and I'm sure about that." Harrington replied that he too recalled the transcript and was positive that Colby did use the term. To be sure my recollection of the testimony was correct, I obtained the transcript and reviewed it a dozen times. Colby was right. On September 16 the *New York Times* ran a CIA-Chile editorial which used the "destabilize" term five times, each time in quotations. Colby wrote a letter to the *Times*, published on September 18, in which he disclaimed responsibility. But "destabilize" has become a part of the international political lexicon and remains so today—meaning, in effect, the process of undermining to the point of collapse a foreign government by CIA. It was not long before the adjective and noun began even to creep into CIA cable traffic. It was an apt enough term for the United States policy for a few weeks in 1970, but not for the period from then until the coup.*

The second part in the series of Chile revelations was also written by Mr. Hersh and appeared on September 20, 1974 in the *New York Times*. It read:

> The Central Intelligence Agency secretly financed striking labor unions and trade groups in Chile for more than 18 months before President Salvador Allende was overthrown, intelligence sources revealed today.... Among those heavily subsidized, the sources said, were the organizers of a nationwide truck strike....

No other reporter of repute has ever confirmed Mr. Hersh's allegation on this, if I recall correctly. Thus, together with "destabilization," it is now almost universally believed that CIA funded and encouraged the strikes which were the major factor in Allende's downfall. Certainly it is believed everywhere in Latin America, with the Chilean truckers themselves possibly being excepted. These are not the facts. There were proposals from Chile and Washington pointing out that the truckers' strike—they were protesting that the Chilean government refused to allow them to purchase spare parts and that the Communist Minister of Transportation advocated nationalization of the trucking industry—could well ensure Allende's downfall. Such proposals were routinely passed up the line in CIA, occasionally for presentation to the Forty Committee. This one was too, with my personal recommendation that CIA and the

---

* There is nothing that will change the current usage of "destabilization," but I would like to add a minor historical footnote for etymologists. The term was first used by Congressman Harrington. I base this on the recollection of a phone call from then Deputy Assistant Secretary Harry Shlaudeman on June 12, 1974— some six weeks after Colby and I testified on Chile in April 1974. Harry had been Deputy Chief of Mission, the number-two man, at the American embassy in Santiago, serving there until shortly before Allende fell. He had just testified before the Latin American subcommittee of the House Committee on Foreign Affairs.

Harry said, "I was really roasted today by Michael Harrington. He kept asking me about the 'destabilization' of the Allende regime. Have you people given Congress anything to indicate that 'destabilizing' was the plan?"

I assured Harry that I never heard of the term and soon forgot the conversation. But when Harrington's leaked summary of the April 22 testimony established "destabilization" as a new word in the political arena I recalled the phone query from Harry. When the *Congressional Record* was published, I reviewed the Shlaudeman testimony. Indeed, Harrington had used the word "destabilization" three times, before he attributed it to Colby.

254

United States government not become involved. The proposal was not acted upon.

The Chilean coup and its aftermath was not the only WH Division flap during my tenure as chief of Latin American operations. In early 1974 a subcommittee of the Senate chaired by Senator Howard Baker conducted an investigation of possible CIA participation in the Watergate break-in, beyond the assistance given a year previously to Howard Hunt with the Ellsberg psychological study, both grievous CIA errors. The investigation was triggered because of a handwritten annotation on a CIA document seen by a member of the Watergate Select Committee chaired by Senator Sam Ervin. The scribble, on the margin of the document, read, "This refers to the WH flap." The White House flap? Watergate? Senator Baker thought he heard but could not see, nor ultimately find, animals thrashing around in the forest.

The "WH" in this instance meant Western Hemisphere (my division), not White House. Some twenty-two witnesses and two thousand pages of testimony later the Baker subcommittee released its findings on July 2. A thorough review of this document reveals that no evidence was found of CIA complicity in the Watergate break-in, but the general tone of the report suggested that there might still be some unseen but noisy creatures in the woods. It certainly did nothing to dispel lingering doubts on Agency involvement in Watergate, most of which, it would appear, were bruited by Charles Colson, a man who CIA people believed (as Abe would have put it) lacked the essentials of greatness.*

Well, there will never be another "WH flap" in CIA. On assuming the job of Chief of the Western Hemisphere Division I felt uncomfortable with the designation. James Reston once described it as "the most intriguing title in town," the inference being of CIA domestic jurisdiction. Certainly WH was not appropriate for a division which did not include Canadian matters in its bailiwick.

The annotation leading to the Baker investigation was not the first time the WH of Western Hemisphere Division had been confused with the WH of White House. When John McCone was DCI, he once was about to speak before the National War College in Washington. As he walked toward the podium an aide, who had been manning the radio in

* Three years later in 1976 Senator Baker added a footnote to his investigation in an addendum to the Senate Select Committee's final intelligence report: "The investigation of Watergate and the possible relationship of the Central Intelligence Agency thereto, produced a panoply of puzzlement. While the available information leaves nagging questions and contains bits and pieces of intriguing evidence, fairness dictates that an assessment be rendered on the basis of the present record. An impartial evaluation of that record compels the conclusion that the CIA, as an institution, was not involved in the Watergate break-in."

McCone's limousine, stopped the DCI, saying, "Colonel J. C. King [then Western Hemisphere Division Chief] wants you to call him immediately." McCone said, "Tell King that I'm about to give a speech. I'll call him later." Director McCone was only a few minutes into his discourse when the aide scurried down the aisle of the auditorium, interrupting McCone. He was breathless. "The President is furious! He says to hell with the speech. He needs to talk to you right now."

The radio message received in McCone's automobile had contained the double-talk instruction: "Have the Director telephone Number One at WH right now." The aide had interpreted this to mean, "Call Colonel King of Western Hemisphere Division," and not as it was meant to be, "Call the President at the White House."

So that's why there will never be another WH flap at CIA. I changed the name to one more accurately describing the area responsibility for operations in Latin America and the Caribbean.

Several times I had further business with Jim Angleton. At one meeting I said, "Have you forgotten that you were going to give me"— I unconsciously lowered my voice to a whisper—"The Briefing?" Angleton looked at his watch. "That's right. But can't do it now. The Briefing takes several hours."

While the hullabaloo and brouhaha continued, the critical responsibilities of CIA remained. There was work to be done abroad. At the moment, my particular division did not enjoy the priorities of other areas, but this did not lessen the requirement to recruit agents, especially where there was a Soviet, Cuban, or Bloc presence, to acquire the intelligence demanded by policy makers, to conduct liaison with Latin American security services, and to mount a very few covert action operations.

At one of our stations, CIA was called upon to "intercept" a meeting between a Soviet KGB officer from the local embassy and an indigenous KGB agent. That is, knowing of the planned encounter, a CIA officer was to pose as a Soviet, in order to learn more about the relationship between the Soviet embassy and the local agent and his political party. Our man, exploiting his ability to speak Russian, met the agent on the pretext that the regular KGB case officer was ill, and that he was taking his place on an emergency basis. To add authenticity to the scenario, another CIA officer, also a Russian speaker, sat behind the wheel of a black automobile of the type used by the Soviets—the ubiquitous Russian chauffeur. There was an exchange of money, and then a forty-five-minute conversation. When the meeting ended, the Latin American agent said to the CIA officer, "You know, I've been working for the KGB for six years—and you are the most professional KGB officer I've ever met!"

256

Two weeks later in another country it was necessary for a four-person team to conduct a surreptitious entry—an illegal break-in—in an effort to obtain vital high priority intelligence data from the offices of a hostile power. I say four-person, since one of the CIA officers involved was a female. The team used the cover of electricians making repairs. As there are no female electricians in Latin America, our woman was disguised as a male, complete with phony mustache.

An international meeting was to convene in February 1974. The positions to be taken by countries not completely friendly to the United States was an intelligence requirement with obvious benefits for American negotiators at the conference. In one Latin American country, the CIA station obtained a photostatic copy of that country's position, but it was a lengthy document and there was no time to translate and cable it to the site of the meeting, thousands of miles away. The Station Chief summoned his most junior officer and instructed him to board the next international flight to hand-carry the vital piece of intelligence. The young man went to the airport and encountered the marvelous circumstance which every CIA man dreams of—there were no seats available in the tourist section and he had to travel first-class. Only under such emergency conditions can Foreign Service officers below ambassadorial rank enjoy such luxury. On the plane the young officer kept touching the breast pocket of his coat, where he carried the purloined document. He had reason to be nervous. Directly across the aisle, close enough so that the CIA officer could have leaned across and touched him, was the foreign minister of the country in which he was stationed, also flying to the conference. The foreign minister spent the flight thumbing through *his* copy of the position paper!

One reason CIA is necessary in third world countries is to counter terrorism. Unless one has lived overseas in a country where violence is endemic, it is difficult to appreciate the pressure under which foreigners, especially diplomats and businessmen, live when terrorism is rampant. In Guatemala in 1968 an American ambassador, John Gordon Mein, and two United States Army officers were murdered, as was my friend Karl von Spretti, the German Ambassador in 1970. Captain Charles Chandler was killed in Brazil in 1968, and Dan Mitrione was executed by Tupamaros in Uruguay in 1970.*

Kidnappings of American and other foreign officers have been frequent: Colonel James Chenault in Caracas, Ambassador Burke Elbrick in Brazil, Lieutenant Colonel Donald Crowley in the Dominican Republic, Ambassador Knox in Haiti, and my friend and former colleague in Mexico, Terrence Leonhardy, all were victims. British, German, and

---

* Though the film *State of Siege* suggested otherwise, Mitrione was not a CIA agent.

Swiss ambassadors have been abducted in Uruguay and Brazil. American and foreign businessmen are not immune to terrorist brutality. In Argentina alone there have been dozens of such kidnappings, among them a Ford executive who was assassinated, two Coca-Cola executives kidnapped, one of them *twice*. To the assassinations, kidnappings, and murders, add explosive bombs, fire bombs, assaults on offices and private homes, and threats to wives and children.

In Argentina a USIS official in Córdoba in 1974 was kidnapped and wounded by terrorists who believed him to be CIA (he was not). In 1975 the honorary American Consul in Córdoba, John Egan, was abducted and murdered. The small action cells of extremists, seldom members of the traditional Communist parties which are closely monitored by CIA and local services, have learned over the years how careful they must be of penetrations of their groups. When a terrorist action squad plans to kidnap a foreign diplomat they take extreme precautions. Thus a CIA penetration agent might actually participate in such an attempt and have no way to warn his CIA case officer. A theoretical but valid situation: the agent is summoned by a very few conspirators involved and told that he is about to assist in kidnapping an American official. He is also told: "Don't go to the john, don't phone your wife, don't leave our eyesight." Thus, should a kidnapping occur, the CIA agent who might actually be guarding the American will have had no opportunity to communicate in advance his vital information.

Difficult as the countering of terrorism is, CIA has developed techniques and capabilities which are quite useful. On a 1974 inspection trip of stations in Latin America I was summoned by the President of a country I shall call Plaza Brava. This chief executive had worked with CIA in the past, in the sense of gratefully accepting training and technical assistance to prevent (successfully) an attempt by a hostile foreign power to aid extremists trying to overthrow his government. The President of Plaza Brava had a new problem. He had heard, he told me, fragmentary but disturbing reports that the first attempt at violence by Arab terrorists in Latin America was planned for his country, and this during a time associated with an international conference to be held in the capital city of Plaza Brava. The President said he would appreciate any assistance CIA could provide in thwarting any such action, pointing out that coverage of Arabs who might enter Plaza Brava from abroad was far beyond the capabilities of his own service. This seemed unlikely, as there had never been Arab terrorist activity in the Latin American area. But I promised that we would monitor the radar screen of international terrorism.

Returning to Langley I thought about the request of the President of Plaza Brava. One day a routine cable report from a Latin American country near Plaza Brava noted an Arab was visiting from the Middle East, and the station asked headquarters for information on the traveler. The next day, on my outgoing cable board the response: an Arab known to have terrorist connections sometimes used an alias similar to the name reported. I instructed my Chief of Operations to alert all stations. Soon a station in another country reported the suspect Arab had arrived there and was meeting with local Arabs known to be violence prone. From still another country in Latin America a cable advised that a woman of Arab extraction departed for the capital city where the others were meeting. The cable also went to a Middle East station that might be interested and evoked an immediate response from there: the woman was known to be a courier for one of the most active international terrorist groups. Finally came a report that the entire group had departed for Plaza Brava. Grandmother was on the roof.

Then an unexpected development. From surveilling the group's movements, we found that their intention was to travel to a nearby area where a major energy installation, we assumed, might be their target. CIA, through liaison, warned the authorities of that country and appropriate defense measures were taken. I instructed the CIA station in Plaza Brava to advise the President that the terrorists were using his country as a staging area and to let him know where they could be found. They were arrested, jailed, and then expelled from Plaza Brava, there being no evidence against them which could be used in court. We hadn't directly helped the President, but at least we had frustrated the first Arab terrorist action planned for Latin America.

Some weeks later a report came in from a station halfway around the world. The terrorists, on their return to the Middle East from Plaza Brava, indiscreetly discussed their foray, and the gist of the conversation reached the local CIA station. Indeed they had used Plaza Brava as a staging ground, but the terrorists had abandoned the original plan, formulating a new one for terrorist action in Plaza Brava, an act which suggested itself when they read of the important international meeting— the same meeting the President of Plaza Brava had mentioned to me in expressing his concern some weeks previously. His arrest of the terrorists based on CIA information had not after all thwarted the third country action, but the last-minute substitution of terrorism within Plaza Brava.

At about the same time another terrorist incident in Latin America demanded that CIA respond to three basic overseas responsibilities of an American intelligence service—acquisition of intelligence, liaison with a foreign government, and the use of covert action. In order to protect sources and methods I will fictionalize the following account, which is an accurate reflection of what occurred.

Newspaper accounts from Nuevo Gerona described the kidnapping of a senior United States official in the capital of Valencia. Linda Marsh was the first female American diplomat abducted by terrorists anywhere in the world. She was spirited to a farm where she and several other hostages were held by local Marxists. The terrorists demanded one million dollars and the release of twenty political prisoners. Otherwise, they threatened, Linda would be executed.

Local military and police officers planned their strategy, early in the game leaning toward a solution by force; that is, storming the farmhouse. This type of reaction usually solves the problem, but seldom guarantees the safety of hostages.

Working closely with the American ambassador, the CIA station in Valencia proceeded with the first order of business—the acquisition of intelligence. Authorities sent into the farmhouse a Pepsi-Cola case with the soft drink bottles filled with water. A CIA technician bugged the case: an audio device was embedded in it, rather like that apocryphal olive which is supposed to transmit from a martini. But we soon lost the audio device because Linda Marsh protested vehemently to the leader of the terrorists that her captors were behaving inhumanely since they were drinking most of the meager water supply while she and her fellow hostages were allowed little. The terrorist leader agreed with Linda and set things straight by putting her in charge of the water supply. Linda promptly hid the Pepsi-Cola case in a remote closet, covering it with blankets. We could no longer hear. Another of the hostages suffered from a stomach disorder and asked for warm tea. We bugged the Thermos in which it was sent. In short order we acquired two vital pieces of intelligence concerning intentions and capabilities: that the kidnappers were frightened and confused and did not wish to harm the hostages unless forced to do so, and that they had enough explosives in the farmhouse to blow it sky-high if it came to that.

Next CIA conducted liaison. Our information was passed to the appropriate local authorities, who then abandoned plans for attacking the farmhouse and adopted a new strategy of negotiation and wait-and-see. Linda's future became brighter.

CIA learned from the bug which radio station the terrorists, anxious to know what was being said about their caper, were listening to. Covert action came into play. Our officers in Valencia and abroad monitored comments in Marxist newspapers and magazines about the kidnapping. Some of these comments were critical of the Nuevo Geronan terrorists. CIA arranged that they were repeated on the local station which we knew the extremists were tuned to night and day. One scathing denunciation of their action focused on the lack of machismo in a situation where Latin males were threatening a female. Over a period of days the terrorists heard only negative comments on their operation, deprecation from their ideological allies. They heard nothing from those who supported them. Regular reports on the atmosphere within the farmhouse redoubt reached the President of Nuevo Gerona.

Several days later the President made an announcement—we heard the terrorists hearing it—that he had decided not to pay the million-dollar ransom and not to release the political prisoners. He would, however, allow the terrorists safe-conduct from the country if the hostages were released unharmed. That's what happened. When the terrorists arrived in Panama, en route to Cuba, a group of newsmen were at the airport. The Panamanian government did not allow the reporters to interview the terrorists, but their leader managed to pass a written message to a journalist before he was led away. The note read: "Our operation failed because fellow revolutionaries would not support us."

Linda Marsh, plucky, fine Foreign Service officer that she is, stayed on in Valencia to finish the job she had been sent there to do.

In October 1974, Philip Agee gave a press conference in London, a few weeks after his fifth trip to Cuba. It was attended by a number of British and Latin American journalists as well as radio and television reporters. Agee, apparently too anxious to get about his anti-CIA business to wait for the publication of his book, read a list of thirty-seven people he claimed worked in CIA's Mexico City station. He said the list had been compiled "by a small group of Mexican comrades whom I trained to follow the comings and goings of CIA people before I left Mexico City." The Fleet Street cynics listened to Agee, but decided they didn't like what he was saying or doing, and there was no publicity in Britain except in leftist publications after the conference. But the Latin American correspondents wired the story home and it was headlined throughout South and Central America. Four Mexico City newspapers printed the list, to which Agee had conveniently added home addresses and telephone numbers of the people he named in Mexico. The newspapers repeated Agee's exhortation to the Mexican people to "neutralize" the CIA personnel, and "to drive them out of the country."

Agee's list was substantially accurate, but not completely. A black State Department officer Agee named, for instance, will now undoubtedly find it difficult to become an ambassador in many places after being tainted with the false allegation that he is CIA. In an interview with Agee in *People* magazine, the reporter asked Agee if he were not concerned that some physical harm might befall his ex-associates in Mexico because of the exposure. "That is beside the point," Agee is quoted as replying. "These are grown men I'm talking about. They can take care of themselves." In fact twelve of the persons named by Agee were women, the majority very young secretaries on their first overseas tour.

They were understandably nervous, as terrorism had escalated in Mexico City. Only a few weeks before Marxists had kidnapped the father-in-law of the President of Mexico. The wives and teenaged children of CIA officers were upset too. Agee later boasted in print on several occasions that as the result of his exposé the CIA Station Chief and his deputy had departed Mexico City abruptly. This was not true: none of the CIA staff moved as a result of his revelation, they simply went about their business under new and more difficult circumstances.

Agee's book went to press in London. We learned that he intended to identify persons as CIA officers, agents, or "collaborators." In describing the "collaborators" he did a great disservice to a number of patriotic Latin American officials who dealt with CIA in very valid and mutually beneficial liaison arrangements over the years, mixing them indiscriminately with agents who did work for the CIA. My name—why I cannot explain—was not on the list.

I became increasingly frustrated over Agee's revelations. Agee was exposing my people to physical danger, especially in countries such as Argentina where terrorism directed against Americans was a real concern; and he was besmirching the reputations of many fine Latin Americans, among them three presidents. From intelligence available to CIA it was obvious to me that Agee was in contact with the Cuban intelligence service and, by implication at least, indirectly with the KGB. I wanted to do something to publicize this connection. Senior officers and Agency lawyers told me that as Agee was an American, CIA had best not do anything which could be construed as interfering with his civil rights, which were being stoutly defended by an official of the American Civil Liberties Union. So Agee continued his crusade of revealing identities of my officers and placing CIA people and their families in jeopardy. And, I was intrigued to note, he was being joined in the campaign by some of the other vocal critics of the CIA, principal among them Victor Marchetti and John Marks, co-authors of *The CIA and the Cult of Intelligence*.

As 1974 drew to an end, the second of the series of newspaper revelations which led to the presidential and congressional investigations of CIA was published. On December 22 Seymour Hersh wrote in the *New York Times* of CIA "massive illegal domestic" operations.

That did it. Overnight CIA became a sinister shadow organization in the minds of the American people. Visions of a CIA payroll swollen with zealous and ubiquitous cloak-and-dagger villains impervious to good judgment and outside control arose throughout the country. CIA was seen as what the detractors had been so long claiming: unprincipled spooks threatening American society. That was not the CIA I knew, but

I realized that any image less sinister would never really be believed by Americans still stunned by Watergate.

Gina was dismayed. She asked, what is this all about? I told her that I could not say for sure, as domestic operations had never been in my purview, and had to admit that I knew of some past activities that fit the pattern of the charges. We would have to wait and see. Younger officers in the Division came to me the next and following day, Christmas Eve, their eyes troubled, asking if the story were true. They were disturbed and dismayed. So was I.

Stories in the press and whispers in the halls that CIA had been involved in assassinations proliferated. I was shocked; I couldn't and didn't want to believe them. Gina reminded me that I promised long ago that I would resign if ever convinced that assassination was a CIA practice.

In the air force during World War II there was an expression denoting a sad state of affairs: "My mother told me there would be days like this, but she never told me there would be so many in a row."

When I left the building on Christmas Eve it was dull and ugly outside; obviously there would not be a white Christmas. I paused briefly near the statue of Nathan Hale. I squinted at the bronze patriot, the spy who had not been a very good one.

"Merry Christmas, Nate." I spoke loudly enough that a passing guard glanced at me, with a smile, as if forgiving me for too many drinks at an office Christmas party. I wished him a Merry Christmas too and went home to help Gina wrap presents.

10

WASHINGTON 1975

I missed Abe. With almost thirty years of government service behind him, the CIA veteran retired in the summer of 1974. On the standard form which every CIA officer fills out each year with his or her preference for future assignments Abe had written: "This time next year I expect to be on the Outer Banks at Hatteras where, if you are not careful, a bluefish will jump into your pocket." The more compelling reason for his retirement before the mandatory age of sixty, Abe confided, was that he had decided that he owed his wife—the young girl he had met in Czechoslovakia and disguised as a soldier to bring over the border—some time and attention after the years of long hours on the job and neglect of home life. It is not an uncommon reason for many CIA officers retiring early.

The accuracy of Seymour Hersh's characterization of CIA involvement in domestic operations as "massive" in the December 1974 *New York Times* story was the subject of considerable, and sometimes acrimonious, debate. One thing was certain: the Hersh story, I found on returning to Langley after the Christmas holidays, had produced massive cracks in what had been up to that time a fairly monolithic intelligence establishment.

One of Hersh's allegations was that Jim Angleton was in charge of the CIA effort to gather information on American dissidents.

At the first DDO staff meeting in 1975 Jim Angleton sat in his customary seat to the right of Bill Nelson. There were a few routine announcements; then Nelson told us without any preamble that Angleton had submitted his retirement papers. There was a shocked silence. Angleton impassively lighted another of his filter tip cigarettes. Nelson went on to explain Jim's departure had no connection with the Hersh charge in the *New York Times*—it was coincidental. The senior CIA officers around the conference table were instinctively skeptical; the intelligence profession does not exactly condition one to accept coincidence as an explanation for a sequence of events.

But, as it turned out, Nelson had once more aired a delicate internal matter in his characteristic fashion: truthfully and without embellishment. The inevitable conflict between Angleton's Cold Warrior attitude and William Colby's intention to create a new American service had come to a head in late 1974. Colby told the counter-intelligence chief that he was to be assigned to other tasks, with another officer taking over the Agency's counter-intelligence functions and liaison with the Israeli service. Angleton chose to retire. The move was delayed until the last day of the year so that he would receive the benefit of a cost-of-living adjustment in his annuity. The Hersh revelations on domestic operations did come, coincidentally, in the interim. Angleton, we learned also, had not been in charge of the controversial program of investigating American citizens. The line of command had opted to bypass him in favor of another counter-intelligence officer.

Angleton addressed the meeting. It was what some in CIA called his "Nature of the Threat" speech—dire predictions, grim warnings, and suspicion of détente. It was a gloomy forecast. We were uncomfortable; while most of us felt the counter-espionage expert to be inordinately inflexible, we also knew that he possessed an incubus of deep secrets and a better understanding of the Soviet Union's intelligence operations than any man in the West. When the meeting was over we all left hurriedly, almost as if escaping.

My parking space in front of the main entrance of CIA headquarters was one removed from Jim Angleton's. Leaving the building that night I caught up with Angleton, who was walking very slowly through the darkness to his black Mercedes. We talked for a few minutes, standing in the diffused glow of a distant light. Angleton's head was lowered, but occasionally he glanced up from under the brim of his black homburg at the looming CIA building. Although he would stay on for a while until his successor returned from overseas, Jim Angleton had officially separated from his beloved intelligence service when he had walked out of the door a few minutes earlier.

"You know, Jim," I said, "you never did give me The Briefing."

"I didn't?" Angleton smiled wanly. "That's right."

We then rambled on about nothing in particular. I thought to myself that I had never seen a man who looked so infinitely tired and sad. We shook hands. And, I got into my car, backed out of the parking space, and drove toward the exit. In the rear-view mirror I could see Angleton's tall, gaunt figure growing smaller and smaller. He was still standing beside his car looking up at the building when I turned a corner.

Early in 1975 I traveled south to visit the CIA stations in Latin America. Everyone seemed busy enough, but morale was low. "All we see in the local papers," one CIA chief told me, "is what Agee and Marks and Marchetti are saying about the Agency. Why isn't someone speaking out to put the record straight?"

I boarded a plane for a flight between capitals. An old friend and retired colleague sat next to me; it was a pleasant surprise. I had worked with him a number of times while he was CIA Station Chief in half a dozen countries. When he had retired, he had stayed on in Latin America and gone into business. It was obvious that he was doing well: he was wearing a cashmere suit.

"What the hell is going on in Washington?" he asked. "All I hear is horror stories."

I admitted that things weren't going well.

"The spy business used to be the most satisfaction and, at the same time, fun a man could have," he said. "Remember?"

I said I did.

"Why, I remember when I was COS in"—he named a small Andean country—"back in the late forties. The naval attaché flew in from Panama with a flock of turkeys for Thanksgiving. Not those frozen Butterball birds you guys can get now in an embassy commissary, but real live cackling turkeys. Each family in the embassy was to get one. But one night my people and I—there were three of us in the station—got drunk and decided to have some fun. We stole the naval attaché's turkeys, the whole bunch. A turkeynapping. The naval attaché had to go tell the Ambassador the turkeys were missing."

"The Ambassador was really upset," my friend continued, warming up to his story with a martini. "Not about the turkeys so much, but he was worried about the attaché's security practices. 'If you can't watch out for a bunch of turkeys,' he asked the attaché, 'how can you take care of your classified files?' So the Ambassador sent a bomb of a cable to Washington, asking for some guards to help watch the embassy.

"Then the Ambassador called me into his office. I had a monumental hangover. 'Hate to do this,' the Ambassador said, 'but I want you to put your best agents on the trail of the missing turkeys. I want them back by Thanksgiving.'

"Fortunately, we hadn't eaten the turkeys. They were stashed away in the back yard of a safe house. So I got 'em back. The naval attaché was relieved, and the Ambassador was satisfied. But it was too late: because of the Ambassador's cable, two Marines were already on a plane, assigned to our embassy as security guards.

"And that's why," my friend concluded, "American embassies in Latin America today are taken care of by Marine guards."

"You're a liar," I said.

He held up his palm, as if to fend off my accusation. "It's the God's honest truth," he averred.*

In Lima, Peru, Dick Welch met me at the airport. He turned off the main road and we drove for half an hour through the shanty-slums of Lima, then into the area where the rich Peruvians lived. It was Dick's custom to give senior visitors this tour. After having the newcomer absorb the squalor of the slums he would let him marvel at the luxury of the oligarchs' homes.

"The important thing," Dick would then say, "is to remember that the answer to this country's future lies somewhere between the two extremes."

Dick confided to me that there was one assignment he coveted more than any other: he wanted to return to Athens as Chief of Station. I promised to do what I could. When I returned to Langley I wrote his fitness report. Knowing Bill Nelson and Bill Colby would see it, I noted in the final paragraph Dick's desire to serve again in Athens.

During my trip to Latin America I had seen how frequently the organization known as the Fifth Estate and its publication, *CounterSpy*, were quoted in Spanish newspapers. One *CounterSpy* issue printed the names of more than one hundred CIA chiefs around the world. Its listing was largely accurate—Dick Welch's name was included—but there were mistakes. A Department of State officer, for instance, was labeled CIA Chief of Station in Moscow. He would have a hard time doing even the most routine task now.

The disclosures and investigations proliferated. President Ford established the Rockefeller Commission to check out the Hersh story. Congressional committees began planning investigations.

In February of 1975 morale at CIA plummeted to a new low.

An unclassified notice was circulated by the Agency's legal counsel to all CIA employees, at home and abroad. The first paragraph described the probable scope of the investigations and noted that each employee must be reminded of his rights under the Miranda decision. The Miranda decision? That was for *criminals!*

---

* In 1975 I contacted the Historical Office of the United States Marine Corps in Washington. The historian confirmed that the first permanent Marine guard service to U.S. embassies began in the year my friend was in the country concerned. He could not find a record indicating which country was first and knew nothing about turkeys.

"Technically," the memorandum read, "the so-called Miranda Warning is not required unless the person being questioned is in custody. This being so, employees who are questioned or volunteer information in the course of our own investigation, if not warned, might incriminate themselves and find the information they have provided admissible as evidence in a subsequent criminal proceeding."

A précis of the notice was attached:

> The purpose of this investigation by the Agency is to collect facts as required for submission to the President's Commission, various congressional committees, and the Department of Justice. The Department of Justice is reviewing certain past Agency activities for possible conflict with the criminal code. Before you answer any questions, we would like to be sure you know you have the constitutional right to remain silent and that anything you say and any statement you make may be used as evidence against you. Of course you have the right and privilege to confer with private counsel prior to answering any questions. Do you understand and do you have any questions?

There certainly were some questions. Many of them were put to me by young officers, distraught and incredulous, seeking an explanation of what was happening. Senior officers were equally disturbed. One of the weekly DDO meetings became a shouting match, as veteran managers gave vent to their frustration—one of them saying, desperately, "Why can't we *do* something?" The session closed on a note of gloom.

Leaks sprang everywhere. I accompanied Bill Colby to the Department of State, where he gave a classified briefing to a conference of American ambassadors assigned to Latin America. An extremely accurate summary of what Colby said appeared two days afterward in the Washington *Star*.

Two weeks later I attended another meeting at the Department—a routine, weekly session in which we discussed problems of mutual concern and especially any CIA plans for covert action in Latin America. I described an uncontroversial proposal—covert action with a small c, small a—which was being prepared at Langley. It involved the use of an agent of influence in an operation which might have saved American taxpayers some money.

A Deputy Assistant Secretary, an old friend, said that the Department of State preferred that the project not be undertaken because of the high risk factor involved.

"High risk?" I was surprised. "But there's practically no flap potential. The agent is reliable; he has worked for us for years. I see little chance the operation will become known or backfire."

"I agree," my friend from the Department said. "There's little chance of the operation being compromised abroad. I'm talking about the probability it will leak here in Washington."

I had no rejoinder. The proposal was shelved.

A foreign intelligence officer stationed in Washington invited me to lunch. He represented one of the world's major intelligence services, and liaison lunches between us were routine. "I really hate to bring this up," he said while we had our coffee. "But I must ask you to do me a favor. Would you return to me the documents I've passed CIA during the past couple of years?"

Reports from the field indicated that CIA agents were nervous. Some resigned from the spy business.

I went to see Bill Colby. I submitted for his consideration the thought that any organization with a public-relations problem of the magnitude of the one tarnishing CIA's image needed some kind of public-relations effort to keep matters in perspective.

"You're right," Colby replied. "But we can't do it. Remember *The Selling of the Pentagon?* The furor which arose when it was revealed that the Defense Department had such a massive PR effort? We're just going to have to take the heat. Institutionally, we aren't geared to that type of undertaking in any event."

At home Gina and I prepared for a family conference. Debbie was fifteen. It was time to talk to her.

It is a myth that the wives and families of intelligence officers are ignorant of their profession. A spouse plays such a vital role that she or he must know. Children, when they reach a certain age, must be told. There is a practical aspect to this: a teenager left in ignorance might say something in the presence of a foreign visitor which could cause professional damage, such as, "Dad, who was that Mr. Gonzalez who telephoned last night?" Depending on circumstances, location, and the maturity of the child, teenagers should be informed if at all practicable that their father or mother is an intelligence officer.

Often the divulgence is a relief for the children. For the first time they are disabused of the notion that their father is an unsuccessful business nomad who can't seem to hold a job or settle into a career. Or, they will understand why he has not become deputy chief of mission or an ambassador, enjoying a long black car with flags flying from the fenders. My first four interviews had a tremendous positive impact. With Maria, David, Jr., Atlee, and Christopher the reaction, tinged with admiration, had been, "Gee, my old man in the same league with James Bond and *Mission Impossible!*"

Debbie sat on the floor in the living room while I explained to her that I was not really an officer of the Department of State, but an intelligence officer. That I worked for CIA.

Debbie's reaction was quick: "But that's dirty."

Gina blanched and reached out to touch my hand. She knew how deeply the unexpected response would affect me. Of course, to me, Debbie's reaction represented the current perception of anyone in CIA being an uncontrolled zealot, impervious to good judgment and engaged in every kind of immoral and unscrupulous trickery. At best, I felt it was a pretty meager reward for twenty-five of the best years I could muster working for my country.

For the next three weeks I was dejected. I watched the television talk shows as Marks and Marchetti, and Seymour Hersh and Daniel Schorr excoriated the CIA. Only two former intelligence officers debated the issues with them to set the public record straight: Ray Cline and Harry Rositzke, a retired operations officer. Both had been out of CIA service for several years. It occurred to me that it would be useful if another senior officer, with more recent field experience, would join them in the arena.

Philip Agee was featured on Tom Snyder's NBC "Tomorrow" show, which I knew was popular with college students. The interview had been taped previously in Canada because Agee had been advised by his lawyer not to return to the United States. Agee gave his usual spiel, stressing the canard that CIA encouraged torture in Latin America. At one point Agee mentioned—for the first time in public, I believe—that he had visited Cuba while writing the book in which he exposed the identities of more than two hundred American and foreign agents. I sat on the edge of my chair; I knew that Agee had been in Havana five times, not once.

When Agee said he had been in Cuba I waited for Snyder's next question. Certainly the experienced TV journalist would ask, "Why?"

Instead, Snyder's reaction was a chuckle and, "Oh? How was Fidel?"

There was another family conference—this time just with Gina. I described my frustrations. I told her I wanted to leave CIA in order to participate, somehow, in the public controversy about intelligence.

Gina nodded understandingly and waited. I explained that my $36,000 salary—I had recently been promoted to GS-18—would be cut in half upon retirement. The drop in income would be only a part of the reduction; retiring eight years early would mean that my pension would be much smaller than it would have been otherwise with additional years of contribution to the retirement fund. The best chance of new income would be from lecturing; I could contact the lecture agent in New York who had represented me more than two decades before. Things might be rough. There were five more college careers to finance.

Todd, born in Brazil, would be graduating from high school when I was about sixty-five. Even if I could obtain lecture dates, they would not begin until the following fall. The first summer, I told Gina, might be very thin financially.

Gina got up and went into the kitchen to pour herself a drink. I presume it was a stiff one. Then she came back and said, "I know where I can get a summer job."

Then she added, "Go!"

I went, first, to Bill Nelson to advise him of my plans. Later I intended to tell Bill Colby, but that visit became unnecessary when the DCI walked into Nelson's office near the end of our session. Nelson recounted for Colby my intention to resign, and what I planned to do: lecture, write some, and form an organization of retired intelligence officers from all U.S. services. There was some discussion about whether, instead, it might not be better for me to remain in CIA. I said that I had already made the decision. "In that case," Colby said, "I wish you well." I had the feeling the soldier-priest was not completely unhappy.

I flew to New York to talk with the lecture agent. It had been more than twenty years since our last meeting. I asked him how much revenue I could expect from a year of lecturing about intelligence, attempting to set as much of the record straight on CIA as I legitimately and honestly could.

"I expect you can make between five and ten thousand dollars," the agent said. "But what about speaking *against* the CIA? That way I can promise you between fifty and a hundred thousand dollars the first year."

I knew then I had made the right decision.

After disclosing my intention to retire, I selected early May as my departure date so that the Agency would have sufficient time to select and have in place a new Chief of Latin American and Caribbean Operations.

During April I worked evenings and weekends on plans for my post-retirement future. Using our Christmas card list as a start, I began to send announcements to retired CIA friends, asking them to join me in forming an organization of ex-intelligence people from all U.S. services. My letter read, in part:

… Under the circumstances, there is little doubt that a thorough Congressional review is the best, if not the only solution even though some leakage of sensitive details on foreign operations seems almost inevitable. A few of our documents from the Cold War period will make for pretty heady reading today. As for our present activities, I am convinced we have no problem. In the meantime our capabilities

271

abroad are being damaged. More and more of our agents and friends
—many of them fine people who cooperate on the basis of ideology
—are saying thanks but no thanks. Friendly liaison services are
beginning to back away from us. The Marchettis and the Agees have
the stage and only a few challenge them. . . .

The press soon had the story. Shortly thereafter I received a telephone call at my home. A woman introduced herself as an editor on the
program staff of one of the major TV and radio networks. She asked,
"Are you the man who is going to deny everything about the CIA?" I
had no intention of denying accurate versions of CIA history, no matter
how disturbing, nor to attempt to defend the indefensible—and said so.
But after our telephone conversation I began to catalogue CIA mistakes,
and to prepare for what I suspected would be a barrage of questions about
them once I entered the public debate about CIA. As an intelligence
officer I had learned long ago that where there is smoke there is usually
fire—but also that sometimes there is a smoke-making machine responsible for the haze. I began to sort out fires from smoke-making machines.

Certainly the first issue that had to be met head on was assassination.

In early 1975 I did not know the details of the two abortive assassination schemes CIA concocted against Fidel Castro in Cuba and Patrice
Lumumba in Africa. But I had picked up enough circumstantial evidence
from conversations with other officers and from reading a portion of the
Skeletons list to feel the charges were probably true.

CIA "involvement" in attempts against foreign leaders had already
been discussed extensively in the press. That subject I felt prepared to
handle. When I triggered a toggle switch of a B-24 bomber during World
War II I was "involved" in the death of I don't know how many persons,
but I emerged from the war with my personal code of ethics intact. I
knew that when CIA backed a foreign group plotting against an incumbent regime, as in the case of the Dominican Republic when Trujillo was
killed, or in Chile when General Schneider died, it was not always possible to put limits or ON and OFF buttons on the cabal being dealt with. I
knew a CIA Station Chief abroad was derelict if not in contact with—
in the sense of having an agent reporting what was happening—any
movement that manifested the ability and intention of overthrowing a
government.

Rationalization or justification in other respects was something else.
For example, I could understand in the case of Castro why a very few
men might weigh the merits of disposing of one man at the same time
two American Presidents had approved the Bay of Pigs—where many
died and which could have resulted, in the event of civil war, in the
death of thousands. But how those few men in CIA could have been so

stupid as to make a connection with the Mafia for that purpose I cannot explain. A tenet of intelligence tradecraft is to avoid association with those who might later resort to blackmail. As I understand it, it was CIA's Office of Security which established the connection between the Agency and the underworld. Perhaps officers from the Clandestine Service might have squashed the proposal. But a few of the DDO people did take over this program during the period when Bobby Kennedy was telling the CIA "to get off its ass" and do something about Castro. I do not know if President Kennedy and his brother knew Castro's assassination was contemplated.

I decided to come right out and say that assassination is unacceptable either as a practice or concept in our society. It could not even be justified under the "such other functions and duties" clause in the Agency's charter that had been used—legitimately in my opinion—to sanction many activities not spelled out in the law.

There was another indefensible area: CIA operations in the United States which were unconstitutional and violated the rights of Americans. We now know that these violations were not "massive"; the undisputed findings of the Rockefeller Commission established less than a dozen cases which could be described as clearly illegal. But there were a number of questionable areas, such as the practice of infiltrating CIA agents into domestic dissident groups so they could obtain radical credentials and cover for use overseas and try to find out, for Presidents Johnson and Nixon, whether there was a foreign connection with the unrest in American cities and on American college campuses. In short, I decided that any violation of the Constitution, including opening mail to and from Communist countries, should not be tolerated in our country. There is no reason an intelligence officer should not go to prison if he violates the laws of the United States. However, the gray areas which inevitably evolve in pursuing a mission that is illegal abroad from a home base in the United States must be dealt with *a priori*. Just take the routine matter of a deep-cover agent applying for a U.S. passport as an American businessman. Technically, he is in violation of U.S. law when he lists his occupation as "businessman" instead of "CIA deep-cover agent" in his passport application. Or, what is this same individual going to do when he is caught up in a U.S. census survey requiring subterfuge on his part? Many situations that are more complex and tricky—and consequently grayer—arise frequently. Yet there is absolutely no intent to violate U.S. law, but to pursue U.S. interests overseas through clandestine operations that, unfortunately, require cover to be developed on home soil. If there are any legal questions on the functions CIA performs and how it goes about them, then ground rules should be established by some authority outside the Agency. This is especially important

273

with respect to the controversial "such other functions and duties" dangling as an authorization for almost anything.

Drug-testing? This I could rationalize, knowing that LSD was invented and marketed in the early 1950's by a single scientist and a single laboratory in Switzerland. The United States found that most of the production of the new drug was being shipped to Moscow. There were many questions to be answered, especially after brainwashing emerged from the Korean War. Without question, conducting the drug research on unwitting persons or in a manner that could lead to suicide, as in the instance of one man, was unjustifiable.

Dart guns and shellfish toxins? In early 1975 I had never heard of either.

Chile. That, I knew, would be the subject of much concern, because the United States' covert action program—Capital C, Capital A—had built into it the full range of covert techniques. I decided that the CIA program in Chile could reasonably be divided into three phases. The first I call the debatable period: the decade-long financial support by the CIA to the Christian Democratic Party. I feel sure that President Kennedy and his advisers saw the creation of a healthy Christian Democratic system in Latin America as a possible answer to the perennial problem of military coups, and as a political philosophy and movement dedicated to democracy and social justice, not dependent on caudillos, and with deep roots in the masses. Perhaps Kennedy recalled the successful CIA backing of Christian and Social Democratic groups in Europe after World War II. In any event the program, which continued under Presidents Johnson and Nixon, is one which is a valid subject for debate; I suspect the conclusion most interested Americans settle upon will depend ultimately on whether one endorses or condemns covert action as a principle.

The next period in CIA's Chile program I label as the inexcusable. Track II in 1970, and the first time in my experience when a U.S. President used his intelligence arm to conduct foreign policy without advising his Secretary of State. I was emotional about that period and my role in it. Three of my children had been born in Chile, and I admired Chileans and their unswerving devotion to the democratic process—so unusual in Latin America. Track II was the only episode in my CIA career which disturbed me to the point that I even considered resigning in protest.

Finally the third period, which I like to think of as the correct. Thanks to Abe's cables of May 1973, and perhaps to the fact that Richard Nixon was preoccupied with Watergate, CIA distanced itself from those who eventually toppled Salvador Allende. Despite Congressman Harrington's characterization of the CIA program as "destabilization," the intent

274

in 1973 was just the opposite—to stabilize by keeping alive democratic institutions until the elections then scheduled for 1976.

A discussion of whether the CIA should or should not have been involved in Chile usually leads in the end to consideration of whether the United States should maintain clandestine operations at all or at least without change. But, despite the avalanche of words published and broadcast on the subject, few outside the Clandestine Service, including many in the other services of CIA, really understand what they might be abolishing or letting stand—in short, what clandestine operations are, and (equally important) what they are not, their limitations, and why they exist.

And that's understandable. The debate over this country's clandestine operations reached its climax in 1975 in a high tide of confusion—with the wreckage of those activities strewn over the Washington landscape and on many foreign shores as well. Some criticisms of the seamy side of our intelligence agency's behavior had been deserved. Others were ill-founded but sincere. A small minority seemed to be the product of deliberate obfuscation.

While Congress pondered a resolution of the dilemma secret foreign operations pose for a democracy, subject matter and issues were being obscured—if not lost—in an esoteric jargon borrowed by Congress and the media from the intelligence subculture. As with most trade talk, intelligence terminology such as *clandestine operations, covert action,* and *black box* is highly technical and has developed nuances not easily inferred from the words themselves.

If such terms were confusing even within the intelligence community I would have to presuppose even greater consternation in the public mind. Confusion usually begins with what the Clandestine Service does. It basically does two things: (1) collects intelligence needed by policy makers to formulate policy; and (2) undertakes programs to assist policy makers in carrying out a policy.

The first is known as "espionage" and the second "covert action." Both involve the use of clandestine operations. Espionage seeks information important to the United States government which some foreign entity wishes to keep secret. Covert action endeavors to persuade a foreign entity to take action or to refrain from an action. Circumstances and the nature of the persuasion preclude the attribution of covert action to the United States government. Propaganda in its many shades of gray (that is, degrees of concealment of sponsorship) may accomplish a covert action objective. Secret agents dealing directly with individuals in a position of influence are more likely to do so.

275

Strictly speaking, paramilitary operations—such as supporting a secret army—should not be classified under covert action. They relate to covert action as war compares to diplomacy. Paramilitary endeavors belie sooner or later the one condition essential to covert action, secrecy, and flout the old maxim that one should not attempt to cover a hippopotamus with a handkerchief. Nor, as I had discovered during the Bay of Pigs, can a handkerchief cover a tank on a Caribbean beach. Unless the U.S. government was prepared to sponsor overt intervention in Cuba, the Bay of Pigs should have remained essentially a psychological warfare project rather than a military incursion.

The funding of foreign political parties, however, should be considered a covert action even though it is difficult to maintain secrecy in such a passionate milieu. Usually the passage of money is arranged through a "black bag" operation, i.e., a secret, under the table transaction.

Some critics have contended that the United States government should not be ashamed to support democratic forces overseas and, therefore, should fund deserving political parties openly, if at all.* Although refreshingly straightforward, this approach overlooks one reality. The beneficiaries of such aid would be the first to insist that it be given discreetly. It would be political suicide for them to accept foreign assistance, just as it would be for a party in this country to do so. (On the other hand, I found in serving in eight countries abroad that handsome subsidies given by the Soviets to Communist opposition parties surreptitiously are accepted as a fact of life by nearly everyone, including most governments and peoples of the countries concerned.)

Clandestine operations have been condemned as immoral in principle and illegal in practice. This attitude naïvely sidesteps the problems of existing and, indeed, surviving in a world whose history continues to be determined by nations promoting their own interests at the expense of others—the League of Nations, United Nations, and similar laudable endeavors notwithstanding. More to the point, it would have the United States, blindfolded and with one hand tied behind its back, compete in the international arena under rules of engagement which, at best, are minimal and flexible. This grim state of affairs is not likely to improve much in our time nor, for that matter, in our children's or grandchildren's. Until it does, the nations of the world will continue to insist on their sovereign right to defend and advance their interests through clandestine operations, restricting any question of immorality or illegality to cases uncovered within their own national boundaries.

Sincere critics, including several of my friends who work in CIA,

* A leading advocate of this course is Morton Halperin, a former aide to Henry Kissinger on the National Security Council. Halperin, a vocal critic of CIA, lives across the street from my home in Bethesda.

276

have tried to establish a legal distinction between covert action and intelligence collection. Under their criterion, covert action is objectionable because it involves "dirty tricks"; intelligence, on the other hand, *can be* collected "innocently" and "decently." Their argument usually rests on one of two premises, both of them false. The first views intelligence collection as a passive activity subjecting the United States to less involvement than covert action. The second claims that, since most intelligence comes from open publications, the residue from clandestine sources such as spies could be sacrificed without harm.

The notion that intelligence collection is inoffensive when it is passive assumes the use of "black boxes" (i.e., inanimate technical methods of spying) and precludes the employment of secret agents. Satellite snooping is the most striking and effective example of the black box approach. But satellite spying, however remote from the target, is basically no different from the means employed in Francis Gary Powers's ill-fated U-2 flight over the Soviet Union. The Soviets tolerate our satellite observation of their secret installations because, as with all the U-2 flights that preceded Powers's, they have no way of stopping it. They will not allow, for example, a U.S. reconnaissance aircraft to overfly their territory to perform precisely the same task as the orbiting satellite.

The contention that most intelligence is gleaned by diligent, skilled analysts from overt sources in the press and technical journals begs the question. The DDI people, intelligence analysts with whom I worked in CIA, of course must be quite familiar with what appears in the open literature in their field of competence. Their task is to begin from that point in order to distinguish what unknowns remain to be collected by clandestine means, that is, black boxes or agents. At this juncture, they frequently face the most vital and difficult aspect of intelligence: secret intentions and plans not readily deducible from the evidence at hand. Thus, intelligence analysts do require and utilize information from clandestine sources. This "protected information," as it is called in the espionage business, is an essential component of the analyst's intelligence product. None of my DDI friends ever suggested to me that he could perform his duties without intelligence provided by spies.

I have found in discussing these issues that the debate is usually reduced to these terms:

> If we consider it important to this country to have an *adequate* intelligence capability, we must recognize resorting to clandestine means, including espionage specifically, is inevitable.
>
> If we feel as a nation we can accept some clandestine means, such as espionage, but not others, such as covert action, at least our rationale should be clear.

If we decide that covert action is wrong because it constitutes meddling in other people's affairs, we should re-examine not only our intelligence activities but our entire foreign policy, our foreign aid program, and our tariff policies (to mention only a few examples) because any aspect of each of these can have a profound effect on the internal affairs of any number of countries and very often is designed to have just such an effect.

One CIA officer, with a European background, put it to me another way: "CIA is only one instrument of a United States foreign policy grounded on what Karl Marx identified as *realpolitik*, 'politics based on the realities of national interest.' One may argue whether or not the United States should practice *realpolitik*. The fact is that every other nation on the globe does. *Realpolitik* is the practical acknowledgment that, undesirable as it may be, there are relatively few recognized, and no enforceable, international laws. *Realpolitik* refuses to concede that one nation can be bound by the laws of another, so legality is not at issue in *realpolitik*." (But even my *realpolitiker* colleague acknowledges that officials and citizens of a country should abide by their own national laws. And this is a point on which everyone must agree with CIA's critics on domestic operations and related issues.)

Even while disagreeing with CIA's critics, I can conclude that they have raised valid issues, most of which are overdue a searching examination. It really comes down to the fact that if clandestine operations are worth continuing, they should be defensible and at least capable of absorbing reasonable modifications without any serious loss in effectiveness.

Obviously, my personal view is that our country must practice espionage as a vital adjunct to foreign policy. And I believe that in special situations the option of covert action should be open to American Presidents.

Détente with the Soviet Union became a practical possibility when American intelligence developed the satellite capability to monitor Soviet adherence to arms and nuclear agreements. In America there are many perceptions of détente. Some view it with suspicion, some advocate it fervently. All of us, I am sure, are convinced that it is better than the disaster of a nuclear war. But the French word *détente*, when translated into Russian comes out as "unload the gun." It does not mean unload the gun and melt down the bullets. Good intelligence is indispensable to the U.S. in an era of détente and every indication is that it will continue to be so for generations.

General Vernon Walters often told the story of the two Americans who visited the Moscow zoo. They were amazed to find a large bear and a small lamb in the same cage. They summoned the zookeeper.

"This is amazing," the Americans said. "We have never seen a bear and a lamb in the same cage."

"Oh, yes," the zookeeper replied. "This is to prove that co-existence is possible. This demonstrates that détente can work."

"Well, it is incredible," the visitors said.

The zookeeper looked about, to be sure he was not being overheard. Then he added, "Of course, we have to change the lamb every day."

In the final analysis, someone has to look after the lambs of the world.*

Dick Welch visited Washington and invited me to lunch, curious about my decision to retire and what my plans were. Satisfied on that

---

* While sorting out fires from smoke-making machines, I found it difficult to evaluate the influence, for good or for bad, that modern Directors of CIA have had on the Agency's policies and practices. Those who had worked closely with one or another of the CIA chiefs were inclined to be fiercely loyal, or, in some cases, subjective in condemning them. I decided to poll retired colleagues, not on that facet of their leadership but on how they rated five Directors of CIA as personalities. The Directors I chose as subjects for the survey were Allen Dulles, John McCone, "Red" Raborn, Richard Helms, and William Colby. (James Schlesinger was not included: opinions about him are easy to come by, especially from those who were the victims of his purge of "Old Boys.") My poll was based on the recollection of G. K. Chesterton, who among other British literary figures was asked what book they would most want to have with them if shipwrecked. One selected the poetry of Keats, another Shakespeare, a third the Bible, and so on. Chesterton nominated a volume entitled *How to Build a Boat.*

The first question of my survey was, "If I were to be shipwrecked on a desert island, a pleasant one with abundant food, good climate, a supply of scotch and every hope a ship would pass by, I would choose to be with..."

Allen Dulles won handily, with almost 75 percent of the 57 votes. Most respondents mentioned how pleasant it would be to listen to the genial spy-master; eight applied the word "raconteur." Dulles was a great storyteller, his best yarn being the one of opportunity lost when he skipped the chance to talking with Lenin. Other CIA people remarked that Dulles was a comfortable, old-shoe type. Several noted he was somewhat more inclined to be a supervisor than a doer. "What a schemer! He would devise a plan to get us off, but arrange it so I would have to implement the plan." Another said, "Dulles would be selecting all the places *I* should be digging for clams to keep us both alive."

The second question was, "If I were to be shipwrecked on a terrible desert island, with little food and no amenities, with scant hope for survival and I wanted to escape badly, I would choose to be with..." Dulles plunged to third place, and Helms led Colby slightly. One respondent, reflecting a general sentiment, split his vote between them. "Helms would also be selecting places to dig for clams," continued the mollusk fancier, "but I would have a better chance of persuading him he darn well better dig with me...." A few noted Helms would be aloof and keep his distance. One said, "I credit myself with enough skepticism to not let him get off the island alone." Second-place Colby won his votes from those

279

score, he abruptly changed the subject of our conversation. Between bites of his fish, he asked me what I thought about death.

"Dick"—my own mouth was about half full of food—"do we really want to talk about that now?"

"Why not?" Dick replied.

We decided that our views coincided with what Dick dubbed Thurber's Thanatopsis. Agreement came after I told Welch about reading many years before James Thurber's personal credo in a book entitled *This I Believe*. Thurber likened life to a trip on a train. Most people rode in the coaches, some in the pullman, and a lucky few in the club car sipping a glass of scotch. Sooner or later the train would enter a dark tunnel. Then it would stop, and the conductor would shout, "All out for Oblivion!"

"When that happens," Thurber said, "I'll take a final swig of my scotch and soda and step out, unafraid, into the darkness."

"That'll do," Welch said. "I don't feel like a scotch, but what about a brandy?"

Over the cognac Dick Welch thanked me for my efforts on his behalf. My recommendations had led to a cherished new assignment—Athens.

---

who admired the soldier-priest's courage and compassion. Several choices were pragmatic: McCone is a ship-builder ("He'd build a boat out of seaweed...."), Raborn was an admiral, and Helms, I was reminded, a navy navigator.

As a companion on the pleasant island, a majority of fourteen women intelligence officers wanted to be stranded with Allen Dulles, some expressing maternal concern—"I would not want to see him subjected to the rigors of the other island." One, noting that she had known Helms socially, asked, "Would any woman *not* delight in being shipwrecked with Richard Helms?" Unlike the men, women preferred Dulles for both islands.

Finally, I separated the opinions of the dozen most senior respondents to the questionnaire. These included a former Deputy Director, four Directorate Chiefs, and some senior staff people. In the more junior category of Division Chiefs, I held my own vote in abeyance. The eleven who worked most closely with the ex-Directors voted this way for the pleasant island: six wanted to share it with Dulles, four with Helms, one with McCone, and none with Raborn or Colby. I then cast my vote for Helms as the most stimulating man to be with in a tropical paradise.

Then the senior respondents chose their partner for the terrible desert island. Dulles did not receive a vote. Nor did Raborn. The eleven votes were split: four for McCone, four for Helms, three for Colby. I could have broken the deadlock by voting for either McCone or Helms. But I thought about Chesterton and his island. What if a volume entitled *How to Build a Boat for One Passenger* should float ashore on my desert island? With that in mind, my vote did not break the deadlock, but created a three-way tie. I selected Colby. He would get us both off that island. Certainly he would never entertain the notion of building a boat for one or, if he did reach that point, he would later stand in the surf and wave good-bye—a faint smile on his thin lips—after pushing me out to sea.

Late in the afternoon of May 9, 1975, my friends said farewell to me at a retirement party in the Executive Dining Room at Langley. The tables were pushed against the walls so the room would accommodate the crowd of colleagues. "Wally," with whom I had worked in Chile, Mexico, and the Dominican Republic, was there as well as "Hector" from Guatemala days. And "John," who had chortled so when we heard the Communist flatulence in Mexico City. And many others.

Of course Abe was there. He mixed with his old friends and heard their glum talk. Many seriously doubted that CIA would survive. Suggestions that the Agency be abolished were being heard from its critics, some of them honestly convinced that was the only remedy. The men and women of CIA were despondent. Many feared that their years of work at home and abroad were about to be chucked, and intelligence responsibilities might be given to another agency.

As usual, Abe had a story for the occasion. He told about a U.S. government official who had been assigned to take the census in a remote mountain section of Tennessee where classic hillbilly types still abounded.

One day the census taker came upon a dilapidated shack clinging to the mountainside. A clutter of bearded figures—barefooted, in tattered overalls, and with moonshine jugs and rifles close at hand—were sprawled out among an assortment of hounds on the porch. He approached the most senior-looking, announced his business, and asked how many persons were in the family.

The head man scratched and reckoned for a moment before allowing, "Twenty-two."

The census taker's reaction was one of disbelief. "The government only wants the figures on immediate members of your family," he explained. "That is, your wife and children."

"Twenty-two," the mountaineer insisted, but the census taker quite obviously remained unconvinced.

So, the mountaineer slouched out into the yard and whistled loudly —whereupon children appeared from all quarters and lined up in two ranks. A count was made. Only twenty-one. Who was missing? Finally, someone announced it was Little Luke, the two-year-old. Everyone scattered to look for Little Luke. Soon there was a shout from the outhouse nearby; Little Luke had fallen through the privy's hole.

The mountaineer took the census taker over to the structure, pointed down the hole to Little Luke floundering in the morass at the bottom and said, "Twenty-two." And then, he casually walked away.

The census taker grabbed the mountaineer by the arm and protested, "But, wait a minute! What about Little Luke? Aren't you going to pull him out?"

The mountaineer shrugged. "Aw, hell, mister," he replied. "It's

281

easier to have 'nuther one than to try and clean him up."

Abe then went on to conclude, "In many ways, this story represents the Agency's situation, and Little Luke's dilemma is ours at the moment. But, I'm sure in the end good judgment prevailed and they didn't leave Little Luke in that predicament nor will they us."

It was time to turn in my badge. As we passed the guard post near the main foyer of the building, a security officer took it and Gina's temporary visitor's badge as well. We walked on past the thirty-one stars carved into the wall of the marble hall; they represented the CIA officers who had died in the line of duty.

Outside, I left Gina and walked over to the statue of Nathan Hale.

How appropriate. The statue in front of CIA was that of a man with his hands tied behind his back.

Poor Nate. He had called intelligence a "peculiar" service. He was a lousy spy. He hid his secret writing in his shoe, where the British easily found it, and arrived on Manhattan Island too late to accomplish his mission.

But he did say, "I wish to be useful. And every kind of service, necessary to the public good, becomes honorable by being necessary. If the exigencies of my country demand a peculiar service, its claims to perform that service are imperious."

I stood there for a long time.

Finally Gina called. "Come on. It's time to leave."

EPILOGUE

The first thing I'm going to do, I promised myself, is fix the front screen door. It had been askew and sagging for months. Repairing it seemed an appropriate chore for a retired bureaucrat who no longer had to go to the office every morning.

But the very first morning after my retirement party turned into a hectic one. I appeared at a press conference at a Washington hotel. When it was time to begin I was terrified. The large hall was packed with journalists, photographers, and technicians. I counted seventeen microphones on the podium. Five television cameras eyed me.

What I wanted to do was to talk about the need for perspective in the intelligence controversy and shed some light on what CIA is and, in particular at that time, what it is not. That morning, however, most of the questions concerned assassination, Chile, the violation of Americans' civil rights, drug-testing, and the opening of mail. I was so busy handling hot potatoes, I never did have an opportunity to give an organized version of my points.

A few days later, I flew to Paris for a debate with John Marks and others on the French national television network.

The following night in London I sparred with Philip Agee on BBC. On arriving at the studio I learned that the first five minutes of the twenty-minute program was a film strip of an interview with Carlos Rafael Rodríguez, a Cuban Communist. Rodríguez claimed CIA was responsible for "more than one hundred" assassination attempts against Fidel Castro. I countered with the story of the time I warned Castro about an attempt against his life.*

* The wire services carried the account and, predictably, I had a reaction from Florida. A man named Max Gorman Gonzalez told Associated Press in Miami that

Next, on the *Today* show Douglas Kiker asked me first about Chile, and then assassination.

After that, I participated in a panel discussion with Philip Agee, John Marks, and Jack Anderson on ABC's "AM America." The telecast was introduced with Anderson's scoop on CIA's use of Johnny Roselli and the Mafia in an attempt against Castro. Despite this, Jack Anderson, who lived not very far from my home in Bethesda, was eminently fair to me for the remainder of the program. Agee, still concerned about entering the United States, had been interviewed in Canada; and Marks, Anderson, and I were to appear live after the film of Agee's Canadian interview had been shown. At one point Bill Beutel, the anchorman, asked Agee what he thought about me and my statement that he, Agee, was "the first CIA defector." Agee replied, "...I will bet you within a year or eighteen months, he will have a much different attitude. Who knows but what he'll be agreeing with his daughter, who right now is against him."

Jack Anderson and I were watching the Agee videotape on a monitor. The journalist turned to me, his face stern. "What's that low blow about your daughter?" Anderson had reason to be interested. His son Randy and my daughter Debbie ("but that's dirty") had been dating for several months.

As the weeks passed I grew weary of rehashing the assassination topic: on the Martin Agronsky show, CBS television, numerous radio broadcasts, and during the question-and-answer sessions after a number of lectures around the country. Something I did want to comment upon didn't seem to be of any interest: the Fifth Estate and its publication, *CounterSpy.*

Agee continued to identify American intelligence officers and agents abroad. Marchetti, Marks, and their Fifth Estate colleagues beguiled college students and journalists with their slanted versions of CIA policy and practice. *Playboy* magazine ran four anti-CIA pieces in one issue; all were written by members of the Fifth Estate. I decided it was time to give the publicity efforts of the Fifth Estate and *CounterSpy* a boost. I believed the media and the public would be skeptical about allegations coming from men supporting a program with the purpose of exposing United States intelligence personnel in such places as Prague, Budapest,

---

he planned a million-dollar suit against CIA because he had been "thrown to the wolves" by CIA when an assassination plot he was involved in had to be aborted. Asked about my statement, Frank Sturgis (of Watergate fame) said the scheme I talked about on BBC was "very possibly" Operation Sword, in which he had conspired with Gonzalez. On numerous occasions Sturgis has made sensational allegations based on knowledge he gained as a CIA agent. In fact, Sturgis never worked for the CIA.

and Bucharest, not to mention those third world nations where endemic terrorism was a latent threat to any American official and more so to identified intelligence officers.

Retired Colonel L. Fletcher Prouty told Dan Schorr on CBS that Alexander Butterfield was CIA's chief contact and secret informant on the White House staff. It was sheer nonsense—but received heavy play in the media. After it became obvious that Prouty's story had no merit, the headlines and brouhaha evaporated. To most, this incident represented just another summer weekend sensation concerning CIA which enhanced the credibility of such ridiculous charges as CIA had been the intellectual Godfather of Watergate, or, had been involved somehow in the assassination of President Kennedy. During all this not one newsman or TV journalist mentioned that Colonel Prouty, too, was a member of the Fifth Estate with his name listed on the masthead of *CounterSpy*.

I wrote a short article on the Fifth Estate which I proffered, unsuccessfully, to the Washington *Post* and the Washington *Star*. In one part of the article, I pinpointed my fears about the consequences of that group's crusade against CIA: "Why does all this bother me so much? In the first instance there is my concern that inevitably Messrs. Agee, Marchetti and Marks and their colleagues are going to be responsible for the unnecessary death of an American intelligence officer abroad. They are already responsible for untold worry and even anxiety on the part of CIA families...." The article, written six months before the death of Dick Welch in Athens, finally appeared in an in-house publication of the Association of Retired Intelligence Officers, the organization of former intelligence people I started when leaving CIA.

In September of 1975 our group—known as ARIO (the initials of the organization and not another code word)—held a reunion in Alexandria, Virginia. It was the first national convention of ex-spooks in history. Former CIA and military intelligence officers from all over the country convened at a Ramada Inn. Much like Rotarians, we wore name tags and, as far as I could tell, there wasn't an alias or pseudonym among the lot. We held a press conference in which a panel of eight ARIO members fielded questions from the journalists. I thought it was a rather unique news story and was disappointed when the convention was not mentioned in the *New York Times*. The Washington *Post* did cover the meeting on the obituary page in its fourth section.

The convention was fun. Abe came out of his retirement in the bluefish country to attend. Beforehand, I had talked to him on the telephone and asked that he draft a brief statement I could use to close a speech. I wanted some thought that would be appropriate for ex-intelligence officers huddled together in the midst of an onslaught of sensational publicity and congressional revelations.

When Abe arrived he handed me the statement he had scrawled on the back of one of his son's school homework papers. He watched me over the rims of his bifocals as I read it:

Sincere people on all sides of the U.S. intelligence issue may disagree radically. But, I think—and hope—we can agree that: First, while an intelligence system may function with much greater ease and effectiveness in a closed society, it's in support of the wrong cause. Secondly, that the difficulties the U.S. intelligence system may encounter from time to time are far outweighed by the values which create these problems and make our job of defending them under any circumstances worthwhile.

"Is that okay?" Abe asked.
"Yes," I said. "It's just right."

In late 1975, Senator Frank Church's Select Committee on Intelligence released its findings on CIA activities in Chile. Three phases of U.S. policy were highlighted: the debatable program in which the Christian Democrats were supported for more than a decade; the inexcusable era of Track II in 1970; and the correct stance of noninvolvement in the uprising that toppled Allende in 1973—thanks to Abe's two cables sent that May and CIA prudence in not becoming involved with the strikes that finally triggered the coup.

I was delighted to see an editorial entitled "The CIA in Chile" in the December 7 issue of the *New York Times*. The first paragraph read:

Revolutions and counter-revolutions inevitably produce political myths. Like all myths that succeed in getting hold of the popular imagination, these legends contain an element of truth; but they also contain large amounts of exaggeration, invention, and imported emotion that is derived from other situations or historical analogies.

It mirrored my own sentiments.

In fact, six months previously, the *New York Times* had published on its Op-Ed page an article I had written in which the theme was identical. In that piece I said:

Perhaps soon the CIA can fade back into the position of somewhat less prominence and interest to the news media, with which we have had and undoubtedly will continue to have our unique problems. Responsible, factual stories we can endure stoically, even though we find painfully gratuitous the exposure of active operations or agents. Egregious, sensationalist ones we can also endure because the ridiculous is patently short-lived. The type that really bothers us is the hybrid (fact and fallacy) story that refuses to die or be straightened out, and sinks into the public subconscious as a durable myth....

The December 7 *Times* editorial also supported CIA's contention that it was not responsible for the ouster of Allende:

The staff report of the Senate Select Committee on Intelligence has now placed the activities of the United States Government in Chile in recent years in some perspective. The central fact that emerges is that although the United States did inexcusably interfere in the Chilean political process, the United States still was not basically responsible for the overthrow of President Salvador Allende. Despite the left-wing myth that this country was the prime mover in that event, the coup was actually conceived and carried out by Chileans acting for reasons of their own....

Later during the month of December Gina and I received a letter from Dick and Kika Welch. They invited us to visit them in Athens and stay in their "somewhat notorious" home. I didn't realize until later that Dick was referring to the fact that a local newspaper had identified him as the CIA Chief of Station and printed his home address.

Late on the afternoon of December 23, Gina and I were driving through the Maryland countryside. The radio announced that Dick Welch had been gunned down on his doorstep in Athens.

Gina gasped. "The bastards have killed him!"

On Christmas Eve our living room was filled with television camera crews, and I suggested that the Fifth Estate and *CounterSpy* had at least some responsibility for Dick Welch's death even though I didn't know who pulled the trigger. The editor of the Athens newspaper that exposed Dick said first he had obtained the name from "an anonymous Greek friend." When a Washington *Post* reporter interviewed him a second time, the editor admitted his first statement was erroneous: that he had "checked out" a Fifth Estate list of CIA officers.

If the murderers of Dick Welch are ever apprehended, I predict they will be political extremists who no longer believed the myth that CIA would or could strike back.

Whatever the case, the edition of *CounterSpy* which fingered Dick as a CIA Chief of Station also contained an exhortation by Philip Agee:

The most effective and important systematic efforts to combat the CIA that can be undertaken right now are, I think, the identification, exposure, and neutralization of its people working abroad. Working through careful analysis of the U.S. government employees country by country abroad, the CIA people can be identified

and exposed through periodic bulletins disseminated to our sub-
scribers, particularly individuals and organizations in the foreign
country in question. Photographs and home addresses in the foreign
capital or Consular cities should be included. Having this information, the peoples victimized by the CIA and the economic exploita-
tion that CIA enforces can bring pressure on their so-often compromised governments to expel the CIA people. *And, in the absence of
such expulsion, which will not be uncommon, the people themselves
will have to decide what they must do to rid themselves of CIA.*
[Italics are mine.]

In twenty-five years as a professional intelligence officer I had seen
a number of similar statements overseas. Most of them had been drafted
in foreign capitals for use by indigenous radicals of the extreme left in
local propaganda publications.

Critics of intelligence often ask why Dick Welch was not returned
to the safety of the United States once he was identified as a CIA man.
The question begs the real issue of why he was exposed in the first
place. Of course, neutralizing his ability to function was just what Agee
and his friends desired, and is the rationale they have given for their
sordid campaign since Dick's death. Dick Welch didn't come home because he had a job to do in Athens. American ambassadors, consuls, and
military attachés have been the victims of terrorist violence for more
than a decade; they have been kidnapped and assassinated. Several times
while serving overseas I warned embassy officers of plots against them.
Not once did one suggest he should abandon his post and scoot back
to a safe haven in Washington. And that's the reaction CIA officers must
have. This is quite aside from the basic fact that the Clandestine Service
simply cannot afford overnight to start yanking and replacing scores of
its people because they have been exposed by the Fifth Estate. It lacks
the immediate personnel resources in terms of numbers, experience, and
language to conduct that kind of massive transplantation securely and
effectively. And, the savor of such a great success undoubtedly would lead
the Fifth Estate to repeat the exposure cycle as soon as the new contingent of Station Chiefs and operational personnel settled in. In brief,
the Clandestine Service could not possibly provide the kind of intelligence support the United States must have while riding a merry-go-
round operated by the Fifth Estate. Unfortunately, the individuals who
must remain at their posts naked* will find their jobs infinitely more
difficult, but there is no alternative.

* In intelligence slang, the connotation of "naked" is unprotected, without
cover, exposed.

288

On CBS's *60 Minutes* show Morley Safer asked me if Dick Welch would have pictured himself as a hero. No. But Dick did think of himself as an intellectual Marine.

Dick was a bright hope for the future of the CIA. He had such a zest for life and work that sometimes I thought I could almost detect a twinkle in his blind eye. He not only had the desire but the requisite talents to make CIA a better organization. Those of us who knew him felt he was so intelligent, honest, and perceptive that, whatever the circumstances, there would have been no excesses and few mistakes on his night watch.

Much has been made of the fact that Dick Welch was an erudite man. Indeed he was. Once a cable came into CIA and the last sentence was in Latin. Everyone scurried around looking for Dick, obviously the man to answer it. He did, and the last sentence of his message was a quotation from Shakespeare—translated into impeccable Latin. Dick also was fond of citing Lord Macaulay; in one CIA meeting someone suggested bringing an adversary group to terms for some reason or another and Dick settled the matter by saying, "Let them be. Their reward is to be what they are."

When the Congressmen returned to Washington in early 1976 after the Christmas holidays, they brought back with them a new appreciation of their constituents' reactions to the barrage of criticism the intelligence community had endured during the previous year. The tide seemed to have turned.

In Chicago a television commentator, preparing me for a filmed interview after I had spoken to a college audience, told me he would be asking two questions. I had little doubt what the two subjects would be and only wondered which would be first: assassinations or Chile? His first query was indeed about assassinations. Then the second: How did I feel about détente? Indeed, things were changing.

My son Christopher, now nineteen, returned from a trip to Europe. He looked at the title page of the draft of this book.

"I like the title," Chris said. "I saw Rembrandt's *The Night Watch* at the Rijksmuseum when I was in Amsterdam. Some nut slashed it to pieces in 1975, but now it's restored and on view again."

I went to visit Bill Colby, who had also become an ex-intelligence officer by then. It was another resplendent Washington spring, and I drove past blooming azaleas to his small home in Bethesda. I wondered if he would greet me with the customary "friend."

Colby opened the door. "Hi, friend. Come on in."

Barbara Colby was leaving to shop. She chatted with us for a

289

moment about the ice cream in molds she planned to purchase for the family's Easter dinner.

Colby and I talked about a number of things. Through the window behind him I could see the Church of the Little Flower.

Most of what the former DCI said he will want to reveal, if at all, in due time in his own way. But I did talk with him, for the record, about Dick Helms. When I mentioned the name Colby's eyes hardened.

"That talk about my throwing Helms to the wolves?" Colby the soldier was responding. "I've said over and over again that he didn't perjure himself. He had his job to do in different times, and he was forced to give answers which might have been thin but were not perjury. There were some things I had to tell the Department of Justice about that era."

I told Colby there were two schools of thought in CIA and the intelligence community about his role during the investigations. The first believed he had acted correctly, having no choice in the post-Watergate atmosphere other than being as open as he had. The other school contended that he should have kept quiet and volunteered nothing.

"A lot of people wanted me to be quiet," Colby said. "One prominent fellow said later he thought I should have stonewalled the problem areas.* That wouldn't have worked. There are three kinds of secrets: nonsecrets, good secrets, and bad secrets. The bad secrets were going to come out anyhow. There was no other way. For a while I didn't think we were going to make it. You were with me during some of those times."

Colby looked out past the dogwood to the church.

"No," he repeated, "there was no other way."

Driving home I thought about the difference between the CIA of Dick Helms and the CIA of Bill Colby.

Helms was Director during a period when it was axiomatic almost to respond any way possible to Presidents. He had learned to understand them. And, in the process, he had held the umbrella to catch the crap so CIA's people could get on with their job. The institution had not been in jeopardy.

Colby had been Director after Watergate when a telephone call from the White House signaled caution. He saw his job as protecting the Agency in a furor which threatened its very survival. Candor was his umbrella.

I am of the school that believes Colby's course was the correct one,

---

* In plain English, keep quiet and reveal as little as possible, and then only when forced to. There are perhaps two or three people in Washington Colby would describe as "prominent."

even if he might have started too fast too soon. But there was no other way in the end.

I visited Abe. Fishing had been good. "The blues *and* the channel bass are running!" he exclaimed. After we had a drink in hand we talked about old times while his wife prepared a reunion dinner.

"How's it going?" Abe looked at me over his glasses. "Are you hanging in there?"

"Some days have been longer than others," I admitted. "There have been a couple of times on college campuses when I didn't think I'd get away with all my skin. But it's getting better."

"You've been on the Hill a lot," Abe said. "Are the investigations about over?"

"Pike's House committee is dead. Suicide. Church's Senate committee has come out with its recommendations. Now we'll see."

"What kind of grade would you give the Church committee?"

"A good one." I thought about that for a moment. "It kept secrets, the staff was serious and responsible. I suppose they deserve a B, maybe a B+."

"What about Church himself?" Abe asked.

"He's the reason the committee doesn't get an A. Church is a decent and sincere man, but he is also sanctimonious and self-righteous. All that circus atmosphere—waving around the dart gun in front of the television camera. Abe, do you remember how we used to laugh about the hypothetical Operation Penis Envy?"

Abe chuckled.

"Well, I keep having a recurring nightmare. I keep dreaming that I'm going to see another investigation on television, and that Senator Church will be brandishing a memorandum entitled Operation Penis Envy, citing it as characteristic of CIA covert action programs."

"You've been seeing most of the journalists on the intelligence beat," Abe said. "How do you feel about them?"

"The Fifth Estate people have written a lot of nonsense in *Playboy* and *Penthouse*. Did you see that Colonel L. Fletcher Prouty is the International Editor of *Genesis*?"

"Is that a religious magazine?" Abe asked.

"No, Abe, it's a girlie magazine."

"What about the more serious press?"

"The Agency got the lumps it deserved from the *New York Times* and the Washington *Post*, but their editorials have been fair and objective. But I fault the *Times* and CBS for letting advocacy journalism color their coverage. Hersh is a damned good reporter but there was bound to be a pernicious aura in anything he wrote about intelligence. On a television talk show with Ray Cline, Hersh said he believed all intelligence gathering should be abolished. You can't expect an objective story from that kind of an advocate any more than the DDI could expect an objective estimate from a biased intelligence officer."

"CBS?" Abe asked.

"Dan Schorr has been delivering some cheap shots," I said. "All those staged interviews with unidentified masked sources. And Schorr saw to it that his stories came out the way he wanted them to be from the outset. At Dick Welch's funeral he was standing outside the chapel when everyone filed in. That night on CBS he said, 'A notable absence of representatives of Congress, especially the investigating committees...' I don't know how he missed them, but seated near Gina and me were Senator McC. Mathias and Bill Miller, staff director of the Church committee. And not far away Congressman McClory of the House committee."

I followed Abe into the kitchen and we talked while he mixed a drink.

"What do you hear from the troops?" Abe asked. "How is morale at Langley?"

"They tell me it's improving," I said. "The younger people were staggered when the horror stories were revealed one by one. But they feel better now that it's clear that all of these matters, including the things Hersh had in his original story, were rooted out by the Agency itself and stopped before the revelations occurred. They now realize that the system worked and set itself straight. And it's clear to them also that the Agency was working for Presidents during those periods and was used as an instrument of foreign policy. They understand that there were zigs and zags...sometimes the policy was good and sometimes it was bad. They know the Agency had some tough chores to perform."

Abe smiled. "Yup. Presidents seem to believe that in the international arena you just naturally must end up cultivating your friends and castigating your enemies. What was it Kennedy said? 'Help any friend, face any foe'?"

"Abe," I said, "at colleges I invariably find myself in a rap session with the students. The one thing that always comes up is the business of personal morality. I just can't convince young people that I've worked all these years in intelligence and come out of it without having any inferiority complex or reservations about my ethical standards. The students always say that there must have been times when I was asked to do something I didn't believe in. And then, they ask, 'Why didn't you quit?'"

"Abandon ship?" Abe removed his bifocals, and began to clean them, slowly and thoughtfully, with a paper napkin. "If you and I had quit in 1970 we wouldn't have been around in 1973. Sure, there have been times when I've been asked or told to do something with which I didn't agree. Anyone has, if they've worked very long for a business, a government agency, a church, or almost any other human institution. But you don't quit unless the differences are so frequent and of such a nature that they overwhelm one's sense of common purpose and satisfaction with what he's doing and can do in the future. What I'm trying to say is, in that respect, working for intelligence is no different from working for any other challenging profession—law, journalism, politics."

"There are some people," I told Abe, "who really believe CIA should be abolished."

"You tell those people something for me," Abe said. He was polishing his bifocals furiously. "Tell them that American Presidents are strong-willed men. They wouldn't get there if they weren't. If they don't have an intelligence service they will create their own. It might not be very big, and not very good, and they might have to reach into the loony bin to find the people to run it. But they will have one. They might even call it 'the Plumbers'!"

I had to smile. "Abe," I said, "be careful. You're going to break your glasses."

In late February of 1976 I debated Victor Marchetti on a television show in Philadelphia. I was surprised that he had agreed to the confrontation since previously he had declined my challenge to a series of college campus debates. Apparently he was seeking a public forum in which he could change his spots: during the show he disassociated himself from the Fifth Estate and *CounterSpy*.

I had a business appointment in New York after the show and caught the first train coming through the Philadelphia station. It turned out to be the Metroliner from Washington. I sat next to a man in a gray suit. My fellow passenger was talkative, and I was intrigued by his heavy foreign accent.

"Are you Russian?" I asked him.

"Yes," he said. "I work at the Soviet embassy in Washington." He gave me his card. "What do you do?"

"I was in the Foreign Service," I told him. "Now I'm retired."

"Very interesting." The Russian diplomat asked a number of questions, but I avoided detailed answers. But he persisted. "Have you been to Europe?" he asked.

"Many times."

"Have you ever visited Moscow?" he asked.

"No."

"You should. Why not?"

"Too expensive," I told him.

"There's a charter flight from Washington for only six hundred twenty-two dollars," the Russian informed me.

Suddenly I felt a tingling at the back of my neck. I was being asked the same kind of questions I had put to numerous foreigners, sometimes to Soviets, in ascertaining if they were worth cultivating for recruitment! Was I dealing with a KGB officer? The fact that he was a Soviet diplomat in Washington made the odds pretty close to fifty-fifty that he was an intelligence officer.

I decided to find out.

"My specialty in the Foreign Service," I lied, "was science and technology."

The Russian's eyes opened with delight. What a choice morsel had fallen unexpectedly on his plate! Code books and secret plans were once the staple in an intelligence officer's diet—today it is research and development or science and technology which most satisfies.

"That charter flight to Moscow," he said eagerly, "you must take it. Perhaps I can arrange a discount."

I began to laugh.

"Why is it you laugh?"

I couldn't help it. My Russian companion had really been the victim of monumental bad luck. Uninvited, a man who could instantly recognize the pattern of a cultivation approach had sat next to him on a train.

"The truth is," I told him, "I recently retired after twenty-five years of working for the CIA."

He blanched. His eyes narrowed. His neck reddened.

Finally, he was able to sputter, "You are me joking?"

"I am not you joking," I assured him.

The Russian regained his composure. He cast his eyes heavenward. "What an amazing country! I sit on a train and a CIA man sits beside me. And he even tells me he is a CIA man! That would not happen in my country."

We talked, understanding each other as two professionals can. Then the Russian shook his head.

"What an amazing country!" He shook his head again. "You know, I even read in the newspapers that in this country there is a public organization composed completely of intelligence officers."

"That's right." I reached into my pocket, pulled out an application for ARIO, and offered it to him. "I'm the president. Have a brochure."

As the train entered the tunnel for New York the Russian spoke. "You know, I have wasted a calling card on you. May I have it back?"

"No," I said. "You keep my brochure. I'll keep your card."

294

As we shook hands in Pennsylvania Station the Russian shook his head again. "An amazing country!" I watched him dart into the nearest telephone booth.

Ours really is an amazing country, where anything can happen. I even am beginning to suspect that American intelligence will survive the incredible adventure of having to run secret operations in Macy's window.

In fact, I'm sure intelligence will survive if all Americans ponder the meaning of the peroration Abe wrote for my speech and are willing to take that a little further: While those of us who worked in American intelligence—especially the men and women of the Clandestine Service of CIA—must understand that our problems resulted from the sanctity of our country's values, other Americans must realize what intelligence people have been doing all this time. They have been in dark alleys working hard—with some mistakes and some success—to protect those values.

Yes, American intelligence will survive.

And, one of these days, I'm going to get around to fixing that screen door.

INDEX

Abe, 87, 89 and *n*., 90, 93, 97, 104, 106, 110–11, 125–6, 133–4, 154–5, 158, 177, 178–9, 180, 187, 200, 220–1, 222–3, 236–8, 240, 241, 251, 255, 264, 274, 281–2, 285–6, 291–3, 295
Abel, Colonel Rudolf, 61
Adele, 157
Africa, 81, 187, 204, 226, 272
Agee, Philip, 238–9, 251, 261–2, 266, 270, 283–5, 287–8
Agency for International Development (AID), 180, 215
Agronsky, Martin, 151, 284
Ahern, Deborah, 199, 269–70, 284
Al, 190–1
Alcott, Colonel, 95, 101–2 and *n*., 104, 109
Alessandri, Jorge, 220
Alexandria, Virginia, 285
Algeria, 216
Allende Gossens, Salvador, 28; coup against, 185, 237–8, 246–51, 252–4 and *n*., 274, 286–7; death of, 247–8; election of, 220–3
Allende Gossens, Mrs. Salvador, 247, 250
Alvim, General, 163
"AM America" (TV show) 284
American Broadcasting System, 284
American Civil Liberties Union, 262
Amiama Tío, Luís, 145, 165
Amory, Robert, 191
Anderson, Clark, 127–8, 156, 160, 179, 184
Anderson, Jack, 284
Anderson, Randy, 284
Angleton, James, 189–90, 202, 205, 239–40, 246, 256, 264–6
Arab terrorists, 258–9

Araucanian tribe, 27
Arbenz Guzmán, Jacobo, 34–5, 36, 40–8, 51–4
Argentina: terrorism in, 258, 262
Arica, Chile, 249
Arms Control Disarmament Agency, 197–9
Asia, 187, 225
assassinations: and CIA, 91, 138–9 and *n*., 208 and *n*., 209, 263, 272–3, 283–4 and *n*., 289; by terrorists, 184, 185, 217, 257–8, 287–8
Association of Retired Intelligence Officers (ARIO), 271, 279 *n*., 285–6, 294
Athens Greece, 194–5, 211, 267, 280, 285, 287–8

Baghdad Iraq, 75
Baker, Howard, 255 and *n*.
Balaguer, Joaquín, 177–81, 184
Balmaceda, José, 247
Barnes, Tracy, 34 and *n*., 35, 36, 49, 51, 53, 55–7, 58, 86–8, 90, 91, 99, 101, 106 and *n*., 107, 109, 123
Baruch, Bernard, 14
Batista, Fulgencio, 63–4, 74, 77, 80, 92, 158
Bay of Pigs operation, 53, 86–112 *passim* 118, 119, 138, 145, 222, 272; air strikes for, 100, 103, 104, 105–9, 110 and *n*.; Brigade 2506, 95, 99–103, 106–9; failure of, 100 *n*., 107–12; government-in-exile planned, 87, 92, 101; infiltration team, 97–8, 109; intelligence for, 95–6, 99; internal attack deception, 105–6; landing site for, 95 100; landing site changed, 102, 110–11; military

Bay of Pigs operation (*cont.*)
plan changed, 101–4, 107–9, 110;
paramilitary planning for, 93, 95,
99, 276; propaganda for, 86, 87,
88–91, 96–7 and *n.*, 101–9 *passim*,
112

Beirut, Lebanon, 67–76

Bell, Ian, 182, 184, 185

Bell, Ruth, 182

Bender, Frank, 87, 91–3, 95, 96, 99,
101

Bennett, Tapley, 152, 154, 158, 161,
163, 168, 172, 176

Berle, Adolf, 103

Berlin Wall, 205

Beutel, Bill, 284

Bill, 95, 98, 100, 102, 104, 109

Bissell, Richard, 36, 38, 53, 86–91, 97,
99, 100, 101, 102, 104, 105, 107–10,
113, 119, 123, 133, 197–8, 239

Blake, George, 205, 207

Blatty, William Peter (*The Exorcist*),
73

Block, Martin, 7

Board of National Estimates, 125

Bob, 19, 20–5, 26, 28–9

Bolivia: CIA in, 209; Communism
in, 133; Guevara in, 81, 188, 204,
209–10

Bosch, Juan, 145–6, 163, 172, 177–81

Bowdler, Bill, 185, 241

Bowers, Rick, 14–15, 26, 28, 61

Bowles, Chester, 103

Brad, 3–4, 8–10, 15, 18, 19, 28, 30, 33,
36–7, 38, 49–50

Bradley, General Omar, 6

Brasília, Brazil, 214, 224, 226

Brazil, 60, 117, 245; CIA in, 213–19,
223–4; Communism in, 133, 216;
in OAS, 152, 161, 162–5; terrorism
in, 216–17, 257–8

British Honduras, 35

Brookings Institute, 243

Brownell, Herbert, 50

Bryan, 157

Bucharest, Rumania, 285

Buckley, William F., 113

Budapest, Hungary, 284

bugging, 11, 134–7, 260;
disadvantages of, 134–5; and Soviet
Union, 135; telephone, 134, 227

Bundy, McGeorge, 107

Bundy, William, 58

Bunker, Ellsworth, 154, 158–77
passim, 181, 185, 186, 244

Butterfield, Alexander, 285

Caamaño, Colonel Francisco, 148–9,
152, 156, 158, 159, 163–4, 174–5,
176, 184

Cabell, General Charles P., 86–7,
97–8, 101, 107–8, 110

Cantinflas, 41–2

Caracas, Venezuela, 183, 226–7, 229–
34, 257

Carroll, Madeleine, 174

Castillo Armas, Colonel Carlos, 34,
36, 42–8, 50, 52, 53–4

Castro, Fidel, 54, 81, 83, 89, 99,
124, 142, 145, 176; and Bay of
Pigs, 96, 103, 104, 105–9, 110 *n.*,
111; CIA plots against, 87, 91,
114, 138, 139 *n.*, 142 *n.*, 208 and *n.*,
209, 272–3, 284; and Communism,
77–8, 80; Cuban opposition to,
81–2, 93, 95, 97 and *n.*, 100, 101,
103, 130, 165, 208–9, 283, 284 *n.*;
and Cuban revolution, 64–5, 73–4,
76–80; demanded honesty, 80, 134;
encouraged export of revolution,
53, 125, 133, 158, 188, 227, 237;
see also Cuba

Castro, Raul, 64, 77

Central America, 34–5, 40, 43, 50–1,
52–4, 103; *see also* individual
countries

Central Intelligence Agency (CIA),
61 and *n.*, 78–9, 116, 123, 149–50,
191–2, 228–9, 243, 244, 277; and
American citizens overseas, 127–8,
139–43, 238, 262; assassination
plots of, 91, 138–9 and *n.*, 208 and

Central Intelligence Agency (*cont.*)
n., 209, 263, 272–3, 283–4 and n.,
289; blacks in, 226, 240, 242;
charter of, 35, 273–4; Chiefs of
Station, 8, 19, 69, 116–17, 133,
153–4, 155, 210, 216, 219, 226, 230,
242, 272; Clandestine Service
(Directorate of Plans), vii, 3–4,
12, 34, 55–6, 79, 112, 123, 149, 169,
192–3, 200–12, 213, 224–6, 230–3,
234, 242, 256–61, 273, 275–8, 288,
294–5; and Cold War, 8, 14, 56–
60, 120, 238, 271; criticism of, vii,
238, 244, 251–5, 261–93; defectors
from, 238–9, 284; defense of, 244,
270–93; destabilization charge
against, 252–4 and n., 274; dirty
tricks of, 55, 91, 120–1, 133, 206,
212, 234, 277; domestic operations
of, 62, 156, 262, 264–5, 267–8, 273,
278, 283; and drug-testing, 274,
283; ethnic groups in, 226, 242;
families of employees of, 9, 61,
156, 187, 202, 226, 262, 264, 269,
285; and FBI, 3, 23, 155–6, 160,
171, 186; field stations, 117, 119–
23; grade structure in, vii, 34, 51,
57, 227; and leaks, 268–9, 271;
investigations into, viii, 139 n.,
251–5 and n., 262, 267–8, 271, 273,
286–7, 290–1; liaison with other
intelligence services, 116, 189, 207,
256, 259–60, 262, 265, 269, 272;
and Mafia, 273, 284; and mail
opening, 273, 283; and McCarthy,
58–9; morale in, 58–9, 236, 238,
245, 251, 266, 267–9, 292; and
morality and ethics, viii, 22, 34–5,
52–3, 206, 222, 276, 292–3; officers,
12, 34, 35–6, 38, 52, 56, 59, 86–7,
119–20, 190–3, 201, 207, 224–6, 288;
offices, 13, 37–8, 58 and n., 85–
113 *passim*, 118 n., 137, 147, 149–
55 *passim*, 171, 200, 228; plumbing
operations of, 92 and n., 95; and
presidential visits, 121–3; public

Central Intelligence Agency (*cont.*)
identification of agents of, vii, 169,
238–9, 251, 261–2, 267, 270, 284–
8; public relations of, 101, 242–3,
269; Secrecy Oath of, 57, 76 n.;
security in, 85–6, 92, 189, 205,
236–7, 239–40, 242, 246; and State
Department, 37, 55, 56, 61, 62, 67–
9, 214–18, 225, 230, 241, 248 n.,
261, 267, 268; supported foreign
parties, 272, 274, 276, 286; training
programs of, 10–14, 87, 143, 144,
146, 184, 206, 210–12, 230, 242;
and U.S. Presidents, 118, 223, 233,
256, 274, 290, 292–3; used as instrument of foreign policy, 14,
220–3, 274, 292; and Watergate,
233, 234, 236, 238, 243, 245, 251,
255 and n., 263, 285, 290; Western
Hemisphere Division, 36, 86–7,
93, 112, 133, 149, 170, 182, 187,
208 n., 213, 220, 222, 234–8, 240–2,
246–61, 268–9; women in, 58, 139–
41, 157, 206, 225–6, 242, 257,
261–2, 280 n.; *see also* individual
countries, Directors, operations
Chandler, Captain Charles, 257
Cheeseman, Carlos, 46
Chenault, Colonel James, 257
Chesterton, G. K., 279 n.,–280 n.
Chicago, Illinois, 62, 289
Chicago *Tribune*, 168–9
Chile, 3–4, 7–8, 14–29, 128, 240, 274;
and CIA, 3–4, 8–11, 15–16, 18–25,
27 n., 28, 219–23, 237–8, 246–51,
252–4 and n., 255, 272, 274–5,
283–4, 286–7; Communism in,
19–25, 28, 222, 237, 254; coup in,
185, 237–8, 246–51, 252–4 and n.,
274, 286–7; economy of, 237, 249–
50; election in, 219–23; military
of, 223, 246–7; and Nixon, 220–3;
and Soviet Union, 11, 20–1; truck
strike in, 237, 252, 254, 286
China, 114, 126, 206
Church, Frank, viii, 139 n., 286, 291

Churchill, Winston, 205
CIA. *See* Central Intelligence Agency
CIA and the Cult of Intelligence,
  The (Marchetti and Marks), 262
Cliff, 86–7, 89 *n.*, 93, 95–8, 101–2
  and *n.*, 104–5, 107–10
Cline, Dr. Ray, 191, 270, 292
Colby, Barbara, 244, 289–90
Colby, William E., vii–viii, 27, 233,
  234, 239–53 *passim*, 254 *n.*, 265,
  267, 268, 269, 271, 279 n., 280 *n.*,
  289–91
Cold War, 8, 13–14; and CIA, 8, 14,
  56–60, 120, 238, 271
Collier, Bernard, 156
Colombia: Communism in, 133
Colson, Charles, 255
Columbia Broadcasting System, 284,
  285, 289, 291–2
Columbus, Christopher, 60
communications, 227–9, 258; between
  agents, 15, 188, 205–6, 225; brush
  pass, 12, 225; danger signals, 12;
  dead drops, 12, 206; pissing contest,
  37; recognition signals, 12, 31, 129,
  130, 230–1, 240; safe houses, 9–11,
  12, 20, 30, 31, 39, 67, 79, 131, 225;
  see also radio
Communism, 13, 36, 183, 240; in
  Latin America, 14, 81, 113, 133,
  258; *see also* individual countries
Congo, the, 204
Connett, Barton, 162
Connett, Bill, 162, 184
Conte Aguerro, Luis, 164–7, 184–5
Córdoba, Argentina, 258
Costa Rica, 62–3, 152, 184
counter-intelligence, *see* intelligence
Coventry, England, 205
cover for agents, 4, 12, 61, 79, 218,
  224–5, 229–30, 288 and *n.*,
  corporate, 90; deep, 27 *n.*, 37, 60,
  67–9, 73 *n.*, 99, 119, 215, 273; false
  documents, 30–1, 37; false names,
  10, 12, 22, 31; at home, 202–4, 273;

Cover for Agents (*cont.*)
  light, 61, 130, 214, 233; official, 37,
  116, 117, 214
covert action, vii, 36, 55–6, 100, 198,
  204, 207, 215, 230, 234, 256–60,
  268–9, 275–8; in Bay of Pigs, 100,
  111–12; in Chile, 220–1, 252, 274–
  5; in Cuba, 188; in Dominican
  Republic, 159–60, 182–4; in
  Mexico City, 113–14; *see also*
  espionage
Craig, 139–41
Crimmins, John, 176, 178
Crowley, Colonel Donald, 257
Cuba, 54, 60, 63–7, 93–4, 99, 126,
  142, 158, 184, 216, 250, 256, 261,
  270; American firms in, 63, 74, 77;
  and CIA, 60–1, 63–7, 76–83, 97, 99,
  187–8, 204, 208–9; Communism
  in, 77–8, 80, 144, 154, 198, 222;
  defectors from, 130–2, 199;
  influence of, 53, 123, 125, 133, 145,
  152, 187–8, 204, 209; intelligence of
  (DGI), 130–2, 133–4, 182–3, 204,
  206, 208, 239, 250, 262; Mexican
  embassy of, 113–15, 125, 127,
  133–4, 139–41; middle-class
  opposition in, 63, 64, 74, 77–8, 100,
  101, 103; military of, 63, 64, 74,
  77, 101, 103, 104–9, 111; missile
  crisis in, 124–5; and Oswald, 139–
  40, 142; Radio Havana in, 152;
  repression in, 63, 65, 83; revolution
  in, 64–5, 73–4, 76–80; Soviet
  influence in, 78, 97, 124–5, 130,
  208; student opposition in, 64, 78,
  93; *see also* Bay of Pigs; Castro,
  Fidel
Cuban exiles, 64, 78, 86, 87, 92, 95–6;
  in Bay of Pigs, 87, 88, 92–3, 95–6,
  99–103, 105–9; Castro assassination
  plot of, 208–9, 283 and *n.*; *see also*
  Bay of Pigs
Cummings, E. E., 239
Cushing, Dick, 27, 61, 65–6, 94–5,
  186, 191

Cushing, Nancy, 27, 61, 65–6, 94–5, 191
Cushman, General Robert, 91 n., 201
Czechoslovakia, 43, 89 n., 114

Dajabón, Dominican Republic, 150
Dallas, Texas, 139 n., 140, 142 and n., 178
Damascus, Syria, 71–2
dangle operations, 11, 15–16, 19
Dean, John, 245
defectors, 114, 126–32, 205
Detroit, Michigan, 195
Devine, Frank, 184
Dewey, Thomas E., 38
Díaz Lanz, Pedro, 78
Dietrich, Marlene, 239
Dillon, Douglas, 102
Dominican Republic, 143–86, 197; CIA in, 123, 126, 143–87, 214, 228, 272; civil war in, 144, 146–68, 174–5; Communism in, 148–9, 150–1, 152, 158, 163, 167, 168, 170–3, 174, 176, 182–4; election in, 164, 173, 177–81; interior of, 147–8, 149–50, 152, 156, 157–8, 171, 174, 179; military of, 148, 152, 153, 163, 167, 174–5; OAS in, 152, 154, 158–81 passim; provisional government of, 158–9, 162–81 passim; Radio Santo Domingo in, 152–3; terrorism in, 257; U.S. troops in, 144, 149, 150, 152, 155, 156, 157, 158, 159, 161, 169–70, 171, 177, 222, 228
double-agents, 15–16, 72, 189, 204–7, 225
Douglas, 99, 101
Drake, Sir Francis, 189
drug: testing, 274, 283; -trafficking, 134, 238
DuBois, Jules, 168–9, 179–80
Dulles, Allen, 34, 36, 38, 49–51, 53, 55–6, 58 and n., 59, 79, 86–7, 97, 98, 99, 100, 102, 106, 108, 110, 118 and n., 119, 123, 137, 204–5, 248 n.,

Dulles, Allen (cont.)
279 n., 280 n.; Craft of Intelligence, The, 119
Dulles, John Foster, 49, 53, 56, 59, 248 n.

East Berlin, Germany, 56, 205
Ecuador, 238
Edgar, 13–14
Egan, John, 258
Egypt, 65, 72
Ehrlichman, John, 245
Eisenhower, Dwight D., 67, 76, 99; and Bay of Pigs, 86, 87, 99–100, 145, 272; and Guatemala, 35, 49–51, 53, 111
Eisenhower, John, 50
Elbrick, Burke, 216, 257
Eliot, T. S., 101
Ellsberg, Daniel, 233, 236, 255
El Salvador, 35, 162–5
Embajador Hotel, Santo Domingo, 144, 149, 156, 157, 159, 161–2, 167, 173, 176, 179–80, 181
Enrique, 127–8, 134
Entebbe airport raid, 208 n.
Equal Employment Opportunity Commission, 242
Ervin, Sam, 255
espionage, vii–viii, 55, 126, 187–8, 234, 275–8; in Bay of Pigs, 95–6; by and in closed societies, 114, 204–6, 225, 276, 286; and defectors, 114, 126–32, 205; by democracies, viii, 275–8, 286; and double-agents, 15–16, 72, 189, 204–7, 225; history of, 188–9; money for, 128–9, 130, 205, 207; and penetration of opposition, 129, 130, 131, 135, 150–1, 158, 170–1, 205, 238, 239–40, 258; and street men, 12, 27; and surveillance, 12, 23; and walk-ins, 128–32, 141–2, 240, 250; see also communications; intelligence gathering; recruitment of agents

Esquipulas, Guatemala, 46
Europe, 13–14, 29, 187, 189, 274

Federal Bureau of Investigation, 5,
    33, 92, 114, 127–8, 142 *n*., 150, 154,
    184, 245; and CIA, 3, 23, 155–6,
    160, 171, 186
Felix, Maria, 41–2
Fifth Estate, 267, 284–5, 287–8, 291,
    293; *CounterSpy* of, 267, 284–5,
    287, 293
Figueres, Jose "Pepe," 62–3 and *n*.,
    78
Figueres, Karen, 62–3 and *n*.
FitzGerald, Barbara, 155
FitzGerald, Desmond, 123–5, 133,
    138–9 and *n*., 144, 146, 148, 149,
    151, 153, 154–5, 170–1, 181, 185,
    201, 239, 244
FitzGerald, Frances, 155; *Fire in the
    Lake, The*, 155 *n*.
Fleming, Ian, 135
Florida, 168, 208
Ford, Gerald, 267–8
Foreign Affairs, 13, 59
Foreign Broadcast Information
    Service (FBIS), 147
foreign correspondents: in
    Dominican Republic, 157, 168–9,
    179–81; in Guatemala, 46; in
    Lebanon, 71–2
Fortas, Abe, 59
Fort Lauderdale, Florida, 30–3
Fort Worth, Texas, 4–5, 7, 30, 61
Forty Committee, 204, 220–1, 248
    and n., 249, 254
France, 65, 72, 92, 189
Frankfurt, Germany, 51
Frei, Eduardo, 220
Fulbright, William, 103

Galindez, Jesús, 182
García-Godoy, Héctor, 162–4, 167–8,
    170–4, 176–81 *passim*, 185, 186
Gavin, General James, 197
Genesis, 291

Germany, 257; in World War II, 5–6,
    205, 247
Giles, 231
Goering, Hermann, 6
Gonzales, Max Gorman, 283 *n*.
Goodwin, Richard, 103
Great Britain, 65, 72, 257, 261;
    defectors from, 72, 189, 205, 207;
    Secret Intelligence Service of, 72,
    128, 189, 205, 207–8, 234
Guantanamo naval base, Cuba, 208–9
Guatemala, 34–54, 197–8, 237; and
    Bay of Pigs, 87, 93, 95, 99–100,
    101, 112; and CIA, 34–54, 56, 87,
    89, 103, 111, 119, 201; Communism
    in, 34–5, 40, 51–2, 133, 185; Cuban
    influence in, 53, 204; Labor Party
    of, 34, 43; military of, 34–5, 43–9,
    53; rebels of, 34, 36, 42–8, 50, 52;
    repression in, 42–5, 53; Soviet
    influence in, 34–5, 43, 52–4;
    terrorism in, 185, 257; and Voice
    of Liberation, 40–8, 52–3
Guatemala City, Guatemala, 34, 36,
    37, 38, 41, 43–8, 50, 51, 54, 211
Guevara, Dr. Ernesto Che, 54; in
    Bolivia, 81, 188, 204, 209–10; in
    Cuba, 64, 77, 80–1
Gulf Steamship Company, 90–1, 96

Haig, Alexander, 221
Haiti, 145; terrorism in, 257
Haldeman, H. R., 245
Hale, Nathan, 189, 251, 263, 282
Halperin, Ernst, 110 *n*., 197
Halperin, Morton, 276 *n*.
Hanoi, North Vietnam, 183
Harrington, Michael, 252–3, 254 *n*.,
    274
Harvey, 39–40
Havana, Cuba, 60, 63–7, 74, 76–83,
    86, 88, 91 and *n*., 93–4, 97, 100,
    101, 103, 110 *n*., 114, 132, 141, 148,
    188, 204, 250, 270
Heath, Donald, 68
Hector, 49–51, 52, 281

Helms, Richard, 38, 65–6, 86–7, 89–90, 119, 138, 147–8, 151, 153, 154–6, 171, 198–9, 200–1, 204, 221, 223, 233, 239, 279 *n.*, 280 *n.*, 290
Hemingway, Ernest, 65
Hersch, Seymour, 253–4, 262, 264–5, 267, 270, 291–2
Hiss, Alger, 251
Hitler, Adolf, 37, 92
Hoffman, Paul, 182
Hollywood, Florida, 30–1
Honduras, 35, 90, 98–9
Hoover, J. Edgar, 160, 170–1, 173; resentment of CIA, 3, 155–6
Hotel Matum, Santiago, 174–5
Humphrey, Hubert, 177–8, 199
Hungary, 65
Hunt, Dorothy, 38
Hunt, E. Howard, Jr., 34–6, 38–9, 51, 53, 87–8, 90, 91 and *n.*, 92–3, 95, 96, 99, 101, 109, 113, 140 *n.*, 201–2, 227, 233, 236, 255; *Give Us This Day*, 88 *n.*, 91 *n.*

illegal break-ins, 233, 257
Imbert, Antonio, 145, 152, 159, 163–7, 172, 184
Indio, El, 49, 51
intelligence gathering, viii, 35, 114–15, 135, 231–3, 259–60, 275, 277–8; black boxes for, 275, 277; counter-, 35, 52, 72, 93, 189, 205, 207, 239–40, 265; dangle operations for, 11, 15–16, 19; illegal break-ins for, 233, 257; and intuition, 117–18, 124–5; lipreading for, 231; microdots for, 43; radar for, 126, 139, 238, 258; routine work in, 115–16, 231–3; satellites for, 229, 277, 278; U-2 operation for, 61, 87, 90, 106, 125, 277; *see also* bugging; espionage; individual countries
International Red Cross, 150
Iran, 51, 111, 233
Is Paris Burning? (Collins and Lapierre), 217 *n.*

Israel, 65; Mossad of, 207–8 and *n.*, 265
Italy, 5, 105, 245

Jack, 11–13
Jake, 27 and *n.*
John, 130–2, 136–7, 142, 143 *n.*, 281
Johnson, Lynda, 185
Johnson, Lyndon B., 59, 138, 148, 199, 222, 252, 273, 274; and Dominican Republic, 144, 147, 149, 150, 153, 154, 155, 161, 170, 177–8, 180–1, 185–6, 222
Jorden, Bill, 241, 246, 248
Juan, 21–5, 28, 128, 222

Karamessines, Thomas, 195, 201, 221, 223, 233, 239
Kennan, George F., 13
Kennedy, Jacqueline, 122
Kennedy, John F., 100, 122–3, 138, 145, 214, 252, 273, 274, 292; assassination of, 139 *n.*, 140–2 and *n.*, 143, 238, 251, 285; and Bay of Pigs, 97 *n.*, 100–1, 102–3, 105–10, 112, 118, 272; and Cuban missile crisis, 124–5
Kennedy, Robert, 109, 112, 195, 273
Key West, Florida, 83–5, 105
Khrushchev, Nikita, 56, 65, 125, 138, 204–5
kidnapping, 115, 215, 216, 232 and *n.*, 257–8, 259–61, 288
Kiker, Douglas, 284
King, Colonel J. C., 36, 49, 60, 76, 87, 93, 112, 133, 200, 256
King, Martin Luther, 195
Kissinger, Dr. Henry, 193, 204, 221, 241, 248, and *n.*, 249–50, 276 *n.*
Knox, Clinton, 257
Korean War, 274
Korry, Edward, 220
Kubisch, Jack, 241, 246
Kurzman, Dan, 156, 157, 181

Laird, 153–5, 157, 158, 161
Lancaster, Burt, 243

INDEX

Langley, Virginia: CIA headquarters in, 38, 58 n., 118 n., 137, 171
Laredo, Texas, 116, 139
Latin America, 18, 23, 34, 144, 146, 163, 171, 181, 226, 237, 261, 268; and CIA, vii, 3, 209, 210, 218, 225, 235, 241, 254, 256, 262, 266, 268, 270, 272; Communism in, 14, 81, 114, 133, 258; Cuban influence in, 53, 123, 125, 133, 145, 152, 187–8, 204, 209; Soviet influence in, 11, 14, 20–1, 23, 34–5, 43, 50–1, 52–4, 78, 97, 113, 124–5, 130, 204, 208, 276; terrorism in, 184, 185, 210, 216–17, 232, and n., 257–61, 262; see also individual countries
Lebanon, 67–76; CIA in, 67–76 and n.; civil war in, 74–6
Lem Jones Associates, 101
Lemnitzer, General Lyman, 102
Len, 57–60, 84–7, 95, 102, 104, 109
Lenin, Vladimir Ilich, 87, 279 n.
Leonhardy, Terrence, 257
Lester, 174–5, 176–7
Liebling, A. J., 69
Life, 46
Lima, Peru, 267
Linda, 9–11, 15–16, 19–20
Lippmann, Walter, 13
Lloyd's of London, 47 and n.
London, England, 163, 176, 184, 234, 262, 283
London Daily Telegraph, 71
Long, Ted and Phyllis, 27, 232 n.
Lumumba, Patrice, 272
Lyon, France, 6

Macaulay, Lord Thomas, 289
Macmillan, Harold, 72
Madrid, Spain, 51
Mafia: and CIA, 273, 284
Malcolm X College, 243
Managua, Nicaragua, 142
Mann, Thomas C., 102
Marchetti, Victor, 238, 251, 262, 266, 270, 284–5, 293

Mario (Mario López Otero), 38–48, 52, 53–4
Marks, John, 238, 251, 262, 266, 270, 283–5
Marsh, Linda, 260–1
Marshall, George, 55
Marshall Plan, 14
Martin, John Barlow, 152
Marx, Karl, 278
Marxism, see Communism
Massachusetts Institute of Technology, 196–8
Mathias, Charles, 292
McCarthy, Joseph, 58–9, 114
McClory, Robert, 292
McCone, John, 118–19, 123, 124–5, 138, 147, 255–6, 279 n., 280 n.
McCone, Mrs. John, 124
McGovern, George, 227
McNamara, Robert, 102
media: and investigations of CIA, viii, 251–4, 261–5, 267–70, 272, 283–93
Mein, John Gordon, 257
Merrick, David, 7
Mexico, 35, 41, 54, 64, 113–14, 155; terrorism in, 257, 262
Mexico City, Mexico, 41, 122–3, 139, 140–3; Chilean embassy in, 240, 250; CIA in, 113–43 passim, 156, 238, 261; Cuban embassy in, 113–15, 125, 127, 133–4, 139–41; Latin American exiles in, 92, 114; Soviet embassy in, 113–14, 139–41
Miami, Florida, 30, 35, 90, 105–6, 112, 164–5, 169; Cuban exiles in, 78, 86, 87, 92, 95–6
Middle East, 67, 187, 192–3, 204, 225, 259; see also individual countries
Miller, Bill, 292
Mitchell, John, 204
Mitrione, Dan, 257 and n.
Mongolia, 114
Montevideo, Uruguay, 130
morality and ethics, viii, 22, 34–5, 52–3, 222–3, 263, 272, 274, 276, 292–3

Morgan, Thomas E., 253
Moscow, USSR, 20, 148, 274, 293–4
Mossadegh, Mohammed, 111
Mowinckle, John, 217 and *n.*, 218 and *n.*

Napoleon's (restaurant), 60, 86, 104, 112
National Broadcasting Company, 7, 270
National Intelligence Daily (NID), 245 and *n.*
National Security Council, 35, 199, 241, 276 *n.*
Nedzi, Lucien, 252
Nelson, Bill, 239, 241, 264–5, 267, 271
Neruda, Pablo, 22
Newark, New Jersey, 195
New York City, New York, 5, 11–12, 26, 91, 92, 177, 199, 206, 230, 271
New York Times, 46, 156, 169, 179, 182, 253–4, 262, 264–5, 285, 286–7, 291
Nicaragua, 141–2, 152; and Bay of Pigs, 87, 103–4, 105–8, 112
Nicholas I, Czar of Russia, 189
Nicosia, Cyprus, 211
Nixon, Richard M., 50, 91 and *n.*, 199, 273; and Chile, 220–3, 248, 249, 252, 274; and Watergate, 233, 245, 274
North Korea, 126, 183
North Vietnam, 183
Nuremberg, Germany, 5

O'Brien, Larry, 185
Okinawa, 240
O'Leary, Jerry, 168, 180
Onassis, Aristotle, 73
Organization of American States (OAS): in Dominican Republic, 152, 154, 158–81 *passim* O.S.S. (Office of Strategic Services), 13, 34, 56, 58, 92, 123, 207, 228, 239, 244

Oswald, Lee Harvey, 139–40 and *n.*, 141–2 and *n.*, 143

Palmer, General Bruce, 154, 161, 163, 175
Panama, 169–70, 241, 261
Paraguay, 152, 185
Paris, France, 126, 139 *n.*, 217 *n.*, 283
Paris *Herald Tribune*, 194
Paul, 13, 23
Peace Corps, 215, 216 *n.*
Pedro, 152–3
Peking, China, 148
Penkovsky, Colonel Oleg, 125
Pentagon, *see* U.S. Defense Department
Penthouse, 291
People, 261
Pepe (José Toron Barrios), 38–48, 52, 53
Pepito, 188, 196, 204
Perez Friman, Earle, 130–2, 136
Peru, 267; Communism in, 133
Peter, 37, 49–51, 52, 92
Philby, Kim, 72 and *n.*, 116, 189, 205, 207
Phillips, Atlee, 26, 60, 65, 67–8, 70, 85, 187, 195–6, 269
Phillips, Christopher, 65, 67–8, 85, 94, 188, 199, 204, 269, 289
Philips, David Atlee: as an actor, 5, 7, 8, 9, 15, 60, 133, 182, 227; in army, 5–6, 272; arrest of, 30–3; background of, 4–7; and Bay of Pigs, 85–112; in Brazil, 213–19, 223–4, 226; as Chief of Station, 143–4, 154–86, 213–18 and *n.*, 219, 223–4, 226–8, 230–4; in Chile, 3–4, 7–11, 14–29, 222; and Chilean coup, 237–8, 246–50; and Chilean election, 219–23; cover for, 15, 27 *n.*, 57, 60–2, 67–70, 73 and *n.*, 80, 82, 116, 119, 122–3, 202–4, 221–2, 233, 269; in Cuba, 60–7, 76–83; and Dominican Republic,

Philips, David Atlee (*cont.*)
143–86; family of, vii, 9, 26, 65,
67–9, 75, 83, 88, 93–4, 156, 175,
187–8, 195–6, 199, 204, 219, 224,
227, 235, 269–71, 284; and
Guatemalan revolt, 34–54; in
Lebanon, 67–76 and *n.*; as lecturer,
26, 50, 57, 61, 62, 270–1, 284, 291,
292; in Mexico City, 113–43
passim; morality and ethics of, 22,
34–5, 52–3, 222–3, 263, 272, 274,
292; as part-time CIA officer, 3–4,
8–9, 13, 15–16, 18–25, 28–34, 76; as
permanent CIA officer, 55–60, 86,
113; in political-military game,
196–9; received medal, 78–9;
resigned from CIA, 74, 76, 82, 84;
retired to defend CIA, 270–95;
training of, 10–14, 143, 144, 146,
206, 210, 230; in Venezuela, 226–8;
230–5; on Western Hemisphere
Division (Washington), 55–60,
187–208 and *n.*, 209; as Western
Hemisphere Division chief, vii,
208 *n.*, 234–42, 246–61, 266–9; as
writer and editor, 4, 7, 8, 15, 25,
271, 285, 286
Phillips, David, Jr., 26, 60, 67–8, 85,
187, 195, 199, 269
Phillips, Gina, 199, 204, 213, 218, 219,
224, 227, 242, 243, 246, 263, 269–
71, 282, 287, 292
Phillips, Helen, 7–9, 16, 18–19, 26–7,
28–9, 60–1, 65, 67–8, 74–7, 80,
82–3, 85, 88, 94, 110, 113, 122, 127,
187
Phillips, Maria, 26, 60, 63, 67–70, 85,
175, 187, 195, 199, 269
Phillips, Todd, 219, 271
Pierre, 5–6
Pike, Otis, 291
Plan Centaur, 240, 250
Playboy, 230–1, 284, 291
political action, 13, 59, 87, 92, 99, 101,
144; *see also* propaganda
Pound, Ezra, 239

Powers, Gary, 61, 277
Prague, Czechoslovakia, 284
Preston, 164, 182, 183, 184
propaganda, 13, 36, 114, 275, 288;
for Bay of Pigs, 86, 87, 88–91,
96–7 and *n.*, 101–9 *passim*, 112;
leaflet drops, 40, 43, 88, 97, 101,
103–4, 107–8, 112; for
psychological warfare, 47–8, 52, 59,
88–9, 97, 102, 103, 105–6, 276;
Soviet, 253; *see also* radio
Prouty, Colonel L. Fletcher, 285, 291
psychological warfare, 47–8, 52, 59,
88–9, 97, 102, 103, 105–6, 276;
see also radio
Puerifoy, Jack, 52
Puerto Barrios, Guatemala, 46–7
Puerto Rico, 106, 156, 163, 168
Pyongyang, North Korea, 183

Raborn, Admiral William, 147–8,
149–50, 153, 154–5, 156, 170–1, 173,
180–1, 200, 279 *n.*, 280 *n.*
radio, 59, 227–9; and Bay of Pigs,
88–91, 96–7, 101, 103, 108, 109,
112; black broadcasting, 13;
clandestine, 13, 36, 40–8, 52–3; and
Guatemalan revolt, 36, 40–8, 52–
3; progress in technology in, 206,
229, snuggling, 47
Radio Swan, 90–1, 96, 98–9, 101, 108,
109, 112
recruitment of agents, 3–4, 8, 12,
20–5, 80, 128, 160, 188, 193, 205,
208, 222, 226, 256; false-flag, 206–
7; target studies for, 20–1
Reid, Donald, 145–6, 152
Reston, James, 255
Richelieu, Armand, Cardinal and
Duc de, 189
Rickey, Branch, 242
Ridgway, General Matthew, 50
Rio de Janeiro, Brazil, 213–19, 223–4,
245; *see also* Brazil
Roa, Raul, 106
Rockefeller Commission, 267–8, 273

Rodríguez, Carlos Rafael, 283
Rogers, William, 220
Rome, Italy, 76, 244
Roosevelt, Kermit, 111, 123
Rosa (maid), 27
Roselli, Johnny, 284
Rositzke, Harry, 270
Rostow, Walt, 199
Rountree, William, 217
Rowan, Carl, 151
Rush, Kenneth, 249–50
Rusk, Dean, 102, 107–9, 198

Safer, Morley, 289
Saigon, South Vietnam, 154, 185, 192, 244
St. George's Hotel, Beirut, 71–2
Salvador, David, 78 and *n*.
San Cristóbal, Cuba, 125
San Francisco de Macorís, Dominican Republic, 157–8, 171, 174
San José, Costa Rica, 62–3
Santiago, Chile, 3–4, 7–11, 12, 14–29, 223, 238, 240, 246–7, 249–50, 254 *n*.
Santiago de los Caballeros, Dominican Republic, 147, 149, 173, 174–5, 176–7
Santo Domingo, Dominican Republic, 143–84 *passim*, 188, 214, 222, 228; *see also* Dominican Republic
Sao Paulo, Brazil, 216, 217
Saudi Arabia, 71
Scammon, Richard, 180
Schlesinger, Arthur, Jr., 103, 106; *Thousand Days, A*, 106 *n*.
Schlesinger, James, 233–4, 242, 279 *n*.
Schneider, General Rene, 223, 272
Schorr, Daniel, 270, 285, 292
Schweiker, Richard, 143 *n*.
Scorpio (film), 243
Scott, Winston, 113, 116–18, 121, 123, 126, 129, 131, 134, 140 and *n*.
Selling of the Pentagon, The (TV documentary), 269

Shlaudeman, Harry, 161, 162, 167, 168, 173, 174, 176–7, 181, 185, 220, 241, 254 *n*.
Shumlin, Herman, 7, 8
Simon, William, 248–9
Sinai Peninsula, 65
"60 Minutes" (TV show), 289
Snyder, Tom, 270
Somoza brothers, 142
Southeast Asia, 13, 37, 58, 144, 226; *see also* Vietnam War
South Pacific Mail, The, 4, 8, 14–15, 16, 22, 25–6, 29, 61
Soviet Union, 43, 126, 256, 277; and Bloc countries, 14, 21, 206, 256; and Cold War, 8, 13–14, 56–60, 120; and Cuban missile crisis, 124–5; defectors from, 125, 128; and detente, 240, 265, 278–9, 289; espionage of, 114, 135, 189, 204–5, 207; and Hungary, 65; influence of, in Latin America, 11, 14, 20–1, 23, 34–5, 43, 50–1, 52–4, 78, 97, 113, 130, 204, 208, 276; intelligence of (KGB), 11, 14, 23, 72, 113–14, 120, 129, 135, 189, 204–6, 208, 229, 233, 239, 256, 262, 265, 293–5; embassy of, 113–14, 139–41; and Oswald, 139–42; propaganda of, Mexican, 253; use of bugging, 135
Spain, 144–5, 189
spies, *see* espionage
Spretti, Count Karl von, 182, 185, 257
Stalag 17 (show), 7, 8, 133
Stalin, Joseph, 8, 56
State of Siege (film), 257 *n*.
Stettin, Poland, 42
Stevenson, Adlai, 103, 106 and *n*., 107
Stewart, Allen, 27, 62, 232 *n*.
Stewart, Marian, 27, 62
Stilwell, General Joseph, 123
Stimson, Henry, 207
Strategic Air Command, 125
Sturgis, Frank, 284 *n*.
Sun Tzu, 188

Susskind, David, 91
Sutton, Willie, 128
Swan Island, 90, 96, 98–9
Switzerland, 34, 87, 258, 274
Syria, 71–2
Szulc, Tad, 156; *Compulsive Spy*, 140 *n.*

Tampa, Florida, 106
Taylor, General Maxwell, 112
Taylor, Admiral Rufus, 201
Teguicigalpa, Honduras, 98
telephones: secure and sterile, 153; taps, 134, 227
terrorism, 115, 207–8, 215, 285, 287–8; and CIA, 134, 210, 216–17, 226, 257–61; in Latin America, 184, 185, 210, 216–17, 232 and *n.*, 257–61, 262
Texas Christian University, 5
Thomas, Norman, 181
Thurber, James: *This I Believe*, 280
Time, 203
"Today" (TV show), 284
Tokyo, Japan, 51
Tomic, Radomiro, 220
"Tomorrow" (TV show), 270
tradecraft, 6, 11–14, 37, 92, 120, 132, 210–12, 230, 273
Trinidad, Cuba, 95, 100, 102, 110
Trujillo, Rafael Leonidas, 145, 152, 158, 163, 165–6, 177, 182, 184, 272
Truman, Harry, 35

United Fruit Company, 53
United Nations, 103, 106 and *n.*, 107, 276
United States, 25, 26, 114; citizens of overseas and CIA, 127–8, 139–43, 238, 262; civil unrest in, 195, 264, 273; and Cold War, 8, 13–14; defector from, 126–8; and detente, 240, 265, 278–9, 289; domestic operations of CIA in, 62, 156, 262, 264–5, 267–8, 273, 278, 283; foreign policy of, 13–14, 53, 99, 220–3, 274, 276, 292; and political-

United States (*cont.*)
military game, 196–9; and Southeast Asia, 13, 58, 144, 146, 154, 197, 222, 244–5; *see also* individual Presidents
U.S. Army, 209, 217, 222; in Dominican Republic, 144, 145, 150, 152, 155–61 *passim*, 169–70, 171, 179, 222, 228
U.S. Congress, 289; investigations into CIA, 251–5 and *n.*, 262, 267–8, 271, 275, 291; *see also* U.S. Senate
U.S. Defense Department, 55, 90, 95, 100, 112, 149, 221, 248–9, 269
U.S. Information Agency (Service), 36, 65, 73, 149, 151, 157, 215, 217, 258
U.S. Justice Department, 268, 290
U.S. Marines, 76, 144, 149, 150, 152, 157, 159, 161, 171, 177, 267 and *n.*
U.S. Secret Service, 121, 143, 177–8
U.S. Senate, 59, 145; Church committee, viii, 139 *n.*, 286–7, 291
U.S. State Department, 36, 42–3, 58–9, 67, 100, 119–20, 209, 220–1, 229, 274; and Bay of Pigs, 89, 97, 103, 107; and CIA, 55, 56, 214–18, 225, 230, 241, 248 *n.*, 261, 267, 268; and Dominican Republic, 147, 149, 150, 157, 166, 175; foreign embassies of, 37, 61, 62, 67–9, 121–2, 126–7, 130, 214–19, 232 *n.*, 288
University of Chile, 8
Uruguay: CIA in, 88, 238; Communism in, 133; terrorism in, 257–8
U-2 operation, 61, 87, 90, 106, 125, 277

Valdivia, Pedro de, 27
Valparaiso, Chile, 4, 7, 8
Varon, Benjamin and Miriam, 182, 185
Venezuela, 204, 227; CIA in, 226–7, 230–4; Communism in, 133; terrorism in, 232 and *n.*, 257
Vesco, Robert, 63

Vienna, Austria, 75
Vietnam War, viii, 13, 144, 146, 154, 197, 222; Operation Phoenix, 244–5
Voice of America, 90, 150–1, 158, 186
Voice of Liberation, 36, 40–8, 52–3

walk-ins, 128–32, 141–2, 240, 250
Wally, 27, 114–15, 123, 125, 143, 150–1, 158, 161, 162, 281
Walsingham, Sir Francis, 189, 207
Walters, General Vernon, 91, 201, 245–6, 278
Warren Commission, 141, 142 *n.*
Washington, D.C., 91, 92, 94–5, 181, 195
Washington *Post*, 146, 169, 179, 218 *n.*, 222, 253, 285, 287, 291
Washington Special Action Group (WSAG), 248 and *n.*, 249–50
Washington *Star*, 168, 180, 268, 285
Watergate, viii, 227, 233, 234, 236, 238, 243, 245, 251, 255 and *n.*, 263, 274, 285, 290

Wayne, John, 93 *n.*
Welch, Kika, 287
Welch, Richard, 193–5, 201, 210–12, 216, 222, 251, 267, 279–80, 287, 289, 292; murder of, 285, 287–9
Wessin y Wessin, General Elias, 152 158, 159, 163–4, 167–70, 172, 184
West Palm Beach, Florida, 62
Weyrick, Colonel Joe, 168–9
White, Dr. Paul Dudley, 67–9
Wiesbaden, Germany, 6
Willard, 158, 161
William and Mary College, 5
Wisner, Frank, 36, 38, 55–7 and *n.*, 58, 65, 86, 89, 123, 239
World War I, 87
World War II, 5–6, 13, 34, 57, 58, 89 *n.*, 92, 93 and *n.*, 95, 105, 109, 205, 217 and *n.*, 228, 239, 245, 247, 263, 272

Youngblood, Rufus, 178

For twenty-five years DAVID ATLEE PHILLIPS stood "the night watch" as an agent in the arcane profession of espionage. As a Central Intelligence Agency officer he rose to become director of the Western Hemisphere Division, a post he occupied at the time the Allende government was overthrown in Chile in 1973. He retired in 1975 to write *The Night Watch*.